BOLSHEVIK
FEMINIST

BOLSHEVIK FEMINIST

The Life of
Aleksandra Kollontai

BARBARA EVANS CLEMENTS

INDIANA UNIVERSITY PRESS
BLOOMINGTON AND LONDON

Manufactured in the United States of America

This book was brought to publication with the assistance
of a grant from the Mellon Foundation.

Library of Congress Cataloging in Publication Data
Clements, Barbara Evans, 1945–
Bolshevik feminist.
Bibliography:
Includes index.
1. Kollontai, Aleksandra Mikhailovna, 1872–1952.
2. Socialists—Russia—Biography. I. Title.
HQ1662.K6C55   335.43′092′4 [B]   78–3240
ISBN 0–253–31209–4   2   3   4   5   83   82   81   80

For my father

Contents

PREFACE

Aleksandra Kollontai belonged to the generation of European feminists who won major advances in suffrage and social welfare programs for women. She participated in the campaigns for female emancipation and she made a contribution to the literature on the woman question by exploring the relationship between sexuality and liberation. Yet Kollontai vehemently denied that she was a feminist; rather, she saw herself as a Marxist revolutionary who sought freedom for women as part of the freeing of all humankind from the control of capitalism. Thus she set herself apart from those other members of her generation who pursued reforms for women, becoming instead a socialist, in truth a socialist feminist.

The distance that Kollontai put between herself and the feminists accounts in part for her being relatively unknown among Western European and American students of the woman's movement. Furthermore, her most original writing gained prominence in Europe only in the twenties, at the very time that it went out of favor in her own country. In 1923 criticism of her theories on female personality began to appear in the Soviet press, because Communist Party leaders were trying to destroy her political influence and also because they were reacting against the sexual exploration of the revolutionary years. They gave Kollontai a choice—to stop propagating her ideas or to leave the party—and she chose to submit. Thereafter her feminist socialism, always divorced from feminism by Kollontai herself, was relegated to obscurity within Soviet communism. Only in the late sixties did Western feminists begin to rediscover her ideas and the woman herself.

Western feminists in search of Kollontai found very little to guide them—two sympathetic but reticent biographies by friends, some unrevealing Soviet studies, and memoirs written under the constraints of politics and fading memory.[1] Yet the story of her life was there, behind the official pictures, in Kollontai's prolific writings and in the documents of Soviet history. The search for her led through these remnants to an extraordinary woman whose life deserved retelling. She was an original feminist, despite her disavowals; she espoused a utopian Marxism which came into conflict with the imperatives of industrialization; and she lived a life that resembled melodrama more than reality. Awakened to an interest in her by the revival of feminism, then tantalized by her romantic obscurity, students of the woman's movement began to ask, "Who was Kollontai? What did she leave us?"

Kollontai was born in 1872, into an aristocratic Russian family. Her mother, Aleksandra Masalina, was the daughter of a Finnish merchant and a Russian noblewoman. Her father, Mikhail Domontovich, had Ukrainian ancestry. An army officer, he eventually attained the rank of general. His wife owned an estate in Finland, and the family lived well, surrounded by servants and partaking of the amenities of upper-class life amidst the poverty of Russia. It seems an unlikely milieu to nurture a revolutionary, but Russia was spawning revolutionaries by the thousands in just such aristocratic homes in the 1870s. That the privileged young could turn against the status quo was indicative of the society's grave problems.

The vast majority of Russia's people, the peasants, lived in constant debt with small prospects for improvement. Aleksandr II ended serfdom in 1861, but in so doing he saddled the peasants with redemption dues, forty-nine yearly payments for the land they had received from the nobility. This financial burden, combined with inefficient farming methods, a growing rural population, and a lack of effective governmental support, kept the people of the countryside in economic bondage. Although Aleksandr II understood that the emancipation had not created a class of truly free farmers, he could not attempt more major land reform without alienating the nobles, who gave the monarchy its most consistent support. Like his forefathers, he hoped to import from Western Europe technology and ideas that would enable the Russian government to become more efficient, the elite better educated, and the masses more productive, but he also wanted to preserve autocracy.

In one of these tasks, Aleksandr II and his father Nikolai I succeeded admirably. They did generate an educated elite, for the Russian upper classes studied European ideas more zealously than the emperors had ever intended. Some of the children of the 1830s became Hegelians or utopian socialists; their children of the 1860s were the feminists, liberals, and nihilists who became populists, or even terrorists, in the 1870s. An important segment of the Russians privileged by birth or talent turned their education toward a critique of their society, and the Russian intelligentsia was born, that bright, visionary, sometimes lunatic group from which came great artists and great revolutionaries. Their defining characteristic was alienation. Kollontai wrote, "Just because there was a kind of abyss between foreign countries ... and everything that we, the Russian youth, saw all around us, we learned never to accept any statement blindly, never to believe only what some authority preached."[2] In opening Russia to the West, therefore, the autocracy created the educated nobility it wanted, but that nobility in turn generated a gadfly group of intellectuals who pushed for more reform than the monarchy would grant.

Kollontai grew up in a family of the liberal intelligentsia. She came of age in the 1890s, when Marxism was attracting large numbers of young people, and she became a Marxist because the ideology offered a more systematic explanation of Russia's ills and a more certain hope of rectification than did her parents' liberalism. As she dabbled in quasi-legal educational projects among the workers of St. Petersburg, Kollontai gradually realized that her vocation lay in revolutionary politics. In 1898 she left her husband and son to go to Zurich, in order to study Marxism. Returning to Russia one year later, Kollontai joined the Russian Social Democratic Labor Party, and spent the first decade of the twentieth century engaged in Marxist analyses of the Finnish economy and in illegal political organizing. She fled Russia to avoid arrest in 1908 and spent the years 1909 to 1917 in Western Europe. There she wrote her most important articles on the relationship between female sexuality and female subjugation.

Marxism already possessed a rich analysis of the oppression of women in Friedrich Engels's *The Origin of the Family, Private Property, and the State* and August Bebel's *Woman Under Socialism*. Kollontai added a sensitive portrait of the psyche of woman. She understood the pull of her traditional upbringing, and she saw that the human need for intimacy often led to female subordination, because women and men could not treat one another as equals. Kollontai knew how difficult it was to be a "new woman," who could be independent without being stifled by doubt or loneliness. She wrote about women's emancipation in a way the male theorists did not, because she felt its personal cost and rewards, as they did not. This insight enabled Kollontai in the years before World War I to add to the economic analyses of Engels and Bebel an exploration of the psychological dimensions of woman's condition and her emancipation, which was a contribution to feminism as well as to socialism. Unfortunately few feminists read her work. Kollontai addressed it to the Russian socialist movement, within which psychology remained distinctly subordinate to sociology.

Kollontai's prewar writing did not deal exclusively with female personality. She also made a reputation as an expert on reform in maternity care and as an advocate of organizations for women within socialist parties. When the Bolsheviks seized power in Russia in 1917, Lenin chose her to head the Commissariat for Social Welfare. In that position she authored decrees that committed the Soviet state to full funding of maternity care from conception through the first year of life. Kollontai also advised other commissariats on laws establishing the legal and political equality of women and reforming the marriage code. The foundations for female emancipation laid in those first days of the Bolshevik Revolution were substantial, but Kollontai was not satisfied. She and Inessa Armand led the campaign for a woman's bureau within the Communist Party, and in 1920, after Inessa's death, Kollontai became its head. She used this position to apprise women of their new rights, to draw them out of the home into political activity, and to push for the promotion of women into positions of leadership in the government and the party. From the beginning of the Russian Revolution until her departure from the country in 1922, Kollontai was a leader in the great Soviet experiment in female emancipation, and that experiment, in turn, was one of the most far-reaching efforts to free women ever undertaken.

Kollontai left her post at the Zhenotdel (the Woman's Bureau) because she had become a central figure in a debate on party democratization and industrialization. Communists disagreed on the means for modernizing Russia and on the degree of dissent tolerable within their own ranks. Kollontai advocated worker-run factories and full freedom of opinion so vocally that the party leadership appointed her to a diplomatic post that was essentially an exile. She wrote a number of articles and short stories in 1923, but soon these too fell under attack, and for the rest of her life Kollontai confined her career to diplomacy.

These are the contours of the shadowy figure sought out by students of the woman's movement. Aleksandra Kollontai was a daughter of the aristocracy who chose to become a revolutionary, and went on to make an important contribution to feminist literature and female emancipation. She was an anarchistic Marxist who raised fundamental questions about the infant Soviet state, a revolutionary who saw her revolution come, then become something less than she had dreamed. Her life was a drama, acted, perhaps, with the women of the future in mind, in the hope that they would seek to understand the struggle of their grandmothers' generation.

Until February 1918 Russia used the Julian calendar, which in the nineteenth century was twelve days and in the twentieth century thirteen days behind the Western European (Gregorian) calendar. Dates will be given in the Old Style, i.e., according to the Julian calendar, until the narrative reaches 1918, when the Soviet government shifted to the Gregorian. In transliterating, the Library of Congress system will be adhered to, with some simplifications, except in the case of well known proper names (e.g., Trotsky, not Trotskii).

I should like to acknowledge the support of the University of Akron Faculty Research Fellowships and the American Council of Learned Societies-Social Science Research Council Soviet Studies Grants. I should also like to thank those friends who gave me their comments on the manuscript at various stages—Barbara Alpern Engel, Peter Kenez, Sheldon Liss, Philip Pomper, and Richard Stites. Their help was generously offered and gratefully received. Sam Clements has lived with Kollontai for ten years, helped with translations, searched through libraries, typed and proofread, all with good grace and unfailing patience. And finally, thanks go to Garnette Dorsey, who typed all the drafts of this book without complaint, even though she does not really approve of Kollontai.

Illustrations

Shura, age 5. From A. Kollontai, *Den första etappen* (Stockholm: Bonniers, 1945).

Aleksandra Kollontai with husband Vladimir and son Misha, 1897. From A. Kollontai, *Iz moei zhizni i raboty*, ed. I. M. Dazhina (Moscow: Sovetskaia Rossiia, 1974).

Vladimir Kollontai. Courtesy of Maria Jul Andersen.

Kollontai circa 1910. From *Stormklockan*,
April 6, 1912.

Kollontai in 1912. From *Iz moei zhizni i
raboty*.

A meeting of the Council of People's Commissars in early 1918. Kollontai is seated to Lenin's left. Dybenko is standing behind and to the left of Kollontai. From *Iz moei zhizni i raboty*.

Kollontai at a nursery in Kiev, 1919. From *Iz moei zhizni i raboty*.

With Dybenko and his family, 1919. From Gustav Johansson, *Revoltionens ambassadör: Alexandra Kollontays liv och gärning, åren 1872–1917* (Stockholm: Arbetarkultursförlag, 1945).

Inessa Armand.
From *Kommunistka*, October 1920.

Clara Zetkin.
From *Kommunistka*, October 1920.

Aleksandr Shliapnikov. Courtesy of Craig Nation.

Ambassador Kollontai, before presenting her credentials to the Swedish court, 1930.

In Stockholm, 1944. The portrait is of Kollontai's mother. Courtesy of Sonya Baevsky.

At the Norwegian Embassy in Moscow, June 1946, after presentation of the Norwegian Order of Saint Olaf. Sovfoto.

BOLSHEVIK
FEMINIST

1

Girlhood

ALEKSANDRA KOLLONTAI was born on March 19, 1872, in St. Petersburg, the capital of the Russian Empire. It was a stormy night in a stormy decade. The city of Peter the Great lay frozen in the grip of the northern winter, its broad streets and pastel buildings blanketed with snow. In cold student apartments young revolutionaries gathered to plan ways for winning the peasants to socialism, while behind the gates of the Winter Palace, Emperor Aleksandr II sought to solve the pressing problems of his country without tearing apart her traditions. Between the palace and the garrets of the revolutionaries stretched the storm-crossed streets of St. Petersburg, whose inhabitants would eventually choose between tsar and revolutionary.

The baby Aleksandra seemed destined to support the emperor, for she was born into the nobility, into rank and privilege and wealth. Her father, Mikhail Alekseevich Domontovich, came from a Ukrainian family which traced its ancestry to the thirteenth century. Born in 1830, Domontovich had been graduated from the Petro-Poltavskii Cadet Academy and had pursued a career in the cavalry. In school he read illegal socialist literature, as did many young men, but age mellowed him into a liberal with a strong commitment to English constitutionalism. He believed in monarchy, in the emperor, and in peaceful change. His wife, Aleksandra Aleksandrovna Masalina, shared his liberalism. Thus few observers would have predicted that their baby would become one of the most radical opponents of the society that sustained her parents and offered her a gracious life.

An omen of Aleksandra's revolutionary future may have been the fact that her parents had stirred up a storm of their own in order to be married. They met at the opera in St. Petersburg more than ten years before their child's birth, but Aleksandr Masalin, Aleksandra Aleksandrovna's father, had blocked their courtship. Because Domontovich was from a better family than Aleksandra, Masalin thought the young man did not intend to marry her. When Domontovich received a new assignment outside the capital, therefore, Masalin forced his daughter into marriage with an engineer named Mravinskii. That union lasted some ten years and produced three children, but when Domontovich returned to St. Petersburg in the late 1860s, his love affair with Aleksandra Aleksandrovna was rekindled. By now her father was dead. Refusing to bow once again to duty, she obtained a divorce, presumably on grounds of adultery. She bore the baby Aleksandra before the divorce was final.[1]

This defiance of convention marked the Domontoviches as unusual. For the same crime Tolstoi had the Russian nobility ostracize Anna Karenina and destroy Vronskii's military career. Neither Mikhail Alekseevich nor Aleksandra Aleksandrovna suffered such dire consequences for their love. Domontovich continued to move forward in the cavalry, and St. Petersburg ladies did not snub Aleksandra Aleksandrovna. Their marriage accomplished, the Domontoviches settled down to provide a home for their new daughter, to protect her from the turmoil of the times and to assure that she would have a placid, secure future.

The baby, nicknamed Shura, was a fair-haired, blue-eyed, pretty child. She was bright, energetic, imaginative, stubborn, and not a little spoiled, for she was surrounded by a household of adults. Her immediate family included her parents, her half-sisters Adele and Evgeniia, and a number of maternal great aunts. Living with the family were two other women, Elizaveta Ivanovna, a former companion to Shura's grandmother, and Miss Hodgson, Shura's English nanny.[2] From 1872 to 1877 the Domontoviches spent winters in St. Petersburg and summers at Aleksandra Aleksandrovna's estate in Finland. In this comfortable world Shura grew.

The person she loved above all the others in her large family was her father. Tall, bearded, and handsome, Domontovich seemed godlike to his daughter, and this impression was strengthened by the fact that he paid little attention to her when she was young. Like most men of his class, Mikhail Alekseevich expected his wife to manage his household and rear his child. At home, he spent his time reading history or discussing politics with male friends in a room that was off limits to curious little girls. Sixty years later Kollontai wrote: "I remember how one time I sneaked on tiptoe into my father's study. He did not notice me. I stood on tiptoe and kissed him on the forehead. Father looked up surprised, as if he had never seen me before. Then he smiled."[3]

Domontovich was a scholarly man who dabbled in history. In the early 1880s he wrote a study of the Bulgarian war for independence, which was confiscated by tsarist censors, apparently because Domontovich did not sufficiently praise Russian policy in the Balkans. A liberal, Domontovich often discussed politics with brother officers, even though occasionally his opinions, like his book, provoked retaliation from his superiors. When not engaged in work, study, or conversation, he enjoyed long walks through the woods at Kuusa, his wife's estate in Finland. All of these facets of her father's life Shura adopted—his love of books, his liberalism, his appreciation of nature. "I cannot talk about my childhood without thinking about my father," Kollontai wrote. "If ever a man had an influence on my mind and development, it was my father."[4] She adored him from a distance, and grew into a young woman who shared his intellectual bent and his concern for social issues.

Shura's relationship with her mother was far more problematical, both because her mother was as dominant as her father was aloof and because mother and daughter had similar, fiery temperaments. Aleksandra Aleksandrovna had shown her strong will most dramatically in leaving her first husband and bearing a child out of wedlock, but even before that scandal she had defied convention sufficiently to raise eyebrows in St. Petersburg. She managed a dairy farm at Kuusa and sold the products in the capital, which was considered sinfully bourgeois behavior for the wife of a tsarist officer.[5]

No doubt gossips explained Aleksandra Aleksandrovna's bad taste by pointing to her merchant parentage. Her mother came from the Russian nobility, but her father, Aleksandr Masalin, was a Finnish peasant who had made a fortune selling wood. When he died, his daughter inherited the estate in Finland, which he had bought as a symbol of his rise in society, but which he left encumbered with debts. Aleksandra Aleksandrovna could not bear to sell the land, so she paid her father's bills with the proceeds from the dairy farm. She found the work so satisfying that she continued to manage the business long after Kuusa was hers free and clear.

Aleksandra Aleksandrovna had other interests. She worked in charity projects among military widows and orphans, organized a school for young ladies, and read widely about modern scientific advances, particularly in medicine. Louis Pasteur was one of her heroes. To her daughters from her first marriage, Adele and Evgeniia, and to Shura, she preached the virtues of education and self-reliance, although she also expected each girl to make a career of marriage. She was an intelligent woman, more independent than most women of her class, possessed of strong opinions and an equally strong will.

The relationship between Aleksandra Aleksandrovna and Shura was so filled with conflict that forty-five years after her mother's death Kollontai still described her with resentment, softened only slightly by admiration. "My mother and the English nanny who reared me were demanding," Kollontai wrote. "There was order in everything: to tidy up my toys myself, to lay my underwear on a little chair at night, to wash neatly, to study my lessons on time, to treat the servants with respect. Mama demanded this."[6] Her mother was always demanding, dragging Shura to orphanages to play with the children there, forcing her to take art lessons, hiding her books so she would not become a bookworm. She worried over her child's shortcomings, complaining that Shura was nervous, that she could not sing, that she daydreamed too much, that she was too shy.

Aleksandra Aleksandrovna may have been so concerned about her daughter because Shura was her youngest, and because the two other babies of her marriage with Domontovich died in infancy. She fussed about Shura's health, she said that the child's faults were indications of frailty, she kept her at home for all of her education. Yet she tempered her protectiveness with tolerance, so much so that the daughter grew up just as strong-willed as, and considerably more independent than, her mother. Aleksandra Aleksandrovna taught Shura to value originality and orderliness, and she passed on enough of her own strength that the little girl developed a fierce need to break free.

Aleksandra Aleksandrovna also gave her daughter into the care of an English nanny, Miss Hodgson. Her presence eased the friction between Shura and her mother, and provided the child with the uncritical love her mother could not give. Shura trusted Miss Hodgson, for the nanny was discreet and comforting. Once, while in Bulgaria, after having seen a crowd of prisoners pass by on their way to execution, the little girl became convinced that she should have gotten her father to stop the firing squad. She could not confide her fears to her mother, but she could tell Miss Hodgson. "I confessed to her that I was guilty for the fact that the partisans and other prisoners had been shot, and all because I was a foolish person. Miss Hodgson, with her usual patience, asked about everything, she gave me some sugar water to drink, and I fell asleep holding her hand."[7]

Miss Hodgson was a Victorian Englishwoman of definite opinions and definite prejudices. Kollontai knew very little about her background beyond the fact that her father had been a sea captain. A modest person, Miss Hodgson refused to bathe with the Domontovich women at a bathhouse because she believed that one should not undress in public. She was a capable woman and helped Aleksandra Aleksandrovna run the household. Kollontai remembered her as scornful of much of Russian life; she thought the Russians were uneducated, brutal, and distinctly inferior to the British. Shura thus learned from her nanny, as well as from her father, to admire England as the seat of a civilization superior in many ways to her own.

Under the watchful eye of her mother and the protection of Miss Hodgson Shura grew into a bright, active child. Until she was five she lived in St. Petersburg, where her father taught at the cavalry school. Then in 1877 Domontovich was transferred to combat duty in the Russo-Turkish War. For two years the Balkans had been racked by rebellions against Ottoman rule, and Russia supported the Slavic independence movement. When the Turks began to win, Russia intervened on the side of the Rumanians, Serbs, Montenegrins, and Bulgarians, tipping the balance in their favor, but only after bloody battles. The Domontovich family anxiously awaited news from the front, and as each dispatch came, Aleksandra Aleksandrovna called them all together to hear it read aloud. After the Peace of San Stefano was signed in March 1878, Mikhail Alekseevich stayed on as a member of the Russian staff advising the constituent assembly that was to establish a government in newly independent Bulgaria. In 1878 the family joined him.

Describing this time in her life, Kollontai later wrote, "In Sofia I started to observe and think and my character began to take shape."[8] The six-year-old girl was bombarded by new impressions—the excitement of a long trip to a reunion with her father, the sights and sounds of an unfamiliar country, the social upheaval of a city recovering from war. She began to listen now to the family's political discussions, and she remembered for the rest of her life seeing the partisans who were about to be executed. More important than politics for a little girl, however, was finding a playmate among the children of the Russian colony in Sofia. Zoia Shadurskaia, the five-year-old daughter of a Russian diplomat, became Shura's constant companion; they would remain close friends until Zoia's death in 1941. Delighted by Zoia and by the adventure of life in a new place, Shura spent a happy year, until her father was ordered home in disgrace.

Domontovich had incurred the disfavor of the emperor by advocating a liberal constitution for Bulgaria. He returned to St. Petersburg in 1879 to await a new assignment, and the family settled into a large, dark house, sparsely decorated with gloomy Victorian furniture. Shura understood vaguely what had happened: she knew that her parents were irritable, that her half-sisters had gone to live with their father, and that no one was paying any attention to her. She told Miss Hodgson that the tsar who punished her father was a wicked man. Miss Hodgson replied that such talk could cause her father's arrest, and the little girl promised that she would go to jail with him. "In order to make it easier for myself," Kollontai wrote, "I called the tsar all the ugly names I could remember."[9]

In a few months, Domontovich received a post in the capital, reportedly because he earned favor with Minister of War Dmitri Miliutin. The family moved to an apartment on one of the canals that cut through St. Petersburg, and Aleksandra Aleksandrovna cautioned everyone in the household to behave, for her husband's position was still insecure. Less than two years later, Aleksandr II was assassinated.

Kollontai remembered vividly the hush that descended on the city as its inhabitants waited into the evening of March 1, 1881, to learn if the emperor had died. Candles were lit, and police clattered down the deserted streets. Everyone talked in hushed, frightened voices. Shura's aunts cried for the fallen tsar, then pronounced that his death was God's judgment for his marriage the summer before to his long-time mistress, Ekaterina Dolgorukaia. Petersburg society had never forgiven Aleksandr the indiscretion of marrying beneath him. Shura took in the sorrow in the faces around her, and in the days that followed she listened to her mother and sisters discuss the fate of Sofia Perovskaia, a well-born young woman who had participated in the murder. Then the little girl felt the crime touch her family directly. The police arrested her mother's first husband, Mravinskii, for complicity in the assassination.

Mravinskii was an engineer, and he had been inspecting water pipes in the basements of St. Petersburg buildings, or at least that was the official purpose for his entering the homes and stores of the city. In fact, the men who assisted him were not sewer workers, but police searching for tunnels dug by the *Narodnaia volia*, the group which killed the tsar shortly thereafter. Aware of the terrorists' plot to plant dynamite under the streets, the police hired Mravinskii and devised the phony plumbing inspection as a way to search secretly for explosives.[10] Of course the ruse failed. Members of *Narodnaia volia* did dig a tunnel which went undetected, and they would have detonated it, had not the tsar changed his customary route home. Aleksandr did not go down the mined street, but the terrorists, anticipating that possibility, had stationed people throughout the city. One of these persons, Grinevitskii, killed Aleksandr and himself with a hand-thrown bomb. In the wave of arrests that followed, Mravinskii was charged with deliberately misleading the police.

Because of their connection with Mravinskii, and probably because of their liberalism, the Domontovich family found themselves again ostracized. Friends avoided them, the aunts moved out, Adele complained that no one would ever marry her. Aleksandra Aleksandrovna said Mravinskii would not have gotten into such trouble if she had stayed with him. She urged Domontovich to use his influence to help her former husband, but Mikhail Alekseevich hesitated, fearing he would jeopardize his own insecure position by supporting a man accused of treason. After some quarreling between the two, in which she accused him of jealousy, he yielded. Mravinskii was found guilty, probably because of the flood of emotion surrounding the assassination rather than because of any convincing evidence that he had protected terrorists from the police. Domontovich's intervention saved Mravinskii from Siberia. Instead, he lost all the rights of his class and was sent to exile in European Russia.[11]

Shura, now nine years old, felt the tension between her parents, even though Miss Hodgson tried to divert her. Always an imaginative child, she fantasized a brilliant solution to the crisis: she would rush up to Aleksandr's widow and beg for Mravinskii's freedom. "Everyone would be glad and I would be a heroine." When Zoia came to visit, she and Shura planned Mravinskii's rescue together. "We sat on my bed in our white, very long nightshirts (of English style). We had no light in the room other than that fluttering low in the little red glass of oil that hung in front of an icon in the corner of the nursery." Zoia had just read a book about the storming of the Bastille, so she suggested that they enlist the aid of revolutionaries to lead an assault on the prison where Mravinskii was held. Although both girls thought that a fine idea, they found on reflection that they did not know any revolutionaries.[12]

After the sentencing, Aleksandra Aleksandrovna left St. Petersburg for Kuusa, her refuge from the hostile city. Shura went too, having now experienced a second family crisis brought on by her parents' confrontation with the monarchy. Many aristocratic young Russians learned about English constitutionalism at home, but few knew the price of political opposition so personally. Shura did not simply hear criticism of the tsarist system, she saw her family life disrupted, her father and another man close to her mother directly threatened by the government. Such events strengthened the anti-tsarist attitudes she had already learned from her liberal parents, but equally important, they taught her to see opposition activity as heroic. Thus her childhood fantasies took on a political tone; she had once daydreamed about rescuing people from a shipwreck, now she would save a man by pleading with the tsar's wife. Many of the experiences of her young life—her parents' conversations, the partisans in Bulgaria, the assassination of the emperor, Mravinskii's victimization— were teaching the growing child to see political action as highly esteemed and to perceive political injustice as personally threatening.

The two political crises may have been heightened in Shura's consciousness by the fact that the family suffered social ostracism as well as government disfavor. Although not condemned as severely as Anna Karenina and Vronskii, the Domontoviches must have had a reputation for unconventional behavior. They were from different social strata. They had committed adultery openly. Domontovich held political opinions that annoyed the emperor, and now Aleksandra Aleksandrovna's former husband was implicated in the assassination. In the aftermath of the murder, few members of the government and military circles within which the Domontoviches moved wanted to associate with people of such questionable reputation. Aleksandra Aleksandrovna withdrew from this atmosphere, taking her daughter with her, and Shura may have added to her antipathy toward the monarchy a feeling that she did not quite belong to the nobility. Perhaps her renunciation of her class in adulthood was made easier by this early exposure to its hostility.

These times of strain were important in Kollontai's development, but they did not make her childhood an unusually difficult or stormy one. She passed the 1880s peacefully in St. Petersburg, growing into an attractive, intellectual adolescent. Shura was a good student, particularly interested in history, her father's avocation, and in languages. She spoke French with her mother and sisters, English occasionally with her nanny, Finnish with the peasants at Kuusa, and she was studying German. She loved to read, so much so that her mother was afraid she would become too intellectual to appeal to young men. To round out her education, Aleksandra Aleksandrovna took Shura to dancing, music, and drawing lessons, none of which were successful. She was bored by art, she could not sing on key, and she disliked ballet. Her mother despaired of making a lady of her. "You'll ruin your eyes from reading so much," she told her. "Sit up, don't slouch. You'll become a hunchback."[13]

In these years of late childhood and early adolescence, Shura became closer to her half-sister Evgeniia, or Zhenia, who was some six years older. Like Adele, Zhenia spent much of her life in social activities—balls, picnics, theater parties. Involved in this world and in formal education, neither girl had a great deal of time for Shura. Both felt their younger sister was spoiled and headstrong; they used to say that she always got her own way. Zhenia showed a greater interest in Shura than did Adele, and Shura learned to respect her sister's independence. Although Aleksandra Aleksandrovna wanted Zhenia to become certified as a teacher and then to find a husband, Zhenia chose to study opera. Eventually she made a career for herself in St. Petersburg and abroad. While still a girl, she taught her little sister music and conspired with her in defiance of their mother.

Zhenia also introduced Shura to Maria Ivanovna Strakhova, a governess hired to prepare Zhenia for the examinations that would earn her a teaching certificate. Strakhova was the first person Shura knew who talked about a truly radical transformation of Russian society, including the full emancipation of women. Aleksandra Aleksandrovna was ambivalent, advocating both independence and dependence, but Strakhova was an open exponent of full female self-reliance. She rejected physical vanity, dressing in dark clothes and thick boots. She wore her hair simply. When she came to the house in 1880 or 1881, she seemed so different from the other women there that Shura was frightened of her. From the first, however, Strakhova showed concern for the child and that, combined with Zhenia's approval of her new tutor, melted Shura's reserve. Finally, when she saw that her father enjoyed discussing politics with Maria Ivanovna, Shura was completely won over. She did not understand the arguments, but she was impressed that her father treated Strakhova as an equal, and that Strakhova had the courage to argue with him.

As she grew into adolescence, Shura was the intelligent, well-educated child of a loving, if rather unconventional, family. Her childhood had been happy; as an adult Kollontai would complain only that she was lonelier than most children because she had no friends her own age except Zoia, who was rarely in St. Petersburg. She also resented her mother's constant supervision, and later felt she had been sheltered and fussed over excessively. To escape from her parents, Shura daydreamed. "I preferred to ramble alone in Kuusa's shady park and find big and exciting events in which I was the heroine," Kollontai wrote.[14] She could bow more easily to the demands of the adults if afterwards she could retreat into a place where she was in control. "I said that I was a rebel from my earliest childhood," Kollontai wrote. "But outwardly and formally I was very obedient. I did not want to be scolded, for it would have hurt my pride in front of my older sisters and brother. I did what I was told like a nice, obedient little girl, but I revolted inwardly."[15]

When Shura was about thirteen, the family moved back into the house where she had been born, Sredniaia podiacheskaia 5. It belonged to one of Mikhail Alekseevich's cousins, "a very cultivated and refined gentleman." Shura did not like her father's cousin, but her sister Adele did, and when she reached twenty she married him, even though he was forty years older than she. Kollontai wrote that her mother was very pleased with the match.[16]

Aleksandra Aleksandrovna planned a similar future for Shura. The girl would take the examinations to certify her as a teacher when she was sixteen years old; the certification would guarantee that she could always support herself. Aleksandra Aleksandrovna knew her daughter wanted to take university courses, but she refused permission on the grounds that young people encountered too many radical ideas in higher education and that further formal schooling was unnecessary for a woman. Once she had passed her examinations, Shura should enter society to find a husband.

Shura did not reject her mother's pushing her into a social life, but she had no intention of marrying a man of sixty. She intended to marry for love. When she was fifteen, she fell in love with Vania Dragomirov, the nineteen-year-old son of General Mikhail Dragomirov, who had fought with Domontovich in Bulgaria and was one of the most admired of Russian military strategists. Shura met Vania through his sister. She was drawn to him because he liked to talk about reforming Russian society and because he had the temerity to criticize his parents. Although they were not forbidden from seeing each other, Shura and Vania met secretly, while she was on afternoon walks with a female companion, and they communicated in invisible ink.

At first Shura must have felt she was living her daydreams, for she had found a boy with whom she could share her adolescent rebelliousness, and the two invested their relationship with all the trappings of illicit love to heighten its glamor. The romance faded, however, as Shura realized that Vania was disturbed by enormous guilt feelings. He told her that he was not worthy of her because he had stained his honor. Worried about his depression, Shura neglected her lessons to the point that Strakhova, now her governess, scolded her. She took her exams, but received lower scores than she had expected. Even in history, her best subject, Shura made only a four instead of the top mark of five.

Shortly afterward Vania shot himself to death. "When you get this letter," he wrote to Shura, "I shall no longer be found alive. What happened today [he had kissed her] showed what a wretch I am, how little self-control I have. I cannot live without you, and I can never possess you. I sacrifice my life for you. Be happy, my angel, and never forget me. Farewell forever."[17]

It seems unlikely that closely watched young people like Shura and Vania could have done anything sufficiently scandalous to warrant his consuming guilt. The boy had been seriously ill. The Domontoviches and General Dragomirov blamed themselves for not sensing his depression, and they did all they could to ease Shura's grief. Aleksandra Aleksandrovna took her to Kuusa, Mikhail Alekseevich gave her a horse, and Zhenia sent her a riding habit. At the end of the summer of 1888 her mother arranged a trip to Stockholm. Such solicitude quickly revived the girl. "When the first shock and pain over Vania's suicide passed," she wrote, "and I found myself in Kuusa surrounded by the beauty of early spring, I felt strangely free and full of life. It was the first time that death's shadow had passed so near me, but it only made me notice life's beauty more strongly."[18] She was sixteen, she was alive, she was looking forward to growing up, and she was resilient. Perhaps she even enjoyed the attention that her role as a bereaved young lover had earned her within the family.

When the Domontoviches returned to St. Petersburg that fall, Sonia Dragomirova and Shura enrolled in the courses for young women that had been organized by the historian K. N. Bestuzhev-Riumin. They were the equivalent of a university curriculum, separate from the regular university because women were not allowed fully equal coeducation. Although disapproving, Aleksandra Aleksandrovna gave permission for Shura to attend and also for her to be tutored by Viktor Petrovich Ostrogorskii, a professor of literature. At first Ostrogorskii doubted the seriousness of this stylish young lady, but as they worked together he realized that she was interested in her studies, and he stressed to Kollontai a reverence for the Russian language. The course and Ostrogorskii's encouragement strengthened the decision she had made to become a writer.[19] She did not intend to pursue that goal by herself, however, and in 1890 or 1891, after a few years of flirtations at St. Petersburg parties, she fell in love with Vladimir Ludvigovich Kollontai.

Kollontai was the only son of Praskovia Il'inichna, one of Mikhail Domontovich's cousins. He came to St. Petersburg to study engineering at a military institute, and there he met Shura. To her, he was a romantic relative from a different world, since his Polish father had been exiled to Tiflis for participation in the Polish rebellion of 1864. Praskovia Il'inichna had supported her son by teaching, but they were poor, and now Vladimir was determined to complete his engineering degree and then repay his mother's sacrifices.

Cheerful and handsome, Kollontai won Shura quickly. "My heart used to swell with indignation and warm sympathy when Kollontai talked about how badly he had lived during his childhood. What could I do so that my admirable cousin would forget all the suffering and all the injustices?"[20] Unlike the other young men she knew, he had nobility of purpose, he needed her help, he could take her out of the familiar world where she felt confined.

Possibly this infatuation would have cooled, as had another since Vania's death, but Shura's parents refused to let her see Kollontai on the grounds that he was not a suitable prospect for marriage. Their denial heightened her resolve, as her love for Kollontai now merged with her need for independence. Years later she wrote that she had married him "as an act of protest against the will of my parents."[21] Determined, Shura launched a campaign to win their approval. Her father opposed the match because he felt Vladimir was not as intellectually inclined as she, and thus the two would have little in common. Shura replied that he could learn to read the books she enjoyed. Aleksandra Aleksandrovna objected because the young man was so poor, and her daughter retorted that she would work as a teacher to augment their income.

"You, work!" my mother sniffed. "You, who can't even make up your own bed to look neat and tidy! You, who never picked up a needle! You, who go marching through the house like a princess and never help the servants with their work! You, who are just like your father, going around dreaming and leaving your books on every chair and table in the house!"[22]

"We had a long, hard battle, my mother and I," Kollontai wrote, "a battle which lasted two years." Her parents forbade her to see Kollontai and even sent her on a tour of Western Europe so she would forget him. Finally they accepted her decision, but Aleksandra Aleksandrovna did not capitulate gracefully. She was convinced that her pampered daughter was marrying because she wanted to assert her own will, not because she loved Kollontai, and that time would prove her right. Meanwhile, she continued to express her disapproval. She told Shura they would starve. She said she would not plan a big wedding, since such ostentation was an unseemly way to launch the marriage of paupers. She bought her child a trousseau of "practical outfits" because she said penniless young people had to wear the same clothes for years. She even refused to wear her best dress to the wedding. "This is not a big day," Aleksandra Aleksandrovna declared. "This is only the stupidity and obstinacy of a stubborn girl. And if her father had been willing to prevent this stupidity, Shura would have been thankful one day."[23] Such carping only strengthened Shura's resolve, and in 1893, at the age of twenty-two, she married Vladimir Kollontai.

After a honeymoon visit to his relatives, the couple moved into an apartment near the Domontovich house. Kollontai decorated it with her parents' spare furniture. The couple had a servant named Annushka who had worked for Aleksandra Aleksandrovna, and Mikhail Alekseevich sent them money every month. Yet despite all these ties to her parents, Kollontai at first fancied herself free. She had achieved the prescribed goal of every young woman—marriage. She wrote in her memoirs:

I remember when I was a girl of thirteen or fourteen I used to think, I shall marry for love. I shall be very happy. I shall have two small girls. And afterwards? What shall I do later? I always had a dim awareness that after a time it would be very boring.[24]

That awareness remained dim at first. She became pregnant shortly after her marriage and bore a son, Mikhail, in 1894. Before the baby's birth she had planned for Annushka to handle most of the time-consuming details of child care so that she could continue studying. She was reading populist and Marxist authors and she was writing fiction. Once Misha was born, however, she found herself increasingly involved in housewifely responsibilities. Not only did she have to spend far more time with the baby than she had expected, but Vladimir naturally wanted her to entertain their friends and to be with him in the evenings. "I worshipped my cheerful and handsome man, who was so happy at last to have me completely to himself," she wrote. "But I was not as happy as he. I longed to be free. What did I properly mean, to be free?" Slowly Kollontai began to name the source of her discontent. "'I hate marriage,' I used to complain to Zoia. 'It is an idiotic, meaningless life. I will become a writer.'"[25] When Zoia told Vladimir that his wife had to have time to write, he replied that he wanted her to be happy, and he offered to hire more servants so she could pursue her studies.

Those studies bored him. Although he would listen patiently to her reading aloud about socialism, Vladimir never debated the issues so important to her. He was an engineer, and he looked with disdain on intellectuals who discussed political abstractions. Such people, he felt, rarely accomplished anything. Shura talked instead to Zoia or to a friend of her husband, a fellow engineer whom Zoia nicknamed "the Martian" because he was "short, pale, and ugly, but with an intelligent face."[26] It was the Martian who encouraged her to write her first short story.

She wrote it as a protest against "the double standard" of Victorian morality. In the story an older woman takes a trip to Western Europe with a younger male friend. En route she proposes that they have an affair for the duration of the journey, then resume their separate lives after returning home. Strakhova pronounced the story good, but too "daring."[27] After encouragement from other friends, Kollontai sent it to V. G. Korolenko, the respected populist writer who also edited the journal *Russkoe bogatstvo*. Korolenko rejected the story as being more a polemical pamphlet than a work of fiction. Her friends agreed and advised

Kollontai to turn to other kinds of writing. Hurt by their criticism, she began working on an article about education.

Kollontai was becoming distant from her loving husband and the comfortable world of her parents. The first step had taken her out of her childhood home into marriage. With that choice she had rejected her mother's control but not the traditional role of married woman. She had seen Vladimir as a liberator and the life of wife and mother as a free existence which would enable her to pursue her vaguely defined ambitions. She could write or study while giving her husband the love he deserved, much as her mother had engaged in her manifold activities within a happy marriage. Only after she had experienced domesticity did Kollontai realize that she could not find the fulfillment she needed as wife and mother.

At the same time she was moving away from her parents' liberalism toward socialism. Kollontai later wrote that she found liberalism "too shallow, too passive, powerless in some way."[28] It did not answer the passionate demand of her youthful character for total, immediate solutions to Russia's problems, and it belonged to her parents. Kollontai was examining all the values they had taught her—their political beliefs, the proper destiny of women—with the independent intelligence they had also nurtured in her, and in that examination of fundamental verities she was not alone. Many contemporaries were engaged in the same process.

Kollontai described herself as one of the Russian youth "who longed for a great mission in life. We reached out eagerly for a new belief."[29] Young intellectuals of the 1890s, like their predecessors in the 1860s and 1870s, were seeking an explanation for Russia's injustices as part of their formation of adult consciousness. For some, the adoption of a revolutionary ideology, "a new belief," made sense of their world and gave them a place in it. Among these youth, the ideology that had greatest popularity in the 1890s was Marxism, primarily because it addressed itself to the process of industrialization then underway in Russia. Marxism was also modern, it was European, it was systematic, it was sophisticated, and it was revolutionary. Thus it served the needs of the heirs to the revolutionary movement, members of the intelligentsia educated to seek Western European solutions to Russian problems.

Kollontai did not immediately choose Marxism over liberalism upon reading Marx, Engels, and Bebel, and the Russian Georgii Plekhanov.

At first she flirted with the older and more Russian populism, but in the nineties, populism had few effective advocates. It was an agrarian socialist ideology built on the premise that society should be organized around the peasant commune. According to the populists, the peasants were the revolutionary class. Yet in the 1870s the peasants had not responded to populist propaganda efforts. Thus in the nineties, many young radicals turned away from populism, because it seemed out of step with the rhythms of industrialization and because it placed its revolutionary faith in a class that had not demonstrated sufficient militance. Marxism seemed more appropriate to the times, and gradually Kollontai too came to accept the Marxist analysis of society.

Some young intellectuals in Moscow or St. Petersburg were content to discuss Marxism in study circles, others made tentative efforts to propagandize among the poor or, by the middle years of the decade, to organize workers for strikes. The most activist radicals greeted the labor unrest that arose in 1896 with enthusiasm, and although many of them, including the young Lenin, were arrested, the first Marxist revolutionary party, the Union of Struggle for the Emancipation of Labor, had been founded. Kollontai was then at home, taking care of her baby, but as she became less satisfied with marriage, she became more interested in doing something to help the poor. She began by working with her sister Zhenia and her former governess Strakhova several hours a week at a library that supported the Sunday classes teaching workers basic literacy and a little socialism. The library loaned maps, globes, textbooks, and other materials to groups meeting in various parts of the city and sent out illegal populist and Marxist tracts under the cover of the legal activity. The organizers also smuggled communications to the political prisoners at the Schlüsselburg Fortress. Kollontai took on the unglamorous jobs of pasting labels on exhibits of dead insects, cataloguing pictures for a magic lantern show, and delivering mineral collections to schools around the city.[30]

At the library she met Elena Stasova, also one of Strakhova's students and later a prominent Bolshevik. Although Stasova and Kollontai worked together intermittently, they never became close friends. "Elena knew what she wanted from life," Kollontai wrote. "She had found her way. I was still seeking mine." Stasova was a stern, somewhat forbidding figure, who would later bear the nickname "Absolute." She and the more mercurial, emotional Kollontai had very little in common save their upper-class origins. In the mid-nineties, Stasova was already involved in underground political activity through the library, but when Kollontai tried to gain access to that phase of the work, she found herself rebuffed. "Sometimes Elena used me as a messenger to take some package of illegal writings to an unknown person who gave the right answer to my password, took the package, and not once said goodby or shook hands. Was this revolutionary work?"[31]

Apparently Stasova and Strakhova realized that Kollontai was still a young lady playing at revolution. When she finally convinced them to allow her a greater role in their illegal activities, Stasova invited her to a secret meeting. The plotters gathered in Stasova's mother's "red plush salon" and "drank tea just like ordinary guests." After the refreshments, Stasova asked Kollontai to dun her friends for money to print an illegal pamphlet. Kollontai left "both disappointed and indignant."[32]

Her first exposure to the forbidden politics of her acquaintances was disillusioning. She experienced no sudden revelation that here lay the purpose she sought, and she later blamed her lack of enthusiasm on the failure of her friends to take her seriously. Yet Kollontai herself was not fully committed to the dangerous and often frustrating work of educating the poor. She still devoted most of her time to her home and studies, remaining within the unconventional but scarcely revolutionary pattern of her mother's life. Unlike her mother, however, she had begun to chafe at the limitations of marriage. Because she was an intellectual and because she had learned to value social conscience, in short because she had become one of the intelligentsia, Kollontai turned to the typical activities of the intelligentsia—studying, writing, charity—but she shrank from a final break with hearth and home. Torn by feelings of discontent, she complicated her life still further by becoming involved in an affair with her husband's friend, the man identified only as "the Martian."

Kollontai asserted later that their relationship never went beyond his declarations of love, but she was always discreet when writing about her personal life. She did admit that in her youth she was often torn between two men. She could not break free of one before turning to another. "Did we really love both?" Kollontai wrote, referring to her entire generation. "Or was it the fear of losing a love which had changed to friendship and a suspicion that the new love would not be lasting?"[33] The motive was probably deeper than either of the possibilities she considered; it was a need for intimacy that compelled Kollontai, and most women, to seek love relationships even though they felt confined by the traditional rules governing those relationships. The alternative was a life alone. Furthermore a young woman learned that establishing a marriage and a family were her most important goals, the indices of her worth as a woman. If Kollontai struck out on her own, she risked loneliness, and she also turned her back on her feminine destiny, as society had taught her to define that destiny. Thus she could not leave one man without going to another, because she feared isolation and because she had not yet shaken loose from the ties of tradition.

Perhaps a woman who had transcended her society's standards could defy those standards without inner conflict. Such a person was the mythical "new woman" whom Kollontai would later praise, whose very self-definition proceeded from self-established criteria. Through a conquest of submissiveness, she could assert both her independence and her womanhood without feeling a need to sacrifice one to the other. Kollontai was never able to achieve that degree of autonomy, and she later admitted to being torn most of her life between "love [subordination] and work [independence]." She wrote:

> It was vouchsafed to our generation to make a fetish of erotic love. Oh, how much energy and time we lost in all our love tragedies and love complications! But it was also we, the generation of the 1890s, who taught ourselves and those who were younger than we that love is not the most important thing in life for a woman. And that if she must choose between "love and work," she should never hesitate: it is work, her own creative work, which gives her the real satisfaction and makes life worth living.[34]

The entanglement with her husband's friend did not result then simply from incompatibility with Vladimir or from a search for physical pleasure. Kollontai wanted independence, but she feared its price, and over the years she devoted a major portion of her work to exploring the psyche of a woman so trapped. In the late 1890s she resolved her dilemma by deciding that she had to leave her husband and her lover in order to study. The affair was a stage through which she moved, from which she emerged. She had begun her search by marrying, then had gone on to read socialism, to write, and to seek out revolutionary politics. By the summer of 1897, when she traveled to the Urals with Strakhova, Kollontai had determined "to set myself free." She had finished the article on education begun after the rejection of her short story, and the journal *Obrazovanie* accepted it for publication in three installments. That achievement may have given her the confidence she needed, and Zoia told her, "The first step is taken. Now you have only to follow your own way."[35]

Entitled "The Basic Principles of Child Rearing in the Views of Dobroliubov," the article proposed an environmentalist approach to child care drawn from the writings of Nikolai Dobroliubov, the social critic of the 1860s. Kollontai asserted that since the infant came into the world a *tabula rasa*, society had only to structure his or her environment properly in order to improve the life of the human race. Dobroliubov had correctly observed that human personality was totally "a product of society." The tsarist regime distorted individual growth by encouraging dishonesty and practicing despotism, but tsarism was losing its hold on the mind of Russia. Now parents could give their children a humanistic education to foster the development of independence and a loving concern for human welfare. Such education would promote "the great and crucial cause— the moral and intellectual development of future generations."[36]

Kollontai's social conscience sounded very clearly throughout the article, as did a conventional nineteenth-century materialism which was not notably Marxist. Later she would scorn the fundamentally individual-istic approach to social reform she had proposed in the article and the liberal thinkers from whom she had drawn inspiration, among them Herbert Spencer. Nor would she feel comfortable with sentences that bore witness to her aristocratic origins: "A child growing up in a family where humane, truly humane, relations extend not only to the people of his own circle but also to the servants will, of course, develop a correct understanding of man and of humane relations with people."[37]

Throughout the article Kollontai stressed the need for parents to encourage independence in their children. A peasant child, she wrote, could develop more self-reliance than a gentry child, since "no one has time to meddle in his spiritual world." She would have been more accu-rate had she said that his poverty denied a peasant child the luxury of a spiritual world; Kollontai really knew very little about the life of the poor. She was generalizing from her own, narrow experience. In the most revealing passage she made the connection between independence and dedication to social welfare. Drawing no distinction between girls and boys, she asserted that a dependent, weak-willed person could never succeed in life. "No, such a person will never take courage, will not have the desire to go against predominant beliefs; he will not begin to search for new ways, he will not begin to fight for new truths, and without such a fight there will be stagnation; humanity will never go forward and no perfection will be possible."[38]

Here was Kollontai's link between personal independence and reform. A child dominated by his parents could not develop autonomy, she wrote. With autonomy, however, he could dedicate himself to "new truths" and drive humanity forward. There was in Kollontai's mind a connection between independence and commitment to social reform; one had to become free in order to work for the improvement of society. These thoughts reflected her own experience, wherein the establishment of an adult identity had involved first the rejection of parental control, then the adoption of a radically reformist ideology, and now full dedication to that ideology. The importance she attached to personal freedom would subsequently make her a Marxist with an abiding distrust of authority. She would become a Marxist for whom the establishment of communism, a time without rules and a place without limitations, would be a prime imperative.

Soon after the article was accepted, Kollontai resolved to leave Russia to go to Zurich, where she could study Marxism freely. She told her father that the trip meant a final break with her husband. Mikhail Alekseevich did not want her to go, but he promised to send her a little money every month, and he asked her to agree that she would reconsider ending her marriage. Together, they told Aleksandra Aleksandrovna that Shura was going abroad to a spa. After moving her son and his nurse Annushka into her parents' house and saying goodby to her friends, Kollontai departed for Zurich in August 1898. On the train she wrote a letter to her husband, who was in the south on an assignment, informing him for the first time that she was leaving. She also wrote to Zoia that she did not intend to return to him. It was a cruel and somewhat cowardly way to begin her new life.

Nevertheless, the independence Kollontai's parents had taught her had now enabled her to set out on her own. Her family's willingness to defy convention, their protective but tolerant love, her own intelligence and ambition, had made of Kollontai a restive wife and mother. She looked at the ferment of her homeland and found purpose in the activities of the intelligentsia, in their Russian blend of scholarship and politics. Although not yet an active revolutionary, Kollontai had already made the choice between emperor and revolutionaries.

2

Social Democrat

KOLLONTAI'S JOURNEY to Western Europe to study Marxism was a pilgrimage made by many Russian radicals, for abroad they could read and talk freely. Women especially had been going to Switzerland for thirty years because Swiss universities were open to them. In Western Europe Kollontai could also hope to meet the leading Marxists, including the Russians Georgii Plekhanov, Pavel Akselrod, and Vera Zasulich, who were in exile in Switzerland. By attending lectures at the university and talking with the masters of revolutionary politics, she would complete her education in scientific socialism.

The late 1890s was an exciting, if fractious, time to begin the serious study of socialism, for European socialist intellectuals were then embroiled in controversy. During the year that Kollontai spent in Switzerland, she became absorbed in the argument raging around her between orthodox and revisionist Marxists. According to Marx's orthodox followers, the working class was becoming steadily poorer and capital more concentrated in a few hands, in prologue to inevitable revolution. This was the position adopted by the German Social Democratic Party (SPD) in the Erfurt Program of 1891.

In 1899 the German socialist Eduard Bernstein attacked orthodoxy in a work that came to be known in English as *Evolutionary Socialism*. Bernstein argued that both Marx and Karl Kautsky, the architect of the Erfurt Program, were wrong in their predictions of proletarian impoverishment. In fact, the proletariat had improved its wages and living conditions and property was becoming more widely distributed; he concluded that the possibility existed for a peaceful transition, or evolution, to socialism by enlarging the gains already achieved. Bernstein's analysis was a response to the situation prevailing in Germany in the 1890s, where, after a decade of repression by Chancellor Otto von Bismarck, the SPD was able to participate in parliamentary politics, and where, furthermore, capitalism was flourishing.[1]

Bernstein stood as the central, catalytic figure in an SPD debate over "revisionism," that is, the revision of Marx and Engels, which had been developing throughout the nineties around a variety of practical and theoretical issues. Because the SPD was the leading Social Democratic party in Europe, the issue of revisionism swept outward from Germany to influence socialists throughout the continent. In Russia revisionist questions coexisted with the argument over economism, a dispute of Russian origin which, like revisionism, questioned the extent to which revolutionary change was necessary. The economist controversy began in 1898 when Ekaterina Kuskova, a young Russian socialist studying abroad, wrote a "Credo" asserting that revolutionary parties should aid the workers' efforts to improve their living conditions and achieve constitutional reform. Kuskova circulated her ideas among her friends rather than issue them in full defiance of the established party view, as Bernstein had, but both her notions and his arose from observing the amelioration of proletarian life in Western Europe. She and another young Russian, S. N. Prokopovich, went on to argue that parliamentary reform could educate Russian workers politically and that the poor would respond more quickly to demands for economic improvements than to calls for revolution. Revolutionary strategies for Russia's immediate present were deemed impractical as well as dangerous.[2]

The leaders of the Russian Social Democratic Labor Party (RSDRP) —Plekhanov, Akselrod, Zasulich, Vladimir Lenin, Aleksandr Potresov, and Iulii Martov—attacked economism with all the considerable polemical skill they possessed. Plekhanov warned that this was a resurgence of the old populist notion that the masses could carry out a revolution without political struggle; Lenin declared that Marxism must preserve its revolutionary dimension or it would fail in Russia.[3] Over the next four years the majority of the party would come to agree with Plekhanov and Lenin, but when Kollontai arrived in Zurich in 1898, the debate over economism and the new ideas from Germany had just begun.

By her own account, Kollontai rejected revisionism from the first.[4] She met revisionists in Switzerland, including Heinrich Herkner, the professor with whom she studied, and in 1899 she visited England, where she contacted the Fabian socialists Beatrice and Sidney Webb; but despite this broad exposure Kollontai was impressed by the antirevisionists —Rosa Luxemburg, Kautsky, Akselrod, and Plekhanov. She did not find evolution a realistic course for Russia; in the articles she wrote shortly after her stay in Switzerland she clung tenaciously to the notion of inevitable revolution. She asserted that inevitability granted hope, and she expressed a distrust of gradualism that was deeply ingrained in both the Russian revolutionary tradition and her own impatient soul.[5] She may also have found revisionism too reminiscent of the liberalism in which she had been reared.[6]

In 1899 Kollontai returned home, now well versed in the fundamentals of Marxism and acquainted with many of the leaders of Social Democracy. She journeyed back to St. Petersburg through Finland, where she met Finnish Social Democrats and promised to raise money for striking textile workers.[7] Finland would occupy much of her attention for the next several years. She had begun studying the Finnish economy at Professor Herkner's suggestion, both because of her own background and because of repressive tsarist policies that were then earning the Finns much sympathy.[8] Finland had been part of the Russian Empire since 1809, but the tsars had allowed the country substantial autonomy. The government of Nikolai II had reversed that policy by requiring Finns to serve in the Russian army and then violently suppressing Finnish protests.

Kollontai worked on her study of the Finnish economy during the winter of 1899–1900. The extent of her revolutionary activity at this time is unclear, but the evidence suggests that Kollontai was primarily engaged in raising money among the wealthy and in arguing ideology with other Social Democrats.[9] Her father supported her, both financially and morally; the old general even hid illegal literature for her.

Kollontai's difficult relationship with her parents had eased now, and her father accepted his daughter's choices with remarkable tolerance. The new harmony did not last long, however, since Aleksandra Aleksandrovna and Mikhail Alekseevich died within a year of one another. In early 1900

Aleksandra Aleksandrovna lost a long battle with heart disease. She left Kuusa to Adele, Zhenia, and Aleksandr, some said out of guilt for having divorced their father.[10] Kollontai never disclosed whether she and her mother became truly reconciled. A year later, in the summer of 1901, Kollontai and her father traveled together to the Ukraine to visit relatives.[11] From there Kollontai went abroad to meet foreign Social Democrats; she saw Luxemburg, Kautsky, Paul Lafarge (Marx's son-in-law), and again Plekhanov. She also published several articles on Finland in *Neue Zeit*, the leading German Social Democratic newspaper, and in *Zaria* and *Iskra*, Russian émigré periodicals. Shortly after her return to Russia, her father died in an accidental fall.

Kollontai mourned for that gentle, tolerant man. They had grown closer in his later years, as finally she earned both his attention and his approval.[12] She wrote, "With the death of my father, I knew the pain of despair from irrevocable loss."

> The most terrible moment came when we returned from the funeral. The house met us terribly calm and deserted. Tea waited for us in the dining room and the lamp burned as usual, lighting the snow-white tablecloth.
>
> I went to my father's study; as always four candles under a green shade burned on his desk. Father's beloved, deep, roomy armchair was drawn up to the round table with the lighted lamp, and an open book, *Macedonia and Eastern Rumelia*, lay on the table. Everything in the room awaited the coming of the master. There, only in that minute, did I understand with full force that my father would never come back to his table.[13]

She sold all the furniture at Sredniaia podiacheskaia 5 and moved with Zoia into a small apartment. Annushka the maid had married, but Kollontai talked her into coming to work for her again. Mikhail Alekseevich left her a small inheritance, which she supplemented with the proceeds from her writing. She was growing ever more estranged from her sister Adele, and Zhenia traveled a great deal, so of her family Kollontai had only her son. Misha, now eight, lived with his mother. During the day he attended a school noted for its progressive pedagogy and at night she took him to political meetings.

Kollontai continued the research on Finland, which culminated in a substantial book, *The Life of the Finnish Workers*, published in 1903. It was a great triumph to have it accepted by a press, but when she went for the first time to see the editor, he suggested, "Don't you think it would be better if your papa himself came to discuss the statistical tables and not do it through an intermediary?"[14] Kollontai had to convince him that she had written it.

The *Life* and the series of articles on Finland, published separately, constitute an exhaustive study of the Finnish economy from the orthodox Marxist perspective that Kollontai had wholeheartedly adopted. She argued that Finland had entered the capitalist stage of development and thus possessed a working class, but that, since it had experienced industrialization only recently, the country lagged behind Western Europe. Among the workers, class consciousness continued to be retarded by the remnants of "primitive patriarchal relations," i.e., by the traditionalism of the peasantry.[15]

Capitalist economic growth, Kollontai continued, was leading to the increasing impoverishment of the proletariat, and poverty would create revolutionary awareness. Here Kollontai accepted the Marxist premise that Bernstein had rejected. In her analysis of the Finnish economy, she dissected every aspect of working-class life. Statistics on wages, housing, and factory conditions were given in detail, to prove that worsening economic conditions and the socialization of production were generating the class consciousness that would lead the workers to revolution.[16] Although the works published in Russia did not mention revolution—such an indiscretion would have brought their confiscation by the police—revolution was the underlying concern. Beneath the scholarly Marxism, the charts and tables, the careful analytical work, lay Kollontai's passionate concern for social change. The salvation of the worker could come only from shaking off his chains, so she searched through the extensive data for the key to liberation.

Kollontai had to use some ingenuity in applying an orthodox Marxist analysis of decaying capitalism to Finland's emerging capitalism. She also had to deal with the peasants, whom Marx had condemned as nonrevolutionary because of their attachment to private property. Kollontai asserted that the impoverishment she viewed as crucial to revolution was affecting the peasants as well as the proletariat. The growing poverty of the landless agricultural laborers of Finland resulted directly from capitalist development, she wrote, because that development was causing an intensification of agricultural as well as industrial production. As smaller landowners were displaced, the poor were driven to the cities, where they provided a labor supply for the factories. The competition for jobs among the members of this burgeoning proletariat increased the workers' awareness of their plight, raised their class consciousness, and thus, by implication, hastened revolution.[17]

Marx and Engels had paid little attention to the peasantry, so Kollontai's efforts to see them as sub-groups variously affected by capitalism were creative, reflecting a common concern among the Social Democrats, most notably Plekhanov and Lenin, for analyzing the revolutionary potential of the Russian Empire's agrarian society. Kollontai advanced her ideas tentatively, however, and she clearly stated that the workers were the only revolutionary class. A landless peasant had to be absorbed into the industrial work force to have any chance of improving his lot or, by implication, of acquiring proletarian consciousness.[18] Kollontai's articles contained little of the theory advanced by Lenin and Trotsky that the poor peasants could be allies of the proletariat in the overthrow of the feudal monarchy. Orthodox and therefore unoriginal, the Finland studies did demonstrate Kollontai's grasp of Marxism and established her intellectual credentials within the Russian Social Democratic movement.[19]

In the fall of 1903, she went abroad, again at a time when controversy was dividing the Russian Social Democrats. Kollontai had heard of the split between Bolsheviks and Mensheviks at the Second Party Congress in the summer of 1903, and she was probably acquainted with the ideological battle that had preceded it. In 1902 Lenin, in his famous pamphlet *What Is to Be Done?*, expounded the theory that, to succeed in Russia, the Social Democratic Party should be a tightly knit association of full-time revolutionaries. The police would destroy an open political movement. Lenin linked this tactical premise to an ideological one. The revolutionary party was a vanguard, he wrote, which fought the inroads of "trade union mentality" among the workers by awakening them to the reality of their oppression. Both Lenin and Bernstein saw that the reforms to which capitalism had acquiesced in the last years of the nineteenth century were wooing the proletariat of Western Europe away from the notion of revolutionary change, and both inferred that revolutionary change was not altogether inevitable. Lenin refused to say so openly, but his "vanguard theory of the party" sprang from the belief that current alterations in the economic structure of society might slow the development of revolutionary consciousness.

At the Second Congress of the RSDRP, debate over these issues, and over the position of national groups like the Jewish Bund, led to a split, from which Lenin emerged as head of a temporary majority, the

Bolsheviks. He soon lost his advantage, but the labels continued to distinguish the adherents to Lenin's position (Bolsheviks) from those who disagreed with him (Mensheviks). Plekhanov, the leading Menshevik, argued that Lenin's vanguard would not be an elite of the working class but a group of bourgeois intellectuals—Jacobins who would impose their will on the masses. To encourage formation of such a group contradicted the fundamental orthodox position that class consciousness developed among the workers as a result of economic change. Martov, agreeing with Plekhanov, charged that Lenin was questioning the spontaneous nature of revolution. Furthermore Martov and Akselrod contended that a tightly knit, highly centralized party such as Lenin envisioned would not be a mass party; the Social Democrats, if they had no large membership after the bourgeoisie overthrew the monarchy in Russia, would fail as a political movement. The party itself would become undemocratic, dominated by its leadership, as tyrannical as the institutions it sought to destroy.

Kollontai became a Menshevik, in part because the leaders she admired—Plekhanov, Akselrod, and Martov—were Mensheviks, but also because she found the Menshevik position more convincing.[20] It is true that Lenin's theory implied the possibility of accelerating history through personal intervention, thus introducing an element of voluntarism that should have appealed to Kollontai's commitment to revolution. But she could not accept a theory which diminished the spontaneous, inevitable quality of social change and implied a managed revolution. She wanted revolution as fervently as Lenin did, but it was to be a great, democratic upheaval organized and led by the masses. Kollontai would countenance neither the revisionists' questioning of the need for revolution nor Lenin's attempt to force it. Thus she denied that trade unionism had weakened the appeal of radicalism in Western and Central Europe, and that Lenin's conspiratorial party was better suited to the reality of Russian repression than was the Menshevik concept of a mass movement. Kollontai would have spontaneity, democracy, and revolution—the central images of nineteenth-century socialism and of Menshevism.

Throughout 1904 Kollontai worked as a speaker in St. Petersburg.[21] She discussed revisionism and economism at socialist meetings, gave lectures on Nietzsche and neo-Kantianism to more mixed audiences of intellectuals, and taught socialism at workers' study circles. Kollontai did not participate in the conspiratorial side of party life—the smuggling of illegal literature and the clandestine assignment of party workers, which was then being managed in St. Petersburg by Elena Stasova. Instead, Kollontai took to the roles of speaker and writer, higher in status among Social Democrats and also less open to women. Stasova said later that she chose to be a party secretary because she lacked ability as a theorist.[22] Kollontai had theoretical ambitions from the outset; thus she gravitated toward the intellectual side of revolutionary politics.

Meanwhile, unrest in Russia was mounting. Economic stagnation in the early 1900s resulted in a new round of strikes, demonstrations, and repression. Intellectuals and professional people were calling for reform, and the inept monarchy compounded its problems in 1904 by blundering into a war with Japan. The Japanese victory only increased public discontent. In December 1904 a strike began against the management of the mammoth Putilov steelworks in St. Petersburg. The strikers were led by a priest and union organizer named Gapon, who in early January 1905 drafted a petition to Nikolai II. Gapon called for an eight-hour working day, civil liberties, and the right to organize and bargain collectively. On Sunday, January 9, a crowd of icon-carrying workers marched to the Winter Palace to deliver the petition to the Emperor. Kollontai was among them.

> I noticed that mounted troops stood drawn up in front of the Winter Palace itself, but everyone thought that did not mean anything in particular. All the workers were peaceful and expectant. They wanted the tsar or one of his highest, gold-braided ministers to come before the people and take the humble petition.[23]

Tsar Nikolai had left his palace, however, and the frightened soldiers fired on the unarmed crowd. Kollontai ran in panic with the rest.

> At first I saw the children who were hit [by rifle fire] and dragged down from the trees. But I still had not grasped what was happening. I saw terror in my comrades' faces, I tried to encourage them.
> "Courage, comrades, it's only stray shots." . . .
> We heard the clatter of hooves. The Cossacks rode right into the multitude and slashed with their sabers like madmen. A terrible confusion arose.
> I have no clear idea what happened then. It was indescribable. I don't even know how I got out of the open square. But I was one of those who managed to escape being hit or ridden down.[24]

The Bloody Sunday attack catalyzed anti-tsarist feeling, and 1905 became a year of turmoil in all sectors of the Russian population. Unions were set up, the peasants seized land from the nobles, liberal leaders called for a constituent assembly, army and navy units mutinied. It seemed as if the revolution had begun. Revolutionaries like Kollontai set to work with enthusiasm in an effort to lead the proletariat, who had started the protest without them. She helped raise money for the St. Petersburg Committee of the RSDRP, served as liaison with the Finnish Social Democrats, and wrote for party publications.

In January 1905 Lenin instructed A. A. Bogdanov to recruit Kollontai as a contributor to a Bolshevik newspaper, and throughout the year she worked closely with the Bolsheviks.[25] She did not adopt their position on party organization and its relationship to the masses, however; the more she saw of the St. Petersburg Bolsheviks, the more critical she was of them. Particularly, Kollontai disliked their approach to the trade unions and factory committees that were springing up almost daily. The Mensheviks viewed these genuinely proletarian organizations as groups that could be educated in Social Democracy, then allowed to operate autonomously within the party hierarchy. Theoretically, they would form part of a broad coalition of various groups under Social Democratic leadership. The Bolsheviks, distrustful of weakening professional revolutionary cadres by enlarging the party organization, wanted to use the unions and factory committees chiefly as vehicles for agitation. The party would continue to be tightly organized.

The distinction between factions remained more important in theory than in practice, for in fact both groups sought to dictate union leadership and decision making.[26] Kollontai herself felt that when union "spontaneity" led workers to pursue nonrevolutionary goals such as parliamentary reform, the party should intervene; revolutionary spontaneity was fine, nonrevolutionary spontaneity not so fine.[27] Yet the Mensheviks and the Bolsheviks did differ on the union question, and Kollontai found the Bolsheviks too inclined to advocate strong leadership with this specific issue and generally.[28] Although she worked with them in 1905, she did not become a Bolshevik.

Nor did she rise to prominence as a Menshevik agitator against the Bolsheviks. Still a minor figure in party politics, Kollontai avoided factional infighting. She wrote about the questions at issue between the two groups, but without bitter partisanship. She never attacked other Social Democrats by name, unlike the leading Bolsheviks and Mensheviks, whose work was cluttered with mutual harangues. As she would do for the rest of her life, Kollontai saved her venom for other parties, and deliberately remained on the periphery of the squabbles that racked the RSDRP.

In 1905 Kollontai published several articles in which she departed from her concentration on Finland and revealed in full for the first time the variant of Marxism which had become her ideology. In two agitational pamphlets, *On the Question of Class Struggle* and *Who Are the Social Democrats and What Do They Want?*, Kollontai presented Marxist fundamentals to the working-class reader. "The doctrine of historical materialism and the labor theory of value," she wrote, "are the theoretical bases of the class struggle." Quoting Luxemburg, she repeated the basic antirevisionist argument—that capitalist competition was becoming increasingly anarchic, that by contrast production was being socialized, "creating a positive base for the future socialist structure," that the proletariat's consciousness was growing toward the awareness necessary for revolution. She stressed the development of this consciousness, just as she had in her work on Finland. But *Class Struggle*, published in the revolutionary year 1905, did not have to be as circumspect as her earlier studies, and its revolutionary goals were stated more explicitly. The growing contradictions of capitalism would awaken the proletariat, who would then destroy the old order. Denying Lenin's vanguard theory, Kollontai wrote that the untutored "class psychology" of the workers was "the greatest weapon in the historical process."[29]

As evidence that the awakening of the working class had begun, Kollontai cited the same reforms that revisionists used to justify an evolution into socialism. Yes, there had been improvements, but only because the workers demanded them. Regardless of the concessions the bourgeoisie might grant, their interests and those of the proletariat remained antithetical. As long as capitalism existed, it would exploit the workers, and as long as there was exploitation, there would be class struggle. Only destruction of the existing system through revolution could usher in the true harmony of absolute equality. In pursuit of that goal the proletariat recognized "class struggle as a fact of life, class politics as a tactical principle."[30]

Kollontai discussed her vision of society after the revolution in *Who Are the Social Democrats?* Again the basic argument about capitalist decay appears. Again the key to the future is seen to lie in rising proletarian consciousness. Here Kollontai's position was still more clearly Menshevik; far from being an elite of professional revolutionaries, the Social Democratic Party was composed of all workers who understood Marx and who "consciously join the general proletarian liberation movement." She stressed the inevitability of revolution because inevitability gave hope to people weighted down by the burden of a seemingly omnipotent capitalist system. In so doing, Kollontai called attention to another quality in Marxism that had attracted her. Marx had proved, she wrote, that "socialism is not a vision, not a dream as many think, but a living, real necessity." The just society was not only possible, it was inevitable, and that knowledge allowed the socialist to deal with daily disillusionment. "The good will of people is not necessary to change all the existing conditions and relationships," she wrote. "No, for that it is [only] necessary that the definite conditions be present, for life itself at its depths develops the rudiments of a new order." With the requisite economic conditions, socialism would come regardless of human frailty. Kollontai wrote, "The merit of Marx consists precisely in the fact that he grasped in our present foul order the seed of a better future, that he showed how life itself, the economic needs of mankind, lead it inevitably to a socialist order."[31]

Under socialism all people would own everything in common, and they would work together to produce goods in response to the society's needs. The growth of technological mastery over the environment and the existence of truly equal opportunity would assure each individual the ability to develop to his full potential. Above all, "First place will be occupied not by competition, but by solidarity, the unity of people who can put the general good ahead of the personal, the particular."[32]

Nothing in Kollontai's description of socialism seems particularly unusual either as theory or as agitation. The lack of precision, the hortatory quality, even the terminology, are familiar Marxism; the pamphlets were a rehash of the arguments against revisionism and, more obliquely, economism, that had been made repeatedly by Kautsky, Luxemburg, Plekhanov, Lenin, and many others since 1899. The articles are important, however, for an understanding of Kollontai's outlook. Taken together with her assertions of the inevitability of socialism, the passages on the character of socialism reveal the enduring elements of her Marxism.[33] For Kollontai the achievement of a communal, just society was of paramount importance. She had embraced Marxism as an ideology because it promised revolution; she believed in the innate virtue of the workers and in their revolutionary consciousness; she hated the bourgeoisie and all dictatorial institutions because they stood in the way of the ultimate good.

What private need made Kollontai so sensitive to social ills? In her earliest writing she had linked dedication to social reform with personal independence: a life struggling for social justice would be possible only if one were free. Conversely, such a life was also, for her, a means of achieving independence, of escaping the control of family, husband, and tradition. Having a strong need for autonomy herself, Kollontai was sensitive to the chains that bound other people and eager to aid in their destruction.

Her drive for independence had been nurtured by her childhood. So too had the perception that her own fate was linked to the fate of her society. Kollontai was sensitive to the bondage around her because her family, like so many Russian intellectuals, had taught her to feel a connectedness between the individual and society, an intimate involvement in the whole. Furthermore she had experienced social wrongs personally as a child. Thus when she became a revolutionary, she built an ideology which stressed those elements most important to her individual psychological life. Kollontai did not imagine injustice: it was real, but she felt it as a greater threat than did many people of her class. She did not pursue independence only for herself, she stressed its importance for others because she knew its importance for her.

Independence and self-esteem were not the only goals Kollontai sought in socialism, however. Repeatedly in 1905, and for the rest of her life, she stressed "solidarity" as the chief virtue of a just social order. She wanted a world where everyone would work together "for the general good," that is, for a society where private isolation would be broken down. This too was an abiding Russian vision with special meaning for Kollontai, who had felt alone through much of her childhood. Under communism she would resolve her vacillation between dependence and independence because there connectedness would not require sacrifice of self.

The attraction of collectivism for Kollontai is far more explicit in her later writings. As she grew older and established her autonomy, she came increasingly to value community. Nevertheless the attraction to communal togetherness, born out of childhood loneliness and her Russian heritage, can be seen in 1905. It appears in her descriptions of both communism and the working class, and her great faith in the innate virtue of the proletariat may have sprung in part from her seeing it as a comradely group. This was a perception, some would say an illusion, common among socialists.

The same elements—freedom and solidarity, independence and dependence—play a central role in two articles Kollontai wrote for the sophisticated socialist journal *Obrazovanie*. She was pursuing a different goal here—to defend Marxism from the frequently leveled charge of amorality. In the 1870s, German philosophers had sponsored a revival of the ideas of Immanuel Kant, seeking to generate an ethics and epistemology that would replace the simplistic materialist determinism common in the late nineteenth century. In 1899 Bernstein attempted to awaken socialists to their own philosophical shortcomings by declaring that they should avoid dogmatic use of the dialectic and consider moral norms to have independent validity. Bernstein does not seem to have understood Kant well enough to be called a disciple,[34] but the discussions he provoked became part of the revisionist controversy, finding their way to Russia along with the more general neo-Kantianism that was common in nonsocialist intellectual circles. Critics attacked orthodox Marxism for founding ethics on a constantly changing material base. Following their master, the neo-Kantians believed in the need for moral absolutes, for categorical imperatives. There could be no ethical action, they felt, without universal standards of right and wrong.

The two articles Kollontai wrote for *Obrazovanie* were intended to clarify the grounds for Marxist morality. The first, "The Problems of Morals from the Positivist Point of View," appeared in two installments in the fall of 1905; the second piece, "Ethics and Social Democracy," was published in 1906. In both essays, Kollontai referred to the Marxists as positivists, that is, people whose ethics had a "positive," material foundation. Thus she linked them to the philosophical positivists, the disciples of Comte, Mill, and Spencer, who rejected traditional metaphysics in favor of scientific empiricism. Countering the neo-Kantians, Kollontai argued correctly that idealist ethics were based on unproven and unprovable "teleological" principles and a priori absolutes. Being metaphysical, idealism was unverifiable; being unverifiable, it was meaningless. By contrast the positivists drew their ethics from the scientific study of society. They understood "that morality arises because of the real mutual relations of people, that it develops under definite socioeconomic conditions, that for its existence it is dependent not on the individual but on society, since social cohabitation of people appears its source, cause, and even goal."[35] Moral laws enabled human beings to live together peacefully; without them the individual would pursue his self-interest to the detriment of group harmony and therefore group survival. As social needs changed, morality would change, and different norms would be learned by society's children.

At an early stage of social development, Kollontai wrote, people were unaware of this process. Individuals accepted the rules of society as absolutes, because they had no sense of their identity apart from the group. Group imperatives were internalized so perfectly that the individual will barely existed. The growing sophistication of human intellect, however, brought some thinkers to question the grounds of morality, asking why they should obey, and the conflict between personal interest and social good arose. Out of self-awareness came a drive to understand moral questions which reached a climax in bourgeois assertions of individualism. Kant and the other middle-class philosophers had proclaimed the primacy of the single will but had also tried to establish reasons for dedication to social welfare. They did not succeed, for they relied on metaphysics. The only sound basis for moral, socially beneficial behavior was a scientific understanding of that behavior, an acceptance of the empirical observation that moral rules furthered social harmony.

Obliquely in this article and openly in the later one, Kollontai wrote that the empirical search for morality would lead to the discovery of two conflicting codes in contemporary society—the bourgeois and the proletarian. In a world dominated by class struggle a morality "above classes" became a "logical absurdity." The moral norms of the proletariat represented the highest development of society to date and were the hope of the future. "The Social Democrats maintain," Kollontai wrote, "that under current socioeconomic relations, in this phase of the historical development of society, *the interests of the proletariat and of no other class whatever*, are nearer than anything else to answering the highest and most general interests of mankind, that their leading principles, and not the principles of another class, more closely coincide with fundamental moral criteria." The mores of the proletariat promoted the good of humanity. Within the proletariat itself, values "serve one single task, pursue one single goal—to validate and support community, i.e., the social cohabitation of people." The virtues of the working class were therefore "solidarity, unity, self-sacrifice, subordination of particular interests to the interests of the group."[36]

From unconscious obedience, history had brought humankind through bourgeois individualism to a conscious acceptance of duty to the whole. The ultimate goal lay ahead. "In this new world, still far from us, there will no longer be a place for compulsion; personal desire will coincide with social imperatives."[37] Marx promised that when people understood their power to control the economy, they would be free. Kollontai prophesied that when individuals submitted to social imperatives out of a conscious commitment to the good of the whole, they would be moral. The achievement of such perfection required the abolition of private property. Branding Nietzsche the ultimate embodiment of bourgeois individualism, Kollontai wrote that "the true Superman is possible only as the creation of new, approaching, living forms, fastened together by widely understood principles of community, imbued with the mighty idea of socialism."[38]

For Kollontai, there existed no ethical god, no moral absolutes, no universal design based on ideas. There was only the rational working out of the unordained human purpose—a society in which the autonomous individual found community. The traditional virtues had value only insofar as they promoted that end. "As a goal, self-sacrifice, self-restraint, and self-denial in the name of society seem moral from the positivists' point of view only when they flow out of living social interests by natural necessity."[39] Kollontai did not explain how determined events could have a moral dimension. If proletarian behavior occurred because of "natural necessity" without the operation of individual choice, how could it be called moral? From the time of the ancient Greeks, philosophers had recognized that a person must choose a right action of his own free will for his action to be ethical. Kollontai implied that as one recognized the utility of moral rules and chose to conform to them out of that realization, one became moral. Presumably one had a choice whether or not to dedicate himself to promoting social harmony.

In a burst of unconscious self-revelation Kollontai wrote, "We overthrow the former gods in order to set up in their place our deity—society."[40] In the second article she added a corollary, "When society as a whole is threatened with danger from one social group, then the act of self-defense, in whatever form it takes, should be recognized as moral; then the principle of nonresistance to evil is the greatest moral crime."[41] Thus in fighting for the good, all weapons became acceptable, indeed virtuous, and all obstacles evil.

Kollontai's naiveté, her breezy self-confidence, reflect a life which up to this time had been free of truly difficult ethical choices. Declaring that "we overthrow the former gods to set up in their place our deity—society," she did not perceive that society could be a bloodthirsty god which would demand sacrifices. Instead she saw "society," or at least a properly constituted society, as a purifier of human personality. "Only in the new social labor order," Kollontai wrote, "in which the concern of society will be directed to the creation of conditions favorable to the flourishing of personality, will the social atmosphere be formed in which the realization of the higher moral person, now inaccessible to us, will be possible." In the meantime, "society, being the source of morals, serves for [the positivist] as the next, immediate goal; outside of social cohabitation there are not and there cannot be ethics."[42] This position was easy to take in 1905, when the evils of tsarist oppression were clear; it would be harder to live by in 1922, when the imperatives of Kollontai's cherished "society" came into conflict with her personal values. Yet even then she would remain faithful to her belief in the absolute priority of social imperatives. She would cling to her amorphous concept of "society," that notion which blended Rousseau and the communal elements of Russia's heritage, and which embodied the idea that there was a great human mass, trampled under foot now, but capable, given the right conditions, of building a perfect community where individual will and general will would coexist harmoniously. Kollontai never realized that these were mystical conceptions, touched with faith and sadly unamenable to proof. Like so many materialists, she thought that her philosophy rested on "objective" science. She had found the nonmetaphysical path to ultimate truth, for she did not recognize that all ultimate truths are ultimately metaphysical. She thought that faith could be based on logic and that evil was economically determined.

The popular pamphlets and the philosophical studies express Kollontai's variant of Marxism; the premises would remain central to her ideology throughout her life. She accepted the orthodox Marxist scheme of history, stressing the virtue of the working class and the achievement of revolution. In her vision of the future, she attached great importance to a change in human relationships from competition to cooperation. The final goal was the creation of both mutual dependence and freedom; the process had already begun within the proletariat. It was a strongly determinist ideology forged by ardent belief.

Yet as her ideology stood in 1905, it lacked one central element: the set of ideas for which Kollontai was to become famous. There was nothing in the writings of 1905 about women. The absence does not mean that Kollontai came to the woman question after her ideology had formed, for rebellion against traditional female roles had helped make her a Marxist in the first place. But she did not embark on organizational work among women until the winter of 1905. Only several years later did she realize that she could make a contribution to the Social Democratic approach to the issue. By 1905 Kollontai had established herself as a revolutionary, a Social Democrat, a Menshevik. Thereafter she became a socialist feminist.

3

Socialist Feminist

THE "WOMAN QUESTION," to which Kollontai would add her socialist feminism, had a rich history in Russia. It began to develop in the 1830s and 1840s, when the intelligentsia read the work of Charles Fourier, the utopian socialist who asserted the right of women to equality with men. The controversial woman novelist George Sand was also influential, although not permanently so, for her free love theories consisted largely of a demand for recognition of woman as an erotic creature. Sand did not make a systematic analysis of woman's position, nor did she support any fundamental reform in the legal and political spheres; still, she and the utopian socialists were discussed by Russian intellectuals in prologue to the emergence of a debate on the woman question in the late 1850s.

Throughout Europe, feminism began as a question of emancipation for upper- and middle-class women. Peasant women in Russia, as elsewhere, were too downtrodden to rebel. They endured all the privations of poverty and endless labor which their menfolk suffered, and they were burdened with abuse by those men, who felt themselves entitled to treat their wives as chattels. To upper-class women, however, Russian society allowed some small independence, and that fact may help explain the rise of feminism there. A degree of ambivalence in a society's judgments of women's capacities and roles may be required to enable women to formulate demands for change that do not meet with total rejection. Russian women could own property, a right for which early feminist movements in England and the United States struggled. Women managed extensive estates and controlled their inheritances. They also ran charities, organized schools for peasant children, and collected money for revolutionaries.

Such liberties were allowed to an upper-class woman so long as she performed her duties as wife and mother, the roles for which she was believed suited by virtue of her allegedly innate capacities to be submissive and maternal. She could keep her property, but she was taught to be subordinate and she was hedged in by legal and social restrictions to guarantee her status. A married woman could not apply for a passport without her husband's permission, a serious limitation since passports were required for movement within Russia as well as abroad. If a marriage failed, divorce was difficult; the Church recognized as grounds only adultery, desertion, impotence, or criminality, and successfully bringing any of these charges was more difficult for a woman than a man. In order to prove impotence, for instance, a woman had to establish her virginity; proof of adultery required two witnesses to the act. In court, a woman's word was valued less than a man's, for the law read, "When two witnesses do not agree, the testimony of an adult outweighs that of a child, and the testimony of a man that of a woman."[1]

These legal impairments enforced woman's inequality. So too did the lack of educational opportunities; until the 1870s most upper-class women had access only to finishing schools and domestic tutors who taught social graces and a smattering of languages, history, and mathematics. It was to education that advocates of improvements in woman's position turned their attention in the late 1850s, when Aleksandr II launched the reform debates preceding the emancipation of the serfs. The initial articles discussing educational reform came from N. I. Pirogov, a pedagogue who argued that women should develop their minds so as to be better mothers. His was a position common throughout Europe in the mid-nineteenth century, when middle-class literature was stressing motherhood as a vocation for which women should be trained. Advocates of such professionalized domesticity wanted not an alteration of women's traditional roles, but a development of women's "feminine" capacities. Pirogov was a moderate reformer; his objective was a literate wife and mother.

M. L. Mikhailov, a poet, presented far more thoroughgoing proposals for the emancipation of women in the late 1850s. He called for equality in civil rights, education, and the professions, and justified these demands by arguing that woman was man's equal intellectually, emotionally, and morally. Any seeming inferiority in will or intelligence sprang from inadequate education. If given freedom to develop her potential, she would be a better mother and a partner in marriage, rather than a dependent. Mikhailov did not call for the abolition of the traditional family, but neither did he stop at Pirogov's well-educated helpmate. He proposed equalizing the relations of women and men by removing the restrictions on women. It was a liberal program, influenced by Harriet Taylor and John Stuart Mill and addressed to the upper classes. Mikhailov did not openly consider extending the luxuries of equal opportunity to the enserfed peasantry. He also accepted Pirogov's stress on education, seeing it as a principal means to female emancipation.[2]

Mikhailov did influence more radical thinkers, however, most notably Nikolai Chernyshevskii, author of the famous didactic novel *What Is to Be Done?* (1862). Dedicated to social good, rational to a fault, totally selfless, the protagonists of this novel furnished generations of young Russians with models of revolutionary personalities. Vera Pavlovna, the central figure, was a sheltered young woman who left her home to become the organizer of a dressmaking shop where profits were shared among the workers. Thus liberated, she went on to study medicine in preparation for a life dedicated to the people, a life she shared with a husband of equally lofty purpose. This vision of woman's emancipation, together with the emerging revolutionary activity of the Russian intelligentsia, marked the beginning of a radical position on the woman question in the 1860s. Pirogov and Mikhailov advocated moderate to liberal changes for upper-class women. Without fully realizing it himself, Chernyshevskii linked female emancipation with the emancipation of all society. Women influenced by Vera Pavlovna's example drew two conclusions —that their bondage was part of the general injustice of Russian society, and that they could become free by working for the liberation of all people. When radicals organized illegal political groups, called "circles," in the 1860s, therefore, women joined. In the 1870s they comprised twenty to twenty-five percent of the populist movement.[3] Women who became involved in populism were aware of their own inequality, they saw it as related to the inequality of the masses of the Russian people, and they thought improvement was possible only through revolution.[4]

Thus as discussion of the woman question continued into the 1860s, a fundamental difference of opinion emerged between the reformers, on the one hand, and the revolutionaries, on the other. The reformers, represented by Pirogov and Mikhailov, sought education as an immediate goal, peaceful change as the means. From this position came Russian feminism, a movement which had female equality as its primary objective. By the 1870s, through applying pressure in intellectual journals and petition drives, female and male feminists had secured the establishment of segregated secondary schools (gymnasia) for women, advanced lectures affiliated with the major universities, and a medical school. Aleksandr III closed the medical school and refused further concessions, but after his death in 1894 feminist groups began to organize again. The most prominent, the Russian Women's Mutual Philanthropic Society, was led by a physician, Anna M. Shabanova, and was dedicated to educational reform and charity work. The Society also favored political and legal equality for women, but its members could not openly work for those ends without risking arrest. They concentrated instead on politically less sensitive issues —prostitution and the dreadful living and working conditions of factory women. Generally their efforts took the form of housing, feeding, and tutoring those girls who found their way to shelters in the major cities. By the turn of the twentieth century, therefore, Russian feminism had much in common with feminism elsewhere in Europe; it favored reform rather than revolution, sought education first, then civil rights, and appealed largely to upper-class women, although it attempted to reach across class lines and ameliorate the problems of the poor.[5]

The radical position on the woman question dismissed feminism as a self-interested effort by bourgeois women to gain equality with their bourgeois brothers. Socialists believed that women would be liberated only when all people were free, and that the means to that end was the abolition of private property through revolution. Russian populists and Marxists scorned the feminists' charity projects, just as they scorned all attempts to improve a fundamentally unjust social order. Handouts could not better the lot of the poor, and the people who gave them did so out of guilt and a selfish desire to quiet the masses. In the feminists' efforts to emancipate women, therefore, the revolutionaries saw, with some justice, a program aimed at the needs of the propertied classes. The Russian socialists, like their comrades elsewhere in Europe, considered the woman question to be part of a larger problem of social injustice and sought its resolution in the restructuring of the entire society.

Kollontai had come to revolutionary politics because she was dissatisfied with her life as wife and mother, and because she believed that revolution would liberate women and men. So completely had she subsumed the woman question in the general question of emancipation that her early writings paid no special attention to women workers in Finland or to any particularly female issue. Kollontai accepted the socialists' low evaluation of feminism, and therefore when feminist groups became politically active in 1905, she attended their meetings to argue against them.

In that revolutionary year the Russian Women's Mutual Philanthropic Society openly called for female political equality. It was joined by new feminist groups, the Women's Progressive Party and the Union for Women's Equality, which were composed of younger and more impatient professional women. The Union, organized in Moscow, made a strong effort to build an alliance of women from all classes by coupling its demands for equal rights with calls for a constituent assembly and land reform, and by organizing clubs to aid poor women. Kollontai viewed these initiatives with alarm, for she perceived that the feminists were moving away from what she judged to be their narrowly bourgeois concerns toward appeals to the working class, and she saw them gaining support thereby. Such activity had the potential for weakening the appeal of the Social Democrats.

Responding to this threat, Kollontai attended feminist meetings and publicly branded feminism bourgeois. She also attempted to counter the feminists' organizing activities with Social Democratic programs, and in that effort she met with failure. Although the party platform called for complete female equality and for reforms in working conditions which included maternity and child care benefits, the party was making little effort to draw women into its ranks. When Kollontai argued that something must be done to prevent the feminists from wooing away the female proletariat, her comrades responded that all their activities were open to the entire working class. Women were as welcome as men to attend meetings, read party propaganda, and become members.[6]

This argument overlooked the fact that proletarian women were not flocking to Social Democracy in numbers representative of their participation in the labor force. Although the largest source of employment for women was still domestic service, women made up a significant percentage of the employees in textile mills, tobacco factories, bakeries, and luxury goods workshops. Numbering between twenty and thirty percent of the Russian working class, women endured more difficult living and working conditions than the men.[7] Generally, they held the least skilled jobs. Where they did the same work, they were paid less than men, and in addition to enduring the dirt, noise, danger, and disease of Russia's factories, they had to cope with pregnancy, child care, and household chores. A pregnant woman either continued working or risked losing her job. Management docked her pay for days missed when the baby came. After the birth the mother could turn her child over to a relative or to a local babysitter or simply lock it at home all day. Many women were the sole support of their families; they often went undernourished in order to feed their children on starvation wages. Forced to contend with all these difficulties, working-class women had no time left at the end of the day for attending socialists' meetings.

Furthermore, working-class women lacked the political awareness of men. They had learned to be submissive, they did not consider it proper for their sex to be involved in politics, and they had little confidence in their own abilities. The men among whom they worked, including those involved in radical politics, discouraged their wives and other women from moving beyond the narrow world of factory and home. Thus, because of their special burdens and the traditional attitudes of the proletariat, women were less responsive than men to the revolutionaries who appealed to the industrial labor force. Those women who went to the shelters run by the feminists of the Union for Women's Equality or signed Union petitions for the vote probably did so because the Union made an effort to talk to them, and because the charity projects were tailored to their immediate needs.

When Kollontai began to think about countering the feminists in 1905, she soon realized that the Russian Social Democrats had no plans for organizing women workers that would break down the barriers of suspicion and apathy. She decided that she needed to formulate an organizing strategy especially designed for women, and in 1906 she went to the congress of the German Social Democratic Party to ask for guidance. The German Socialists were pioneers in work among women. As early as 1891 they had published a paper for women workers, *Die Gleichheit*, sent out agitators trained for female audiences, and lobbied for a woman's department within the party. Clara Zetkin's formulation of reforms for women—the vote, legal equality, full funding of maternity and child-care expenses, and working conditions tailored to protect women's health—had been adopted by most European social democratic parties, including the Russian. Thus in September 1906, when Kollontai went to the SPD congress in Mannheim, she found herself among people dedicated to a cause to which she was just coming, people years ahead of her in experience, yet willing to listen sympathetically.[8]

Kollontai returned to St. Petersburg much impressed by the German women and determined to establish a woman's bureau modeled on theirs within the Russian party. After some argument with the party leaders she got permission to hold a meeting to discuss the formation of a woman's bureau, but when she and her friends arrived at the room assigned to them, they found it locked. On the door was a sign that read, "The meeting *for women only* has been called off. Tomorrow a meeting *for men only*."[9] Although her small group did eventually manage to meet, Kollontai could not generate enough support within the party to establish a woman's department. The Petersburg leaders did not forbid her work, but neither did they support her.

For the next two years Kollontai made more modest efforts. Through contacts among the textile workers, thousands of whom were women, she organized lectures and discussion groups in the spring of 1907; but when one such meeting voted a resolution of support for a strike, the police banned them.[10] In the fall of 1907 Kollontai established the Society of Mutual Aid for Women Workers, a club patterned after workers' clubs organized by feminists the year before. It offered lectures, a reading room and buffet, and even summer trips to the country. The Society soon had three hundred members, of whom one hundred were men and women from the intelligentsia and working-class men. Although she managed to attract only a small number of working women, Kollontai hoped that the club would educate them, build their confidence and initiative, and ultimately draw them into party and union activism.[11]

It is ironic that the police remained tolerant of this venture, while Kollontai had difficulty with her own Social Democratic comrades. Despite her invitations to Bolsheviks and Mensheviks to participate, the local party leadership refused her any help and she had to finance the club with private donations. On opening day Vera Zasulich, one of the most prominent Social Democratic women, told Kollontai that she was wasting time and diverting party strength. Tensions were also developing within the club itself, between the workers and the intellectual organizers. In the spring of 1908 some of the proletarians demanded that nonworkers be excluded from membership. Disgusted with the endless bickering, Kollontai quit the project altogether.[12]

She was enormously frustrated. For two years she had pushed her party to pay attention to women workers. There were precious few working-class women who had any interest in political activism, and the feminists had won many of them over. Even some Social Democratic women were supporting the work of the Union for Women's Equality, which had organized public dining rooms, aid to the unemployed, and other social projects that in Moscow alone from May 1905 to May 1906 disbursed 10,000 rubles.[13] The feminists seemed to be taking all the initiatives toward women workers. When Kollontai spoke on the woman question in 1905, she spoke at feminist meetings. When she organized her own meetings in 1907, she was following the feminist lead. When she established the club in 1907, she was copying an earlier feminist experiment.

Kollontai could take heart only from the continued vitality of the female organizers in the German party. She followed Clara Zetkin's work closely, and hailed her successes. In the fall of 1907 Kollontai went to Germany to attend the Stuttgart Congress of the Second International. There, in her first speech to the international association of socialist parties, she proclaimed the solidarity of the "Finnish and Russian women-comrades" with the Germans and declared that the feminists in Russia presented a real challenge to "progressive" women who wanted "to drink the blood" of revolution. Feminism was growing, but Kollontai pledged that the revolutionaries would struggle against it.[14]

When the International passed a resolution calling for women's suffrage, and also authorized the staff of Zetkin's newspaper *Die Gleichheit* to serve as a woman's secretariat, Kollontai was jubilant. She saw these measures as "a victory for the principle of equality in civil rights for all members of the proletarian family."[15] Enfranchisement would allow women to become more politically active, and the International, in supporting the vote, reaffirmed its commitment to women. Kollontai also backed Zetkin's demand for the establishment of women's bureaus in each national party, because, she wrote, women's bureaus could involve women in the party and goad the men into paying more attention to women. By becoming involved in their own emancipation, women would advance the cause of revolution. This was Clara Zetkin's position: an attempt to blend socialism and feminism and argue for female autonomy in pursuit of female goals within the working-class movement. Although Zetkin would have strongly denied it, she was a feminist, if "feminist" is defined as a person who seeks female emancipation as a primary objective. She differed from the feminists in her socialist interpretation of the origins of women's oppression and in her commitment to revolution. Rather than a reformist feminist, she was a socialist feminist, for she dedicated her career to the liberation of women through socialism. By 1907 Kollontai had become her disciple.

The International approved Zetkin's suffrage resolution and the establishment of a Woman's Secretariat, but its action did not move the Russian party to support Kollontai's projects. When she returned from Stuttgart, the reaction to her proposals was as negative as before. Most Russian Social Democrats viewed a woman's bureau, campaigns for reforms that benefited only women, or even propaganda aimed at women, as feministic. They considered that their platform contained the most far-reaching program for female emancipation advanced by any political party and that their ideology had analyzed the determinants of female oppression fully. Women would be freed by revolution. To achieve that end, they should join the general proletarian movement, not ask for special treatment. Kollontai did not dispute the assertion that revolution was the ultimate emancipator, but she argued that if women's burdens were not attended to, women would not join the class struggle. Other Social Democrats replied that it was un-Marxist to claim that women suffered any more than men did under capitalism.

For support, Kollontai and her opponents drew on the two classic Marxist analyses of the position of women—Friedrich Engels's *The Origin of the Family, Private Property, and the State* and August Bebel's *Woman Under Socialism*. Kollontai had read the books in the 1890s, as had most of her contemporaries, and it was from them that she took both her attacks on feminism and her advocacy of programs for women. Like so many theoretical statements, however, these two provided no clear strategy for organizing proletarian women. Thus Marxists, varying in their attitudes toward the woman question and in their ideological systems, drew different conclusions from the same texts.

The contents of the two books must be examined in some detail, therefore, before the arguments between Kollontai and the party majority can be understood. In *The Origin of the Family, Private Property, and the State*, Engels synthesized anthropologist Lewis Morgan's analysis of family evolution with economic determinism to produce a coherent picture of the historical development of family institutions and the position of women. As a fundamental premise he posited:

> According to the materialist conception, the decisive factor in history is, in the last resort, the production and reproduction of immediate life. But this itself is of a twofold character. On the one hand, the production of the means of subsistence, of food, clothing, and shelter and the tools requisite thereto; on the other, the production of human beings themselves, the propagation of the species. The social institutions under which men of a definite historical epoch and of a definite country live are determined by both kinds of production, by the state of development of labor, on the one hand, and of the family, on the other.[16]

The stages of family development should correspond to the stages in productive relations. Morgan had discovered three general family types: (1) total promiscuity; (2) group marriage; (3) monogamy. Engels added a fourth, the family under communism. He asserted that in the period of primitive communism, before the development of private property, the pattern of relations between men and women was an important, independent social determinant. Then society had changed fundamentally, as private property proved more productive of the means to sustain life than the gender-linked economic forms of the communal stage.

> The old society based on ties of sex bursts asunder in the collision of the newly developed social classes; in its place a new society appears, constituted in a state, the units of which are no longer groups based on ties of sex, but territorial groups, a society in which the family system is entirely dominated by the property system, and in which the class antagonisms and class struggles which made up the content of all hitherto *written* history now freely develop.[17]

The first two stages of family structure, therefore, are coterminous with primitive communism, and monogamy with the rest of history, indeed with all "written history." Engels believed that human reproduction had been as important a determinant of social organization in the primitive past as the ownership of property was in historical society. Thus he asserted that society knew two kinds of production, babies and material goods. This declaration threatened to undermine the fundamental postulate of economic determinism, because it introduced into his analysis a noneconomic factor of primary causal power, the human form of organization for physical reproduction.[18] Engels never clarified the ambiguity.

Accepting Morgan's pioneering but incomplete research, Engels erroneously believed that under primitive communism women had lived as equals with men. In some cases he asserted that they even held positions of greater power, for their importance in reproduction brought women honor and power. In fact, later anthropological research has shown women to have been subordinate to men in most tribal cultures, even those using matriarchal inheritance patterns. With the invention of private property, Engels wrote, control over the means of production replaced physical reproduction as the source of power, and patriarchy replaced matriarchy. "The overthrow of mother-right was the *world historical defeat of the female sex*," he asserted. "The man seized the reins in the house also, the woman was degraded, enslaved, the slave of the man's lust, a mere instrument for breeding children."[19]

Monogamy then developed as the means to patriarchal control. In the early period of slavery, the stage of history introduced by the invention of private property, women were passed from man to man, and in reaction they pressed for premarital chastity and a single husband. Men were willing to accept the principle of monogamy for women because it made possible the determination of paternity, which is essential for property inheritance. Thus women became monogamous. Men remained promiscuous, by developing the time-honored customs of prostitution and adultery. A piece of property herself now, the wife served as "domestic slave" and bought lover. This process was no minor feature in Engels's analysis; he saw it as a major element in the creation of social divisions.

> The first class antagonism which appears in history coincides with the development of the antagonism between man and woman in individual marriages, and the first class oppression with that of the female sex by the male.

He added:

> In the monogamous family, in all those cases that faithfully reflect its historical origin and clearly bring out the sharp conflict between man and woman resulting from the exclusive domination of the male, we have a picture in miniature of the very antagonisms and contradictions in which society, split up into classes since the commencement of civilization, moves, without being able to dissolve and overcome them.[20]

The bourgeois family saw this development reach its peak, since capitalism had destroyed the traditions which sanctified marriage and openly revealed its economic essence. Though the worst stage, capitalism was also the last, for the family was disintegrating among the bourgeoisie and the proletariat, prior to its abolition in revolution. After the dictatorship of the proletariat, the universal destruction of private property would remove both the basis for male supremacy and the economic functions of the family. Women would then work as full equals; through their labor they would become free. Public organizations would assume all services previously performed in the home, including child rearing. Engels wrote:

> The care and education of the children becomes a public matter. Society takes care of all children equally, irrespective of whether they are born in wedlock or not. Thus, the anxiety about the "consequences," which is today the most important social factor—both moral and economic—that hinders a girl from giving herself freely to the man she loves, disappears.[21]

Prostitution and the slave relationship between man and woman would disappear also, but society would not then return to promiscuity. Marriage would continue as an institution based on "sex love" between equals, unlimited by any restrictions save those the couple themselves established. When love ended, the marriage was over. "If only marriages that are based on love are moral, then, indeed, only those are moral in which love continues," Engels wrote. Sexual intercourse should be "judged" as "legitimate or illicit" by determining "whether it arose from mutual love or not." In a passage that may reflect personal experience, Engels wrote, "The duration of the impulse of individual sex love differs very much according to the individual, particularly among men; and a definite cessation of affection, or its displacement by a new passionate love, makes separation a blessing for both parties as well as for society."[22]

Engels ended his discussion of sexual relations under communism with a theme that would reappear throughout Kollontai's writing on the subject.

> That [i.e., the sexual behavior of communist society] will be settled after a new generation has grown up, a generation of men who never in all their lives have had occasion to purchase a woman's surrender either with money or with any other means of social power; and a race of women who have never been obliged to surrender to any man out of any consideration other than that of real love, or to refrain from giving themselves to their lovers for fear of the economic consequences. Once such people appear, they will not care a rap about what we today think they should do. They will establish their own practice and their own public opinion . . . and that's the end of it.[23]

The other classic Marxist analysis of the position of woman was August Bebel's *Woman Under Socialism*, a book that went through multiple editions and numerous translations, to become more widely read than Engels's study. Bebel followed Marx's and Engels's theory that female subjugation arose with the institution of private property, but he explored the history of women in more detail. He saw the Middle Ages as a period of liberalization, marked by a "healthy sensualism" of which Luther was the prime spokesman.[24] Calvinism killed this spirit by introducing the inhibited, repressed sexual attitudes that came to dominate the nineteenth century. Simultaneously, capitalism produced the dehumanizing system in which sexuality was fettered by considerations of property and, for males, vented in widespread prostitution. Bebel excoriated prostitution as the prime example of bourgeois society's double standard, for although officially condemned, it was tolerated to a degree that almost sanctified male promiscuity. Furthermore, since most prostitutes came from the working class, Bebel believed that they had been forced to sell their bodies by poverty, and he contended that their existence was one more example of capitalist exploitation. Like Engels, Bebel saw that woman was the ultimate victim, for government punished her and not the men who bought her.

> This protection by the State of man and not woman, turns upside down the nature of things. *It looks as if men were the weaker vessel and women the stronger, as if woman were the seducer, and poor, weak man the seduced.* The seduction-myth between Adam and Eve in Paradise continues to operate in our opinions and laws, and it says to Christianity: "You are right; woman is the arch seductress, the vessel of iniquity." Men should be ashamed of such a sorry and unworthy *role*; but this role of the "weak" and the "seduced" suits them;—*the more they are protected, the more may they sin.*[25]

Bebel followed Marx and Engels in believing that the bourgeois family structure was disintegrating. To support his argument, he cited a decreasing birth and marriage rate, rising divorce rate, and the presence of more women than men in national populations. In the proletariat the necessity to work outside the home had broken up marriage and family, leaving in its wake "immorality, demoralization, degeneration, diseases of all natures, and child mortality."[26] Out of this morass and out of the proletariat's growing consciousness the new family was emerging, based on the common struggle of husband and wife for the liberation of society.

Bebel's analysis of contemporary conditions included an examination of female personality, in which he attempted to establish that woman's "inferiority" to man, that is, her emotional and physical "weaknesses," stemmed from centuries of deprivation. Human personality had evolved in a process of natural selection, the desired characteristics determined by social values, which in turn were determined by property relations. Throughout history man was taught to develop his reason and will, woman her emotionalism. "As a consequence," Bebel wrote, "she suffers from a hypertrophy of feeling and spirituality, hence is prone to superstition and miracles,—a more than grateful soil for religion and other charlataneries, a pliant tool for all reaction." Confined to her house while her husband grew in contact with society, the woman became "mentally stunted and sour."[27] But just as her brain had evolved toward its emotionalism in response to societal demands, after the revolution it would develop new characteristics. Surely few men set so ambitious a project for socialism—to alter the structure of the human brain.

Of course it is easy to find foolishness in the ignorance of another age, and Bebel's belief in "natural female deficiencies" should not obscure the truly liberating message emanating from his phrenological jargon. In his view woman under socialism would be fully equal in law and work. Maternity would be considered a social function, and therefore the services necessary to insure healthy pregnancy and childbirth would be provided to all. Likewise, education would be universal, but the family would continue to exist, and parents, free of economic worries, would have leisure time to devote to their children. They would also have democratic control over the institutions caring for and educating those children.

Without property, sexual relations would be based on love, "which alone corresponds with the natural purpose." Bebel thought the sex drive, "the impulse to procreate," was a natural human instinct on the same level as the need to satisfy hunger and thirst. To develop normally, humans had to gratify it. But, like Engels, Bebel did not preach promiscuity. Under socialism a couple in love would marry; to have intercourse without "spiritual affinity and oneness" was "immoral."[28]

On what grounds can a materialist characterize one form of sexual union as moral and others as immoral? For Bebel and Engels, the standard seems to have rested on "the natural," a legitimate materialist position: whatever is natural is right, whatever unnatural, wrong. Then, unconsciously true to their own bourgeois Victorian sensibilities, they unhesitatingly declared that heterosexual, monogamous love relationships were the most "natural." Engels and Bebel accepted the long-lived Western norm that pleasurable gratification must have a purpose—procreation —and must be based on a "higher," nonphysical, nonanimal source— "spiritual affinity."

If married partners ceased to love one another, Bebel believed that their relationship became immoral and should be dissolved. The dissolution should not require elaborate divorce proceedings or state intervention. Bebel, like Engels, believed strongly that marital matters were private and should be regulated only to prevent disease, injury, or exploitation. All other aspects of love relationships were the concern only of the lovers.

Bebel concluded with a ringing summary of the socialist position on female emancipation.

> The complete emancipation of woman, and her equality with man, is the final goal of our social development, whose realization no power on earth can prevent,—and this realization is possible only by a social change that shall abolish the rule of man over man—hence also of capitalism over workingman. Only then will the human race reach its highest development.[29]

Engels, Bebel, and, to a lesser extent, Marx equipped socialism with a thorough analysis of the position of women. Despite its shortcomings it surpasses in depth and scope the analyses furnished by other political philosophies. Why then did Kollontai meet such resistance when she attempted to persuade her comrades to support efforts to reach working women? It was in part because Marx, Engels, and Bebel were committed to the emancipation of the entire working class, within which they considered women the more backward element. Of the three men, only Bebel really put a high priority on organizing proletarian women, and all three theoreticians favored a unified movement of the entire working class. Despite the fact that they acknowledged women's conservatism and the difficulties of women's lives, the socialists did not want to admit that propaganda aimed at "the entire working class" reached primarily men. To examine that fact too closely would call into question the myth of proletarian solidarity. The working class was a "brotherhood," united across all barriers of religion, nationality, and gender by its common misery, and destined to draw from that unity the strength necessary for successful revolution. A demand for separate organizations for any group within the proletariat, therefore, threatened to weaken the movement.

Furthermore the call for special programs for women had the heretical implication that women carried a special burden—sexism—in addition to the capitalist yoke they shared with men. Engels and Bebel recognized the existence of gender-based discrimination, of course, and they posited that it, like capitalist exploitation, derived from private property. They implied that women suffered under the dual oppression of sexism and capitalism, but they wrote far more often about the common struggle of all workers. Their followers could therefore argue that since men and women were equally downtrodden, women should make no special demands. They would be freed by revolution; until then they should work with men to foment revolution.

Thus Kollontai met resistance because many of her colleagues judged her efforts a separatist threat to socialist unity. Given the Marxist analysis of revolutionary change, that charge had considerable ideological validity. Were there other, nonideological reasons for it? Were the Marxists in fact sexists who harbored a judgment that women were basically less important than men? In terms of their ideology, the answer is no. Nowhere did Marx, Engels, or Bebel allow the notion of female inferiority to influence their analysis of the past or their predictions for the future. Aside from Engels's naive assertion that men are naturally more promiscuous than women and Bebel's attempt to analyze female hysteria through phrenology—a standard fixture of Victorian medicine—there are remarkably few sexist judgments in their writing. Even these lapses are not integral to the ideology of either thinker; they are merely unfortunate asides.

In their personal behavior, the great theoreticians were no more consistently liberated toward women than they were consistently revolutionary. Marx, Engels, and Bebel all lived conventional bourgeois lives full of conventional bourgeois peccadilloes. Marx treated his wife like a servant, Engels was attracted to working-class women, and Bebel thought women weak and hysterical.[30] Of course none of this would be significant were it not symptomatic of the socialist movement as a whole. While the Second International paid lip service to female emancipation, few of its members saw any more need to translate that commitment into concrete action than did the founding fathers. They genuinely believed organizing efforts to be dangerously separatist, they thought the woman question would be resolved through revolution, and they did not consider women's problems an issue of great importance because they harbored traditional attitudes toward women. Thus they refused to acknowledge the obvious truth of Kollontai's charge that the party's programs were not attracting the female proletariat. Some socialists even shrank from the degree of female emancipation advocated by Marx, Engels, and Bebel, believing instead that woman's proper roles were marriage and motherhood. And finally, all these attitudes, common among European socialists, were heightened in the Russian party by its chronic shortages of members and funds. The Russians had to allocate their meager resources where they felt they would be most effective in gaining workers' support, and most Russian socialists, for the combination of ideological, personal, and practical reasons discussed above, did not consider organizing working women to be a worthwhile investment.

Why did Kollontai disagree? What made her advocate work among women? At first the feminist threat seems to have been decisive. Kollontai believed the Social Democrats were neglecting half the proletariat. Thus she studied the Germans' programs and attempted to convince her party to adopt them. Failing in that effort, she tried some unsuccessful organizing of her own. In the course of this work she moved from her initial belief that the party should do more to attract working women to Zetkin's notion that women should organize within Social Democracy to press for their rights now. In 1908, when feminists announced a congress to bring together women's groups from all over Russia, Kollontai decided to counter the feminists with a book presenting the socialist position on the woman question. Here for the first time she developed at length her argument for socialist feminism.

The Social Bases of the Woman Question explored four themes: "the fight for the economic independence of women, marriage and the family problem, the protection of pregnant women and women in childbirth, and the struggle of women for political rights." Each chapter presented Marxist theory and program, then attacked the feminists for insensitivity to the needs of working women. Kollontai began by discussing the economic position of women because, in Marxist fashion, she believed that economic factors caused women's subordination. She supported her position with an examination of women's history based on Bebel and on a study by the German feminist and socialist Lily Braun, which reinforced Bebel's analysis with a detailed examination of the role of women in medieval society. Braun's work was condemned in Germany by Karl Kautsky and Clara Zetkin, because she and her husband Heinrich were revisionists, and because she talked about cooperation with feminists, but Kollontai found her research valuable. Using examples from Braun, Kollontai asserted that medieval women were relatively free because they were able to become self-supporting as artisans or as ladies of the manor. The development of cottage industry reduced poor women to a new dependence, from which the factory system later began to release them. Female consciousness rose with the economic autonomy women gained when employed outside the home, and working-class women thus awakened participated in the French and American revolutions.

By contrast bourgeois women remained quiet. Only in the nineteenth century, as capitalism impoverished more and more of the middle class, did women of the bourgeoisie feel a need to earn their "crust of bread." When they tried to enter the professions controlled by their brothers, the men resisted. Kollontai wrote, "This struggle bred 'feminism'—the involuntary struggle of bourgeois women to unite, to rely on one another, and with common strength to rebuff the common enemy—man."[31] These were the decisive characteristics of feminism—a perception of men as the enemy and a campaign for bourgeois privileges by bourgeois ladies. The feminists were unaware that the proletariat had begun the fight when it entered the factories, and that without that fundamental change feminism would not have arisen.

Although she believed that women advanced historically when they left the home, Kollontai did not romanticize their lives. "Labor leads woman on the straight road to her economic independence, but current capitalist relations make the conditions of labor unbearable, disastrous to her; these conditions plunge her into the most abysmal poverty; they acquaint her with all the horrors of capitalist exploitation and force her every day to know the cup of suffering, created by conditions of production that are destructive to health and life."[32] Kollontai produced data from the industrialized nations to document the miserable lot of women workers. She pointed out that women were paid less than men, not because of female physical weakness but because society automatically valued women's labor less than men's. Often women worked in formerly domestic industries, where the stigma of "woman's work" stayed with the enterprise even after it moved out of the home. Furthermore, employers assumed, erroneously, that since men were the main support of the family, women needed less money. Even where equally skilled men and women received the same pay, it generally meant that the men's wages had fallen, and not that the women's had risen.

To correct these inequities, women and men in the unions should work together to achieve the reforms advocated in the Social Democratic party platform—an eight-hour day, a forty-two hour week, a ban on over-time and most night work, the end of female labor in dangerous indus-tries, free pre- and postnatal care, ten weeks' maternity leave, nursery facilities in all factories, and breaks in the work day for mothers to nurse their babies.[33] Kollontai did not admit openly in *The Social Bases of the Woman Question* that her own party refused to push for enactment of these reforms. She only testified to the existence of inner-party resistance in her appeals throughout the book for a unified proletarian struggle on behalf of working women.

The second theme of Kollontai's polemic was "marriage and the family problem." She began with a Marxist axiom which not all Marxists accepted: "To be truly free, woman must throw off the contemporary, obsolete, coercive form of the family that is burdening her way."[34] The abolition of the bourgeois family was as important as equal pay or politi-cal rights, for the bourgeois family encouraged man to rule woman.

Kollontai repeated the fundamental argument of Engels and Bebel that in bourgeois society woman could choose only between marriage and prostitution, two forms of the same bondage. She praised the decision of some women not to marry, but she added that "the subjective resolution of this question by single women does not change things and does not brighten the generally gloomy picture of family life." Hope did lie, how-ever, in the fact that the development of capitalism was eroding the eco-nomic functions of the family, so that the bourgeois family currently served only to pass property from one generation to another. The prole-tarian family did not even have property functions, since it owned noth-ing, and drunkenness, debauchery, and prostitution were destroying it. "In the sight of the whole world," Kollontai wrote with ill-disguised glee, "the home fire is going out in all classes and strata of the population, and of course no artificial measures will fan its fading flame."[35]

Kollontai attacked bourgeois feminists for prattling about "free love" rather than proposing genuine alternatives for the masses. Free love among the proletariat would mean that the poorly paid single woman would have to deal with the backbreaking responsibilities of child care alone. The only meaningful changes for her would be those which trans-ferred the rearing of children to public institutions. Then the working woman could begin to know a truly free relationship with a man. Kollon-tai did not oppose the notion that sexual relationships could be sponta-neous and unfettered, but she thought that such independence could be achieved only after fundamental economic change, i.e., revolution.

Kollontai went on to argue that in bourgeois society, individuals did not know how to love. Until men and women were reeducated, love relationships were doomed, because society taught men to treat women like possessions and women learned to subordinate themselves. A woman who wanted to be free would have to remain alone, "an individualist in the very essence of her experience." She might work with "a collective," or group enterprise, but that would not compensate her for her isolation. Only after a revolutionary change in human personality would men and women find the community they presently sought, unsuccessfully, in heterosexual love.[36]

This discussion of love and socialism in *The Social Bases of the Woman Question* was tentative and brief, but it foreshadows the full development of Kollontai's ideas several years later. She would return again and again to the theme of the individual seeking relief from solitude in a love relationship, then fleeing possession, in a fruitless attempt to find solace in a "collective." Kollontai was obviously generalizing from her own experience; she was an individualist who could not reconcile independence and dependence and who therefore looked for a solution in a communal future. She was coming to see the revolution as a transfiguration of human relationships that would remove the possessiveness from love and create a genuine community. Kollontai, like the earlier utopian socialists, wanted human beings to live together harmoniously in groups that had reconciled *eros* and *agape*; her ultimate goal was not technological modernization or political power, but communalization. In 1908 she was just beginning to develop these ideas; it would take another three years before she shaped them into a sensitive portrait of woman's solitude.

The section on maternity and child care in *The Social Bases of the Woman Question* reiterated the Social Democratic proposals for public financing of childbearing and child rearing. The final chapter examined the suffrage question. Kollontai repeated her denunciation of feminism, then defended her own advocacy of the vote for women. She wrote that fighting for universal suffrage was an aspect of the class struggle which could involve women workers in politics for the first time. Female participation would, in turn, enlarge the ranks of the active proletariat and thereby strengthen the workers' political victories.

Kollontai then lapsed into a tedious attack on the feminists. Anyone who considered the vote an end in itself was a feminist, and feminists were bourgeois. Those who were willing to settle for less than universal suffrage as a step toward the final objective she accused of pursuing class interest. Those who appealed to all classes and refused to compromise she accused of hiding their true intentions. Then she trotted out the Marxist charge that no bourgeois could ever rise above class interest. It was an odd claim coming from an aristocrat, but Kollontai did not seem to see the irony.[37]

She was on weak ground in her attack on the feminists, chiefly because she herself wanted the vote as part of the package of Social Democratic reforms for women. She tried to justify women's suffrage as a means to greater proletarian strength, as did Zetkin and other socialist feminists. They sought it, however, not just because it would enhance the class struggle but because they thought it was a woman's right. They argued that women should be allowed to organize separate sections within Social Democratic parties to push for emancipation because they valued emancipation. Here Zetkin and Kollontai came perilously close to the feminists they despised. In their defense, they argued that an autonomous effort by socialist women to gain reforms for their sex would advance the working-class movement by raising female consciousness and female participation. Kollontai wrote:

> The *separation* of the struggle of the female proletariat for its emancipation into a special sphere of the general class struggle, independent to a certain degree, not only does not contradict the interests of the working [class] cause, but is of immeasurable benefit to the general struggle of the proletariat, as the practice has shown in those countries where such a separation has already been carried out.[38]

Kollontai reaffirmed that the vote was a "weapon," not an end in itself. "For the woman proletarian, political equality is only the first stage to a further achievement; her goal is not female rights and privileges, but the liberation of the working class from the yoke of capitalism."[39] Thus Kollontai called for special attention to the problems of women while maintaining at the same time that those problems had no special priority. Suffrage was not a right, it was a tactic. Equal pay, decent working conditions, and maternity care were not merely elementary justice; they were the means to a healthy younger generation. And any reforms for women were part of the revolutionary process, which was, finally, the only true means to female emancipation. The argument was awkward, a bit disingenuous, and less consistent ideologically than the antiseparatist position. Repeatedly in the coming years, Kollontai would argue both for reforms and for revolution, as she attempted to reconcile her feminist commitment to improvements for women now with her socialist belief that women must seek liberation through subordinating their goals to those of a united movement. In 1908, she concluded her book by reaffirming the relation between female emancipation and revolution:

> In her difficult procession to the bright future the woman proletarian—this slave so recently oppressed, without rights, forgotten—at the same time learns to throw off all the virtues imposed on her by slavery; step by step she becomes an independent worker, an independent personality, a free lover. This person, in common struggle with the proletariat, wins the right to work for women; this person—"the little sister"—stubbornly, persistently, opens the way to the "free," "equal" woman of the future.[40]

Maxim Gorky's press, Znanie, accepted *The Social Bases of the Woman Question* for publication. The editors scheduled it for release shortly before the Woman's Congress in December 1908, but they ran into delays in mailing the manuscript to Capri where Gorky lived, and the book did not appear until 1909. Meanwhile Kollontai had begun organizing a Social Democratic delegation for the Woman's Congress.

Although she knew the feminists would dominate the meeting, Kollontai saw it as a good opportunity to present the Marxist position in a national forum while giving women workers who were delegates valuable political experience. Most of her colleagues did not share her optimism. When she went to the St. Petersburg party committee for support, Mensheviks and Bolsheviks accused her of collaborating with the bourgeoisie. Neither faction approved of participation in the Woman's Congress. Kollontai therefore turned to the textile workers and the Trade Union Bureau. Gathering together many of the women with whom she had worked before (Antonova, Solov'eva, Klavdiia Nikolaeva), Kollontai began to organize delegate elections, chiefly among the textile workers.

The elections took place in September and October 1908, in union rooms and private apartments, usually under the pretext of mathematics or sewing lessons. Women workers were afraid of illegal activities, so experienced organizers reassured them by holding small gatherings among friends. In the two months Kollontai and her colleagues arranged fifty meetings, "which at that time was considered colossal work."[41] The task became more difficult when Kollontai learned that the police were seeking her arrest for a pamphlet on Finland, in which she had called for revolution. In the midst of the conference work she went underground, staying with friends and assuming aliases.

Party opposition remained a problem also. Angered by both her defiance and her success, the Petersburg Committee issued a proclamation that women workers should boycott the Woman's Congress. When the committee realized that Kollontai's group had found support, it reversed itself, approving Social Democratic participation; an organizer, Vera Slutskaia, was sent to Kollontai's group, and a new chairman for the delegation was appointed. Kollontai later wrote, "But we had already done the main work in preparation for the congress with the support of the Central Trade Union Bureau."[42]

She never frankly revealed how she handled this last-minute attempt by the Petersburg Committee to co-opt her months of work; she offered only a clue: "Shortly before the opening of the Woman's Congress," Kollontai wrote in 1919, "the representatives of the workers' organizations . . . organized themselves into a separate group of women workers."[43] Separate, that is, from the feminists who would dominate the congress. Kollontai then stressed that the union women drew up their own resolutions, and she implied that Slutskaia was in the group only as a representative of the Petersburg Committee. It seems likely, therefore, that Kollontai encouraged the union women to lead the faction, while subordinating the Social Democratic members of the delegation to the newly arrived committee emissaries. The blessing of the party would enhance their activities at the Woman's Congress, but Kollontai would not allow party interference to change their tactics or rewrite the resolutions they had prepared.[44]

When the congress convened, the Workers' Group numbered forty-five in a total gathering of over a thousand women, most of them middle-class professionals or the wives of professionals.[45] At each point in the debate one of the women workers rose to attack the feminists. The proletarians repeated the fundamental argument that only the class struggle would free women and declared that middle-class feminists knew nothing about the life of working women. Finally Zinaida Mirovich, a conference organizer, shouted in irritation, "Those who don't think it's possible to go along with us shouldn't be at the congress. We didn't invite you."[46]

The Workers' Group presented a number of resolutions calling for complete legal and political equality for women, reform in working conditions, and public maternity and child care. In a statement read for her by another member of the delegation, Kollontai reaffirmed her socialist principles:

There is no independent woman's question; the woman question arose as an integral component of the social problem of our time. The thorough liberation of woman as a member of society, a worker, an individual, a wife, and a mother is possible therefore only together with the resolution of the general social question, together with the fundamental transformation of the contemporary social order.[47]

Since women were divided along the same class lines as men, they could not join a political organization with people of alien interests, regardless of minor concerns held in common. Kollontai concluded that women had to produce the same "value" as men to be equals in the labor force, so they required reforms in wages, working conditions, and maternity care, which would be achieved as part of the general emancipation struggle.[48]

On the last day of the congress, the Workers' Group walked out of the meeting in protest. It was an anticlimactic gesture; members of the delegation had been unable to agree among themselves on the best time to leave, and several women lingered on awhile to hear more of the stormy debate.[49] Nevertheless, Kollontai was satisfied that they had clearly drawn the line between Social Democracy and bourgeois feminism.[50] She had to enjoy the triumph alone, for her presence in the delegation would have meant certain identification by the police. On December 15 Kollontai fled Russia. In her absence her Social Democratic colleagues in St. Petersburg allowed organizing among women to lapse. They criticized the congress delegation for being too doctrinaire, for not using the forum to win over other leftists to Social Democracy. Beyond that, they praised the basic goal of reaching working women, but did not suggest continuing the work.[51]

Alone, Kollontai left Russia. "I remember a wintry, snowy, frosty night at the Verzhbolovo station," she wrote, "and the endlessly long hour when the document check went on. Wrapped up in the collar of my fur coat I walked up and down the platform, which was covered with hoarfrost, with one persistent thought: will I succeed in slipping away or will I be arrested?"[52] The police returned her papers without detecting that they were forgeries and Kollontai went into exile.

Kollontai remained abroad for eight years, during which she lectured and wrote and traveled. She went first to Germany, intending to work with Clara Zetkin. Kollontai did not yet realize that the SPD, which had led the way in establishing work among women, had begun merging the woman's bureau into the party apparatus. Most German Social Democrats were as suspicious of female separatism as the Russians, and Zetkin had won their support primarily because German law forbade women from joining political parties. Any organizing efforts among women had to be separate from legal party structures. In 1908, when the German government legalized female participation in politics, Social Democratic leaders began pushing for an end to the woman's bureau, contending that now separate organizations for women were unnecessary. The leadership and some women members as well had never accepted Zetkin's argument that the woman's bureau should be an advocate for women within the party. Thus gradually Zetkin and her comrades were moved aside, until in 1912 the bureau was abolished altogether.[53]

When Kollontai arrived in Germany, Zetkin was still unaware of this effort to undermine her activities. Kollontai established a close working relationship with her and accepted the German party as the leader in work among women. Her admiration for the SPD was strengthened by a trip to England in the spring of 1909, where Kollontai and Zetkin met with British socialists and argued against British feminists. Kollontai was horrified by the British socialists' moderation. "The English have their own logic, different from ours," she wrote. "They are able to accept the facts, and they only try to make the most beneficial use of them for their own cause."[54] She felt more at home in Germany because the Germans seemed far more resolute and revolutionary.

Returning to Germany, Kollontai established her home base in Berlin. Her son Misha was now attending a gymnasium in Russia, and he visited his mother on summer vacations. Although her cosmopolitan background and command of languages enabled Kollontai to adjust rather easily to émigré life, she was occasionally homesick. In April 1909 she wrote to a friend:

> At times I am irresistibly drawn to you, to Russia, in spite of the fact that for these past months I have lived a highly interesting, intense life, that very different impressions have come one after another, that new, often interesting faces have flown past me, "silhouettes of people" so to speak, who live, in a word, with every fiber of their being. Nevertheless I wish now and then to be by myself, and do the things that I believe in there, at home, among my own.[55]

In 1910 Kollontai went with Zetkin to the congress of the Second International at Copenhagen, as a representative of the St. Petersburg textile workers, with whom she maintained intermittent communication. At the woman's conference preparatory to the full congress, she supported Zetkin's efforts to put the International on record again as favoring female suffrage and to establish March 8 as International Woman's Day, a holiday on which socialists would demonstrate for issues of concern to women, particularly the vote.

Kollontai disagreed with Zetkin only over the resolution for maternity insurance. It called for the package of reforms that had been standard among Social Democrats since the 1890s—an eight-hour day for adults and less for children, the abolition of female employment in industries harmful to women's health, full pregnancy and maternity care paid for by worker insurance plans, sixteen-week maternity leave on full wages, educational classes on child care, free day care.[56] Kollontai, joined by a few Finnish representatives, was of the opinion that the maternity benefits should be extended to unwed mothers. She also wanted the payments to be financed through taxation rather than through contributions to group insurance funds. Kollontai was advocating, therefore, full public funding of pre- and postnatal care for all working-class women, because, she argued, childbearing was a service to society, for which society should pay. "It was important for the conference authorities to stress that maternity be recognized as an independent social function not dependent on the form taken by marital or family life," Kollontai wrote. "This would help clear the way for those new moral norms that are arising in the working-class environment."[57] The majority of delegates disagreed, feeling that to extend benefits to unmarried women would encourage promiscuity and that capitalist society would not accept the financial burden of the tax plan. The argument for complete funding had been raised by Lily Braun as early as 1902; once again Kollontai was following her lead, despite the fact that Zetkin had ridden Braun out of the SPD women's movement years before.[58]

Regardless of her disappointment over this issue, Kollontai thought the conference was a success. She hailed the growth of women's organizations within Social Democracy and she reaffirmed the necessity for them to remain separate.

> There is every reason to hope that the woman's socialist movement, this inseparable and yet independent part of the general workers' movement, at the next, third conference will take on still broader and more impressive dimensions. With full clarity and incontestability it has shown that only

with the preservation of a certain independence for the woman's socialist movement can one hope to fill the ranks of organized workers with the "second army" of women workers, fighting for "the general cause" and for their "special" interests.[59]

Kollontai's optimism also grew from her personal success at the congress. A life-long friend, I. M. Maiskii, described her then: "She was thirty-eight at that time, but she looked like a young girl. Beautiful, intelligent, energetic, full of a spring-like joy in life, Kollontai drew many people to her."[60] At a reception given by the Danish party at the close of the congress, Kollontai particularly impressed her comrades by giving a short talk in German, then translating it into English and French.[61] Her eloquence earned her an invitation to a rally held in Stockholm that same week. Kollontai must have been greatly flattered to be in the company of the leading Social Democrats of the International, among them Jean Jaurès and Keir Hardie. In her Stockholm speech she declared that the revolution in Russia still lived, and the audience responded enthusiastically. A Swedish reporter for the socialist newspaper *Arbetet* noted, "Our Russian brothers could not have been represented by anyone more beautiful than the noble personage of Mrs. Kollontay."[62]

She had less success among her countrymen. After the congress Kollontai conferred with some colleagues about organizing a Woman's Day celebration in Russia. The work among women which she had started in St. Petersburg had not been continued, for the party leadership was not interested in it and most of her co-workers, including Maria Burko and Antonova, had been arrested. All Kollontai could do was write articles which criticized feminist activities such as the conference on prostitution held in St. Petersburg in April 1910.[63] Woman's Day therefore seemed an opportunity to start a new project, a venture blessed this time by the prestige of the International.

When Kollontai broached the idea to fellow Russians, however, she was told that it smacked of feminism. "The general political atmosphere, the tsarist government's repression, the lack of active women workers . . . , the skeptical attitudes of local comrades to the idea of a woman's day, delayed its taking place for two whole years," Kollontai wrote.[64] The only positive response she found was a receptiveness among the Social Democratic Duma delegation to her drafting a bill on maternity protection, and she set about gathering information on that project in the fall.[65]

For the rest of 1910 and 1911 Kollontai traveled and wrote. She spent most of the time in Paris, but she also toured Russian émigré colonies in

Western Europe, gave lectures at the school A. V. Lunacharskii and A. A. Bogdanov had organized in Italy, worked in Germany on the first Woman's Day celebration, and joined French and Belgian demonstrations against high food prices and military expenditures.[66] She also wrote a book on her experience as an agitator, and she explored female personality in several articles. The hasty quality of many of Kollontai's publications notwithstanding, the quantity of her work is impressive. After a lengthy tour, burdened with daily speeches and all the inconveniences of travel, she was able to return home and write prolifically.

In the spring of 1911 Kollontai settled in Paris and began drafting a record of her trips in 1909 and 1910, basing it on her recollections and on excerpts from her diaries.[67] The book she produced, *Around Workers' Europe*, was refreshingly nondidactic, for Kollontai functioned as an observer and her ideology intruded very little into the narrative. She described the towns through which she passed, the people she found there, and especially the party workers and the proletariat. Of the audiences at a socialist meeting she wrote:

> Where have they disappeared, the tired, hopeless expressions of the listeners? The eyes shone with joy—joy and faith in the nearness of deliverance, in the inevitability and truth of victory. How could they live and struggle, where would they get the strength and energy for the difficult, daily battle, without this fortifying, animating faith?[68]

At the same time she recognized the despair of factory life, the brutal conditions that weakened the spirit. On occasion, the misery she saw caused her to question the worth of her mission as lecturer. She described her mood on leaving a mill town:

> And these nineteen days, endless work, already seemed like a dream, a vision. Were they? Perhaps I only read about them. The images of the pale, exhausted faces of the women, the hopeless apathy in the eyes of the men, rose up, flashed before me, revived. Tedious factory cities and towns, the busy hubbub at the party bureau, the gloomy, stuffy workshops.
> A hopeless, monochrome life. After I leave, everything will go on as before, from day to day, from year to year. The joy of life will cool, grow dim.[69]

Party organizers in particular did not fare well in *Around Workers' Europe*. Kollontai generally portrayed them as revisionist parliamentarians, too fond of doctrine. In her account, they spend most of their time fumbling over the arrangements for her lectures and giving orders to the workers. In one typical scene a party functionary advises a factory employee on the slate of candidates in an upcoming election. The party man wants the worker to be careful about choosing people of the proper class affiliation so that the campaign will be effective. Impatient with the outsider's dogmatism, the worker breaks in, "I am a proletarian myself, I drink from this cup every day, and I know that it wasn't agitational speeches but life itself that drew me onto the path of struggle."[70]

This kind of criticism of the German party appeared repeatedly in the book, and it infuriated German leaders when *Around Workers' Europe* was published in 1912. In 1911, however, that storm lay ahead. Upon completing the book, or perhaps while she was still working on it, Kollontai began a series of articles on female emancipation. Discussions of sexuality were common then in European intellectual circles, from Freud's Vienna to Virginia Woolf's Bloomsbury. Kollontai had read extensively on the subject, particularly in literature, and she was also recovering from a love of her own.

She had had an affair with Petr Pavlovich Maslov, a Menshevik economist five years her senior. He had grown up in the Ukraine and had been active in illegal politics since 1889, making a name for himself as a theoretician on agrarian problems. In 1906 Maslov was one of the chief spokesmen for the Menshevik position that land should be "municipalized," that is, turned over to the peasants to administer through elected committees. The Bolsheviks favored "nationalization," or peasant land seizure under governmental supervision. Later, Maslov worked with Martov and other Mensheviks on a collection of scholarly Marxist articles, *The Social Movement in Russia at the Beginning of the Twentieth Century*, to which Kollontai was a contributor. He also published his own attempt at elaborating Marxist economics, *The Theory of the Development of the National Economy*.

A scholar of some reputation, Maslov was also a married man with a sickly wife and five children. He and Kollontai had been colleagues for years, but in 1909 they apparently became lovers. They managed to meet at conferences, during her many trips, and occasionally when she left her work to see him. The affair lasted about two years, until she ended it, even though he offered to divorce his wife. Kollontai told him that she could not take on the responsibility of someone else's children, and she cabled him not to follow her to Paris.[71]

Kollontai said years later that she had been drawn to Maslov by his intellect, and that her sexual longing for him grew out of a need for spiritual closeness to an admired comrade. She felt that his interest in her was only sexual; when he was physically satisfied, he could no longer understand her need to be with him. Nor would he treat her as an intellectual equal, preferring to discuss economics with male colleagues. Gradually the affair soured, as Kollontai found herself interrupting her precious work to minister to a man who loved only her physical presence. He was incapable of thinking of her as an equal, and when she accused him of ignoring her feelings, he replied, "If I do it, it's unconscious, inadvertent. I don't want inequality at all."[72]

Maslov may well have been unable to deal with women as both equals and sex partners; few men of his generation had tried to make such an adjustment. On the other hand, if Kollontai herself harbored doubts about her intellectual abilities, she may have magnified his thoughtlessness into prejudice. She may also have blamed him for her own inability to be intimate without feeling trapped. She was a solitary person. Her aloneness came from her fierce need to be independent and was her way of being independent. He was insensitive, she needed autonomy, they could not live together in peace. Wounded by that failure, Kollontai wrote several articles elaborating the theme of woman's isolation which she had introduced in *The Social Bases of the Woman Question*: "Sexual Morality and the Social Struggle" and "On an Old Theme," published in the journal *Novaia zhizn'* in 1911, and "The New Woman," published in *Sovremennyi mir* in 1913.[73] Taken together, these important pieces presented Kollontai's fully developed exploration of female personality.

In contemporary society, Kollontai asserted, woman's inferiority was imbedded in the pattern of erotic love, the most private of human relationships. She accepted Engels's observation that bourgeois marriage was a fraud based on property and prostitution, but she added that it also destroyed individuality. The married couple, male and female, thought that being married entitled them to possess one another body and soul. No secrets, no privacy, not even close friends were tolerable. In the past, society had chosen monogamy as a way to guarantee the peaceful inheritance of property and had therefore converted woman into one of the male's possessions; bourgeois culture carried that development to the extreme of proclaiming the right to possession of her soul as well.

Was this not the very spiritual closeness Kollontai had demanded from Maslov? No, because the woman had to sacrifice her individuality, while the man did not, to the same degree. He demanded all of her but was unable to give of himself. Indeed, men were taught to devalue intimacy, and they learned to treat women as prostitutes. Seeking only physical satisfaction in sexual activity, they disregarded the needs of the woman. "It [prostitution]," Kollontai wrote, "distorts our ideas, forcing us to see in one of the most serious moments of human life—in the love act, in this ultimate accord of complex spiritual feelings—something shameful, low, coarsely animalistic." Man saw woman as an object through which he could achieve personal satisfaction and therefore "with startling naiveté . . . ignore[d] the physiological experiences of the woman in the moment of the most intimate act." Kollontai wrote:

> The normal woman seeks in sexual intercourse completeness and harmony; the man, reared on prostitution, overlooking the complex vibrations of love's sensations, follows only his pallid, monotone, physical inclinations, leaving sensations of incompleteness and spiritual hunger on both sides.[74]

Men and women needed intimacy, because in modern society all people were dreadfully alone; thus they reached out to each other in their search for someone to break down their isolation.

> We, the people of the century of capitalist ownership, the century of sharp class contradictions and individualistic morals, live and think under the heavy yoke of inevitable spiritual solitude. This solitude among the masses of the crowded, pressing-raging, crying-noisy cities, this solitude even in a crowd of close friends and comrades-in-arms, forces contemporary man with sick greed to snatch at the illusion of a "congenial soul," a soul belonging of course to a being of the opposite sex.[75]

Isolation had a particular poignancy for Kollontai: it reminded her of her childhood. Her need for companionship and intimacy made her feel the solitude of urban society and caused her to respond strongly to the elements of Marxism that promised community in the future. It also made her see erotic love as an important human activity, for she realized that she sought a "congenial soul" to push back the loneliness. Yet this search was doomed to failure, because lovers in the era of capitalism could not avoid attempting to possess one another, and that possession meant treating the other as an object, destroying his or her integrity. Even "free love" did not solve the problem, if those practicing it had been reared on the old values. "Without fundamental re-education of our psyches," Kollontai wrote, "the problems of the sexes will not be solved."[76]

The urge to possess would be overcome when man learned to respect woman as an equal and woman learned to behave as an equal. For generations woman had devoted her life submissively to man. All her education taught her to distrust her own abilities and find satisfaction only in marriage. She gave up her individuality to man's demands because that was what society said she should do, "as if she herself has no value, as if her personality was measured only in relation to her husband's."[77] Her virtues were the passive ones of modesty, chastity, spirituality, and acquiescence.[78]

Kollontai knew from personal experience the pull on a woman of her traditional upbringing. She railed against the "eternally female," "the soft female soul, suppressed, loved, full of feminine contradictions."[79] She realized that a woman's social identity demanded a role more circumscribed than a man's, since for her to be fully female, she had to be subordinate. Practically speaking, that meant being a wife and mother, since any other activity challenged male supremacy. Thus contemporary sexual relations, from their most intimate expression in coitus through the interaction of man and woman in the family, were dependent on male superiority, and bourgeois society considered a woman true to her sex only if she adhered to those strict requirements.

Kollontai's examination of sexual relationships seems far from Marxism, far even from the work of Engels and Bebel. To their analysis of the economic base of bourgeois marriage, she added a lament on urban solitude and the psychological dimensions of female inferiority. She returned to the masters, however, to find a solution; she wrote that all the problems of contemporary sexuality would be resolved by the new morality emerging in the proletariat. As had Engels and Bebel, Kollontai believed that the values of socialist society were developing among the working class. She went a step beyond her teachers, however, in asserting that a new morality must develop before the revolution could be successful. Relations based on "comradely solidarity," and therefore equality, were part of the class struggle.

> Every experience of history teaches us that the working out of the ideology of a social group, and consequently the sexual morality, is accomplished in the very process of the highly difficult struggle of the given group with hostile social forces. *Only* with the help of its new spiritual values, created in the depths, answering the needs of the arising class, will this struggling class strengthen its social position, *only* by means of new norms and ideals can it successfully win power from the social groups antagonistic to it.[80]

These concepts of ideology as a weapon in the class struggle and of new social relations developing within the existing capitalist order were not original with Kollontai. Marx, Engels, and Bebel had all made tentative, unsystematic statements about emerging proletarian morality. Aleksandr Bogdanov, a Russian Marxist with whom Kollontai worked in 1911, had developed a theory of the role of class ideology precisely like hers.[81] She put the ideas together. It accorded perfectly with her beliefs to see that the transformation of human relationships so important to her had already begun, and she continued to stress that the primary change producing proletarian consciousness was the economic deterioration of capitalism.

Because capitalism made traditional family life impossible, the proletariat had been forced to adjust "instinctively." Often the workers chose the same behavior as other classes—prostitution, late marriage, even infanticide—but sometimes they practiced new ideas—free cohabitation, female equality, and above all "comradely solidarity." Here was the new morality. When the bourgeoisie tried to institute sexual reform, they contradicted the basic need of their class for monogamy. On the other hand, when the proletariat abolished monogamy, they served their class interests by allowing women to become "independent representatives of the class."[82]

How could Kollontai believe that such processes existed among the workers? Proletarian men were scornful and often brutal toward their wives, and proletarian women were notoriously submissive. Kollontai knew that, but far more decisive than such behavior, which she attributed to the peasant heritage of the proletariat, was the fact that among the working class, more women were earning a living outside the home than ever before. Kollontai posited, but did not prove, that new economic activity created a new psyche for these women. She ignored that the truly independent "new woman" was the middle-class feminist, who also often held a job. Kollontai concentrated instead on the working class, and stressed that the proletarian woman was economically self-sufficient. That she barely earned enough to survive did not matter; she earned enough to give her a greater degree of independence than women of the past. Because she could support herself, she learned that she could live without total dependence on a man, and that knowledge gave her a sense of worth which her grandmothers lacked. "She is only a poor, single factory girl," Kollontai wrote, "but she is proud . . . of her inner strength, proud that she is herself."[83]

The new woman preserved her own integrity, her own "I," to use Kollontai's oft-repeated word, and as a result she was often alone. "She goes away, quietly smiling to him at parting, she goes to seek the dream of happiness she planned, she goes, carrying her own soul with her, as if

she were alone." Solitude, the curse of modern existence, became for her
a badge of achievement, for she had learned that she could live on her
own resources, regardless of the cost. And cost there was; the new woman
must overcome many obstacles, not the least of them her own traditional
longing to be dependent on men. "The old and the new are found in the
soul of woman in constant enmity. The contemporary heroines therefore
have to fight a battle on two fronts, with the outside world and with the
inclination of their forebears which is deep within them."[84]

The new woman did not solve the problem of sexual relationships
by avoiding them, however; she could enjoy her sensuality rather than
deny it as her mother did. She differed from her mother in that she did
not see monogamous marriage as the goal of her existence. For her there
was whatever work she had chosen, and affairs with men became only
"a phase of life," not its sole purpose.

> But when the wave of passion sweeps over her, she does not renounce the
> brilliant smile of life, she does not hypocritically wrap herself up in a faded
> cloak of female virtue. No, she holds out her hand to her chosen one and
> goes away for several weeks to drink from the cup of love's joy, however
> deep it is, and to satisfy herself. When the cup is empty, she throws it
> away without regret and bitterness. And again to work.[85]

The new woman was constantly leaving men because she made demands on them which they could not meet. She demanded that they
satisfy her physically, and they could not. She demanded that they allow
her to be free, and they tried to reduce her to the old dependence. "The
very woman with whom a man falls in love because of her bold flight,
the originality of her soul, he seeks to fasten to him, to put out 'the sacred
fire' of that exploration which is dear to her, to bring her down to the
level of object of his joy, his enjoyment."[86] Frustrated that men would
not respect her integrity, the new woman searched from one to another,
not realizing that she would find her ideal only in the future, when
human beings had learned to love.

Kollontai saw the existence of the new woman and the new morality
she demanded as signs of the socialist ideology developing within capitalism. When the revolution began, the new morality would come of age,
and the problems of the new woman in traditional society would be
solved. Then human beings would learn how to love. Here Kollontai
reintroduced Engels's and Bebel's concept of purified monogamy, based
on mutual respect, containing eroticism and affection. Couples would live

together so long as love lasted and would separate when it ended. The new society would honor and protect motherhood as a social function unrelated to marriage, and a new joy would suffuse a transfigured sexuality. "Love, in and of itself," Kollontai wrote, "is a great, creative force; it broadens and enriches the psyche of him who feels it and him on whom it is bestowed.'" Indeed, the communal world of communism would increase the human's ability to love his fellow creatures. "There is no doubt that love will become the cult of future humanity," Kollontai declared.[87]

She would cling to this vision throughout her life. Its individual elements were not particularly unique; she combined the ideas of Engels and Bebel with the concepts of emancipated womankind then under discussion in feminist circles, added Bogdanov's notion of the role of ideology in the class struggle, and developed a relatively consistent analysis of female liberation and sexuality. She blunted the effectiveness of her analysis by scattering it over three articles that were also intended as book reviews, but most other Russian Social Democrats, including Lenin, also buried their ideas in harangues on contemporary writers long since forgotten. It is unfortunate, but characteristic of her eternal haste, that Kollontai never brought her ideas of 1911–13 together into a single statement.

Nonetheless, there was lasting merit in her analysis. Particularly important was the force and sophistication of her realization of the ways in which female subordination was imposed by sexual relations. Few contemporaries saw that sexual intercourse often served the man without satisfying the woman. Few contemporaries (Bebel is an exception) admitted that female sexual needs should be satisfied. Fewer still realized that the disregard for the woman's sexuality sprang at best from a judgment that she was less erotic than a man, at worst from a feeling that her needs did not matter as much as a man's. Every aspect of her relationship with him, even the most intimate moment of apparent harmony, depended on her subordination. If she rebelled, she doomed herself to a life-long battle with society and with her own conception of her sexual identity.

This was Kollontai's second great perception, that woman had learned to be a slave. She accepted her inferior status as her due, and every time an ostensibly free woman attempted to love a man, she found herself slipping back into the "eternally feminine"—debilitating dependency. Only by becoming economically independent could she begin to establish the independent worth which was the measure of true individuality.

Other contemporaries, most eloquently Virginia Woolf but also feminists such as the Pankhursts, knew the price of female emancipation, but of the Marxists, only Kollontai gave it a place within the ideology. Into a socioeconomic theory that valued rationality as the road to social liberation, Kollontai introduced an emotional understanding of woman alone in an isolating world. With sometimes excessive sentimentality, she felt the sadness of modern society for women and she tried to incorporate that understanding into Marxism. She did not break free of the comforts of ideology into a poet's tragic view of existence. She continued to see the problems of solitude and woman's struggle for independence as economically determined and therefore as soluble. She remained resolutely an ideologue and an optimist.

From her efforts in 1905 to organize working-class women, Kollontai had moved to accept Clara Zetkin's socialist feminism. She then worked, first in Russia and later abroad, to establish an autonomous women's movement within the larger socialist movement. Now she had produced an analysis of sexuality and female emancipation which blended orthodox Marxism with her own understanding of women's oppression. These were the two aspects of Kollontai's socialist feminism—advocacy of reforms for women achieved by women's organizations and exploration of the psychology of subordination. While she was occupied with her writing about psychology, the opposition of her Russian comrades to work among women began to soften.

In 1912 and 1913 Kollontai studied in depth the question of maternity insurance, in order to advise the Social Democratic Duma delegation on drafting a bill and to prepare a book of her own on the subject. Apparently the Mensheviks were now willing to work to achieve at least some of the reforms advocated in the party platform. At the same time, the attitude of the party toward organizing working-class women also began to change, and Kollontai found that Konkordiia Samoilova, Inessa Armand, and Nadezhda Krupskaia had become interested in women workers. This was not an unmixed blessing, for these women were all Bolsheviks, and now factional rivalry became a hindrance to effective cooperation as well as a spur to organizing women.

Kollontai wrote later that the new attitudes toward work among women came as a response to the increased activism of the Russian proletariat. The deceptive quiet between 1908 and 1911, enforced by tsarist repression, exploded in 1912 in a wave of strikes, to which the government responded with force. The revolutionaries observing this violence believed that more working women were taking part in the demonstrations than ever before. Moreover, the government, bowing to union pressure, had recently decided to allow female workers to vote in elections for the factory committees that administered worker insurance funds. This combination of new activism and new power for proletarian women alerted Social Democrats to the possibilities of organizing them.[88]

At the same time Bolshevik-Menshevik competition was growing more intense, as each group sought support within the unions and as Duma elections neared in the fall of 1912. In both campaigns the Mensheviks came out ahead of the Bolsheviks, and they seemed to command the votes of activist women more than did the Bolsheviks. They may have had an advantage with women because they were supporting maternity legislation, but the exact reason for their popularity and even the extent of that popularity remain unclear. What is certain is that in 1912 and 1913 several Bolshevik women believed that the other faction of the party was winning over the female proletariat.

The first Bolshevik to reach this conclusion was Konkordiia Nikolaevna Samoilova, an editor of *Pravda*. Born in 1876 in Irkutsk to a priestly family named Gromov, she had attended a gymnasium and moved easily into the Marxist and populist circles of her home town. Her ambition, rare in a woman of her social level, took her to St. Petersburg in the mid-nineties to study in the lecture courses for women given by university professors, the Bestuzhev-Riumin courses, which Kollontai also had attended. Arrested at a student demonstration in 1901, Samoilova served a brief jail term, then went to Paris to study with Marxist émigrés. Between 1903 and 1909 she worked as a Bolshevik in various cities throughout European Russia. She also married a colleague, A. A. Samoilov. By 1912 she had settled in the capital.[89] A calm, organized, persuasive woman with a talent for compromise, Samoilova decided in the winter of 1912–13 that her faction must make some overtures toward working women.

She talked about the problem with her co-workers on *Pravda*, and with Inessa Armand, who was then in St. Petersburg. Inessa, as she was usually called, had been born Elizabeth d'Herbenville in 1874 in Paris, the daughter of a Frenchman and a Scot who were music hall performers. After her father died, her mother sent Elizabeth to Russia with her aunt and her grandmother. The two women worked as tutors to the children of Evgenii Armand, and the wealthy and generous Armand family practically adopted the young Inessa. She grew up near Moscow and was educated with the Armand children. By the time she was eighteen, she had a fluent command of English, German, French, and Russian, was a skilled musician, and a beautiful woman. She then married her benefactor's second son, Aleksandr.[90]

Elizabeth lived with her husband for seven years and bore him five children, but she, like Kollontai, was not satisfied with a traditional life. She moved through a Tolstoian phase of ministering to the peasants on the Armand estate, then worked on the rehabilitation of prostitutes in Moscow. Finally she decided to leave Armand in 1904 so that she could study socialism abroad. She came back to Russia in 1905 as a Bolshevik, taking Inessa as a pseudonym, and began the usual round of party work, followed by arrest, followed by more party work, followed by arrest. In 1909 she left Russia, and she settled in Paris in 1910. There she became a friend of Lenin and Krupskaia, his wife. It was as Lenin's emissary that she returned to Russia in 1912.[91]

Inessa was already interested in work among women when she began to discuss the question with Samoilova. In 1911 in Paris she and Krupskaia attempted to organize a school for Russian women working in the city. Lenin approved the idea, but other Bolsheviks responded with the usual criticism that such specialized efforts were feminist; the resistance forced Inessa and Krupskaia to abandon the project.[92] In St. Petersburg in 1912 Inessa and Samoilova worked together on *Pravda*, until Inessa was arrested. She managed to escape abroad in 1913, going to Cracow, where Lenin and Krupskaia were living, and carrying with her a determination that the Bolsheviks should set up some programs for working women. By the fall of 1913, when Lenin held a meeting of the Central Committee and the Bolshevik Duma delegates in Poland, Krupskaia had come to support Inessa. Krupskaia told the Duma delegates that they should publish literature on problems of concern to women workers, establish study circles for them, and bring their own wives to party conferences abroad. A member of the delegation, G. I. Petrovskii, recalled:

> She asked [me] to put her in touch with the deputies' wives and to help them write to her about the needs of the workers' families; she tried to convince me that the Bolsheviks should organize a woman's movement and not concede to the Mensheviks in this matter; she recommended that I make contact with the women doing illegal work in Russia. "This is very important for the party," said Nadezhda Konstantinovna. "We may be driving away those comrades who will lay the foundations for work among women."[93]

Krupskaia, the third Bolshevik to join the new work, had been born in 1869 in St. Petersburg. Her mother was a governess, her father an army officer, and they introduced her early to populism. In the mid-1890s she was working in the Sunday school movement in the capital, where she met Lenin. Arrested in 1896 for strike activity, she went into exile with the young Ulianov, they married, and she spent the rest of her life in his shadow. She is usually described as his secretary, although she herself preferred to say that she was a party secretary.[94] Her chief independent activity was her work in education, but she was also interested in work among women. It was she who wrote the first Russian pamphlet on the subject, *The Woman Worker*, in 1900. It was she who discussed the problem with Inessa in 1911 and pushed the Duma delegation in 1913. She remained suspicious of female separatism, repeatedly cautioning the people in St. Petersburg against feminist deviations, but she stood strongly for the need to establish organizing efforts for women within the Bolshevik faction.

Samoilova took the first initiative by holding a celebration of International Woman's Day in February 1913. To disguise the political character of the meeting, the organizers called it "a scientific morning" to discuss various issues of concern to women. Samoilova even had fake five kopek tickets printed. The meeting consisted of speeches by women workers on subjects of socialist concern—factory conditions, prostitution, peasant life, and the Revolution of 1905. Apparently the police in attendance realized the revolutionary intent of the speakers, for later that night they arrested several of them.[95]

This helped to subdue the organizers, and for the remainder of 1913 neither Bolsheviks nor Mensheviks did any work among the female proletariat. Inessa and Krupskaia were conferring abroad, however, and Samoilova wrote to them suggesting a special newspaper dedicated to proletarian women. The number of letters that *Pravda* received from women had grown so large that the newspaper could no longer print them all, and this allowed Samoilova to argue that a publication for working women would be well received. Krupskaia and Inessa approved the proposal from Petersburg, and Lenin agreed with them. When Inessa left Cracow for Paris in the fall of 1913, they had decided that she and Liudmilla Stal' should draft a plan for the first issue of *Rabotnitsa* (Woman Worker), then send it to Krupskaia, who would act as liaison with Samoilova and the other editors in Russia.[96]

Meanwhile the Mensheviks were making plans to publish a news-paper for women. Kollontai was gratified by the new, though tentative legitimacy that organizing efforts among the female proletariat had ac-quired. No one was talking about a woman's bureau yet, but at least some Bolsheviks and Mensheviks were willing to allow publications and meetings for women. Kollontai exhorted the two factions to coordinate their activities in various articles printed in *Pravda* in 1913 and 1914. She aimed her appeals at those Social Democrats who continued to see the work as feminist, arguing that the party needed not only organizing efforts but a full-fledged woman's bureau. The bureau would involve women in the party and give them a means to work for their own needs: "motherhood, the protection of children, the standardization of child and female labor, the battle with prostitution, . . . the achievement of political and civil equality for women." Only if they were fully equal could women become partners with men in the revolutionary struggle, able to partici-pate under conditions of "comradely feelings between the sexes with full economic independence from one another."[97]

Many Bolsheviks, including Krupskaia, had not accepted Kollontai's argument for a woman's bureau. They did not oppose the improvement of life for working women; the party had been committed to reforms such as maternity care for years, but leading Bolsheviks still denied the utility of any new effort to secure those reforms. Such an effort would only divert scarce resources from the revolution itself; the goal now should be to involve women in the general revolutionary movement. In an article for the first issue of *Rabotnitsa* Krupskaia wrote that "the woman question for men and women workers is a question of how to draw the backward masses of women workers into the organization, how to explain their interests to them better, how to make them comrades in the general struggle sooner."[98] She admitted the need for direct agitation among women, but she continued to resist Zetkin's idea of a woman's bureau which would push for reform now, act as an advocate for women within the party, and in the process raise women's political consciousness.

So did a great many Mensheviks. There was no unanimity on the issue in either faction, since some Bolsheviks such as Samoilova stood closer to Kollontai that did many of her own Menshevik colleagues. Nonetheless, in the winter of 1914, when planning began in St. Petersburg for the two newspapers and for the second celebration of International Woman's Day, the Menshevik staff of *Novaia rabochaia gazeta* began to argue with the *Pravda* people. The Mensheviks wanted the Woman's Day demonstrations to be run primarily by women and to demand reforms for women, especially passage of the maternity insurance bill. The Bolsheviks called instead for rallies dedicated to rights for all people; in other words, they wanted to turn a day set aside for women by the Copenhagen Congress into a general political protest. Samoilova wrote in *Pravda* that special attention to women was feminism.[99]

Given tsarist attitudes, the debate proved academic. Five days before Woman's Day, on February 18, the police broke into a meeting of the *Rabotnitsa* staff, arrested all the women there, and seized the articles they were editing. Of the organizers, only Anna Elizarova, Lenin's sister, remained free, and she managed to put together a newspaper in time for the holiday. Meetings were held in St. Petersburg, Samara, Saratov, Ivanovo-Voznesensk, Kiev, and Moscow with varying degrees of success. In Moscow, the organizers could only have "fleeting gatherings" because the police had refused them permission to meet publicly, and in Kiev for the same reason the women resorted to the custom common among revolutionaries of meeting in a field outside the city.[100]

Rabotnitsa published six more issues, under constant police scrutiny. Elizarova had difficulty paying for the printing because influential St. Petersburg Bolsheviks disliked the notion of a newspaper for women. She managed to fund it with some party support and worker contributions, but in the summer the government outlawed it. At least *Rabotnitsa* succeeded in publishing seven issues; the Menshevik *Golos rabotnitsy* appeared only twice before the police moved in.

While Elizarova was fighting for the newspaper in Russia, Inessa and Kollontai were coming into conflict abroad. In 1910 the International had named Kollontai a member of the Woman's Secretariat and assigned her to report on maternity insurance at the next meeting, scheduled for August 1914. In 1910 Kollontai was the only Russian attending the women's meetings. In late May or early June of 1914, Inessa was appointed to the Woman's Secretariat "in the name of the women's organizations of the RSDRP and the group of Social Democratic women taking part in the trade unions and organizations of the RSDRP, and also in the name of the journal *Rabotnitsa*." Krupskaia signed the accrediting mandate.[101] Since the Bolsheviks firmly refused to allow any "women's organizations" within the party, it it difficult to know precisely what Inessa represented other than the newspaper, but it is not difficult to understand why she was appointed. Sometime before July 9 Lenin wrote to her:

Dear friend!

As regards a common or a separate delegation from the liquidators [Mensheviks], I advise you not to decide now, that is, not to say "The delegates themselves decided." (Of course we shall take two different [delegations]; by the regulations of the International we must first try it together and if they [the Mensheviks] *do not agree*, then the Bureau decides the distribution of the votes.)

As regards Kollontai's report, I agree with you; let her stay, but not from Russia. And you will take the floor first or second in the discussions.[102]

Inessa was going to the meeting intending to split the delegation, then present the Bolshevik position in opposition to Kollontai and perhaps even attempt to discredit her as a representative of Russian Social Democracy. Presumably she would argue against special efforts for women workers that detracted from the revolutionary struggle.

In Berlin Kollontai was working on preparations for the conference, aware that there would be a fight, but not anticipating the full extent of Lenin's intentions. In April representatives of the Woman's Secretariat met in her apartment to make speaking assignments and to complete the preliminary organizational work. After the meeting they held an antiwar rally, but Kollontai could not appear because the police were following her. Life in Berlin was further complicated that spring by the fact that she was arguing with some of her Menshevik colleagues over proper tactics toward the Bolsheviks.[103] In July she decided to go to Bavaria for a weeks' rest prior to the meeting of the Woman's Secretariat.

The Woman's Secretariat never convened, for in July 1914 Europe plunged into World War I, and socialists, including Kollontai, postponed work among women for the duration. She had come a long way since her first tentative steps toward the female proletariat in 1905. She had become an advocate for a woman's movement within Social Democracy, she had written eloquently on women's oppression and emancipation, and she had seen the foundations laid for work among women in the Russian party. She had also found her calling. Kollontai was well on the way to becoming one of the leading feminists of the Social Democratic movement.

4

Internationalist

WORLD WAR I, which destroyed a generation, impelled Kollontai to become a Bolshevik. She had always believed that war in the era of capitalism would be a conflagration in which workers fell victim to the nationalistic hostilities of the ruling classes. Thus she participated with enthusiasm in the conference of the International which met at Basel in 1912 to reaffirm the socialist opposition to war. Shortly afterwards in a letter to her friend Tatiana Shchepkina-Kupernik, Kollontai wrote, "I have had to speak against the war, threaten revolution, the 'red specter,' if the powers risk war." In addition to her ideological interpretation of capitalist warfare, she hated the atrocity of combat. Most socialists felt the same as she, but in their meetings and demonstrations there was also an aura of unreality, a touch of sloganeering and bravado that masked the fact that they lacked an effective program and the power to halt war should it begin. Kollontai too became caught up in the euphoria of making declarations which had no force. In the letter written to her friend after the Basel Conference, she confessed, "You know, it was grand, that protest of the peoples against the war. The marvelous voice of Jaurès, the gray head of Keir Hardie, the revolutionary songs, the processions, meetings, the enthusiastic youth. I lived it all fully."[1]

When the war actually began, in July 1914, Kollontai was vacationing in the Bavarian resort town of Kohlgrub. There she read the newspapers avidly, hoping that the conflict between Austria and Serbia over the assassination of Archduke Franz Ferdinand would be resolved peacefully. There had been crises before, in Morocco and the Balkans, and the Great Powers had somehow managed to find an accommodation. Yet this time many Europeans sensed that their rulers would not compromise. On July 26 Kollontai wrote in her diary:

> No, something fearful is building. The newspapers write seriously of war. No one wants it. Everyone thinks it would be *der grösste Ursinns* [the greatest madness]. Resort life takes its normal course. The ladies dance, stout matrons gossip. It is strange to see how everyone tries to assure one another that war is impossible. But in his soul each is afraid and everyone seems to be waiting for something.[2]

When the news finally arrived that Austria had declared war on Serbia, Kollontai knew that there would be no peace. "And yet I don't believe it, I don't comprehend it, I don't feel it."[3]

She arrived back in Berlin on August 2, the day after Germany declared war on Russia, and she found the city in a rush toward combat. Newly mobilized soldiers filled the trains, the streets swarmed with preparations. In the bellicose mood that gripped the nation, Russians had become enemy aliens.

Kollontai worried first about her son Misha, who was in Berlin. He was now a young man of twenty, and sending him back to Russia meant almost certain conscription, unless he could get an educational deferment. Neither he nor the many other Russian émigrés could stay in Germany, given the hostility toward them there, and yet the government had closed the borders, so it was extremely difficult to leave.

Two days after she returned to Berlin, on August 4, Kollontai and Misha were called to police headquarters for questioning. The authorities soon released her, after an interrogation about her revolutionary activities. Misha remained in jail, however, probably because he was a prime prospect for military service, and his mother could not find out where he was being held. It was a sad, confusing time for her: the dreaded war had begun; her son was imprisoned; Germans had become enemies; and most awful of all, the people of Berlin were turning out to cheer the departing soldiers. Even her socialist comrades offered her no comfort. Only Karl Liebknecht helped Kollontai argue for Misha's release, while the rest of the Social Democrats were deciding how to respond to the war.

On August 4 the German socialists had to choose whether to vote for or against military appropriations. If they approved the government's request for emergency funds, they would, in effect, be voting to support the war effort. For years the Second International had vowed to oppose any war fought for the benefit of the capitalist rulers of Europe. Now, when the time came for the Germans to make a decisive choice, the majority approved the expenditures, justifying them as necessary "for national defense." Kollontai sat in the gallery of the Reichstag that day and watched with disbelief as the illusion of an international socialist community died. "And over everything," she wrote, "like lead, weighed the realization: they voted for war! There is no more international solidarity!"[4] The "collective" in which she put so much faith dissolved before her eyes, leaving her betrayed. "I knew horror and despair," she wrote. "It seemed to me that all was lost. The atmosphere was so stifling and hopeless that it was as if a wall had grown up before me and there was no way ahead."[5]

On August 7 the police released Misha, and Kollontai, along with other Russian émigrés, continued to search for a way out of Germany. One German Social Democrat asked them if they thought they could now organize a successful revolution at home. "I did not like the sudden interest with which he put such questions to us," Kollontai wrote. "Is it possible that he supposes that Russian socialists intend to work at the Kaiser's right hand?"[6] She left Germany in early September, having decided to go to Scandinavia and attempt to contact other Social Democrats who opposed the war.[7]

Apparently she never hesitated in her attitude toward the fighting, was never caught up in the wave of patriotism that swept over Europe to engulf most socialists. In 1926 she wrote, "War seemed to me an abomination, madness, a crime; from the very first, more from impulse than reflection, I have rejected it inwardly and up to this very moment I cannot reconcile myself to it. The frenzy of patriotic feeling remains very strange to me."[8] Although a daughter of the military, she had grown up among various nationalities—Bulgarians, Finns, Russians—and was herself both Finnish and Russian. Her parents had taught her to be at home in several cultures, so she had taken easily to the internationalism of

Marxist socialism. Furthermore, that aspect of the ideology spoke to her longing for a collectivist peace after the revolution. Despite all her rhetoric about class warfare, Kollontai felt a pacifist's abhorrence of violence.

Many socialists, the majority, did not share Kollontai's feelings. For years the International had preached that war only served the interests of the ruling classes, that it was the ultimate expression of capitalist competition. The proletarian had no country; his first loyalty should lie with all other workers, regardless of nationality, for they were his true brothers in misery. When the war began, however, the claims of homeland proved to be unexpectedly strong, and many socialists supported their nation's participation in the conflict, arguing that they must defend themselves from an aggressive enemy. Others, not swept away by patriotism, went along with the war spirit because they doubted the political wisdom of flying in the face of public opinion. Only a few socialists applied the old arguments against capitalist war to this war, and they were a minority now within the Social Democratic parties of the combatant nations of Europe. They wanted to generate some sort of organized opposition to the war, but they were loath at first to renounce their colleagues who supported defensive combat. Thus confused and uncertain, the antiwar elements of the Second International began a vain search for unity in a futile effort to stop the slaughter.

After a brief stay in Denmark, Kollontai went with Misha to Stockholm, where the left wing of the Social Democratic Party, led by Zeth Höglund and Fredrik Ström, shared her opposition to the war. She gave vent to her feelings by writing a passionate declaration to women, which she circulated among the Russian community in Sweden and Denmark and then smuggled back into Russia. In it she called for women all over Europe to unite in demanding a just, democratic peace. "The war is not only booty, power, and devastation," Kollontai wrote, "not only suffering, unemployment, and poverty; it is also the unleashing of all the wild passions among humanity, it is the triumph of raw force, it is the justification for all the cruelty, conquest, and degradation which militarism brings in its wake." She concluded by calling for "a war on war."[9]

That phrase, and the article as a whole, reflected the attitudes of many left Swedish Social Democrats. They and the other socialists throughout Europe who opposed the war were calling for peace and disarmament. The majority of the Swedish party, led by Hjalmar Branting, pursued a quieter policy. The moderate Swedish Social Democrats wanted to keep Sweden out of the fighting, and they felt that this goal, less lofty than

Kollontai's demand for an end to the war but also more attainable, could best be achieved by a national policy of strict neutrality. They therefore sought to avoid friction with the combatant nations at all cost, which meant avoiding contact with the radicals' call for a campaign against the war. Thus they did not welcome Kollontai's declarations any more than did the government.

Ström and Höglund were sympathetic to Kollontai, however, and in October 1914 they sponsored a tour of the country for her and another Russian Social Democrat who was in Stockholm, Aleksandr Shliapnikov. It was possibly on this trip that Kollontai and Shliapnikov became lovers.

Shliapnikov had been born in Murom, a town 150 miles east of Moscow, in the mid-1880s; he was not sure of the year because his parents were members of the Old Believer sect, which refused to register births with the government. His father, a sometime miller, laborer, carpenter, and salesman, died when Sasha was three, leaving his mother with four children to rear. They lived in poverty and everyone had to work. The boy learned to read and write, but his childhood was hard, and made more difficult because other children tormented him for being an Old Believer. "Religious persecution, street persecution, persecution in school, poverty and deprivation in the family—all this disposed my childhood dreams and attitudes to struggle and martyrdom," Shliapnikov later wrote.[10]

He became a lathe operator, moving from factory to factory until he made his way to St. Petersburg in 1901. There he took part in the strikes sweeping the capital in the first years of the twentieth century and read revolutionary literature. He left the city because of its dreadful working conditions, but the seed had been sown, and when he got home he sought out local Social Democrats to learn more about Marxism. In 1903 he began to participate in illegal activities, and soon thereafter became a Bolshevik. In 1908 he went to Western Europe, where he combined party activity with factory work. He returned to Russia briefly in 1914, but in late September of that year he set out for Stockholm in order to work with the Bolsheviks abroad, particularly on establishing better communications between them and the party organization in St. Petersburg.[11]

Shliapnikov was dark-haired, mustached, solidly built and average in height. His comrades liked him for his calm disposition and his kindness.[12] Lenin relied on his considerable organizational ability. He had qualities prized by all political organizations—reliability, sobriety, judgment, and dedication. He was, all in all, a respected Bolshevik.

Kollontai fell in love with him in the fall of 1914, and stayed attached to him until at least 1916, and probably longer. It seems an unlikely relationship, for not only were their class origins different, but he was very different from the intellectual Maslov. He was a genial politician rather than a thinker, somewhat like her first husband in his fundamentally nonintellectual approach to the world. She was in every sense his senior in revolutionary politics. He was more than ten years younger than she, proletarian, not highly educated, and without high status as a Social Democrat; but those qualities may have made him more attractive. Perhaps Kollontai felt that this man could not attempt to dominate her as the others had. Given his kindness, she could expect that he would not even try. In loving him, she would run no risk of raising her tendency to become dependent, and thus she could hope that the cycle of subordination and rebellion that had destroyed her earlier loves would not begin again.

It was Shliapnikov who first put Kollontai in touch with Lenin. After making her acquaintance, he informed Lenin that she opposed the war. Lenin responded on October 27: "I am glad from the bottom of my heart if Comrade Kollontai has taken our position."[13] He was referring to his theory that socialists should work to turn the imperialist war into revolutionary civil wars, wherein the proletariat would rise up and destroy the bourgeoisie. Kollontai had not accepted that idea, although she read several of Lenin's articles in October and began corresponding with him. She was drawn instead to the pacifist demands for an end to all war and for disarmament, demands which most antiwar socialists supported. Kollontai believed that peace would allow the class struggle to dominate national life again, and she thought that peace would be achieved by uniting socialists into an effective international opposition that could mobilize the proletariat to end the conflict. Lenin's theory would prevent unity, because it would alienate socialists who were torn between their hatred of war and their desire to see their country defended. They would only be offended by Lenin's demands for civil war, which he coupled with defiant statements that socialists should work for the defeat of their nation's armies. On November 28 Kollontai urged Lenin to accept the need for drawing all antiwar socialists together.

Now we must have a concrete slogan for everyone close to us, and this slogan can serve the struggle for peace. I think we need to put forward a slogan that will unite everyone, promote the revival of the spirit of solidarity. And what can better unite the proletariat of all countries right now than the demand, the call—war on war? In other words, war with those who lead us to war.[14]

Lenin denounced Kollontai's position as pacifist. He was not interested either in socialist unity or in peace at any price; rather than an end to the fighting, he wanted the guns now in the hands of the poor to be turned against the rich. "War on war" was unproductive or worse, regressive, because its adherents did not see the war as a catalyst for revolution. When Kollontai supported that slogan, Lenin immediately rebuked her. In letters of December 1914 and January 1915 he continued to press his civil war theory. To one of those letters she replied in a conciliatory tone, "I am glad above all that we find points of contact and that therefore we can work together in this hard time. This is especially dear to me now, when there is such ruin and when one feels that at times one is talking a different language even with recently close friends."[15]

If she had disagreements with Lenin, they were minor compared to the rift with her Menshevik colleagues, many of whom supported the combat as necessary to defend Russia from German aggression. Like the other socialist parties of Europe, the Russian was divided over the war, but among the Russians this new issue blurred factional lines and caused antiwar Bolsheviks and Mensheviks to move cautiously toward one another in an attempt to work together despite their differences. Kollontai was one such Menshevik. Thus she corresponded with Lenin and joined Shliapnikov's efforts to communicate with St. Petersburg. She also talked daily with the left Swedish Social Democrats and published in Ström's newspaper *Stormklockan*. So active was she that her rooms became a "staff apartment" for Russians and Swedes.[16]

All this work naturally made the Swedish government increasingly uneasy. In mid-November 1914 the police arrested Kollontai and charged her with meddling in Sweden's internal affairs by receiving large amounts of correspondence, turning her apartment into a "revolutionary club," and publishing inflammatory articles. In this last particular they cited "The War and Our Most Immediate Tasks," an article in which she had described the war as having "surpassed anything that one could imagine even in one's most savage fantasies up until now." Kollontai admitted that socialists had underrated the pull of nationalism on the working class, and she called on socialists to oppose militarism.[17] This could indeed be read as an oblique criticism of the Swedish policy of defense spending, but it was Kollontai's whole pattern of activity that induced the government to use the article as a pretext. She was too vocal and too popular among Swedish Social Democrats.

The police took her first to a prison in Stockholm, then to another outside the city. They threatened to deport her to Finland, to which Kollontai replied that they might as well turn her over to the tsarist police directly. She persuaded a priest to take a message to her friends telling them where she was, but that stratagem proved unnecessary, since Höglund and Ström were already pressuring the government for her release. Branting, the leader of the Social Democrats, said in print that the authorities had arrested an innocent foreigner simply because she dared to criticize Sweden's excessive defense spending.[18] Privately he told his daughter Sonia that he thought the Russian embassy might have complained about Kollontai.[19] Höglund angrily declared that the incident was a victory for militarism, and the Social Democratic Party Congress passed a resolution condemning the arrest. Although conservative newspapers accused Kollontai of being a Russian spy, the protest had its effect; the government declared her *persona non grata* and expelled her to Denmark instead of sending her back to Russia.[20] In late November Kollontai left Malmö for Copenhagen.

Denmark proved no more hospitable than Sweden, for the police followed her constantly. Nor did Kollontai find any congenial comrades among the Danish Social Democrats. She stayed in Copenhagen through January to observe a conference of socialists of neutral nations, then accepted an invitation to move to Norway. There she finally felt at home; the Norwegian leftists were resolutely antiwar, there was a fairly large Russian colony around Christiania (renamed Oslo in 1924), police surveillance was minimal, and the country was beautiful.[21]

Throughout the late winter and spring Kollontai worked with the Scandinavians while trying at the same time to maintain her ties with all the various Russians, Bolshevik and Menshevik, who opposed the war. She became a correspondent to *Golos*, a shortlived newspaper printed in Paris by a Bolshevik-Menshevik coalition, including Akselrod and Angelica Balabanoff. The paper lasted only two months, but in its aftermath the same group organized *Nashe slovo* with Trotsky and Martov as joint editors, and Kollontai contributed to this venture as well. At the same time she acted as liaison in Scandinavia for Lenin and for Krupskaia and Inessa, who were then organizing a women's conference for the spring.

Kollontai was still hoping for a general alliance of socialists, so she continued to call for a struggle for peace and for a new internationalism, without invoking Lenin's civil war theory.[22] That stance brought her into long-distance conflict with Krupskaia, who refused to distribute some antiwar propaganda she had received from Kollontai because it was not sufficiently Leninist.[23] Despite her criticism, however, Krupskaia continued to request Kollontai's help on the women's conference, a rump convention of the meeting originally scheduled for August 1914. Inessa and Krupskaia were hoping to organize the delegates there in favor of Bolshevik resolutions against the war. Kollontai tried to find Norwegian support, but the results were not heartening. In her disappointment she wrote to Krupskaia: "I somehow believe more in the youth in present circumstances. But of course this is not going to make me change my beloved work among women, however thankless it is. It's too difficult for them, for everywhere, everywhere, they are slaves. Even here, where they have the vote."[24]

She managed to find three women who would sign a resolution to send to the women's conference, and she dutifully mailed it to Switzerland. She herself could not get permission to cross France en route to Bern, the site of the meeting. In any event, only twenty-nine delegates came to it. Under Clara Zetkin's guidance, they voted for just the kind of general antiwar resolution Kollontai favored.

Aware of Kollontai's position, Lenin was still trying in the spring of 1915 to gain her as a supporter. In April she published a three-part series in *Nashe slovo* entitled "German Social Democracy in the First Days of the War," in which she bitterly accused the SPD of collaborating with the government to mobilize the masses for combat. They should have used their "colossal, perfectly functioning apparatus" to organize against the war.[25] Krupskaia wrote to her shortly after the series appeared: "Vladimir Il'ich was extraordinarily pleased by your article in *Nashe slovo*."[26] Lenin may have been taken with Kollontai's criticism of the German party because the Russians had always admired it as the leading Social Democratic organization in Europe. Its betrayal of socialist internationalism therefore seemed all the more perfidious. Or Lenin may simply have been flattering Kollontai. He did value her skills as a linguist and propagandist, and in the spring, soon after Krupskaia conveyed his compliments, he asked Kollontai to become a contributor to a newspaper he was founding, *Kommunist*. Her first and only article in the paper, "Why Did the Proletariat of Germany Remain Silent in the July Days?," repeated the charge that the German workers supported the war because both their unions and their party favored collaboration with the bourgeoisie instead of encouraging the workers to think for themselves. The masses did what they were told, marching off to die.[27]

Almost in spite of herself, Kollontai was moving close to Lenin, while trying not to break with former comrades.[28] Lenin's gentle persuasion had less to do with her conversion than did the fact that within Russian Social Democracy she had very little choice between the Bolsheviks and those Mensheviks who supported the war effort as necessary for Russian survival. Martov was attempting to retain his affiliation with the pro-war members of his faction, but in so doing he found himself drifting into an ambiguous stand on the war which Kollontai could not tolerate. As the combat became more bloody, it came more and more to dominate her thinking, and the Russian leader who seemed most resolutely against it was Lenin. The indecision of the Mensheviks contrasted unpleasantly with his absolute conviction and with the relentlessness with which he argued his position. In June 1915 Kollontai finally made the decision to support Lenin and become a Bolshevik.[29] In the face of the all-consuming war, she forgot her earlier doubts about Lenin's vanguard theory, about his denigration of the spontaneous revolution, and about his stress on a highly centralized party. He was right about the war, and the war was her major concern.

Kollontai threw herself into backing Lenin as wholeheartedly as she had embraced former causes. Having made up her mind to follow Lenin, she declared now that he was totally right, that his civil war theory would allow socialists who opposed the war to draw a sharp line between themselves and those who were vacillating. Thus the theory had tactical value. It was a position around which people could gather, a prediction of the revolutionary potential in the war, which could also serve as a rallying point. Kollontai wrote in her diary on July 22: "This is not just 'analysis.' This is tactics. This is action. This is a political program. Above all, in all countries, a break with all social patriots. A decisive and ruthless break."[30] Lenin proposed a clear statement of principles, while other socialists fumbled for a new course and hesitated over disavowing their comrades, the "social patriots." Kollontai had no more doubts. On August 2 she continued to praise her new leader: "For me it is completely clear now that no one is fighting the war as effectively as Lenin. . . . The war can be stopped only by means of an attack by the masses, only by the will of the proletariat."[31] She had come over to Lenin, therefore, because she had given up her earlier goal of generating a broad coalition under the umbrella of general and therefore relatively inoffensive slogans. Now she had decided that Lenin was correct in his insistence that "a decisive and ruth-less break" with the "social patriots" was a necessary first step to unifying the left. What Kollontai disregarded in her euphoria was that Lenin's certainty, which had won her admiration, would be a barrier to socialist cooperation, for he would fight repeatedly in the next two years, not just with "social patriots" but with anyone who did not agree with him completely. The antiwar socialists, that minority in which Kollontai put her faith, could not have ended the war by sparking an uprising of the working class in any case. Divided by conflicts caused in no small measure by Lenin's dogmatism, they fell to fighting among themselves, while the war ground on.

Kollontai herself continued to debate with Lenin, even though she claimed to be his ardent supporter. Her first contribution to the Bolsheviks was a pamphlet, "Who Needs the War?," written in the summer of 1915 and translated into several languages for distribution to the troops. In it Kollontai clearly adopted Lenin's notion that the international war must be turned into a series of civil wars, wherein the workers overthrew the bourgeoisie; at the same time in her letters to him she refused to abandon the call for disarmament. That was a pacifist demand which Lenin considered silly. How could the workers overthrow the bourgeoisie without guns? Kollontai had adopted the civil war theory while still holding onto her earlier, and now contradictory, pronouncements against militarism.[32]

Lenin and Kollontai also disagreed about Lenin's theory of imperialism. The development of colonial liberation movements in India and elsewhere had caught the attention of socialists, who were not entirely sure whether such movements were a truly emancipating force or a bourgeois plot. Lenin believed that the temporary alliance of native bourgeoisie, proletariat, and peasantry in a national campaign to expel an imperialist, European power from a colonial country was a positive step toward revolution, for it would weaken international capitalism. Socialists should therefore support aspirations toward "national self-determination." On the other hand, G. L. Piatakov and N. I. Bukharin, borrowing arguments from Rosa Luxemburg, argued that collaboration with the bourgeoisie anywhere would harm the long-term interests of the oppressed classes and that socialists should not encourage nationalism in any form. Kollontai agreed. In an article in *Nashe slovo* in June 1915, almost a year before general debate over the issue produced Lenin's and Bukharin's most significant publications, she wrote that the cry of "Asia for Asians" was simply a slogan promoted by Asian capitalists to increase their control over their own people. Only a firm commitment to socialist internationalism could stem the tide of "yellow capitalism."[33] Kollontai thus rejected Lenin's theory, which was to evolve into a rationale for the wars of national liberation that would later sweep the colonial world. She proved less tactically astute than Lenin, because she clung more stubbornly to orthodoxy. When she included references to her position in *Who Needs the War?* Lenin edited them out.[34]

Of course, Lenin lectured everyone who did not accept his notions completely, and despite their disagreements Kollontai had really joined the Bolsheviks, although she retained her contacts with the *Nashe slovo* group in Paris. She acted now as Lenin's agent in Scandinavia, translating his writings and working with Swedish and Norwegian Social Democrats. In the summer of 1915 the most immediate task was the Zimmerwald Conference, a meeting of socialists scheduled for late summer. Its very convocation sharply divided Social Democrats, for its sponsors, Oddino Morgari of Italy, the Swiss Robert Grimm, Angelica Balabanoff, and especially Lenin and Trotsky, were attempting to organize antiwar socialists. Morgari had sought the support of the leaders of the Second International, but Emile Vandervelde, chairman of the International Socialist Bureau and a Belgian, refused to countenance even a convocation of socialists from neutral nations, "as long as German soldiers are billeted in the homes of Belgian workers."[35] Morgari, the Russians, and the Swiss decided to meet without permission and attempt to lay the basis for a new socialist unity by drafting a declaration of principle. Kollontai approved of that effort wholeheartedly, and in midsummer she and Shliapnikov met with Norwegian and Swedish Social Democrats in hopes of convincing them to go to Zimmerwald.[36]

Branting continued to support the leadership of the Second International, as did the majority of Scandinavian socialists; thus they avoided any movement toward separation. However, Zeth Höglund and the Norwegian Ture Nerman, head of the Social Democratic Youth Organization, were willing to join the Zimmerwald effort. Kollontai tried to line them up behind Lenin ahead of time by getting them to adopt as their own a draft resolution on peace which Lenin had sent her, but here the Scandinavians balked. Unlike her, they had not become Bolsheviks; they wanted to avoid a final split in their parties, and Höglund especially resented taking orders from abroad. They chose to prepare a resolution of their own, approved by the Central Committee of the youth organization with Kollontai's collaboration, but they also voted with Lenin when the Zimmerwald meeting convened.[37]

While Kollontai was negotiating with Nerman and Höglund in early August, she received an invitation from the German Socialist Federation of the American Socialist Party to tour the United States and speak against the war. She wrote in her diary, "This is so incredibly good that I am gasping with joy and am afraid to believe it." She accepted by return mail, then sent off a letter to Lenin telling him that she had just found a fine new opportunity to spread their views. Almost as enthusiastic as she, he sent back instructions that she was to translate his pamphlet "Socialism and the War" into English, and then attempt to have it published in the United States. She was also to use the tour to rally people there to the Zimmerwald movement and to raise money.[38]

Some of her friends, including Zoia Shadurskaia with whom Kollontai was in constant correspondence, worried about her crossing the Atlantic in wartime, but she dismissed their fears.[39] Anxiously she waited until September 15 for the expense money to arrive from the United States; she lived off the proceeds of her writing, lecture fees, and the remnants of her inheritance, but money was always so short that she could not finance the trip herself. When the bank draft finally came, Kollontai had second thoughts. "Then I will be still farther from Russia. What if things start up? There, on that side of the ocean, I won't know anything," she wrote in her diary.[40] The idea of going off on an adventure soon renewed her spirits, however, and on September 26 she left Christiania on a Norwegian ship.

Kollontai knew very little about American socialism. Immediately after the outbreak of World War I the party leadership had taken an antiwar position that seemed to agree with the European left socialists, but in fact only disguised deep cleavages within the movement. Some U.S. socialists favored the Entente, some the Triple Alliance, but only a few condemned the war as capitalistic. The last faction, which included Louis Boudin, Louis Fraina, and S. J. Rutgers, was in turn divided on the real meaning of the war. Theodore Draper has written of the left wing of the American Socialist Party during World War I, "It is best to think of it as a haphazard collection of individuals rather than as anything resembling an organized group."[41]

Complicating ideological confusion was the fragmentation of the party into autonomous nationality groups, which comprised one-third of the total membership in 1915.[42] A few of these socialists were pro-Zimmerwald, like Ludwig Lore, the head of the German Federation and the man who invited Kollontai, but they did not represent the party majority. Nor were they in touch with the latest developments in the Second International. Lore wrote three years later, "At that time socialist America was intensely ignorant of the conditions and tendencies of European Socialism. The words Zimmerwald and Kienthal were only the vaguest of conceptions even to the more intelligent of American Socialists."[43] Kollontai's task was to convince these people to support Lenin.

She spoke first in New York. At one meeting the Bolshevik resolution she proposed was not even brought to a vote because the party chairman, Morris Hillquit, declared that the session could not speak for the entire party. Nor did Kollontai make a good impression on pro-Zimmerwald people. She was homesick, exhausted, and slightly ill, and she left New York convinced that the United States was full of chauvinists and poorly educated internationalists.[44]

In mid-October she started on a three-month tour that took her from the east to the west coast via Cleveland, Cincinnati, Chicago, Milwaukee, Salt Lake City, Portland, San Francisco, and Los Angeles. Captivated by the country's natural beauty, she filled her diary with descriptions of the scenery. On October 15 she wrote, "The train carries us past huge rivers (right now the Hudson), past unknown cities, places. Beautiful! Wonderful. And it is strange that this is America!" Traveling through Illinois on October 29 she wrote:

> The sun shines dimly through gray haze. The wind whirls, chases clouds of dust, forces its way through the chinks in the train and at the station throws dried leaves at us. The harvested fields spread out desolate and dejected; the brown, dried, cracked land prays for rain. . . . What's American here? These endless fields and these green groves above the ponds and these gray farmhouses—all this immediately reminds me of the central regions of Russia.

In early November she went from Colorado to Salt Lake City.

> I never thought that I would fall in love with the desert. But what I saw today surpassed all expectations! What air and what colors and abundance of subtle, delicate watercolor tones. Today the desert is all sand colored, dry, but cut up by wild, uninhabited mountains. These are desert mountains, monochrome. As though covered with velvet, and velvet of subtle tones from cinnamon to vieux rose, from pale gold to delicate sand.
> I am in love! I am in love with the desert![45]

Nature pleased her much more than the people she met. Although she received ample publicity, including interviews in American newspapers, and although her audiences were large, Kollontai did not feel satisfied with her performance. She was badly overworked and always in a rush. In Chicago, the German Federation scheduled two or three speaking engagements a day, for five days, then put her on a night train to St. Louis. She arrived there at 7:00 A.M., to be greeted by a delegation that took her on a thirty-mile tour of the city. She found it "tidy, showy, and boring."[46] Afterward she had no time to go over her speech, and she felt that her talk was flat.

Neither did she care for most of her hosts. They worked her too hard on a skimpy allowance, and they were not staunch revolutionaries. Many wanted to hear her defend Germany rather than attack the war in general. On December 12 in Cincinnati she wrote indignantly in her diary:

> I just came back from a typical meeting organized by the German comrades. The big hall was filled. Of course! The socialists had announced, "a German meeting," not saying that a Russian was speaking, and besides that an international socialist! All kinds of people had gathered. Many petty-bourgeois German burghers. For several hundred men, ten or so women.
>
> After the meeting it isn't at all like meetings of Americans! There they come up, warmly say, *"a splendid speach [sic]. It's just what we want: more revolutionary spirit in the movement."*[47]

She found the Germans "petty-bourgeois revisionists" for the most part, which meant they would not embrace her call to Zimmerwald. The Russian colonies scattered throughout the United States were no more receptive, although they greeted Kollontai as a countrywoman. Their nationalism irritated her. Nor did it aid her persuasive abilities, for Russian audiences interpreted her calls for an end to the war as pro-German.[48]

Kollontai considered the native-born Americans most congenial and receptive to her message, and she particularly liked Eugene Debs, Bill Haywood, and the members of the Industrial Workers of the World whom she met. Apparently the strongly syndicalist cast of the Wobblies did not bother her in 1915, but she did become impatient with the American socialists' reliance on legal means to power. "No," she wrote, "The Social Democratic movement *is getting too decent for me!* If it is only going to count the voices in elections and preach *pur* [sic] *and simple parliamentarianism*, it will miss everything. I am suffocated with such things! A new International must be built!"[49]

The main theme of Kollontai's speeches and articles was that true socialists must band together to form a new International, dedicated to worldwide worker solidarity and revolution.[50] Those people who had been pro-Zimmerwald before she came responded favorably, while those who supported the war on one side or the other responded negatively. Kollontai changed few minds. Nor was she successful in raising much money or in publishing Lenin's pamphlet in its entirety, although she did distribute Zimmerwald literature.[51] Her greatest success lay in publicizing Lenin's position among Americans who were not in close touch with events in the European socialist community.

Her feelings of being cut off from home and of missing Misha and Shliapnikov continued to plague her. In December 1915 she returned to New York, stayed there six weeks, and then sailed for Norway. In March she wrote to Krupskaia that the trip had been worthwhile. The United States was a great, powerful, young country where the advancement of capitalism surely meant a swift transition to socialism.[52]

Back in Norway, in 1916, Kollontai took up her work with Social Democratic youth organizations and with Russian émigrés. Shliapnikov had been in Stockholm with Bukharin and Piatakov, again forwarding Lenin's messages to Russia, but the Swedish police made the process very difficult. In the spring the Bolsheviks moved to Christiania, where Shliapnikov found the Norwegians polite and interested but unwilling to help in an illegal operation. Chronically short of funding, he could not even print Bolshevik literature successfully there, so in midsummer he set off for the United States to solicit contributions from Jewish socialist groups.[53]

Although the Bolsheviks in Norway could not secure good communications with Petrograd, Kollontai took comfort in the widening rift developing between the left and right Scandinavian socialists throughout the winter of 1915–16.[54] She was also pleased by the completion of one delayed project in the spring of 1916. The book she had finished just before the war, *Society and Maternity*, was finally published. She intended it "to bring the demands for broad maternity insurance into conformity with the basic tasks of the working class, to render a clear account of what place this part of the socialist program plays in the great building of social reconstruction."[55] She had stated the basic ideas in several articles between 1912 and 1914, and even as early as 1908 in *The Social Bases of the Woman Question*.[56] The bourgeois family was decaying, she argued; some of its functions had already been assumed by the state with the establishment of public education. Society should now guarantee healthy childbirth and complete child care. Some governments had already begun to take steps in that direction by instituting maternity insurance, but much more needed to be done. Governments should follow the Social Democratic program for reform in working conditions and medical care. Kollontai documented her argument with extensive surveys of contemporary maternity protection in fifteen countries, including Bosnia-Herzgovina and Australia.

The book was almost six hundred pages long. Like *The Life of the Finnish Workers* and *The Social Bases of the Woman Question*, it was more a catalogue than an integrated analysis—a heaping up of data culled from government documents to support the program first formulated in the 1890s by the SPD. The book did provide some shocking statistics on infant mortality, spontaneous abortion, prostitution, and the other horrors of a factory woman's life, and it did exhort the socialists to act on the issue immediately rather than waiting for the revolution. Its publication had limited impact, however, because the war had forced the postponement of all such projects for the duration.

In the late summer of 1916 Kollontai left her work in Norway to return to the United States. Although she planned to renew her contacts with American socialists and Russian émigrés in New York, she went not primarily in order to work, but to be with her son. When Misha had visited her the previous summer, he had been depressed. His mother wrote in her diary on July 11, 1915, "Life is hard for Mishunia now. Like an older person, he bears on his young shoulders many cares that his father and I should carry for him."[57] Probably a large part of his anxiety sprang from efforts to avoid the draft and remain in training to be an engineer. His officer father was fighting at the front, a general now, but the young man followed his mother in hating the war.[58] In midsummer 1916 when he enrolled in a course in automotive engineering in Paterson, New Jersey, he wrote his mother that he needed her with him. For once in her life Kollontai abandoned her work to minister to her son.

She was not happy with the sacrifice. In the first September days in the United States she worried about whether she would see Shliapnikov, who was in New York, but he never contacted her. "It's strange, it's not painful, but an alarming feeling, that he's somewhere near, in America. Let him go. It will be easier."[59] After she knew he had left, she became depressed at her isolation. Paterson was a dreary town where she found American life tedious. In a letter to her friend Tatiana Shchepkina-Kupernik she complained:

We are in the latitude of Naples, but it doesn't feel like the south. . . .
New York is completely surrounded by swamps. I am living with Misha
on the edge of a city. Here the city is divided by straight little streets, lined
with maples. A row of monochrome wooden cottages stretches along
them, with the inevitable little porches, where rocking chairs are arranged
and where in the evenings American women little occupied with their
housework gossip or simply sit, bored.

At first glance the houses always look comfortable, but then one becomes annoyed with the lack of individuality in them and in their fur-
nishings.

I don't think you would like it here. California is a different story, and
so is the Nevada desert. I fell in love with them, and my dream is to live
there sometime.[60]

To relieve the boredom, Kollontai began to read about American
women and was thrilled by the writings of Margaret Fuller, one of the
guiding spirits of nineteenth-century transcendentalism. She moved on to
American literature, especially "psychological studies." In the evenings
she tried to cheer up Misha. "I don't know how successful this is. It's
difficult."[61] She also used the respite for stock-taking. On November 21
she wrote in her diary:

Recently I looked back over my life and I understood that with all the
diversity in it there weren't any long periods of satisfaction, quiet, bright,
happy periods. All the same, the brightest was girlhood, an era of daydreams, hopes, and dreams. The most deadly period was life in Tavriches-
kaia [her marriage], the turning point. Life is all little pieces, now bright,
beautiful, captivating, then suddenly the brightness falls away and the
phase of suffering, of searching begins, then the period of dead emptiness.

Work has always been the center, and in periods when I am working
my soul is quiet, as if content; it doesn't cry, it doesn't rebel, it doesn't
demand.[62]

In December Kollontai made plans to return to Europe. Initially she
wanted to join Lenin and Krupskaia in Switzerland, but her letter asking
them to help her cross France never reached them.[63] There was one last
flurry of activity before she left the United States. On January 13, 1916,
Trotsky arrived in New York. Bukharin had come in November, taking
up the editorship of the Russian socialist newspaper *Novyi mir*, and in
the process ousting the Mensheviks who had controlled it. Kollontai had
not been working with them because of differences over the war question.
When Bukharin staged his coup, she was delighted and she went into
the city to confer with him about bolshevizing the paper. Much to the

chagrin of the Mensheviks, Trotsky, although ostensibly a Menshevik himself, also cooperated with Bukharin and did not attempt to drive the Bolsheviks off. Kollontai wrote to Lenin and Krupskaia, "A week before my departure Trotsky came, and this raised the hopes of Ingerman and Co. [the Mensheviks] a little. But Trotsky clearly disassociated himself from them and probably will carry on his own line, which is by no means clear."[64]

The Russians were not content with fighting factional battles in New York; they also wanted to help organize the confused American left socialists against the mounting war fever in the United States. Kollontai had already tried to get the German Federation and the other nationality groups to denounce Woodrow Wilson's "preparedness" policy, but at the last minute Lore backed off. The Socialist Propaganda League, led by radicals in Massachusetts with whom she had been in touch since her prior trip, had seemed resolutely against the war, until Kollontai asked them to affiliate themselves formally with the Zimmerwald movement. Then she found that they and the IWW were influenced by "the chaos of anarcho-syndicalism." That meant that they also were leery of announcing any adherence to Zimmerwald.[65]

The U.S. groups were proving less tractable than Kollontai had hoped. Nonetheless, she was willing to keep trying, and on January 14 she attended a unity meeting sponsored by Lore at his Brooklyn home. The most prominent socialists were there—Boudin, Rutgers, Fraina, Sen Katayama. To advise them, Lore invited Trotsky, Bukharin, and Kollontai, in addition to two other Russians, V. V. Volodarskii and G. I. Chudnovskii. The meeting to organize the American left turned into a debate between Bukharin and Trotsky, because the Americans soon gave up on any attempt to get together. "The Russians were in their element," Lore wrote, "and long, drawn out, but intensely interesting theoretical discussions were always in order."[66] Trotsky argued that the antiwar Americans should remain within the socialist party and publicize their views there, while Bukharin advocated Lenin's tactics of a full-fledged split with compromisers. Kollontai stood with Bukharin, but when the vote was finally taken, Trotsky won. Kollontai sourly described his victory as a triumph for "the right wing."[67]

Kollontai left the United States disgusted with the hesitancy of the socialist party there and sure that Wilson would soon have the country at war. She did agree to put the Americans in touch with the Zimmerwald people, but she despaired of their ideological confusion. She left satisfied, however, that she had helped her son. "My mission in relations with Mishunia is fulfilled. Misha is mentally stronger, his health is better. And now he no longer needs me."[68]

When Kollontai returned to Norway, the conflict in the Swedish party had built to the split she had predicted the previous spring. At the party congress in February 1917 Branting's majority demanded that the left faction stop its unauthorized protests against the war. The left refused and withdrew from the party. Just a few days before the crisis, Lenin wrote to Kollontai and asked her to keep him informed.[69] Communications between them remained poor, however, for he learned of the split from the newspapers on March 5.

Lenin wrote to Kollontai again, this time giving her detailed instructions on working with the left. The uneasy alliance between antiwar socialists attempted at Zimmerwald had now disintegrated into open hostility between Lenin and his supporters, advocating civil war, and the more moderate antiwar socialists, whose prime goal was the broadest possible alliance, to be achieved through more conciliatory antiwar declarations. To insure that the Scandinavians not drift into the camp of the Zimmerwald center, Lenin ordered Kollontai to establish in Copenhagen, Christiania, and Stockholm a network of Bolsheviks who knew the languages and could steer the local left in the proper direction, toward his minority within a minority. "A new socialism" must be created now, at this decisive time, Lenin wrote; Bolsheviks must make every effort in that direction.[70]

Lenin was right; a new socialism was in genesis, but the first steps in its creation were not to be taken in Western Europe. On February 28 Kollontai finished her daily work with the Norwegians in Christiania and took the train home to her rooms in the suburb of Holmenkollen. She usually bought a newspaper to read en route, but that day the vendor had sold out. When she took her seat, she looked across at a fellow passenger who was reading an evening daily. The front page bore the headline, "Revolution in Russia."

> My heart began to pound. Immediately I was sure, somehow; this is not a newspaper bluff, this is serious. I leaned toward the newspaper, I tried to read it. It was already too late to buy one, the train had started. I asked my neighbor, "When you finish, could you lend it to me? I am a Russian, naturally I am interested in the news."[71]

For the next two days she read every one of the often conflicting reports from Petrograd.* She wrote out an article, "Who Needs the Tsar?," calling on the Russian people to establish a constitutional monarchy responsive to the needs of the masses rather than the landlords and the factory owners.[72] The next day, March 2, she learned from a Norwegian friend that Tsar Nikolai had abdicated. "I darted out into the hall; we hugged one another. I wanted to run somewhere. We had won! We had won! We had won! The end of the war! It wasn't even joy, but some kind of giddy rejoicing."[73]

Although she still had to arrange passage, Kollontai knew she would be going home, after nine years in exile. She was forty-four, and she had spent nineteen years pursuing a revolution which she thought might not come in her lifetime. She had listened intently to every echo of discontent, hoping to hear the first rumbling of the storm, always disappointed but clinging to the faith that it would happen. Now it seemed her faith had been justified. A new Russia was being born from the ashes of war, just as Lenin had predicted.

---

*In 1915 St. Petersburg was renamed Petrograd; in 1924 Petrograd was renamed Leningrad.

5

Revolution

THE EVENTS OF 1917 bore out Kollontai's bright expectations for Russia and for her own career. The year saw her rise to the top echelons of the Bolshevik Party, which she had recently joined, achieve national prominence as an orator, and begin work to emancipate women. Kollontai reveled in the chaos of the revolution, joining gleefully in demonstrations and shouting her calls for an end to the war to soldiers, sailors, and workers. She felt herself in harmony with the people whose cause she championed. Now all her predictions of a great, spontaneous, democratic upheaval seemed to be coming true, and Kollontai embraced "the new Russia" joyfully.

Her first response to the news of the fall of the Romanovs was to plan her return home. In Christiania she conferred daily with Evgeniia Bosh, Grigorii Piatakov (Bosh's husband), and Liudmilla Stal' on how to travel back to Russia and on whether the tsarist warrants for their arrest were still in force.[1] On March 6, A. P. Hanson, the secretary of the Norwegian youth organization, went to Finland to find out if the émigrés could return without risking imprisonment. Meanwhile Kollontai wrote to Lenin for instructions on the Bolshevik position on the war in this new situation and received the answer, "Of course we remain against the defense of the fatherland. . . . All our slogans are the same."[2]

The next day Lenin wrote again to suggest that Kollontai delay her departure until she received "a set of theses," the first two of the famous "Letters from Afar." These were his directives to the Petrograd Bolsheviks to oppose any continuation of Russia's involvement in the war and to begin agitation against the newly established, moderate Provisional Government. Lenin also wanted Kollontai to organize communications between Switzerland and Russia before she left, for he feared he might not be able to go home himself.[3]

At about the same time Kollontai received the news she had hoped for: a telegram from Petrograd informing her that all political émigrés had been amnestied. Although the Russian consul in Christiania told her and her friends that they would be arrested at the border, Piatakov and Bosh set off for Russia. Kollontai had to wait another week for Lenin's theses to arrive, and she also had to obtain the permission of the Swedish government to cross its borders. She appealed to Hjalmar Branting, who managed to secure a visa. Her old friend Tatiana Shchepkina-Kupernik had already asked Kollontai to stay in her Petrograd apartment when she returned, so her arrangements were complete. The Norwegians saw her off with a rousing rally, at which Kollontai enthusiastically hailed the Russian revolution as the beginning of a transfer of power to the soviets, "the organ of the new power of the workers."[4]

She crossed Sweden by train. At the Finnish border she hid the "Letters from Afar" in her underclothing, then passed through Swedish customs toward the Russian station at Torneo. Home after eight years in exile, she felt her spirits rise.

> Then, March 1917, was a harsh winter. A white, snowy shroud brightened the gloom of the poplar swamp. But it was gay in the belled sleighs, as we crossed the frontier river at Torneo. Ahead, the new Russia. It still was not ours, it was still only bourgeois, but had not the workers' and peasants' will for peace and a basic cleansing of old Russia been displayed in the creation of their soviets? Ahead, struggle and work. Work and struggle. Then, in March, my soul was as bracingly bright and fresh as the snowy, frosty air.[5]

The border guard found Kollontai's name on a list of amnestied émigrés and welcomed her back. As she left the station, the lieutenant of the garrison even kissed her hand. Exhilarated, Kollontai rushed on to catch a train for Petrograd. She arrived in the capital on March 18.[6]

Immediately she took Lenin's theses to the Petrograd Committee, where Shliapnikov gave her a report on party attitudes that verified the absent leader's worst fears. The senior Bolsheviks in the city, Stalin and Kamenev, were favoring accommodation with the bourgeois Provisional Government and the temporary continuation of the war. These men, newly returned from Siberian exile, more moderate than Shliapnikov, hesitated to adopt an inflammatory position until the revolution had stabilized.[7]

Their hesitation was natural under the circumstances, for they confronted a confused scene which they were still trying to understand. Nikolai was gone, that much was certain. Of all the tsars since Peter the Great, he had seemed most paralyzed by the dilemma of modernization, the balancing between change and control. He had taken the throne unprepared to rule, he was neither a good politician nor a particularly intelligent man, and his reign saw the fruition of all the inadequate policies of his forefathers. He had wanted to be an absolute monarch, an Orthodox emperor ruling a technologically modern society of medieval classes; thus he had encouraged Sergei Witte, minister of finance in the 1890s, to industrialize the country, but had forbidden him from making major land reforms. At the same time he had pursued the imperialist incursions into Manchuria which led to the Russo-Japanese War. After that defeat provoked rebellions, Nikolai had granted a legislative assembly, the Duma; civil liberties; and, later, the land reform proposed by the chairman of the Council of Ministers, Petr Stolypin. The Duma and the new freedoms did not fulfill the promises of 1905, for the government rewrote the electoral law to favor the upper classes and interpreted free speech as freedom to say the politically acceptable; but for the conservative emperor these were substantial concessions.

Unprepared to fight a modern war, unable even in peacetime to satisfy the needs of its people, Nikolai's government entered World War I. At first, an outburst of patriotism unified the nation behind the crown. Then, as the carnage continued through 1915 into 1916, the government became increasingly helpless. Only privately organized committees supplying medical care, food, and even munitions were able to improve conditions at the front, and Nikolai treated all such groups with distrust. By 1916 inflation began to affect the urban population. The war was being lost at a dreadful cost in human lives. Rumors circulated that Nikolai's German-born wife Aleksandra was a spy, so hostile had grown the public feeling against her influence over her husband. Gossips also hinted at an illicit relationship between the empress and Rasputin, the Siberian peasant and religious mystic who treated her hemophiliac son and increasingly meddled in politics. In 1916 Nikolai switched his officials from office to office, trying without success to improve the functioning of his administration in a display of impotence derisively labeled "ministerial leapfrog."

By February 1917, when food riots broke out in Petrograd, some of the tsar's own relatives were plotting to overthrow him. The demonstrations seemed at first like many the authorities had put down before—angry women demanding food for their children, socialist agitators and trade unionists leading the crowds—but this time when the Petrograd garrison was ordered to disperse the protesters with force, the unseasoned recruits refused. After bloody skirmishes on February 26, the soldiers of the Pavlovskii, Preobrazhenskii, and Volynskii regiments returned, shaken, to their barracks. They talked through the night about how they were firing on their own people, and the next day they refused their officers' orders. Instead they joined the demonstrations, setting off the defection of virtually all the troops in the city.

Nikolai's government had long since sacrificed its authority because of its repression and incompetence. In February 1917 the emperor had to rely on force to keep his capital quiet. Thus once he lost the troops of Petrograd, he had to act quickly to transfer more reliable men to the city, or the demonstrations would grow. Nikolai did order some units back from the front, but they too melted away in mutiny, and the emperor, hundreds of miles from Petrograd at the headquarters of the General Staff, was unaware of how completely his government had lost control in the capital. On February 28, rather than return to the city to attempt to oversee the restoration of order, he set out for the royal palace at Tsarskoe Selo to meet Aleksandra and their children. The train was diverted to Pskov because revolutionaries held the tracks around Petrograd, but still Nikolai persisted in believing that these demonstrations were no more serious than those he had weathered before. Then, on March 2, his own generals came to him to urge him to abdicate; they now knew that he must give up the throne before order could be restored. Quietly, without argument, finally realizing the calamity he faced, Nikolai agreed. He offered the crown to his brother Mikhail, who wisely refused that dubious honor. The Romanov dynasty had come to an end.

Even before the abdication, a new government had begun forming, as liberal Duma deputies established a Temporary Committee—soon to become the Provisional Government. Simultaneously, workers, soldiers,

and revolutionary intellectuals created the Soviet (or Council) of Workers' and Soldiers' Deputies, an assembly composed of elected representatives of unions, factories, and military units. There was a widespread
feeling throughout urban Russia in March that the nation should become
a republic, with civil liberties, better working conditions, and more food
for the cities.[8] A true and complete reform of the nation's ills finally
seemed possible, but the euphoria that pervaded Petrograd obscured the
fact that the Old Regime had collapsed under remarkably little pressure.
The political parties at the center, primarily Octobrists and Kadets, had
attacked the throne verbally but had not acted decisively to topple it. The
left—Socialist Revolutionaries, or SRs, Social Democrats of all sorts, and
various smaller socialist groups—had led the demonstrations and helped
form the Soviet, but they were not important in fomenting the troop
mutinies which destroyed the power of the autocracy in the capital. Leadership had played a less important role in the demise of the Romanovs
than had simple mass anger and Nikolai's paralyzed refusal to fight his
own destruction.

Leadership was vital, however, for remaking Russia, and the very
spontaneity of the first days of the February Revolution meant that no
recognized authority had yet emerged. This was the basic fact underlying
Kollontai's and Shliapnikov's argument with Stalin and Kamenev. The
Soviet was composed of the workers and soldiers of Petrograd, although
on the very day of its founding, socialists of the intelligentsia, primarily
Mensheviks, began to move into leadership of its Executive Committee.
They saw the Soviet as an organization for the expression of workers'
interests rather than as a governing body, for they felt that the Provisional
Government represented the bourgeoisie, which had now come to power
after the overthrow of the feudal monarchy. Russia was behind Western
Europe in economic development, and until capitalism had been built,
the bourgeoisie must rule, according to orthodox Marxism. Stalin and
Kamenev agreed with the Mensheviks.

Kollontai and Shliapnikov felt little of Stalin's hesitation. They followed Lenin in calling for the soviets to take power from the Provisional
Government because they saw this as the quickest route to international
revolution. Socialists must seize the moment, not collaborate with the
bourgeoisie. By creating a proletarian regime in Russia, they could end
the war and set an example that would fire revolution all over Europe.
If they hesitated, the beginnings in Russia might be stamped out by re-
grouped capitalists. Thus their nation's backwardness and the confusion

of the moment, which caused Stalin and Kamenev to be cautious, impelled Kollontai and Shliapnikov to advocate immediate revolutionary action. Internationalists, they thought of pan-European revolution as the solution for both Russia's lagging development and Europe's war.[9]

Without Lenin's presence the impatient Bolshevik minority could not persuade Stalin's majority. Kollontai was hardly ostracized, however. She plunged enthusiastically into writing for *Pravda*, and a few days after her arrival, V. V. Schmidt, secretary of the Petersburg Committee, suggested that she become a delegate to the Soviet. He scanned a list of unions to see which ones had no representative as yet, and his eyes stopped on a woodworkers' group. Giving her the street address, Schmidt directed Kollontai to go to union headquarters and convince the men to elect her their delegate to the Soviet.

"I went," she later wrote. "The office was like any other in those days: two long, unpainted tables, some benches, located in a basement. It smelled damp; the light struggled weakly through a narrow cellar window."[10] From a woman sitting in the dismal place, Kollontai learned that the union leader, Timofei Ivanovich, was out but was expected back soon, so she waited. The two women struck up a conversation that turned to the war and inflation.

> Of course, I tried to propagandize the watchman's wife. Who had started the war? Why? And so on. She didn't argue, but she didn't show any interest. On her face was written: deliver me from idle chatter.[11]

After several hours Timofei Ivanovich returned. Kollontai made her proposal, and he talked it over privately with other union members. Some of the men were suspicious of Bolsheviks, thinking them all to be German spies because they opposed the war. Then a man strolled in who was plainly not a worker. In a voice that implied he exercised some authority there, he asked the woodworkers if they were going to join the Bolsheviks. Kollontai realized she had stumbled into a union where the Mensheviks already had an organizer. After the newcomer spoke quietly to Timofei Ivanovich, the union leader turned back to her. "Tell your Bolshevik committee not to send us deputies to the Soviet from off the streets anymore," he said. "Whether or not we go to the Soviet is our business, the union's. We are nonparty." The other men agreed, and the Menshevik watched Kollontai leave defeated.[12]

Shortly thereafter Nikolai Podvoiskii, head of the Central Committee's Military Organization which managed agitation among the troops, took Kollontai to speak to a group of soldiers. The success of her appearance prompted him to suggest that she become a soldiers' delegate to the Soviet. Kollontai was skeptical about the men's willingness to have a woman representative, but she underestimated her own powers, for on March 27 a unit sympathetic to the Bolsheviks elected her.[13] Soon after, she was elected in turn to the Soviet Executive Committee.

In early April, Lenin returned to Petrograd. On April 4, at a general meeting of Social Democrats at the Tavrida Palace, he called on the Bolsheviks to demand the transfer of power to the soviets, nationalization of land, abolition of the army and police, and an end to Russian participation in the war. So totally did he reject the notion of cooperation with other political parties that he proposed renaming the Bolsheviks "Communists" to set them apart. Henceforth they must demand "Peace, Bread, and Land" and "All Power to the Soviets." This uncompromising declaration stunned Lenin's own followers. Only Kollontai rose to defend him:

> I was so indignant that I wasn't even nervous, as I usually was during speeches, although I saw the malicious looks, heard the deprecatory shouts at my address.
>
> In the first row sat Nadezhda Konstantinovna [Krupskaia] and next to her Inessa Armand. They both were smiling at me, as if encouraging my speech. Vladimir Il'ich was sitting on the podium, and when I finished my speech, I sat down close to him.[14]

Nikolai Sukhanov, a Menshevik-Internationalist, saw Kollontai's appearance as something less than a complete success. It provoked "mockery, laughter, and hubbub." "The meeting dispersed," he wrote. "Any chance of serious debate had been destroyed." Soon a popular rhyme was circulating: "Whatever Lenin jabbers, only Kollontai agrees with him." Audiences shouted at her, "Leninist, we know everything you're going to say. Down, down!" Foreign correspondents dubbed her the "Valkyrie of the Revolution," while moderate Russian newspapers called her "a mad Bolshevik."[15]

In fact, Kollontai was embarking on the greatest adventure of her life. Within a few weeks Lenin had won most of the party over to his position, and now Kollontai found her desires for an end to the war and the beginning of revolutionary, soviet government shared by a majority of her colleagues. In speech after speech to the sailors at Helsingfors, to soldiers and workers in the capital, she issued calls for action. To an audience of women workers she declared:

The war is still not over and there are so many armless, legless, blind, maimed in the world, so many widows, orphans! So many cities and villages destroyed! They lie, those who talk about the defense of the fatherland. The war is led by the capitalists for the division of the spoils.

Where is the people's money going? To the schools, the hospitals, to housing, to the protection of maternity and childhood? Nothing of the sort is happening. The people's money is going to finance bloody skirmishes. Those guilty of the war are the bankers, the factory owners, the landlord-moneybags. They all belong to a single gang of thieves. And the people die!

Stand under the red banner of the Bolshevik Party! Swell the ranks of the Bolsheviks, fearless fighters for Soviet power, for the workers' and peasants' power, for peace, for freedom, for land![16]

Not all her audiences responded enthusiastically; there were hisses and shouts and once even shots fired into the air.[17] Nonetheless Kollontai was happy. If old friends now ignored her, there were new friends, and riding the revolutionary wave left one little time to regret the costs of partisanship. The Bolsheviks would win; she knew they were right; anyone who disagreed was wrong. At the First All-Russian Congress of Soviets in June, Plekhanov, who had supported the war effort, looked at her sadly, then walked by without speaking. She wrote later of the man she had once venerated as the leader of Russian Marxism:

Political enemies, yes. But isn't there value in the past? For him I am an enemy, a defeatist. He is not the Plekhanov who wrote *Monism* and whom I knew in my student years in Switzerland; he's dead for the revolution. What could I say to him?[18]

Her commitment to the Bolshevism of "The April Theses" was unwavering. Only one field of activity was being neglected—work among women. In March the Petersburg Committee had established a group within the city organization to lead agitation aimed at the female proletariat, but in order to receive approval, Vera Slutskaia, the Bolshevik who proposed the committee, had to promise that this was not a separate woman's organization. Despite the concession, the Petrograd party conference in April refused to discuss the woman question because women did not as yet have the vote. Many neighborhood-level party people distrusted Slutskaia's pledge of solidarity, and their resistance to what they saw as feminist separatism prevented the committee from doing any work in the city.[19]

Kollontai realized that Slutskaia's impotent group was not enough. She believed that the Mensheviks, SRs, and feminists would seek support among women, and to counter their efforts the Bolsheviks would need more than a single, weak committee. Kollontai had reason for concern; the feminists were indeed organizing to press for the vote. On March 19 a demonstration sponsored by the League for Women's Equality marched to the Tavrida Palace to ask the Provisional Government leaders if they supported full civil rights for women. When Kollontai spoke to the rally, the crowd hooted down her criticism of feminism.[20]

In addition to rallying working women to their cause, the feminists also had found receptive listeners among the soldiers' wives of Petrograd, the *soldatki*. These women were struggling to feed their children on military allotments that did not keep pace with inflation. To help them, upper-class women had organized "Associations of Soldiers' Wives," which offered advice on setting up food cooperatives and pressuring the government for more money. Kollontai naturally saw the *soldatki* as potential converts to Bolshevism, and she was alarmed by the support they gave to her feminist rivals.[21] Thus she was present when a group of *soldatki* marched on the Soviet. She decried the evils of the war and inflation and urged the women to support the Bolsheviks, but they listened with scant interest, because her appeal did not seem to address itself to their immediate needs.[22] Speeches by one person could not discredit the practical work of the feminists. Shortly after Lenin and Krupskaia returned to Russia, therefore, Kollontai pressed them to set up a group at the highest party level to specialize in organizing women.

Krupskaia disagreed. The party would not accept a separate organization for women, she said. Heatedly, Kollontai emphasized that she had not asked for a separate bureau, just an organization within the overall hierarchy. Lenin intervened, telling her to continue to work with the *soldatki* and to draw up a concrete plan for a woman's group which they could then discuss.

With Klavdiia Nikolaeva and another worker, Fedorova, Kollontai drafted a proposal modeled on Zetkin's defunct German section. It called for the establishment of a committee within every major party organization to coordinate organizing among women. Kollontai then met with Inessa, Krupskaia, Samoilova, Liudmilla Stal', and Zinaida Lilina (Zinoviev's wife) to discuss the matter. The others voted the proposal down and promised to present an alternative the next day. Kollontai later wrote with some lingering resentment, "Nikolaeva and Fedorova, yes, of course. Inessa wasn't against, but she wasn't for our project. It was all the same to me; let them put together a new one; the important thing was not the wording, but the essence."[23]

At the next meeting she found that the essence had been changed, too, and that the other women wanted to avoid any proposal that could be stigmatized as separatist. They had decided to scrap Kollontai's plan and concentrate on reviving *Rabotnitsa* as a center for work among women, since the party's blessing had already been given to the newspaper in 1913. Kollontai again argued for the committees at a party conference the end of April, but again she was rebuffed.[24]

Disappointed, she continued to work in the Soviet, but her main activity was speaking at meetings throughout Petrograd and from time to time in Helsingfors. This was the year of the agitator, as Russia's people, so long denied the right to meet freely, indulged in an orgy of lectures, demonstrations, and debates. Kollontai rushed from gathering to gathering to urge support for the Bolsheviks. She spoke to the troops, the *soldakti*, and crowds of the Petrograd poor. She attacked the Provisional Government's determination to remain in the war, joining enthusiastically in the demonstrations that caused the fall of the first coalition in early May.[25] She called for measures to end inflation, and spoke before the Executive Committee of the Soviet to ask support for laundresses who were striking for higher wages and better working conditions.[26] She traveled to Helsingfors to agitate among the troops, and to strengthen ties with Finnish Social Democrats.

In June Kollontai emerged as a Bolshevik spokeswoman on the issue of national autonomy, particularly for Finland. She spoke at the congress of the Finnish Social Democratic Party, announcing her conversion to Lenin's theory of national self-determination. She vowed that the way to Finnish independence lay through the defeat of capitalism, an end to the war, and the construction of a new International.[27] Several days later she repeated the same theme at the First All-Russian Congress of Soviets. The Bolsheviks, she explained, supported national self-determination because that would swell the ranks of those willing to fight imperialism, and ultimately the destruction of imperialism would unify, not divide, the international proletariat. She introduced two resolutions on the subject, both of which were defeated, for the delegates to the Soviet Congress had not yet accepted the notion of allowing sections of the Russian Empire to slip away.[28]

In addition to her trips to Finland and her appearances at the Soviet congress, Kollontai stood for election to the Petrograd Duma in June, worked to get out the women's vote, and helped organize an antiwar demonstration with the other editors of *Rabotnitsa*. At the end of the month she spoke to a national conference of union representatives with a call for the delegates to support full equality for working women. She also proposed that the unions form departments within their hierarchies that would bring women into the organizations and promote them to the highest decision-making levels. The conference listened politely, then approved Kollontai's resolution.[29]

The revolution seemed to be accelerating. Throughout the spring the men of the Provisional Government had fumbled for solutions to the chaos around them, but their moderate temperaments and political inexperience made them shrink from the strong action necessary to restore stability. They saw themselves as caretakers until a constituent assembly was elected to form a new government, so they were unwilling to act on fundamental issues such as land reform. Then, as public demands for change grew louder, the leaders of the Provisional Government became increasingly hesitant to call the very constituent assembly on which they staked the country's future. The government delayed, the economy faltered, the military disintegrated, and the Bolsheviks grew from a small party in March to a potent opposition force by late June.

In the midst of this turmoil Kollontai left Russia for Stockholm. The International Socialist Committee (ISC), the titular executive of the Zimmerwald movement, was meeting there in preparation for a socialist unity conference scheduled for Stockholm later that summer. Kollontai, on Lenin's order, went to join Karl Radek and V. V. Vorovskii, then working in Sweden as liaison with the Zimmerwald left. The three planned to propose an ISC boycott of the coming meeting. Instead the Bolsheviks favored a conference exclusively composed of the Zimmerwald leftists who agreed with Lenin. The ISC meeting became a shambles, because many delegates failed to arrive and the rump session that did meet refused to act on the Bolshevik motion. Aside from the pleasure of reunions with old friends Zeth Höglund and Fredrik Ström, Kollontai had little to show for her trip.[30]

On July 5, Radek called her hotel to tell her that violent demonstrations had broken out in Petrograd. These were the July Days, a brief but militant attempt by radical soldiers and workers to oust the Provisional Government. Most of the Bolshevik leadership judged such a rising premature, but when it began, they attempted to exercise leadership, with disastrous results. The majority of the military and police forces remained loyal to the Provisional Government; the crowds were soon dispersed and the leaders arrested. In the political reorganization that followed, Aleksandr Kerensky, a moderate socialist, became prime minister. He set out quickly to complete the rout of the Bolsheviks.

Hours after Radek's call, Kollontai met him and Vorovskii in a Stockholm café. At that distance from Petrograd, they knew very little beyond that the party had suffered a defeat, and they talked worriedly about their future. Ia. S. Ganetski, a Polish Social Democrat, joined them with rumors that Kamenev had been arrested and that Lenin had escaped. He thought they should all stay in Stockholm and try to reestablish a foreign party headquarters, much as the émigrés had done before the revolution.[31]

For Kollontai, however, staying in Sweden was not an option. Because Sweden had declared her *persona non grata* in 1914, she had had to obtain special permission to enter the country, and her visa stipulated that she was there only to attend the ISC meeting. That very evening a Swedish newspaper criticized the government's decision to admit her at all, so she knew she would not be allowed to stay. The next day, July 6, she told Radek and Vorovskii that she was going home. They were sure she would be arrested. Kollontai admitted that it was possible, but she wanted to be in Russia, where, as she wrote to an old Zimmerwald colleague, Heleen Ankersmit, "great events are before us."[32]

Zoia Shadurskaia, Kollontai's childhood friend, had just arrived in Stockholm from Paris: together, she and Kollontai boarded the train for Finland. The same border guards who had welcomed Kollontai back in March met them at the frontier, but this time they searched the train and asked Kollontai and Zoia to stay behind after it left, whereupon the commander of the garrison arrested them on the charge that they were spies for Germany.

Kollontai and Zoia traveled across Finland under guard, and as the word spread that the prisoners were German agents, bystanders at the stations through which they passed shouted insults. One waiter refused to feed them because, he said, spies should be kept on a diet of bread and water. He would not even let them drink his water. Kollontai kept expecting some word that the Soviet had intervened to free them, but it never came. On arrival in Petrograd they were taken to interrogation.

"Have you brought in any spies, Bolshevik?" asked a young officer. "Have you taken German money to betray Russia? You won't succeed! We won't allow it! We won't let you!"[33]

A colonel then took over, demanding that Kollontai tell him everything she knew about A. Ia. Semashko, who had worked with her in agitation among the fleet and who had played a role in the July Days as leader of the rebellious First Machine Gun Regiment. Kollontai replied, untruthfully, that she had met him at a few meetings, that was all. The two officers repeated the same line of questioning with Zoia, who knew nothing. Finally they asked the women if they knew where Lenin was hiding, to which Kollontai and Zoia answered truthfully that they did not. That ended the first interrogation. They were taken next to the office of the city prosecutor, where they were separated and made to wait while bureaucrats filled out arrest forms. Two guards then took Kollontai alone by car to the Woman's Section of the Kresti Prison, in the Viborg section of Petrograd. Zoia, who was clearly innocent, was released.[34]

The government charged that Lenin, Zinoviev, Kollontai, Semashko, and other Bolsheviks had taken money from Germany to finance the antigovernment and antiwar propaganda that had climaxed in the armed uprising of the July Days. To support these accusations, the prosecutor published an order from German authorities opening a bank account for the Russians in Stockholm. Furthermore, the government said it had intercepted damning telegrams between the accused. "Although this correspondence has instructions on commercial transactions, the sending of various goods, and monetary operations," the Ministry of Justice asserted, "nevertheless it offers a sufficient basis to conclude that this correspondence covers up dealings of an espionage nature."[35] Kollontai was also specifically charged with engaging in antiwar propaganda with Semashko among the troops in April, May, and June.

The carefully worded accusation avoided further specifics, promising to reveal them in full at the proper time. What information the prosecutor did volunteer was true; the Bolsheviks had taken money from the German government. The Bolsheviks opposed the war and the Provisional Government. If successful, their agitation would weaken Russia's fighting capacity, thus aiding Germany. What was not true was the charge that the Bolsheviks were acting "with the goal of favoring the enemy"—in other words, that they were spies serving the Germans.[36] They did not report Russian secrets to Germany or seek a German victory in the war. Lenin, Zinoviev, Kollontai, and the others took German money to finance a campaign to accelerate the revolution, and while they were less than honest in admitting the source of some of their funding, they were in no way guilty of ordinary espionage.[37]

Kerensky's ploy worked for the moment, however. Although he probably knew that the Bolsheviks were not enemy agents, he was determined to check their growing strength by all the means at his disposal. Thus he added to the charge that they were guilty of riotous behavior during the July Days the accusation that they were collaborating with the enemy and seeking Russia's defeat. That was a potent combination, and the evidence—the well-known Bolshevik opposition to the war, their role in the uprising, and now documents proving German payoffs—was strong enough to make the party's popularity plummet. Held virtually incommunicado, Kollontai did not know that the Soviet, dominated by moderate socialists, had not intervened to have her freed from jail because it feared incurring public wrath by defending a spy.

The fear, inactivity, and physical privation of prison life wore her down. At night all hope of release gave way to a sense of "deathly quiet, broken by the ringing, distant sounds of the prison void."[38] The authorities denied her newspapers, books, magazines, writing paper, and contact with other prisoners. Nor could she send messages out or leave her cell for exercise. Several times the prosecutor interrogated her, trying to force an admission that she had written antiwar articles to help Germany. He cited as particularly damaging a piece in *Pravda* in which Kollontai had called for humane treatment of German prisoners of war.[39]

She did not know then that various people, among them Gorky and Mikhail Bukhovskii, an officer who had been her childhood friend, were pressuring the authorities to ameliorate her treatment. She suffered from a mild case of angina which could flare up again. Their requests brought Kollontai a visit from a prison inspector named Insaev, a left Kadet she had known years before. He told her that the minister of justice, A. S. Zarudnyi, another of her acquaintances, wanted to release her but could not because Kerensky feared she would go back to stirring up the troops.

Conditions improved shortly after Insaev's visit. Kollontai received food packages and digitalis, though written communication with the outside world continued to be cut off occasionally. Now she could leave her cell for exercise in the prison yard, and at times she could even summon back her customary good spirits.

Night. Day. Night again.

I wake up with uncontrollable cheerfulness. Almost "the joy of life." Probably because it is a bright, bright sunny day. I tidy up the cell. I wait for my walk. And on the walk we make bold with the matron, with the one who has the cat-o-nine tails. The little courtyard now has been turned completely into a storehouse for firewood. But the smell from the freshly piled logs is resinous and refreshing, and if you close your eyes you can imagine yourself in a forest.

I return to the cell. But still there is not the depression of previous days. I have gathered myself together, internally. Three years, so, three years. Five years, so, five years. But it won't be that. Will the Provisional Government really cope with all its tasks? Will it really be able to respond to the demands of the people: down with the war, land to the peasants, regulation of industry, power to the toilers? No, it will mark time, it does not understand that history demands, and demands powerfully, a step forward to a new, socialist future.[40]

Not history's demands but the appeals of her friends got Kollontai released from jail on August 21; Gorky had posted bail of 5,000 rubles. Kollontai later wrote that Kerensky, in Moscow, did not hear of her freedom until it was an accomplished fact. In anger he ordered her to be put under house arrest, with two armed guards posted at the door of the apartment she was sharing with Zoia Shadurskaia and Misha. After several weeks of protest from the Soviet, including an article and a speech by Trotsky, the government lifted that final indignity.[41]

By September 9 Kollontai was free. She found Petrograd rife with rumors of counterrevolution and of Bolshevik successes. An abortive attempt at a rightist coup by General Lavr Kornilov in late August had forced Kerensky to ease his campaign against the Bolsheviks. Instead of prosecuting the left, he needed their help. The Kornilov episode fanned fears of counterrevolution, and in this changed climate Bolshevik popularity among the working classes reached a new high. For the first time, in mid-September, they became the largest party in the Petrograd Soviet.

Kollontai's political fortunes rose with those of the Bolsheviks. At the Sixth Party Congress in late July, while she sat in jail, she became the first woman elected to the Central Committee, polling the sixth highest vote. In nominating her a Bolshevik candidate to the Constituent Assembly, Stalin placed her fifth on the list, after Lenin, Zinoviev, Trotsky, and Lunacharskii.[42] When she was released from prison, *Proletarii*, the party newspaper, welcomed her back by declaring: "Greetings to the fighter, returned to our ranks."[43] Requests came in to the Petrograd offices for her pamphlets, and colleagues acknowledged her as one of their best orators.[44] Pitirim Sorokin, a Socialist Revolutionary who was later to become an eminent sociologist, wrote after losing a debate with her:

> As for this woman, it is plain that her revolutionary enthusiasm is nothing but a gratification of her sexual satyriasis [*sic*]. In spite of her numerous "husbands," Kollontai, first the wife of a general, later the mistress of a dozen men, is not yet satiated. She seeks new forms of sexual sadism. I wish she might come under the observation of Freud and other psychiatrists. She would indeed be a rare subject for them.[45]

Sorokin's anger at Kollontai and the Bolsheviks' admiration for her sprang from the same source—Kollontai's talent as a speaker. She had never been more effective in presenting Bolshevik demands for "peace, bread, and land" and "all power to the soviets." Bolshevik popularity was greater than ever before, and Kollontai, buoyed by sympathetic audiences and by her party's success, rushed happily from meeting to meeting. Her speeches, she felt, "expressed the general striving, the united mass will,"[46] of the crowds who shared her radicalism. The final push by the people toward freedom and community had begun. Both then and later, Kollontai hailed the spontaneity of the revolution. She attributed the party's success to the fact that it simultaneously expressed the will of the people and led their historically determined march.

Few non-Bolsheviks shared her reverent assessment. To most Petrograd residents, it had become clear by the fall of 1917 that the Provisional Government had failed to deal effectively with the rising unrest of all sectors of the population. Soldiers were deserting the army, workers had begun to seize control of the factories, peasants were taking the lands of the gentry, and intellectuals, who had the potential to provide leadership, argued among themselves. Kerensky tried in August and September to rally the moderates into unified support of his government, but he failed. As Bolshevik popularity grew with the radicalization of society, rumors multiplied that the party was planning a coup against the Provisional Government in the name of the Soviet. Despite this challenge, other parties remained disorganized, and the most active elements of the city population fell in behind the Soviet, now led by the Bolsheviks. What Kollontai saw as an inevitable, spontaneous mass movement was actually the leap to power of a party able to obtain support by appealing to the people's desperate needs, and willing to act while others hesitated.

Was she deceiving herself by looking at events through the warm glow of her ideology? Perhaps. There were no preordained happy endings ahead for her country. There was no magic future, no blissful peace of socialism. Yet it was no delusion to think that Russia could be made better, and it was only naive optimism to believe that improvement must inevitably come. Kollontai's ideology was a plausible, intellectually respectable way of bringing order to chaotic reality. Above all, in the midst of the revolution, it clarified the alignment of groups in a way that made action possible. If the ideology was a system of oversimplifications, it was also a powerful force, showing the Bolsheviks the way to change their world.

Armed with her faith, Kollontai spent September and October in hectic activity. She attended the conferences Kerensky organized in September, worked in the Soviet, spoke to unions, military units, and general rallies, wrote articles, and even continued to keep in touch with the Zimmerwald Left abroad.[47] At the same time, she worked with the other editors of *Rabotnitsa* to encourage factory women to vote for Bolshevik candidates to the forthcoming constituent assembly. Kollontai, Samoilova, Stal', and Nikolaeva had decided to call a conference of Petrograd factory women, and they managed to obtain the approval of Iakov Sverdlov, the party secretary, even though other Bolsheviks criticized the project as separatist.[48]

At about 10:00 P.M. on October 10, Kollontai went to a Central Committee meeting at the apartment of the left Menshevik Nikolai Sukhanov. His wife, a Bolshevik, had offered the place to the committee in secrecy, in part because Lenin would be there. Since the order for his arrest had not been rescinded, Lenin was in hiding in a residential section of Petrograd. Unfamiliar with the neighborhood, Kollontai had trouble finding the apartment, and she came in after the meeting had begun. She noticed that the atmosphere was "awfully strained."[49]

The discussion went on into the night. Twelve members of the Central Committee had gathered at Lenin's insistence to decide whether to vote their commitment to a transfer of power to the Soviet in the immediate future, in other words, to vote for a coup against Kerensky's government soon. Lenin felt the time was right. The sailor from Helsingfors, Pavel Dybenko, said that the fleet was ready. Trotsky and two delegates from Moscow agreed. Only Zinoviev and Kamenev counseled caution, fearing another catastrophe like the July Days. When the vote was finally taken, it fell ten to two in favor of Lenin's position. "The tension broke immediately," Kollontai wrote. "We felt hungry. A hot samovar was brought out, we fell upon cheese and sausage." At dawn she went home through the streets of Petrograd in a mood she later described as "solemnly serious. Almost reverent. As if you feel a spiritual foreknowledge that you stand on the threshold of a great hour. It will strike, the end of the old world. Solemn, serious, reverent, and a little nervous."[50]

There was ample reason to feel nervous; most of the Bolsheviks feared that Lenin was pushing them too far, too fast. They had resolved to establish a soviet government, but they were not sure exactly when. If they misjudged the hour and moved too soon, they could send their whole party down to a defeat from which it might not recover. Even after the vote on October 10, therefore, the Bolsheviks continued to consolidate control over the military units around Petrograd, agitate against the Provisional Government, and consider the precise timetable for the uprising, while Lenin fumed at their indecision.[51]

That they would ultimately move against Kerensky no one doubted. Kollontai hurried "along endlessly long avenues, swampy with autumn," to meeting after meeting where she proclaimed the imminent death of the Provisional Government. "I believe the victory will be in our hands," she declared in the Soviet, even before the October 10 Central Committee meeting, "and we shall create a socialist republic." On October 22, a Sunday, she told factory rallies that they would soon seize power.[52] Just two days later the time came. On October 24, after a clumsy attempt by Kerensky to close down the Bolshevik newspaper *Rabochii put'*, the Bolsheviks occupied Petrograd's communication and transportation centers. In twenty-four hours the capital of Russia was theirs.

After arresting the ministers of the Provisional Government who had remained in the city and subduing the few troops that defended them, the Bolsheviks went to the All-Russian Congress of Soviets to declare a new government. There Kollontai, weary after two days of frantic activity at Soviet headquarters, listened to her party pronounce that power had been transferred to the soviets, that an equitable peace was to be made, and that all land was to be nationalized. The vote approving the peace resolution especially touched her. John Reed, an American socialist who was at the meeting, wrote:

Suddenly, by common impulse, we found ourselves on our feet, mumbling together into the smooth, lifting unison of the *Internationale*. A grizzled old soldier was sobbing like a child. Alexandra Kollontai rapidly winked the tears back. The immense sound rolled through the hall, burst windows and doors, and seared into the quiet sky. "The war is ended! The war is ended!" said a young workman near me, his face shining.[53]

Kollontai described the meeting as "the greatest, most memorable hour of my life."[54] The revolution she had greeted with such enthusiasm eight months earlier now seemed to be promising Russia liberty and peace.

6

People's Commissar

W HEN THE exhilarating October 25 session of the Congress of
Soviets was over, a sobering reality confronted Kollontai: she
and her comrades had to begin to govern. The Bolsheviks had taken
power quickly; now they must hold it, in the face of the same problems
that had brought down Kerensky. They had no experience in administration and no well-formulated plans. Kollontai later described the Bolshevik
leaders to a friend by saying, "We were so few that we could all sit on
the same sofa."[1] The seizure of power had been rapid, the Bolsheviks
were left somewhat breathless, and many, including Kollontai, feared that
they would soon face a capitalist counterattack that might well oust them.
While the Soviet government lasted, it should set an example of revolutionary rule for the more advanced industrial nations to follow when
their revolutions came. Kollontai told American reporter Bessie Beatty,
"Even if we are conquered, we have done great things. We are breaking
the way, abolishing old ideas."[2]

The precise nature of the government to be established soon provoked an argument among leading Bolsheviks. When Lenin and Trotsky

announced the names of the commissars who would serve as the executives of the Soviet system, several prominent Bolsheviks, among them Shliapnikov, Zinoviev, and Kamenev, criticized the list as too narrowly Bolshevik. They believed that representatives of other socialist parties should be brought into the government as the best way to guarantee the survival of Soviet rule. Kollontai agreed. She told several people in November that the Bolsheviks should form a coalition with the Mensheviks. She also criticized Trotsky as too impulsive, Lenin as too theoretical. Both men lacked contact with the masses, she said.[3]

Despite her belief in coalition government, Kollontai did not protest as vehemently as Shliapnikov, who resigned his post as commissar of labor. She talked to Bolsheviks and non-Bolsheviks about the need to work with other socialists, and she also argued against the wholesale arrest of opposition politicians. It bothered Kollontai to see her comrades easily adopt the repressive measures that had in the past been used against them. She petitioned so often for the release of jailed men that the Council of People's Commissars (*Sovnarkom*) issued a strong rebuke to her, along with Shliapnikov and Nikolai Podvoiskii. They were admonished to "redouble their efforts to clean out the counterrevolutionary nests and not again stir up the question of changing the policy of the dictatorship of workers and peasants directed against the counterrevolutionary leadership."[4]

Kollontai tempered her protest because, although she had doubts about the wisdom of specific Bolshevik actions, she had none about the rightness of their cause. "Objective conditions" had made the revolution, not the Bolshevik Party, and decisive measures now, in accordance with the forward sweep of history, could set an example for the future. The Soviet revolution was the first in the international revolutionary upheaval that would soon sweep through the more advanced nations of Europe, bearing away the war and capitalism.[5] Whatever mistakes the Bolsheviks might make, whether or not they fell from power, the ultimate outcome was not in doubt. Later, sadly, Kollontai wrote that those early days had been "months so rich in splendid illusion, planning, burning initiative to improve life, to organize the world anew, months of preserving the romanticism of the revolution."[6] Political disagreements seemed less important than the possibilities before them, and particularly before her. On October 28, Lenin appointed her commissar of social welfare. This post, she believed, would give her the power at last to realize her long-planned reforms for women and children.

Kollontai was later to recall her first trip to inspect the building where the Provisional Government's Ministry of Social Welfare had been headquartered: "I don't remember why I went alone; I only remember the sodden October day when I drove up to the entrance of the Ministry of Social Welfare on Kazan Street. A tall, imposing doorman with a gray beard, in gold braid, opened the door and examined me from head to foot."[7] Kollontai asked to see the highest-ranking official present, but the doorman told her that visiting hours were over for the day. She responded that she came on government business, but the old man stood firm. Petitioners were received only from one to three, and it was now five. When Kollontai tried to slip past him, he blocked the way. Defeated, she left.[8]

This inauspicious beginning portended several weeks of frustration. Early the next morning Kollontai answered a knock at her apartment door to find a peasant standing there with a note from Lenin. He told her that before the February Revolution the army had requisitioned one of his horses and promised to pay him, but never had. After the tsar had fallen, he thought surely the new government would pay him, and he had spent two months asking for his money, to no avail. Now he had heard that there had been another revolution, so he had gone to see Lenin. Lenin had given him the note authorizing Kollontai to pay him.[9]

Although she did not know why Lenin had sent the peasant to see her, Kollontai promised him that she would give him his money as soon as she could get it. Again she went to the building on Kazan Street, this time taking several friends. The doorman glowered, but he admitted her. The place was nearly deserted. In protest against the Bolshevik seizure of power, the employees of almost all the Provisional Government ministries had begun a boycott, and none of the commissars had any office staff willing to work. It seemed rather silly to move into a vacant building until she had dealt with the boycott, so Kollontai went back to Central Committee headquarters at the Smolny Institute. There on the door of a small room she hung a hand-lettered sign—"People's Commissariat of Social Welfare, 12–4."[10]

Petitioners appeared that very day, the first a delegation of children in ragged overcoats who demanded food. They said they had been to the ministry on Kazan Street, but that the doorman had told them to talk to the Bolsheviks. Kollontai asked why healthy people expected help from the welfare commissariat, and they replied that the Bolsheviks had promised to feed everyone. Kollontai gave them each 20 kopeks out of her own pocket, then sent them off to the Petrograd militia with a note, "At any rate, feed them."[11]

Next in line was a one-armed war veteran with a plan for organizing artels (cooperatives) that would employ other wounded men. All he needed was some money to buy knitting machines. Again Kollontai asked why he had come to see her. He had run into Lenin in the hall, was the reply. Lenin had liked his plan and had sent him here. Kollontai decided "to act bureaucratically": she told the man to come back in two days. He left, muttering angrily about the Bolsheviks. On the way out he passed two representatives of the Union of Disabled Soldiers, who were pushing into the room to threaten Kollontai with a demonstration. If someone did not help the wounded veterans soon, they said, there would be attacks on the Bolsheviks. "The old boys are rebellious," the men declared. "There's no shelter. They are freezing. It will be a scandal if the old boys start dying."[12]

Then came a man from a factory run by the ministry to demand that the workers be paid, and nurses asking for food to feed the orphans under their care, and teachers threatening to quit unless they received their salaries. "It was noisy in our little room," Kollontai wrote.[13] She could not help any of these people until she had established control over the ministry, which was a haphazard assortment of services flung together by the Provisional Government. Composed of charity committees and welfare agencies, it administered care to wounded veterans, pensions for war widows, schools for young women, orphanages, old-age homes for the poor, leper colonies, tuberculosis sanitoria, maternity hospitals, mental hospitals, aid to the blind, and, to finance all the rest, factories that made playing cards.[14] Before Kollontai could organize this motley assemblage, she had to convince its employees to go back to work.

She conferred with Ivan Egorov, a Bolshevik who led a union of the lower staff, and they decided to gather the strikers together and convince them to stop the boycott. Egorov called a meeting of the janitors, playing-card makers, nurses, teachers, and other employees on the night of October 29. It began in bedlam. "Each defended the interests of the establishment where he worked," Kollontai wrote. "And how he defended it!"[15] Eventually they decided to establish a council, or soviet, composed of representatives of the departments within the commissariat. That group would advise Kollontai and also elect a "college" of top administrators. Several hundred people pledged to return to work in defiance of the boycott.[16]

The day after the meeting, Kollontai moved into the building on Kazan Street and the formidable doorman finally abandoned his post in disgust. With Egorov she led the first meeting of the commissariat soviet in a discussion of whether to give upper-level bureaucrats representation in the college. "In view of the fact that only three of the former bureaucrats were left," Kollontai wrote, "they decided for the time being to leave the question open."[17] Although these early efforts at democratizing the commissariat pleased her, they were not a solution for the problems of the war veterans or the orphans. To tackle those issues, she needed experienced people and money.

Over the next few weeks some employees gradually drifted back to work, unable to sustain their poorly organized boycott and afraid of Bolshevik retaliation. The men with the keys to the strongbox in which the ministry's funds were kept stood firm, however. After two weeks, Kollontai sent sailors to arrest three of the strikers, including the former head of the financial department, who had the keys. When the men refused to yield, Kollontai ordered them to jail. Sitting late in her office, she pondered morosely on her action. Kollontai, the avowed enemy of tsarist jailers, had become a jailer herself. Three days later the men surrendered the keys and Kollontai opened the safe.[18] She now had sufficient funds and personnel to set to work, although some employees continued their strike through December.[19]

While trying to make the commissariat operational, Kollontai also attended the Petrograd Conference of Women Workers, the meeting she and Samoilova had planned before the Bolsheviks took power. Five hundred delegates representing 80,000 Petrograd factory workers came, as well as a few people from Moscow, Ivanovo-Voznesensk, Tula, and Kaluga. In a speech on November 6 Kollontai proclaimed the Bolshevik commitment to public financing of maternity and child care. She began by asserting that the Bolsheviks sought a system "in which the participation of women in the productive life of society will not contradict their natural and also socially necessary task of bearing children."[20] To achieve that goal society must assume responsibility for the care of pregnant women and for child rearing. First, a series of laws would regulate child labor and female labor closely, to protect them. At the same time, women would receive eight weeks' paid maternity leave without loss of seniority and free medical care, together with food and clothing for their infants. To finance the new facilities, Kollontai proposed the establishment of a general fund gathered from a tax on the working classes and administered by the soviets with substantial democratic participation by proletarian women. Such a program would provide for female needs while giving women themselves a role in founding the institutions to emancipate them. The conference passed the resolution unanimously, although the delegates must have realized that the funds for such a major reform lay well beyond the resources of the infant Soviet government.[21]

The meeting was not an unqualified victory for Kollontai, for she had once again attempted, without success, to push the other *Rabotnitsa* editors into creating a permanent structure to organize proletarian women. She proposed a resolution calling on all party committees at the city level to establish groups to work with women, but the conference vetoed her idea. According to Samoilova, they feared "alienating" Bolsheviks who continued to see such proposals as bourgeois feminism in disguise.[22]

By the time the conference adjourned, Kollontai had established enough control over the Commissariat of Social Welfare to begin dealing with the needs of its many clients. Later she admitted the difficulty of the tasks confronting her. "One cannot easily imagine what high demands these problems put on a small group of people who were as yet amateurs in state administration," she wrote.[23] Not only were Kollontai and her top advisers inexperienced, but they were not even sure how far outside Petrograd their authority extended. The local soviets which had sprung up in the provinces often pursued their own policies, oblivious to instructions from the city. Indeed, since the Bolsheviks held only the urban enclaves, they were surrounded by the vast rural reaches of Russia, where loyalties were as yet undetermined.

Aware of these obstacles and wondering how long the Soviet government would survive, Kollontai set out to enact her cherished reforms for women. The tasks of the commissariat were twofold, she announced—to restructure welfare aid "on foundations of spontaneity in the interests of the millions of the working masses," and to strengthen "state power in democratic Russia." Her first step, and one of which she was very proud, was the extension of employee soviets to every branch of the commissariat, to provide a mechanism enabling people at all levels to participate in the decision-making process.[24] Thereby she would transform the spontaneity that had destroyed the old order into a force that would build the new one. In fact, however, the soviets functioned primarily to build loyalty to Kollontai. She herself told Louise Bryant, the American journalist and wife of socialist John Reed, that once the janitors and messenger boys were drawn into the meetings, they would willingly work sixteen hours a day for "the little Comrade," as they had nicknamed Kollontai.[25] No important reform proposals came from the soviets; for those, Kollontai drew on her own ideas and on advice from appointed panels of experts in law, education, and medicine.[26]

To increase the funds at her disposal, she cut salaries, fought corruption, and raised the price of playing cards from 30 to 360 rubles per dozen decks. In the bizarre mood of the early months after the Bolshevik revolution, flourishing casinos ordered the decks by the hundreds.[27] With this limited income, Kollontai and her advisers industriously set out to reform every department under their control. They took on all the functions of the charitable committees left from tsarist times, ordered the establishment of new orphanages for children made homeless by the war and revolution, granted students a voice in school administration, decreed that religious instruction must be voluntary, stopped all funds for church maintenance, reduced priests to the status of civil servants on the state payroll, instituted self-government in old-age homes, created a committee of physicians to reorganize the sanitoria, planned homes for the handicapped, abolished the classification of children as legitimate or illegitimate, and organized a department to deal with aid to minorities.[28]

Many of these decrees never went beyond the confines of Petrograd or the pages of *Izvestiia*; they were primarily declarations of principle, since the government lacked the power and the means to implement them. When Louise Bryant, an American journalist, heard that the old people in the state homes could choose their menus now, she asked Kollontai what that meant in a city chronically short of food. "Kollontai burst out laughing. 'Surely,' she said, 'you must understand that there is a great deal of moral satisfaction in deciding whether you want thick cabbage soup or thin cabbage soup.'"[29]

Kollontai saw the symbolic importance of many of her reforms, and she valued a thorough repudiation of past injustices, even if the first efforts of those early days were ineffectual. But in one area, maternity protection, Kollontai was determined to move beyond gestures to genuine action. Working with Nikolai Korolev, a physician who was her chief medical adviser, she appointed a six-person committee to organize a department for maternity and child care. The committee met throughout January 1918 with the heads of other departments that dealt with children and childbirth.[30] After several weeks Kollontai felt they had accomplished enough to enable her to issue two decrees on maternity protection. On January 20 she declared that maternity hospitals would henceforth be open to all women free of charge. Obstetricians became public employees on the government payroll. She also prohibited physicians from using poor patients in experiments and increased the term of midwife education from one year to two.[31]

In the second important set of reforms, issued on January 31, Kollontai decreed that all the inadequate bourgeois procedures for aiding mothers and children were abolished. "A morning begins as clean and bright as the children themselves," she wrote. From that time onward all institutions dealing with pregnant women and their babies were combined under the Department for the Protection of Mothers and Children, within the Commissariat of Social Welfare. This new section had "one general governmental task—the creation of spiritually and physically strong citizens." Korolev's advisory committee was to propose reforms that would guarantee the health of mothers and children, who would grow together "in the atmosphere of a widely developed socialist community," and those reforms would be carried out by the department.[32]

Kollontai considered this manifesto an important step not only because it consolidated all the various Provisional Government agencies under unified administrative control, but also because it established the "legal foundation" for full state funding of maternity and infant care. By bearing all the cost, society acknowledged that motherhood was a social service, not a burden to be borne privately.[33] Kollontai had sought that goal for years, and she planned more than resolutions to achieve it. In addition to administrative consolidation and declarations of principle, Kollontai organized a free maternity hospital as a model facility.

The hospital, grandly named the Palace of Motherhood, was to be a shining example of the new society, with spacious and clean wards, a library, kitchen, and even exhibits to teach women hygiene. Kollontai and Korolev found room for it in a foundling home that dated back to the time of Catherine the Great. For over a hundred years women had brought illegitimate children to a side window in this orphanage, where a nurse would take the infant and write a number on its clothes. Thereafter the abandoned baby would become an anonymous victim of its parents' indiscretion. Now, under the jurisdiction of the Commissariat of Social Welfare, the staff of the orphanage resented the new government fiercely. Particularly hostile was an old countess who had run the orphanage for years; she felt that Kollontai's decree of equality for illegitimate children was equivalent to sanctioning prostitution.[34]

When the people from the commissariat began to remodel part of the building for a maternity hospital, the nurses and the countess became even angrier, for they were convinced that the Bolsheviks planned to bring pregnant streetwalkers into their decent home. Besieged by mothers asking for a place to have their babies, determined to establish her showcase facility, Kollontai ignored the complaints of the orphanage staff. She also put off the demands of other organizations that wanted space in the building.[35]

In addition to dealing with these administrative problems, Kollontai attended evening meetings of the Council of People's Commissars and listened glumly to discussions on how to make peace. The German army was threatening, the Russian army was demoralized, the commissariats were still suffering from the strike. At one particularly depressing meeting on the night before the dedication of the maternity hospital, Lenin did not make his usual effort to cheer everyone up, and Kollontai returned dejected, hungry, and tired to the grimy apartment building where she, Zoia, and Misha lived. On such nights the euphoria of November seemed far away, and she became nostalgic for her earlier life.

> I went up the stairs feeling that it was no fun to be people's commissar, with all the responsibility and all the excitement. I wondered if there was anything to eat in the house. . . .
> I knew that my room would be cold and inhospitable. And I began to long for the time when I wasn't a people's commissar, but an ordinary party agitator traveling around the world and dreaming of revolution.[36]

Zoia had prepared tea and even some bread as a snack, and Kollontai revived somewhat. Then the phone rang. Korolev told her that the maternity hospital was on fire. After calling for sailors to help put out the blaze, she rushed off to the building. The whole central area containing the Palace of Motherhood was burning; Korolev said it looked like arson because several areas had gone up at once. Wretched and angry, Kollontai stood in the January night, watching her cherished project destroyed. The nurses shouted that it was God's judgment on her for being an anarchist and an anti-Christ.[37]

The next day Pavel Dybenko, commissar of the navy, together with Korolev and Kollontai's secretary Ivan Egorov, questioned several of the nurses about the fire. One old woman said that God was punishing Kollontai for removing the icons from the building. Another nurse said she had seen that same old woman take a paraffin lamp to bed with her, even though the electricity was working in the building. The main witness, the countess, whose wing had escaped the fire, publicly said the conflagration was a pity, but asked what one could expect when the Bolsheviks encouraged lawlessness. Some sailor spending the night with a new Bolshevik nurse had probably started the fire with careless smoking. "Don't you see that it's God's punishment? How can you dare to make a bordello out of a home for poor, innocent orphans?" she demanded. "You will send all the women of the streets here and make our nurses wait on them."[38] Even though Kollontai was convinced the countess had ordered the fire, she had no evidence to implicate her. The hearing ended without result.

Regardless of the fate of the maternity hospital, Kollontai was pleased with the progress that had been made for women by late January, barely two months after the seizure of power. The principles of full public funding for maternity and child care, and for full female political equality, had been espoused by the government. Civil registry of marriage had replaced church marriage, enabling a couple to obtain a divorce by mutual consent and even encouraging them, while married, to choose whichever surname they wished—his, hers, or a combination of both. With Kollontai acting as a consultant, Shliapnikov's Commissariat of Labor had begun instituting protective regulations for women in industry.[39] Complete female equality before the law had been affirmed.

Far less satisfactory were Kollontai's efforts to help the war-wounded who eked out an existence on the streets of Petrograd. She wanted first of all to raise their government pensions, but she did not have enough money at her disposal to go about it. She told Louise Bryant that just to provide a minimum stipend would require 4 billion rubles a year, a sum far beyond the government's resources.[40] Kollontai could only centralize control over all veterans' agencies in her commissariat, try to prevent the stealing of what little money they had, and collect pathetically small contributions from factory workers.[41]

In January the Petrograd Soviet called on Kollontai's commissariat to find housing for the wounded men immediately. One Soviet official, Aleksei Tsvetkov, suggested taking over the Aleksandr Nevskii Monastery, which was large, handsome, and practically empty. Kollontai should have thought carefully about moving into one of Russia's holiest shrines, a place of pilgrimage and a repository for icons and other artifacts dear to the Orthodox, but the demands of the veterans rang more loudly in her ears than the ancient bells of priestly power. She sent two delegations to negotiate with the holy fathers, but each time the priests refused to allow an Orthodox shrine to be converted into a dormitory. They accurately saw the move as a part of the Bolshevik campaign to confiscate church property. The Union of War-Wounded argued with equal anger that the Bolshevik revolution had done them no good as long as they were sleeping in the streets. Egorov, Tsvetkov, and the soldiers urged Kollontai to sign an order authorizing the seizure of the monastery and all its property. She signed, convinced that the priests must not be allowed to obstruct the government.[42]

When fifteen men from the Soviet appeared at the monastery on January 19, the monks refused to let them in. The delegation then demanded the keys, and the monks began ringing the bells in a cry for help. Soon a large and hostile crowd gathered to heckle the armed Soviet emissaries. In the confusion that followed, Kollontai went to the monastery herself, after calling Dybenko for reinforcements. The sailors grew increasingly nervous and angry under the taunting of the crowd; monks circulated among the bystanders, stirring them up to shout at the troops. Finally the armed men fired on the unarmed. The confrontation ended with one priest dead and the monastery unoccupied.[43]

The other commissars were furious when they heard about the incident, for Kollontai had not cleared her plan ahead of time with the Sovnarkom. After ordering Kollontai and Tsvetkov to leave the monks alone, Lenin called the two to demand an explanation of their actions. Kollontai told him that they had planned to win over the lay brothers and move into the monastery peacefully, but Lenin was not appeased. In addition to blaming her for not getting the approval of the Sovnarkom, he disliked her forcing a confrontation with the Church. Kollontai later claimed that because of the incident, the Sovnarkom decreed the separation of church and state the next day, earlier than originally planned. With the priesthood of Petrograd already enraged, the Bolsheviks had nothing to lose by declaring their intention to remove the governmental support on which the Russian church had depended for centuries.[44]

The following Sunday a large procession of priests and lay people, organized several weeks earlier as a general protest against Bolshevik policies toward the Church, wound its way through the streets of the city to Kazan Cathedral, then to the monastery to show support for the embattled monks.[45] In the course of the protest, the priests declared Kollon-tai anathema. Lenin told her wryly, "You're not in bad company; you'll be remembered along with Stenka Razin and Lev Tolstoi."[46]

In truth, the ludicrous affair at the monastery gates and its aftermath were deadly serious, for the episode revealed the dimensions of the tasks the Soviet government had undertaken. The Bolsheviks, like their tsarist predecessors, were trying to reshape Russia. The tsars had not been willing to innovate as much as many Russians desired, but the Bolsheviks wanted to go much farther than many Russians desired. Lenin admitted as much when he criticized Kollontai for provoking a confrontation with the Church. To accomplish anything, the Bolsheviks had to temper their ideo-logical vision with an appreciation of just how much change the people would tolerate, and just how far they could be coerced.

This constant assessment of ideals and realities, this politics of effec-tive change, was a game at which Lenin excelled; few Bolsheviks knew so well the limits of power in Russia. For men like Stalin, on the other hand, politics was a test of personal survival: either one succeeded or one perished. Sensing the ultimate cost of the struggle, Stalin learned caution and coercion with ease. But to Kollontai and the utopians in the party, reality was romantically perceived as a merger of wills into a drive to reform. For them, resorting to either coercion or compromise required an admission that the masses did not give their unquestioning support, that the Bolsheviks, instead of riding a revolutionary wave, faced complex currents of loyalties requiring them to compromise, argue, and wrestle with uncertainty. Such an admission would tarnish "the splendid illusion," and few of the utopians made it easily. Although Kollontai knew that her images of a great proletarian mass movement were oversimplified, she could all too easily be drawn into ignoring Lenin's pragmatism and cling-ing instead to the utopian illusion. Then she blundered into resistance far more hostile than she had anticipated: the Palace of Motherhood burned down, hundreds of people rushed to defend the monks. Angry and saddened, Kollontai was forced to admit that she had underestimated the opposition.

In January Kollontai struggled with the manifold problems of her department and with the hunger and cold of the city. Food shortages affected even the Bolshevik leadership. When some visiting Danish Social Democrats sent the commissars a cheese, they carefully divided it, only to find on returning from another interminable meeting that a guard had eaten it all while they were gone.[47] There was no time to relax with friends, for when the working day was over there were night meetings to attend. Kollontai also entertained foreign socialists visiting the new Russia, translated their speeches, and once even went to calm a dispute between the Sovnarkom and the Baltic fleet.[48] She also found time to get married—to Dybenko, the peasant sailor and commissar of the navy.

Pavel Efimovich Dybenko was born in 1889 in a village of the northern Ukraine. There were nine "souls" in the family, he later wrote, his parents, his aged grandfather, and six children. They farmed eight acres and owned but one horse and one cow. To feed themselves, everyone, including the children, had to hire out as day laborers to a local landlord.[49] Dybenko was the eldest child, and his parents wanted him to have some schooling. They sent him first to a priest's daughter and later to an elementary school run by a teacher with Social Democratic sympathies. His parents then thought he had had enough education, but the boy asked his mentor, the Social Democrat, to persuade them to let him go on to a "city school" for poor children. At age fourteen he completed his studies there, and his parents demanded that he begin contributing to the family's income.

Dybenko went to work for the tsarist treasury department but was fired when the police charged that he belonged to an illegal revolutionary organization, probably a Marxist-tinged reading group. At this point he left the Ukraine to work as a stevedore in Riga. There he moved closer to the Social Democrats, joining strikes in 1910. In 1911 he was conscripted into the navy. He became a Bolshevik the next year.

From 1913 to 1915 Dybenko served on the *Emperor Pavel I*, a ship of the line which sailors nicknamed "the ocean prison." He spent a great many of his off-duty hours teaching his mates about socialism, and in 1915, when a mutiny on the dreadnought *Petropavlovsk* brought a crackdown on troublemakers, he was transferred to a land-based naval unit. In 1916 that unit refused an order to attack, for which it was moved from the Baltic to Helsingfors. When the February Revolution swept the fleet, Dybenko was elected to the revolutionary committee organized by the Helsingfors sailors.[50]

John Reed described him as "a giant, bearded sailor with a placid face."[51] In 1917 he was twenty-eight years old, tall and broad-shouldered, with dark hair and eyes. He was a handsome man, genial, modest, dedicated, and well liked. He was capable of fiery explosions when addressing the fleet, but otherwise he impressed people with the even temper that seemed out of keeping with his size.[52]

Kollontai first met Dybenko in the spring of 1917 when she was in Helsingfors speaking to the sailors. Throughout the spring they worked there, evidently growing more attracted to one another. Dybenko too was jailed for a month because of the July Days, then released and returned to the fleet. After the Bolshevik seizure of power he was appointed commissar of the navy. By early November, according to Trotsky, party gossip said that Dybenko and Kollontai were lovers.[53]

Kollontai saw Dybenko as "passionate, steadfast, and totally decisive," as "the soul of *Petrobalt* [the sailors' revolutionary committee], firm and determined."[54] He was a genuine proletarian, not an intellectual, not even as well educated as Shliapnikov. Kollontai captured his simplicity as well as his abilities when she described him as "a person of natural talent."[55] Although she continued to work with Shliapnikov and to care for him, Kollontai could not resist the admiration of Dybenko, or his considerable vitality. Later she wrote: "Our meetings always overflowed with joy, our partings were full of torment, emotion, broken hearts. Just this strength of feeling, the ability to live fully, passionately, strongly, drew me powerfully to Pavel."[56]

Merely being lovers was enough, according to her, but Dybenko wanted them to marry. He told her it was appropriate for them to be the first couple registered under the new marriage law she herself had helped to draft. He also argued that they could stay together more easily if they were husband and wife. Kollontai admitted she was tired of the gossip about them and hoped that marriage would stop it. But Zoia and Misha, resenting the new rival for her affection, urged Kollontai to remain single. "Will you really put down our flag of freedom for his sake?" Zoia asked. "You, who all your life have been fighting against the slavery that married life brings and that always comes into conflict with our work and achievements." Misha added, "You must remain 'Kollontai' and nothing else." Dybenko won her over their protests by accusing her of hesitating because he was a peasant, and in mid-January they were married.[57]

Of course that did not quell the rumors about them; it only fanned them. Zeth Höglund, who visited Russia in January 1918, noted that the age disparity—seventeen years—had caused "a sensation." Albert Rhys Williams, the correspondent for the *New York Evening Post*, wrote, "We were astounded to find one morning that the versatile Kollontay had married the sailor Dybenko." General Henri Niessel, head of the French military mission, recorded in his diary, "For the first time since the world was made, one sees two ministers marry each other," and added that there were rumors that Dybenko had had the union consecrated by a priest.[58]

Those Bolsheviks who later wrote their memoirs were too discreet to gossip in public; indeed, Trotsky criticized Stalin for tittering over Kollontai's relationship with Dybenko.[59] Gossip in private they did, however, for most Bolsheviks were conventional in their sexual habits. While giving lip service to Marxist pronouncements on the abolition of the family, they lived ordinary domestic lives. When Kollontai married Dybenko, they saw it as the silly infatuation of a middle-aged woman (Kollontai was now forty-five) with a virile younger man, who happened also to be her social and intellectual inferior.

Kollontai herself had foreseen that kind of reaction years before, in 1911. Imagine, she wrote in her article "Sexual Morality and the Social Struggle," that a respected professional man fell in love with his cook and married her. Everyone would praise his generosity in raising the poor woman's standing in society. His status would be enhanced, not diminished.

> Now imagine another situation: a female public figure, a docent, a physician, a writer, it does not matter, takes up with her servant and to complete "the scandal" marries him. How would society take the action of the hitherto respected individual? Of course, it would fall on her with contempt. And notice: God save her if her spouse-servant be handsome or have any "physical quality." So much the worse.[60]

A liaison with one's inferior, seen as noble when a man made it, became a frank confession of carnality when practiced by a woman. It also lowered the woman's status to the man's, whereas the status of the female was raised if she contracted an alliance with a superior male. Of course in 1911 Kollontai was describing bourgeois society, and Dybenko was not her servant, but many Bolsheviks had never overcome the social distinctions they had learned as children. A forty-five-year-old aristocrat sleeping with a twenty-eight-year-old sailor made their tongues wag.

In February Kollontai broke off her work in the commissariat to set off on a trip to Western Europe. The party Central Committee on January 19 chose a delegation composed of her, Ia. A. Berzin, and M. A. Natanson to tour Stockholm, Paris, and London, presenting the Bolshevik demand for treaties without annexations or reparations. Trotsky was negotiating a peace settlement with Germany in the Polish town of Brest-Litovsk, but so far he had made no progress. He and Lenin therefore decided to send envoys abroad to explain their foreign policy objectives to the Entente powers and to foreign socialists. Originally Kamenev planned to head the mission, but toward the end of the month he was reassigned as Soviet liaison in Paris, and Kollontai became the delegate to Sweden.[61]

She went first to Helsingfors, where she met with Finnish Social Democrats, then she boarded a ship for Sweden. An icebreaker to lead them through the dangerous waters never appeared, however, and by evening Kollontai and the rest of the delegation had run aground on one of the Åland Islands. Thoroughly chilled, they found their way to an inn and a hot meal, but they soon had to flee from German troops overrunning the island. A young Finn who helped them escape was subsequently caught and executed. Several dismal days later Kollontai was back in Russia, her mission aborted.[62] Later she described the confusing scene that greeted her return:

> We felt at once that something serious was happening in Petrograd. The newspapers were full of alarming news about the German advance. The front was quickly approaching the capital. At the station I learned that all automobiles, even the cars of the commissars, had been taken by a newly established Evacuation Commission. So the delegation had to wait at the railway station for quite a long time before we could get in touch with Smolny and by special permission, get some cars to take us home.
>
> All sorts of rumors were about. Families were trying to leave town or at least send their children away. The Evacuation Commission was removing, as quickly as possible, the art collections from the Hermitage, the State's jewels, etc. The Government had just decided to leave Petrograd and go to Moscow. Nobody seemed to notice the return of our unsuccessful delegation. It was only I who felt rather miserable as I was not accustomed to failure in a task that was given to me.[63]

She could not have succeeded, for she had to set out to present the Bolshevik peace proposals to the Entente, and by late February the possibility of accommodation with Great Britain or France was dying in the face of German pressure for an immediate treaty. The Bolsheviks had taken power with a call for peace negotiations to begin immediately on the principle of no annexations and no reparations. They had not expected the rulers of Europe to stop fighting, however; their appeal had been designed to encourage rebellion among war-weary soldiers and civilians. The Bolsheviks had expected that the demoralization rampant in the Russian army would soon sweep through the rest of Europe to climax in a great mutiny against further fighting. If the governments resisted, the Bolsheviks proclaimed defiantly, the masses led by the revolutionary So- cial Democrats would launch a revolutionary war to end the capitalist war, destroy capitalism itself, and usher in the new era.

Nothing of the sort had happened, none of the sporadic riots and military mutinies in Europe had led to genuine revolution in November or December, so first A. A. Ioffe, then Trotsky, went to Brest-Litovsk to negotiate a separate peace with Germany, while Lenin maintained tenuous contacts with agents of the Entente powers in Petrograd. At Brest-Litovsk the Bolsheviks met with negotiators representing the German High Com- mand, which was bent on extending German control into much of the Russian Empire, including the Ukraine, the Baltic Provinces, Finland, and substantial portions of Western Russia. Unwilling to accept a Dra- conian peace dictated by the leading capitalist power of Europe, the Bol- sheviks stalled and hoped revolution in Germany would sweep away the need for capitulation. In January, as the German negotiators became in- creasingly impatient, Trotsky returned to Petrograd to tell the party leadership that they should refuse either to fight or to surrender. Lenin disagreed. The Bolsheviks must make peace, however disgraceful, because they had no army. Now they needed a "breathing space" to gather their resources. Rather than stall, they must defend the foothold which Soviet Russia represented. When the international revolution came, as Lenin believed it would, they would be stronger and more able to act effectively in support of their brother-workers abroad.

Trotsky called for "no war, no peace," Lenin for peace at any price, while a third group in the party leadership, the "Left Opposition," whose chief spokesman was Bukharin, advocated the concept of revolutionary war to which the party had been pledged throughout 1917. Specifically, Bukharin proposed transforming the conflict with Germany into a guerilla war fought by partisan armies of workers and peasants. The workers would fight for the ideals of the revolution, the peasants for their land, and their example would spark the people of Europe into rebellion. Thus would begin the international revolution of which the Bolshevik revolu- tion was a part and on which Bolshevik survival depended. The nucleus of the Left Opposition came from the young, enthusiastic members of the Moscow party organization, but they had broad support among Bolshe-

viks throughout the country and on the Central Committee. Their call
to guerilla warfare appealed to people who recognized the disorganization
of the Russian regular army, but who could not bear the thought of sur-
rendering to Germany and thereby betraying both the proletariat of
Europe and the international revolution.[64]

On January 8, at the meeting of party leadership where Trotsky first
presented his "no war, no peace" formula, Kollontai declared that Bukharin's course was the right one. Yet she was not fully committed to his
position, nor had she ever been convinced that Russian forces were capable
of the combat necessary to spark international revolution. In November
she told Jacques Sadoul, a member of the French embassy, that Russian
soldiers would refuse to fight a revolutionary war.[65] On January 7, one
day before the meeting where she openly agreed with Bukharin, Kollontai remained dubious when Sadoul talked about organizing a volunteer
army, although she was more willing to entertain the idea than she had
been earlier. "To sign the peace which Germany prepared would be to
betray the International and reinforce German imperialism," Sadoul argued. "Don't forget that you stand before all internationalists, that tomorrow you must give an accounting."

Kollontai reluctantly agreed that "the Bolsheviks had to prepare
themselves for battle." "It would be very good to end in beauty, to die
fighting," she said. "Yes, that is what must be done—triumph or die."
Two weeks later Sadoul wrote that Dybenko and Kollontai were urging
their colleagues to begin rebuilding the army, which Sadoul, anxious for
Russia to remain in the war, took as a sign that Kollontai's attitude was
changing.[66]

When she left for Western Europe she still hoped that there was
some way to salvage an equitable peace by dealing with the Entente, a
move which Bukharin denounced as another capitulation to capitalism.
The failure of the trip then came as a special disappointment to Kollontai. When she returned to Russia the situation had become much worse.
Convinced that the Germans would be content only with a harsh treaty,
Trotsky had announced on January 28 that the Soviet government would
not continue the war and would not accept the German demands. The
next day he left Brest-Litovsk for Petrograd.

The principled heroism of this gesture was lost on Trotsky's adver-
saries, who almost immediately began preparations for a new offensive.
They moved east on February 17 and encountered so little resistance that
General Max von Hoffman, a negotiator at Brest-Litovsk, described the

advance as "the most comic war I have ever experienced."[67] Trotsky now realized that he had underestimated the enemy's willingness to fight. On February 18, after two days of stormy Central Committee meetings, he turned to support Lenin. That action broke the deadlock between the Left Opposition, led by Bukharin and calling for revolutionary war, and Lenin, who continued to argue for an immediate peace, regardless of its severity. On February 19, the Bolsheviks notified the Germans of their intention to resume negotiations. The response, on February 23, was an ultimatum. The army and navy must be demobilized, Latvia and Estonia granted self-determination, and the Ukraine and Finland evacuated. The Soviet answer must be cabled in forty-eight hours; any further negotiations would be limited to three days, after which the German army would attack again.

When Iakov Sverdlov read the new demands to a Central Committee meeting on February 23, the Left Opposition shouted their anger. Trotsky and Lenin insisted the army could not fight, but Bukharin, backed by many of his colleagues, argued that recent demonstrations in Petrograd and Moscow showed that the proletariat was ready to launch a revolutionary war. Lenin listened, then replied: "I don't want revolutionary phrases. The German revolution still is not ripe. This will take months. One must accept the conditions. If there is a new ultimatum then, that will be in a new situation."[68] He reminded them that they had only until seven the next morning to act on the German demands. With Trotsky's abstention, the resolution to accept was finally passed.

That same night Lenin took his case to an equally stormy meeting of the Petrograd Soviet. Kollontai listened to Lenin hammer home the desperate logic of his position, but she was not convinced. At the Soviet Executive Committee meeting which followed, she poured out her disappointment: "Enough of this opportunism! You are advising us to do the same thing which you have been accusing the Mensheviks of doing all summer—compromising with Imperialism." Impassive, Lenin listened and stared at the floor.[69]

Lenin and Kollontai would never again be friends, for the war which had brought them together had now driven them apart. Above all a realist, Lenin believed that hostilities had to stop immediately, before the Germans took Petrograd and demanded even more. Kollontai rejected that analysis in favor of the notion of a war against war, now that revolutionary war seemed the only alternative to surrender. The Bolsheviks would resist by calling to guerrilla combat all the workers who had recently demonstrated against capitulation, and that sacrifice would stir the enemy troops to mutiny. If the rebellion did not come, if they were destroyed instead, "it would be good to end in beauty."

The vision of mass triumph or glorious death for the good of future generations had swept Kollontai onto a revolutionary wave of her own imagining. Every outburst of discontent in war-weary Europe (and there were many in 1918) fed the illusion for her, as did the presence in Russia of others who shared her vision. Now her variant of Marxism, always a sustainer in battle and an illuminator of reality, had turned into a distorter that threatened the survival of her government. To ignore the fact that the Bolsheviks had no army, that partisans could not prevent the Germans from occupying all the territory they demanded and more, that the Bolsheviks would then have to deal with both their domestic enemies and foreign forces—was to allow ideology to create an illusion of strength where there was none. Furthermore, it was an illusion which, if acted on, would cost human lives.

In believing that the future of the Soviet state depended on revolutionary war, Kollontai sacrificed one facet of her Marxism to another. Throughout the war years she had been strongly pacifist out of a deepseated horror of human suffering. When she clamored for guerilla combat in March 1918, therefore, she seemed to allow her commitment to revolutionary war, a concept she had embraced reluctantly, to overshadow her humanitarianism. In truth, Kollontai was not motivated by her adherence to the notion of revolutionary war alone. Her refusal to countenance the peace came rather from another, more central facet of her ideology, her hatred of compromise with the "enemy." Lenin said quite justly that she and her colleagues were motivated by "feeling, desire, indignation and resentment."[70] The Treaty of Brest-Litovsk was a surrender to the coalition of capitalists and monarchists that ruled Germany and therefore a capitulation to the forces against which she had fought all her life. Rather than betray the proletariat of Europe by making a humiliating peace, Kollontai wanted to stake the Bolsheviks' future on a desperate gamble—that the time for international revolution was now. The Soviet state must put its trust in the masses to end both the war and capitalism by making war.

The Left Opposition trumpeted its call to arms through speeches and newspapers to a receptive audience in the cities, particularly Moscow, but the group lacked decisive leadership. Bukharin frankly told Vsevolod Eichenbaum, an anarchist, that he could not carry the feud to the point

of a split with Lenin and Trotsky, for that would destroy the party.[71] The
Left Opposition sought instead to exert pressure enough to hold the majority, which probably favored their position. Lenin's inexorable logic,
strong will, and personal prestige, however, swayed the votes of many
who deplored the decision. On March 3 the preliminary Treaty of Brest-
Litovsk was signed.

Lenin next sought ratification of the treaty by congresses of the party
and the soviets. At both meetings the Left Opposition called for a repudiation, only to lose to the Lenin-Trotsky majority. On March 7 at the
Seventh Party Congress, Kollontai made her first and last public appeal
for the group. The Bolsheviks had signed the initial treaty, she said, but
the war continued. Peace had become impossible, she charged, because
the international battle between the capitalists and the proletariat, "the
Whites and the Reds," had already begun. The united forces of Germany,
Britain, and France would soon strike against the Soviet government, and
the breathing space which Lenin talked about therefore had become impossible, and even undesirable. "Revolutionary will does not grow stronger
in a period of peace," Kollontai said. "You will not strengthen this revolutionary will with agitation; it is created and grows stronger, develops
only in battle itself."[72] Instead of signing the treaty, the Soviet state
should build an underground "Red Army." "And if our Soviet republic
perishes, another will raise our banner. This will be a defense not of the
fatherland, but of the labor republic. Long live the revolutionary war!"
The Left Opposition cheered.[73]

It was not Kollontai's finest hour. The speech rang with the stock
phrases of the Left Opposition—international conspiracy, defense of the
labor republic, international proletarian solidarity—and all in a cause that
would destroy the very people for whom the revolution had been made.
Kollontai, the life-long anti-militarist, was espousing war as a strengthening experience. She spoke of a conspiracy of the British, the French, and
the Germans, while those nations were slaughtering each other in France.
She and the other Oppositionists were now maintaining that they could
not make a true peace, because the German offer was only a ruse to lull
them into quiescence before the imminent, united capitalist attack. This
was nonsense, but by making war a necessity it soothed their consciences.
Fight, they said, advance the cause or die; you have no choice.

Until the end of February Kollontai's hatred of combat had kept her
from a full commitment to the Left Opposition. She did not attend most
of the Central Committee meetings where the war was discussed in Jan-

uary and February, possibly because she was working at the commissariat or because she had not fully made up her mind. She had never taken an active role in the Central Committee, but earlier she had at least attended.[74] Only when she heard the German ultimatum on February 23 did her anger at the full ignominy of the Bolshevik surrender impel her finally to join the Opposition.

The Party Congress approved the treaty; then Lenin took it to the Congress of Soviets for final ratification. There the Left Opposition presented a statement signed by eight Central Committee members, including Kollontai, charging that the peace would tarnish *"the international meaning of the great Soviet republic."* It would encourage international capitalism and weaken the workers' defenses. Rather than capitulate, the Left Opposition wanted to issue a call for proletarians everywhere to rise up in the defense of the first socialist state. To prevent a party split, however, they promised to abstain in the voting of the treaty.[75] The Congress of Soviets ratified it.

The Left Opposition did not disband after the Congress of Soviets adjourned, for although the treaty was now final, they had come in the course of the debate to view themselves as a permanent voice for the Bolshevik left. At the party and soviet congresses, they had also heard in Lenin's speeches another hint that he was adjusting the ideals of 1917 to suit the reality of 1918. "If you cannot adapt," Lenin said, "if you cannot go crawling on your belly in the mud, you are not a revolutionary, but a windbag."[76] Then he had laid out some of the adaptations the Bolsheviks would have to make in order to build successfully a Soviet state.

Of first priority was the reconstruction of industry. That could be done, Lenin said, by communes controlled by the workers. Each person must have a voice in discussing and implementing policy, but the time had come also to establish efficiency. Efficiency required responsibility, discipline, and the orderly division of functions, and that in turn required hierarchies, so managers must be chosen to supervise the operation of industry. Since the only managers available were those who had worked in industry before the revolution, Lenin was proposing rehiring capitalist-trained personnel who had been expelled from the factories when the proletariat had seized control in the fall of 1917.

This amounted to nothing less than advocating that the Bolsheviks bring the enemy, bourgeois managers, back into industry to supervise the workers. Lenin proposed it because the workers lacked the expertise to run the factories, which were now in a shambles. He considered it an expedient until the proletariat was educated, but he knew that any return of bourgeois personnel, however temporary, would encounter heavy party resistance. To persuade the doubters, he argued in March and April of 1918 that the Bolsheviks now had to temper their revolutionary idealism with practicality. The workers must learn how to get the factories running again, and only the old managers could teach them that. The time for absorption in demonstrations and revolutionary phrase-making was past; the time had come for rebuilding the economy. "We must learn," Lenin wrote, "how to unite the 'public meeting' democracy of the working masses . . . with *iron* discipline during work, with *absolute obedience* to the will of a single person, the Soviet leader, during work."[77]

The Left Opposition disagreed. They argued that industry could be rebuilt by the proletariat without bourgeois managers. Of course the Russian workers had a lot to learn, but rather than study capitalist methods, they should experiment with democratic techniques of production which would pave the way for socialism. Lenin, once again arguing for the most expedient means to his end, this time economic reconstruction, was advocating hierarchy and discipline. He was, as usual, pragmatic, realistic, and authoritarian. The Left Opposition refused to temporize and remained true to the democratic ideal of complete worker control of industry, an ideal which, like revolutionary war, was a major Bolshevik pledge in 1917. That the workers would run the factories was also the central promise of nineteenth-century socialism. Thus this new argument, developing in March and April in Lenin's articles and the Left Opposition's newspaper, *Kommunist*, was fundamental to the future of the Bolshevik Revolution, but it petered out by late spring because the Left Opposition lacked the heart to continue the fight. Shortly thereafter civil war erupted in Siberia and the party leadership united in the face of a new challenge.

Kollontai should have found the Left Opposition's call for democratization in the factories even more attractive than their opposition to the peace treaty. War in any form had always appalled her, while she supported workers' control without hesitation and would fight for it fervently in 1921 as a member of the Workers' Opposition. Yet although she was listed as a contributor to *Kommunist* in its May and June issues, she took no active part in the protest.[78] She had not been a central figure in the Left Opposition; her reticence may have been due in part to her absorption in Dybenko's problems.

In late February the German army began its offensive to force the Bolsheviks into signing the treaty. In a northward march toward Petrograd the Germans neared Narva, the city where Kollontai had lived for awhile with her first husband so many years before. One thousand sailors under Dybenko's command were transferred to the city's defense, swelling the motley force there to 3,500. The German army outweighed them in manpower and equipment. When Dybenko arrived on March 1, he immediately telegraphed Petrograd for reinforcements, then turned his attention to a battle for the railroad stations near the city.[79]

After two days of combat in snowstorms, the Russians fell back in defeat. The inexperienced Dybenko was exhausted and frustrated when he met on March 3 with D. P. Parskii, a former tsarist officer just arrived from Petrograd to command the Narva defense. Parskii mapped out a plan for a march on the city, but the sailor-commissar refused to allow his men to fight again. He also made it clear that he did not want to take orders from a tsarist officer. Infuriated, Parskii phoned Petrograd, demanding that V. D. Bonch-Bruevich, head of the Defense Committee, order Dybenko to obey him.

The Defense Committee responded by confirming Parskii's authority, but the argument had cost the commander valuable time. Nor were his problems with the commissar over, for rather than submit, Dybenko simply departed for Petrograd. His sympathetic Soviet biographer has written, "In the battle around Narva, he underestimated the enemy's forces, made a series of mistakes, and left the front without leave."[80] The members of the Sovnarkom were furious when they received the report of his conduct, and they retaliated by firing Dybenko as commissar of the navy and ordering him to stand trial for insubordination.[81]

Dybenko was brought to Moscow a prisoner. Immediately, his arrest raised a protest from his own men, and a group of sailors went to the new capital, demanding his release pending the trial.[82] Kollontai was angry as well. Coming on the heels of the peace treaty, Dybenko's arrest seemed too much to bear. When Jacques Sadoul met her on March 18, she appeared "tired and despondent." She was on her way to the Kremlin with food for her husband, and as Sadoul accompanied her, she told him she felt Dybenko had been betrayed. Narva was not the actual reason for his arrest; Lenin had simply used that as an excuse. In reality, she claimed, the Sovnarkom had taken seriously rumors that Dybenko planned to raise an army against the German occupation of the Ukraine.[83]

Kollontai ignored the most obvious reason for Dybenko's arrest—he had deserted his post in the middle of a battle. His obstreperous behavior since—he had made defiant statements defending himself—had not improved his standing with his colleagues. His rebelliousness may have made them fear that he would make good his threats to defend his homeland, the Ukraine. The mutiny was, however, ample cause for punishment. Kollontai could not accept that reason for his arrest because it implied, at best, a serious mistake on her husband's part. Rather than admit that he could have panicked in a crisis, she chose to believe that he, of all the opponents of the Brest-Litovsk Treaty, was being singled out for retribution.

Kollontai protested vehemently against Dybenko's imprisonment. On March 18 and 19, in successive Sovnarkom sessions, she reaffirmed her opposition to the treaty and angrily announced her resignation as commissar.[84] After several days she and the sailors obtained Dybenko's release on their bond and his own word.[85] Sadoul wrote in his diary that she was loudly attacking Bolshevik policies as a betrayal of the revolution:

> Vestal of the Revolution, she would like to maintain the flame of the maximalist ideal in all its purity. She has thrown herself headlong into the opposition, she criticizes severely the brutal measures taken by her comrades against the anarchists, and is indignant at the concessions to the moderate and bourgeois opposition allowed more every day by the government.[86]

Tired and frustrated, Kollontai and Dybenko went off to Petrograd for a rest. She told Sadoul they were leaving on April 14, but she apparently forgot to tell the Sovnarkom. When the commissars learned they were gone, a cry went up that the sailor had skipped bail. The two were soon found in Petrograd, oblivious to the clamor their trip had caused.[87] Of course, they should not have left without notifying the government, and the silly episode became another juicy tale for the gossips of Bolshevik society. Louise Bryant, the American journalist who had become friendly with Kollontai, wrote that many Bolsheviks "looked with disapproving eyes upon Kollontai's infatuation for Dubenko [sic]."[88] It was doubtless from these same circles that the story arose that the two lovers, absorbed in each other, had gone off together once before, to the Crimea on a honeymoon during the October Revolution itself. When they returned, according to the rumors, several commissars had wanted them shot for desertion; but Lenin had convinced the Sovnarkom that he knew the most appropriate punishment. Dybenko and Kollontai should be forced to live together for five years.[89]

Of course there was no truth to the story. There had been no "idyll in the Crimea," to use Rhys Williams's phrase. Kollontai's activity in November and December can be documented day by day. Dybenko spent those months fighting various pockets of resistance to the Bolsheviks in the Petrograd area.[90] The couple was not even married until January. The mention of the Crimea in the story coincides with the other rumors linking Dybenko to the Ukraine, and indicates that it was a malicious variation on their April trip. Since Kollontai and Dybenko were involved, gossip transformed their flight from political conflict into a romantic Crimean rendezvous.

A special military court tried Dybenko in May and acquitted him. Witnesses testified that communications, intelligence, and supply had been poor during the Narva battles, and that he could not be blamed for the losses his men suffered. Furthermore his refusal to fight resulted in part from the fact that the orders he received were so confusing that an inexperienced commander could not understand them, much less obey them. Dybenko himself refused to comment on the battle, but he stressed that he had always been a good revolutionary. Apparently he too felt the charges were a pretext to persecute him for his opposition to Brest-Litovsk. Exonerated, he received a new assignment several months later, in the Ukraine.[91]

Over now for Kollontai were "the revolution's first romantic months." She had quit the commissariat, and her impassioned protest of April yielded in May to a retreat from politics. "Little by little," she wrote, "I was freed also of all other work. I lectured again and went over my ideas about 'the new woman' and 'the new morality.' "[92] In April her former department was renamed the Commissariat of Social Insurance, and in August made a subdivision of the Commissariat of Labor. The reforms Kollontai had pioneered—maternity insurance, female political and civil equality, civil marriage and divorce, protection of female and child labor —continued to be government commitments, although the civil war made them increasingly difficult to achieve. Despite substantial progress, however, the first glow of triumph had dimmed for her, and for the rest of her life she looked back to those early months with nostalgia.

It was, in the end, a wonderful time. We were hungry and had many sleepless nights. There were many difficulties, misfortunes, and chances of defeat. The feeling that helped us was that all we produced, even if it was no more than a decree, would come to be a historical example and help others move ahead. We worked for that time and for the future.[93]

Sacrifices only made the struggle more worthwhile, for the Bolsheviks were united in the collective she had always dreamed of. Enemies surrounded them, but the masses were with them as they built a new society. Kollontai had never had a more important role to play nor a larger audience to appreciate her. Throughout 1917 the rescue of an entire society had seemed to proceed from triumph to triumph with her in the vanguard. Then the Palace of Motherhood had burned down, her mission to the West had foundered, her husband was arrested, and the revolutionary solidarity of the party disintegrated into acrimony. The hard-won consensus of November and December disappeared in a humiliating surrender to the Kaiser. On a very personal level, Kollontai began to feel the sting of ridicule.

In fact, the party had not launched the comradely crusade she wrote about later, and the masses were not unanimously behind them. She knew this in 1917, and she testified to it in her talks with Sadoul, Bryant, and Beatty, as well as later, in her franker memoirs. The lyrical descriptions about Great October overstated her case, but they did point to a purity of purpose which she felt was lost in March 1918. "The months of splendid illusion" ended for Kollontai in a peace she found to be a humiliating betrayal of the ideals of 1917. Rather than accept policies she believed to be wrong, she retreated. Never again would she feel as in harmony with her comrades.

Nor would Kollontai ever stand as high in the party as she did in the fall and winter of 1917. She was then one of the top Bolshevik orators and leading reformers. So long as the Bolshevik goal was the destruction of the old order and massive change, Kollontai, with her utopian vision, spoke the will of the majority. But once the means to survival as a government began to divide Bolsheviks, her calls to revolutionary idealism cut her off from many of her comrades. She would not adjust to becoming a politician; she cultivated no following outside her commissariat; she disdained even the factional politics of the Left Opposition. Refusing to accept compromise, she withdrew into solitude.

7

Work Among Women

FROM 1918 TO 1920 civil war raged through Russia, putting the Bolsheviks' determination to hold power and their ability to govern to a savage test. Food became scarce, city dwellers scavenged for firewood by dismantling abandoned buildings at night, Whites and Reds slaughtered one another in vicious combat and visited atrocities on the civilian population. By virtue of their organization, unity, and will, the Bolsheviks won, but they themselves doubted at times that they would survive. In 1919 Elena Stasova, then a party secretary, was ordered to store up a horde of tsarist banknotes and passports so that the party leaders could flee abroad, if they were defeated.[1]

The civil war began in the spring of 1918, in reaction to the Treaty of Brest-Litovsk. Those who had opposed the Bolsheviks before—tsarist military officers, liberal intellectuals, and moderate socialists—saw the treaty as the final betrayal in a series of Bolshevik crimes. In the spring of 1918, in the Ukraine and Siberia, members of these disaffected groups began to coalesce into an armed opposition. The developing civil war gained impetus from an unlikely source. Contingents of Czech troops, who had been fighting on the Eastern Front against Germany in hopes

149

of aiding the Czech campaign for nationhood, were ordered to France, to help win the war. When one group of these soldiers became involved in a fight in a Urals railroad station and Trotsky responded by ordering them to give up their guns, the brigade rose up against the Communists all along the Trans-Siberian Railroad. The Bolsheviks' inability to contain the rebellion was just the display of weakness needed to galvanize their enemies into war and the foreign powers into intervention. By midsummer, opposition governments had been organized in Samara and Omsk; the Germans occupying the Ukraine were aiding anti-Bolshevik groups there; and even Left Socialist Revolutionaries, erstwhile Bolshevik allies, had become so disenchanted that one of them seriously wounded Lenin in an assassination attempt. Russia's bloody civil war had begun in earnest.

This challenge brought most of the Left Opposition, including Kollontai, back to the fold. Her comrades had responded to her retreat from politics in May by ignoring her. She had turned for comfort to a review of some of her early writings and made plans to reprint her three essays on the "new woman."[2] With the outbreak of the civil war, however, Kollontai dropped her silence to begin a speaking tour of factories in central Russia. When she told women workers there about the benefits brought by the Soviet government, she found them less enthusiastic than they had been earlier in the year and more inclined to complain that the Bolsheviks were doing little to help them. There were not enough party workers in the country, there were not enough facilities to help women, the men were going off to war again, and all the burdens would only grow heavier. One woman textile worker suggested that the party deal with these problems by holding a national conference of working women.

Kollontai agreed with that idea and with the general criticism she heard.[3] The government had not followed up its declarations of principle by organizing day-care centers or maternity hospitals, not only because the government had no money, but also because, in Kollontai's view, the leadership was giving a second place to such reforms. Revived by the speaking tour and convinced that work among women was lagging, Kollontai returned to Moscow to argue that the civil war was an opportunity, however desperate, to emancipate women by drawing them into building the Soviet system.

Women workers were not turning out en masse to support the Bolsheviks. Generally, they were more suspicious of the party than were their menfolk, and they often gave as their reason that they had heard the Bolsheviks were atheists who intended to take babies away from their mothers.[4] Involved as always in the struggle of daily life, traditional in their values, women workers looked with distrust on a government that made sweeping promises but did not lower the price of bread. Within the female proletariat, however, there were younger, more literate, often single women who were responsive to Bolshevik organizers. The number of women in the labor force had grown steadily since 1905, particularly during the war years, and by 1917 fifty percent of the factory workers in the central industrial region around Moscow were women.[5] Some of these new recruits were politically more aware than the prior generation. They had turned out for the Petrograd women's conference in 1917, and a few were joining the party.[6] Kollontai was convinced that if these receptive women were told about the virtues of the Soviet system they would spread that message to the women with whom they worked.

She had broader ambitions than simply to propagandize the female proletariat, however. Kollontai wanted to involve the more responsive women in the organization of day-care centers and public dining rooms. Women would be more easily attracted to projects which affected them directly, but that was not the only reason Kollontai proposed putting them to work establishing such facilities. By setting up the services they needed, women would lay the foundations for their own emancipation, raise their consciousness, and participate in building socialism. The point was not that women should do women's work, but rather that women should set themselves free. Kollontai was stressing again, as she had during her days as commissar, the virtues of *samodeiatel'nost'*, of spontaneous mass action, as the most desirable means of social change. "We all wait for someone else to build everything," she wrote in *Pravda* in October 1918, "we are used to living by decree from above, as we lived under the bourgeois order, and we forget that now there is a Soviet republic. And in the Soviet republic the great thing is that the field is wide open for *samodeiatel'nost'*, for the display of initiative."[7] Of course, Kollontai assumed that women would organize day-care centers "spontaneously," once the government taught them the virtues of day-care centers. She always thought that women workers wanted to be liberated in precisely the way she defined liberation; that was a questionable assumption, but it was an assumption she and her comrades had always made about female emancipation and about the emancipation of the entire society through socialism.

Kollontai's vision during the civil war period was that women should aid the defense by building the facilities that would set them free. The first step was to reach the female proletariat, and to do that Kollontai argued in the fall of 1918 for a national conference of working-class women. Inessa Armand, Konkordiia Samoilova, Liudmilla Stal', and Klavdiia Nikolaeva, the Bolsheviks most interested in work among women, supported the conference idea. In fact, they had made plans for such a gathering in February 1918, but the war crisis had prevented them from holding it. Instead, Inessa had settled for several meetings among Moscow women in the spring.[8]

When Kollontai returned from her speaking tour, she talked over the conference proposal with Inessa and with Iakov Sverdlov, the party secretary who had given permission for the Petrograd conference of women workers the year before. Again he was receptive to the idea of organizing the female proletariat. Having secured Sverdlov's approval, Kollontai and Inessa set up the Initiating Group, an organizing committee composed chiefly of representatives from Moscow and Petrograd and soon augmented by the former editors of *Rabotnitsa*—Samoilova, Nikolaeva, Stal', and several others. Their job was to make arrangements for the conference in Moscow and to supervise the establishment of regional subcommittees which would recruit working-class women as delegates.

The difficulties the Initiating Group faced were manifold. They worked out of cramped quarters with a minimal budget and small staff. Local subcommittees suffered from the same shortages and had the additional problem of being less experienced and less sure of themselves than Kollontai, Samoilova, and Inessa. Kollontai drafted every woman she could find to help with the project, and when one such draftee complained that she was on leave from work at the front, Kollontai replied sternly: "The local comrades are occupied in Tsaritsyn's defense, and the women need a lively speech to explain to them the tasks of the congress, tasks which are most general [i.e., relevant to all Communists], dear comrade. The Central Committee of the party entrusts you to deliver that speech in the name of the party."[9] Kollontai managed to send agitators throughout the Moscow region and even as far as Samara in the Urals. She spoke at meetings in the capital, published articles, and sent appeals to Petrograd when the organizational effort there faltered. Inessa had been working in Moscow for a year, and her contacts helped in rallying the Moscow women. In October, after the Initiating Group succeeded in holding elections in Moscow factories to choose delegates, the male leaders of the party began to offer some help.[10]

In addition to organizing elections at the center and supervising them elsewhere, the Initiating Group had to set an agenda for the conference. Inessa, Samoilova, and Stal' agreed with Kollontai that their primary goal was to involve women in the government and the party. Thus the committee chose as a slogan for the conference the turgid but concise message: "Through practical participation in Soviet construction to communism."[11] The committee also drafted a series of speeches and resolutions calling for the usual reforms—maternity care and communal facilities such as dining rooms, laundries, and child-care centers. None of these goals was new, and Inessa and Kollontai knew that resolutions alone would not improve women's lives. The crucial discussions in the Initiating Group centered therefore on putting the reforms into practice. Again Kollontai pushed for a woman's bureau, which she envisioned as a semi-autonomous party department centered in Moscow and administering regional sub-sections. Of course the conference could not create such an institution, but it could pressure the leadership by passing a resolution on the subject. Once again Kollontai was voted down. Inessa felt that the party would still consider a full-fledged bureau feministic and separatist. Samoilova, who now agreed on the need for some kind of organization beyond a newspaper, supported Inessa. They thought that there was more likelihood of getting the leadership to authorize the establishment of "commissions" for organizing women which would be attached, and therefore fully subordinate, to local party committees. To reach women in the provinces, Inessa also advocated a series of regional meetings of delegates elected from the factories. In this way the same kind of conference they were organizing at the national level would be held throughout the country, educating women workers, who would return home to propagandize their friends.[12]

In five weeks the Initiating Group held elections and drafted an agenda that called for the creation of the commissions within the party. They planned for the conference to begin on November 7, but because the All-Russian Congress of Soviets was scheduled to convene that day, and possibly also because of delays in holding elections in Petrograd, the organizers moved the opening session back to November 16. Unfortunately some of the delegates were en route when the postponement was made; on November 7 they began to arrive in Moscow. Kollontai huddled with Inessa, Samoilova, and Stal' to decide whether to go ahead or wait until the sixteenth. They chose to wait, but that meant finding shelter and food for the women who had already arrived.[13]

Moscow was then entering a nightmarish winter. The incessant warfare and the revolutionary upheaval had shattered the economy, and supplying the city population with food was becoming increasingly difficult. Nor was there enough firewood or coal or kerosene. When the delegates to the First All-Russian Congress of Working Women and Peasants convened on November 16, they did so bundled up against the cold of their meeting room. Because postal communication with the provinces was so poor, the Initiating Group expected only three hundred, instead of the eleven hundred who came. The hall that had been reserved was too small and the organizers did not have enough food or lodgings for the women.[14]

There was nothing at all to eat the first day. That night Barinova, an organizer trying to placate the angry delegates, called Kollontai. "If we don't get some food by morning," she said, "there's going to be a revolt against us. They're besieging us now, demanding bread. They're hungry." Kollontai got in touch with Sverdlov, who managed to find some tea, sugar, and bread, but it was not enough. At 2:00 A.M. Barinova called again to say that the women, still hungry, were refusing to go to sleep. Kollontai spent the rest of the night on the phone, trying to locate more food. Eventually she supplied the delegates with meals of soup, a spoonful of porridge, and a small piece of bread.[15]

The congress convened on November 16 with Sverdlov welcoming the women to Moscow. Kollontai sat on the podium with Inessa, Samoilova, and the other members of the Initiating Group. Feeling immense satisfaction and some euphoria, she looked out at the crowd of factory women, most of them dressed in kerchiefs and the shapeless, gray-brown clothing of winter, although here and there was a splash of color from a peasant costume. The women elected a presidium to lead the conference and then cheered Lenin and Bukharin, who came with greetings from the party leadership. The opening formalities completed, the delegates began to debate the first resolution put before them, "The Tasks of Women Workers in Soviet Russia." After asserting that women had no special, separate goals, but only the general purpose of building communism, the resolution declared that it was the duty of women to participate in every facet of Soviet life, including "direct armed battle." In so doing they would achieve their own liberation through building the new society, most particularly such components of it as communal housekeeping and educational facilities. "The conference considers," the resolution con-cluded, "that the woman worker, taking a most active part in all aspects of the new construction, should pay special attention to the creation of new forms of feeding society, of spreading public education, through which she will destroy the old bondage of the family."[16] Women them-selves had to abolish the institutions which held them in thrall.

Thus the resolution that addressed itself to the major topic of the conference, the involvement of women in Soviet life, asserted clearly that women were to work not simply to defend the government but to achieve their own liberation. The resolution assured the conference and the party that women had no intention of pursuing their special interests, that is, they were not advocating separatism or feminism. Rather women's eman-cipation was an integral part of the war effort, as it was an integral part of the building of socialism. That position had been the essence of Kol-lontai's socialist feminism for years, and now it was publicly embraced by a meeting of one thousand delegates from around the country. Inessa too was championing socialist feminism openly. Soon after the conference she wrote that women's emancipation should concern all Bolsheviks:

> As long as prostitution is not destroyed, as long as the old forms of the family, home life, childrearing are not abolished, it will be impossible to destroy exploitation and enslavement, it will be impossible to build socialism.
>
> If the emancipation of women is unthinkable without communism, then communism is unthinkable without the full emancipation of women.[17]

The remaining conference resolutions repeated these basic premises —that women's liberation could be built through setting women them-selves to work on it and that female emancipation was an integral part of the construction of communism. The resolution on the family, prob-ably drafted by Kollontai, proclaimed that marriage would become a "free comradely union of two equal, self-supporting members of the great working family." The "Resolution on the Report on Tasks of Social Welfare" called for full and equal female participation in all institutions, and public child care to make that possible. It also urged the replacement of petty-bourgeois persons in the government with genuine proletarians.[18] The remaining resolutions proposed specific reforms in housing, educa-tion, and maternity care.

On the last day of the conference Inessa and Kollontai led workshops which discussed ways the delegates could carry out the proposals when they returned home.[19] In the afternoon, Samoilova brought forward the resolution on establishing commissions for work among women. She used Zetkin's and Kollontai's old rationale for a woman's bureau: women had lower political consciousness than men and could be reached only by specially trained agitators. The conference delegates therefore petitioned the Central Committee to establish commissions for agitation among women. They also asked for each party bureau or committee to create committees to involve women in socialist construction, particularly in areas such as child care which were of special concern to them. Samoilova urged the delegates to return home and pressure their local party officials to act on the resolution.[20]

Kollontai had had to compromise again on her concept of a strong woman's bureau, but she must have expected that, since the proposal had been turned down so often before. This time she had gotten farther toward her goal than before, and in addition a large group of working and Communist women had endorsed every other facet of her program for female emancipation, including its immediate realization. She closed the meeting by declaring jubilantly, "Our conference should break up with the happy consciousness that this was a conference accomplishing business useful to everyone. The conclusion to the story is that women can do anything."[21]

Kollontai had now emerged from her retreat after Brest-Litovsk and immersed herself again in the work she loved. Lenin had written to her before the women's conference, on October 18, promising to restore Dybenko to full party membership. He did not address her with the warmth of the war years, but he did conclude with a gesture of reconciliation. "Thank you so much for your greetings, and I in turn welcome your return to more active party work."[22] Kollontai had put the disappointment of the spring behind her, and she threw herself into work with women, fortified by her success.

The Central Committee followed the conference with a decree in December 1918 authorizing the establishment of commissions for work among women in every party committee. Apparently the success of the meeting and the pressure of its organizers, with Sverdlov's support, had convinced the party leadership that the commissions would be useful.[23] The Central Committee instruction stressed that these new organizations should seek "to arouse the consciousness of the more backward female working masses and involve them in the political struggle for the full triumph of communism." It did not mention involvement as a means to

female emancipation, which was a cardinal theme of the conference resolutions,[24] probably because mobilization of women to aid the war effort
was a goal most Bolsheviks could accept, regardless of their attitudes
toward feminist separatism. Their ideology had always said that women
should become involved in the revolution. Disputes had arisen—and now
were being cloaked in carefully worded declarations—over the extent to
which women should postpone their emancipation in service to the revolution. The difference between Kollontai's arguments of 1908 and the
situation in 1918 was, of course, that the revolution had begun. Yet the
issue of priorities remained. In a struggle for survival more deadly than
any the Bolsheviks had confronted before, should women join the general
effort or work to free themselves? Kollontai, Inessa, and Samoilova
thought women could do both simultaneously. Other Bolsheviks continued to look on any projects designed particularly for women as divi-
sive. Thus the resolution establishing the commissions and the earlier
conference resolutions had to be loaded with disclaimers of separatist
intent and weighted to stress the rationale of mobilizing backward women
to aid the defense effort.

Despite its continued suspicion of feminism, the party leadership had
authorized groups to specialize in organizing women. It ordered two to
five party members to be assigned to such work in every province, district,
and city party committee. Under the control of the local party officials,
the commissions would conduct agitation, distribute literature, enroll
women in courses, and draw them into unions, soviets, and factory committees. Reflecting the influence of Kollontai and Inessa, the order asserted
that the commissions should make a special effort to involve women in
projects dealing with child care and communal housekeeping.[25]

A Central Commission led by Inessa, Kollontai, and Samoilova went
to work in Moscow in the winter of 1918–19. They placed columns about
women's activities in the newspapers,[26] published pamphlets and collections of articles, and spoke at local meetings of women organizers.[27] They
also attempted to supervise the establishment of women's commissions in
the provinces. They then pressured the commissions to organize delegate
conferences as the primary means of drawing women into Soviet activity.[28]

In the process Kollontai found that it was easier to get Central Committee authorization, however qualified, than it was to get cooperation
from lower-echelon Communists who had not been reconciled to the
notion of work among women by the stress on such activity as necessary

for defense. Regional Communist Party officials had been ordered to help with the establishment of the commissions, but more often than not they simply ignored the female organizers. This meant that they gave them no financial aid and no staff support. A Moscow worker, A. Unskova, later wrote that her job early in 1919 was "difficult and thankless." For the whole of Moscow the commission consisted of one secretary and two agitators. Because of "the stagnation and misunderstanding of the full importance of work among women," these few organizers had to justify every step they proposed and frequently appealed to the Moscow Com- mittee for pressure against local Communists. The hostility they encoun- tered forced the women's commissions to work in isolation from the party committees instead of closely with them, as the initial decrees had in- tended, and thereby laid them open anew to charges of separatism.[29] Nor was it possible under such conditions for these inexperienced organizers to make any real progress in mobilizing women workers.

Kollontai was disappointed by the commissions' lack of success. Per- suading the party leadership had been difficult enough; now their victory was vitiated by the resistance of provincial Communists who were less educated and more conservative than the leaders. The obstacles to estab- lishing work among women were also increased by the effect of the war on the party's resources and the workers' morale. Moscow was starving. In the streets crows devoured whatever carrion they could find, or flut- tered in through broken windows to scrounge for scraps. Cart horses that dropped dead in harness were butchered where they fell. A glass of tea cost thirty kopeks, sugar was twelve rubles a pound, approximately equivalent to $12 in U.S. currency at that time. Money was becoming worthless and being replaced by barter. Large numbers of cold, under- nourished city dwellers sickened, then died, often to be buried in straw mats because wood was more valuable as fuel to warm the living than as coffins for the dead.[30]

The desperate privations of 1919 stilled the revolutionary enthusiasm of those workers who had remained in the factories rather than leave for party or army jobs or flee to the countryside where food was still available. Kollontai found that workers were sometimes bitter about the revolution's unfulfilled promises, but that more often they were lethargic, numbed by the atmosphere of malnutrition and death. In her diary in January 1919 she wrote, "It's not so much the masses turning against us now as it is simply hungry passivity. But I love to overcome such attitudes, as at Tsindel [a Moscow printing plant]; to force women to understand finally that they can help themselves in our state, by raising the issue of nurseries, children's homes, and such." After this outburst of enthusiasm she confessed, "But such a daily struggle with the attitudes of thousands among the masses is tiring; you feel sometimes that there simply isn't the strength to go out again to a meeting."[31]

Life was a little easier for the government leaders. Kollontai spent a bizarre New Year's eve at army headquarters, where former tsarist officers, now in the Red Army, gathered with their "ladies" in dresses bought abroad before the revolution. They feasted on soup and black bread with cheese and on tea with real sugar. The sugar delighted Kollontai, who had a sweet tooth. Afterwards there was a concert.[32]

Her son Misha had stayed in Petrograd to finish an engineering course there, but he visited his mother in January. Kollontai wrote in her diary, "He is living in a dormitory, apparently he's hungry and cold, and I don't have anything to send him; it's agonizing. I want us to live in the same city, but he loves his institute."[33]

The hunger, the cold, the misery of the people for whom they had made the revolution tormented Kollontai. Tsarist officers, somewhat tattered now, still danced at army headquarters, but the workers only looked on sullenly as she tried to exhort them to further sacrifices. What had the Bolsheviks accomplished in a year? That same January she wrote in her diary that she had just seen Louise Bryant. "She asked me to take her to a meeting, but I'm afraid of what the attitudes would be there. I reminded her of the American war for liberation at the end of the eighteenth century. They also had hunger and disruption of the economy and the entire world did not recognize a new, free America."[34]

Kollontai clung to her faith that the building of socialism had begun and therefore that eventually life would improve. "I walk around Moscow and I think how it will be in the future, in two hundred to three hundred years. They won't believe that real hunger ruled in Moscow."[35]

She did find the strength to go to meetings; she responded to the hardships of the war by pressing constantly for the beleaguered people, and particularly women, to become more involved in organizing social services. In March Kollontai sponsored a resolution on female emancipation at the first session of the Communist International, the association of Communist parties founded as a successor to the Second International.[36] At meetings of the committee drafting a new Bolshevik Party platform for passage by the Eighth Party Congress, she pushed for a statement of intention to abolish the bourgeois family and fight prostitution, in addition to a more general commitment to female equality, but the committee turned her down. Lenin argued that it was too soon to talk about changing the family structure; the family was necessary now for child rearing. Although Kollontai was asking only for a written commitment, Lenin must have believed even that would alienate party members and cause an unnecessary row.[37]

At the Eighth Party Congress, Bolshevik attitudes toward female emancipation—a mixture of agreement on the most general goals, hostility toward special efforts, and belief that the whole question was unimportant—became apparent again. On March 20 and 21 the congress delegates met to complete the editing of a Central Committee report on party and government reorganization. A lengthy debate ensued on two supremely important questions: whether the government was becoming too bureaucratic and how the party should control noncommunists who worked in the bureaucracy. After discussing those issues for hours, the exhausted delegates came to the last item on the agenda, work with women and young people. Someone suggested from the floor that since there was no particular disagreement over the proposals, a handwritten copy should be sent directly to the editing committee.

Kollontai objected immediately. She wanted the congress to discuss the programs for women because she wanted to convince the local party officials present to support them. "It would be a terribly unwise step if we did not tell the comrades who have come here from the provinces for the first time about the great work our party has done in this field," Kollontai said. "It is necessary to give the comrades the plan for future work." How could Communists perform the difficult tasks which the other congress resolutions set for them, if women were not involved? And she must have thought, although she did not ask, how would the Bolsheviks involve women if these regional officials continued to thwart the work of the women's commissions? With a hint of criticism Kollontai concluded, "The party, which is responsible for the entire government, should consider step by step the improvements which we can make. We are not conceited people, we have not become hardened and numb, we are proposing a whole series of reforms—let the congress support them with their authority and it will be a real step forward."[38] After a few more minutes of debate M. A. Muranov, the presiding officer, ruled that the question would be scheduled for the next session. Kollontai finally managed to get time to present the report on organizing women in a debate on March 22.

Her audience was different now from the sympathetic delegates of November; Kollontai had to establish the legitimacy of work among women before a group of men who cared very little about the subject. She began with the argument they were most likely to accept. Kollontai said that women were backward, a "counterrevolutionary stronghold" that hindered the proletarian movement. To reach them, the Central Committee had authorized the creation of committees that would use normal agitational tools—meetings, courses, literature—with some adaptations for their audience. Then Kollontai moved on to more controversial and feministic declarations. Both men and women should participate in work among the female proletariat, she said, so that men and women could learn to work together and so that men could come to understand women's burdens. The party should not simply talk about female participation in the general struggle; it should work to emancipate women. Particularly important was teaching new skills by enrolling women in government institutions as trainees. Such programs would allow women to free themselves. "We say to the women workers and peasants," Kollontai declared, " 'Our life now is dark and difficult, we shall study how to help ourselves, how to deliver ourselves from the centuries-long servitude and bondage of women by the household and the family.' "[39]

Drawing women into all spheres of government work would not only liberate them, it would enable the government to expel "the petty-bourgeois elements," the holdovers from tsarist days who threatened to pervert the Soviet system. Kollontai had objected to the employment of "bourgeois specialists" in the spring of 1918, during the Left Opposition debate; she continued to dislike the practice in 1919. "It often happens," she said, "that we put a specialist at the head of an institution, for instance, the children's colonies, or the nurseries. She knows her business, but her spirit is alien. She lacks healthy class instinct." The woman worker, on the other hand, had the "healthy class instinct" that would enable her to experiment with new forms of social organization.[40] For all these reasons, local party officials should help with work among women, Kollontai argued, and she ended her speech by reading a resolution instructing them to do so. The congress passed it.[41] There was no debate on the issue because the party had greater problems to discuss. The delegates might not actively aid work among women, but they were now willing to pass a resolution submitted to them by the party leadership.

Shortly after the congress Kollontai had to leave the work of the Central Commission on Agitation Among Women to go south to the Ukraine. The party was in need of people to mobilize the population there against the Volunteer Army of General Anton Denikin, against

Ukrainian nationalists, and against rampaging partisans. At stake ultimately was the survival of Communist rule in Moscow and its establishment in the rich farmlands of the south. To secure that, the Bolsheviks had to fight regular military battles while cultivating popular support and forming governing structures. It was to the latter tasks that Kollontai turned her efforts.

She went first to Kharkov, a city that had served intermittently as Communist headquarters in the Ukraine for the preceding year and a half. In April 1919 Bolshevik government had been reestablished in Kiev, but Kharkov continued to be an important center for Bolshevik activities on the left bank of the Dnieper. Kollontai met Samoilova, who had come south earlier, and the two began organizing work with women and supervising more general agitation.[42]

In May Kollontai set out on a tour of the Donbass, an important mining area through which Denikin's army was driving. Periodically her train stopped at villages where Kollontai got out to speak, never certain that she would not be ambushed by detachments of the Whites or of the Greens, partisans of anarchist and nationalist persuasion. The car assigned to her group was attached to whatever train was going their way, and it was coupled and uncoupled constantly. Kollontai carried a large sheet of thick white paper embossed with an official seal that was supposed to awe local officials into cooperation, but it rarely did. Often her car sat on a siding while trains crept by, headed in the direction she wanted to go. Kollontai would argue for hours with the stationmaster, pursuing him up and down the dingy platform, ordering him to allow her party to get underway, while knowing full well that in this backwater he had absolute power. "The stationmaster stubbornly repeated: 'The train is overloaded, I can't couple you.' We threatened to get in touch with Kharkov by phone; it didn't work. The stationmaster knew very well that in those days it was difficult to get in touch with Kharkov by phone."[43]

Somehow Kollontai's little group completed its trip and returned in time to flee Kharkov ahead of Denikin's Volunteer Army. She went on to the Crimea, where she worked among the troops and served on a short-lived local soviet. Typically optimistic about the danger they faced, Kollontai became impatient when the Bolsheviks, led by Lenin's brother Dmitri, spent all their time planning the evacuation of the peninsula. She wanted to do "practical work," such as setting up sanitoria, so she toured the facilities already in use to see where improvements could be made.[44] On June 24, 1919, Denikin's forces took Simferopol in the center of the

Crimea and Kollontai had to cancel her plans. She fled with Dmitri Ul'ianov to Bolshevik-controlled Kiev, where she became cheerful again. On July 7 she wrote in her diary, "How happy I am to be in Kiev, to be doing creative work, to see all around me the strengthening of Soviet power." This time she added, "Of course, Kiev is threatened."[45] Two months later the city fell to the Whites, and Kollontai returned to Moscow, her tour of duty as a civil-war worker completed.

Kollontai moved into the Hotel National near Red Square, intending to occupy herself again with work among women.[46] In her absence, the party leadership had authorized the conversion of the women's commissions into a woman's bureau, the Section for Work Among Women, or *Zhenotdel*. Inessa had been appointed its head. Kollontai must have expected a leading role in Zhenotdel, since she had pushed for such a department since 1906, but Inessa had been active in the work for years also, and she was particularly important in gathering a group of women in Moscow who lobbied for support from the male leadership. Furthermore she had impeccable Bolshevik credentials, unlike Kollontai. Nor did Inessa have Kollontai's reputation for radicalism on the woman question. She had been astute enough to settle first for the commissions and allow the party leadership to become used to that idea. Then, when the commissions proved unable to mobilize large numbers of women, she could argue for a woman's bureau on the German model, with headquarters in Moscow and a hierarchy of provincial and local departments which would be more directly under control of the central section than the commissions had been. Inessa had gotten the Zhenotdel established and she was well suited to the delicate task of building it.

What Kollontai probably did not understand was the insultingly minor job she was given when she reported back. She was made the Zhenotdel representative to the Department for Work in the Country, and since the woman's bureau did not have any programs aimed at peasant women, that post could hardly be considered a major responsibility. Perhaps there were no other jobs available. Perhaps some shadow of the disgrace of the Left Opposition still lay across Kollontai. Perhaps Kollontai herself made a high-handed bid for consideration that annoyed Inessa. Although they agreed on the goals for work among women, Inessa and Kollontai were never friends. They had been rivals before the revolution and they were temperamentally different; Kollontai was expansive and emotional, Inessa aloof and a bit ascetic. From time to time the two quarreled.[47] Whatever the reason, Kollontai did not move into leadership in the new woman's bureau, but spent the fall of 1919 making speeches, encouraging workers in the provinces, and publishing pamphlets urging the population to support the war effort.[48] In late November even this rather trivial activity ended when Kollontai suffered a serious heart attack. She did not return to work until the late spring of 1920.[49]

While Kollontai lay ill, Inessa worked strenuously to establish the pattern of projects that characterized the Zhenotdel—agitation, propaganda, conferences, enrollment of women as trainees in government departments, and involvement of them in party work. She attached particular importance to the conferences of women's delegates (*delegatki*). The women elected to attend these meetings would receive crash courses in "political literacy," then the most reliable and energetic among them would move to a soviet or other agency for training. Instructors from the Zhenotdel would supervise their work. After several months of experience the delegate would either go on to permanent employment in the government or return to her regular job, both as an example to her friends and as a reliable, committed supporter of the new society. The delegates' participation would have the added benefit of enlisting hitherto uninvolved masses of women workers in soviet-sponsored projects.[50]

At the Eighth Party Conference in December 1919 Inessa chided Bukharin for not mentioning the Zhenotdel's work in his speech on education.[51] That kind of indifference annoyed her, and continued to plague her, so in December she obtained the support of party secretary N. N. Krestinskii for a series of decrees designed to legitimize the women's sections on the local level. Krestinskii issued a "circular letter" commanding provincial party committees to improve their work among women. He stressed the importance of regular communication between the Central Section and the provinces and between the provinces and the districts. He ordered the local Zhenotdel sections to organize delegate conferences, publish literature, and keep careful financial records.[52]

Inessa followed up Krestinskii's letter with a flood of her own instructions during the winter of 1919–20. She drew up detailed course outlines for training Zhenotdel workers at party schools, even specifying the number of hours to be spent on each topic. She issued instructions on drawing women into such fields as education, food supply, protection of female and child labor, maternity and child care, public health, and defense.[53] Throughout, the decrees stressed that these programs would involve women in socially useful activity, but they also pointed out that through such work women would be emancipated from the burdens of family life. In emphasizing the liberating dimension of their activity, Inessa, Samoilova, and the other Zhenotdel workers returned to the theme of the November 1918 conference: that the party must organize women not just to augment its own forces but to achieve women's emancipation.[54] Furthermore the Zhenotdel operatives were instructed to consider the defense of female interests as an important part of their job. They were to lobby for measures helping women, report women's complaints, and increase the number of women on decision-making bodies.[55] Inessa was attempting to make the Zhenotdel more than a mobilizer of women: she wanted it to be an advocate for women within the party and the government.

The decrees of the winter of 1919–20 dealt in detail with organizing Zhenotdel sections in the provinces. The Central Section even told the district secretaries that they must be at the desk assigned to them at the party headquarters from 10:00 A.M. until closing time.[56] It was an ambitious project for a party that lacked personnel and money and was fighting a civil war, but Inessa remained optimistic. At the second conference of provincial Zhenotdel organizers held in Moscow in late March 1920, she reported that the delegate conferences, "the great core of all our work," were meeting regularly. Inessa did not admit what V. A. Moirova, another organizer, confessed later: that the Zhenotdel workers often could not hold elections of delegates because so few women were willing to participate. "We picked out these women in the places where they worked. . . ," Moirova wrote, "chose them at conferences and meetings, watched their attitudes at these functions, and positively dragged them out of their seclusion into public activity."[57] An organizer in Tver confessed that to get women to come to the conference, "it was necessary to go through the workers' barracks and almost have a separate conversation with every woman worker."[58]

Inessa did assert in her March report that they had established Zhenotdel sections in many districts and virtually all the provinces under Bolshevik control. Now they must focus their attention on involving women in socialist construction, which meant convincing women to cooperate with the program of compulsory labor which the government had recently ordered. In outlining ways the Zhenotdel could bring women into the brigades of workers now being marshaled to aid the war effort,

Inessa again stressed that Zhenotdel personnel should defend the interests of mobilized women. Zhenotdel should complain if women were forced to work under conditions dangerous to their health, encourage women to take vocational courses to upgrade their skills, and push to have women included in party, union, and factory committees and leading government departments, especially in the economic sector. To accomplish all these tasks while drawing the female proletariat into more active support of the Soviet system, Zhenotdel needed more personnel and better organization throughout the country. At this point, in March 1920, they lacked staff for every facet of their work, especially for the training programs.[59]

There was some cause for hope in the resolution passed by the Ninth Party Congress meeting that same month. Instead of the pallid statement Kollontai had pushed through the year before, Samoilova managed to persuade this congress to declare work among women "one of the urgent tasks of the moment and a necessary part of our general party work."[60] The resolution called on local party committees "to pay the most serious attention to and participate actively in work among women workers and peasants" by organizing women's bureaus where they did not exist and strengthening them where they did. The women of the Central Section could take heart, for this endorsement represented the strongest statement of party support they had ever received.

Inessa and her colleagues in Moscow spent the summer reorganizing the center, expanding their provincial work, planning a journal, *Kommunistka*, as a communications link, and increasing other publishing activity.[61] Despite the brave talk, they were untrained, understaffed, and faced a significant degree of opposition from both the local party and government organizations.[62] Many working women also remained suspicious and hostile. There were still rumors that Communists were godless people who wanted to take children away from their mothers and destroy the Church. Those women who felt no real dislike for the party were often exhausted after working all day and struggling to find food for their families. Thus many women avoided the Zhenotdel initiatives.[63] A start had been made, the bureau had been founded, but its viability remained in doubt, and the trust of women workers was still to be won.

Meanwhile Kollontai recuperated from her heart attack. In March she felt well enough to do some writing.[64] In May she took two trips, one to Petrograd to greet a British delegation, the other with Dybenko to his home village to spend two weeks with his parents.[65] After that Kollontai went to Kiev and Dybenko to the Caucasian Front. There was strain between them, for he resented their constant separations. He had also become restive under her tutelage. They fought, and Kollontai was relieved when he went off on an assignment and left her alone with her reading. Gradually they began to move apart, although neither would make the final break until 1923. In letters to him Kollontai described the source of their estrangement and admitted to her ambivalent independence: "I see, I know that I cannot give you full happiness. On the one hand you and I are good, close, and on the other are awkward and sometimes miserable. I am not the wife you need. After all, I am more man than woman. Everybody says so."[66]

She had begun to feel that the sailor should have a traditional woman, or so she told him when he demanded attention. Perhaps she was tiring of the maternal role she had fashioned for herself, and growing resentful of the demands of a man so many years her junior. For his part he was no longer the impressionable peasant of 1917; he had fought a war, was attending the military academy in Moscow, and was ceasing to need a wife who was also a guardian. Slowly the differences between them were separating them.[67]

Kollontai returned to Moscow in time to speak at the first International Conference of Communist Women, held in conjunction with the second congress of the Communist International (Comintern) in July 1920. According to Krupskaia the conference met "under extraordinarily difficult conditions," because there had been no time to hold elections of delegates among the various national parties. The women who attended the brief meeting were simply those at the Comintern congress, many of whom had had no experience and little interest in work with women.[68] They heard lectures on women in the revolutionary movement and passed a resolution that called on the Comintern to establish a secretariat for work among women. Clara Zetkin, now working in Russia, presented the resolutions of the conference to the full session of the Comintern, and under her leadership the secretariat and a resolution on work among women were approved without debate. Both were largely paper declarations lacking real meaning, although Zetkin did go on to set up the secretariat. The Comintern was from its inception bogged down in conflict over the extent to which foreign Communists must follow Russian leadership, and that struggle claimed so much attention that few members had either the time or the interest to devote to building an international woman's movement. Thus this commitment to women became embalmed in rhetoric.[69]

Kollontai had now returned to active work in the Zhenotdel; she spoke as its representative at meetings and participated in the editorial board of the newly founded journal *Kommunistka*.[70] As Kollontai grew stronger, Inessa became more tired, but she did not alter the hectic pace she had set herself until the late summer of 1920, when she went south to rest. Fleeing from enemy troops in the Caucasus, Inessa contracted cholera. By September she was dead.

The funeral was both sad and discomfiting. The inner circle of Bolsheviks believed that Lenin had loved Inessa, and they watched him during the ceremony to see if he would betray his feelings. Kollontai, wondering whether he would humiliate Krupskaia by collapsing on the walk to the grave site,[71] spoke eloquently in tribute to Inessa, her rival and colleague. The woman's cause had lost a powerful advocate, a highly partisan Bolshevik who had also become the most effective organizer of work among women in the party, but for Kollontai, the interregnum was over. With Inessa gone, the Central Committee chose her to head the Zhenotdel.

The prospects of strengthening the department seemed brighter in the fall of 1920 than ever before. During the summer Zhenotdel workers had made significant advances in publishing, establishing courses for organizers, setting up sections on the local level, and holding meetings to coordinate Zhenotdel programs with those of related government departments.[72] The "Central Women," as the leading Zhenotdel workers in Moscow were called, took particular pride in a decree on abortion that had been worked out in several meetings with representatives of the Commissariat of Health, its Maternity and Child Care Department, and the Commissariat of Justice.[73]

The carefully worded decree asserted that "the question of abortion should be decided not from the point of view of the rights of the individual, but from the point of view of the interests of the whole collective (society, race)." Abortion, if performed indiscriminately, might have undesirable effects for society and for the individual woman's health. The decree declared:

Repressive measures against the performance of abortion worsen the situation. On the contrary, in order to bring abortion out of the underground, where it inflicts immeasurable harm on women and the race, abortion should be legalized and should be practiced freely in Soviet medical facilities, where the maximum safety of this operation would be guaranteed.[74]

To assure that abortion not become too common, the agencies involved should work to improve maternity care and prosecute anyone practicing abortion illegally.[75] The new policy was not an endorsement of abortion as a means of birth control; it was carefully drafted to forestall the charge that the Bolsheviks favored the killing of unborn babies. But the Zhenotdel leaders felt that the procedure must be made safe in a period when so many were suffering already and when the number of illegal abortions was rising.[76] Eventually abortion would become a common means of birth control in the Soviet Union, for women burdened with full-time employment, housework, and family responsibilities would refuse to have more than one or two children.

The growth in Zhenotdel activity and the success in arranging the abortion decree were optimistic signs for Kollontai in the fall of 1920. So too was an interview Lenin gave to Clara Zetkin in September, in which he firmly supported the Woman's Bureau. "Unless millions of women are with us," he said, "we cannot construct on Communist lines. We must find our way to them, we must study and try to find that way." He attacked party members who let their wives become "worn out in petty, monotonous, household work."[77] He had nothing but scorn for husbands who did not help at home and for housework itself; in fact, he managed to see housework as a threat to the revolution.

> The home life of the woman is a daily sacrifice to a thousand unimportant trivialities. The old master right of the man still lives in secret. His slave takes her revenge, also secretly. The backwardness of women, their lack of understanding for the revolutionary ideals of the man decrease his joy and determination in fighting. They are like little worms which, unseen, slowly but surely rot and corrode.[78]

In earlier speeches Lenin had also supported the Woman's Bureau and the notion that women must be fully freed from domestic responsibilities. He saw husbands sharing household chores as an interim solution; the real resolution of the problem could come only with the establishment of communal facilities, as yet lacking because of the disruptions of war.[79]

To have Lenin's support was a vital aid to the Zhenotdel. Although he had never helped them the way Sverdlov did, he was willing to speak to women's groups and lend his enormous prestige to their efforts. In his attacks on the triple burdens of women—housework, child care, and factory labor—he set a progressive example for many Communists who were prepared only to mouth slogans about female emancipation while letting their wives wait on them. Lenin did not place any great emphasis on the Zhenotdel programs to upgrade women's job skills, however, and there is no evidence that he favored a concerted effort to have women put into positions of authority. Probably he felt, as did most of his comrades, that if women were freed of their shackles, offered training, and encouraged, they would move into a condition of equality without any special push up the ladder.

Lenin's attitudes toward the woman question reflected the thinking of the party leadership. On this issue he was a moderate among Bolsheviks, so his endorsement in 1920 registered a contemporary acceptance of the Zhenotdel by the top men in the party, the educated, intellectual elite. They were not going to exert any special effort to help the Woman's Bureau, but they were willing to let it do its work with their blessing. Such acquiescence may smack of condescension, it may have been motivated as much by a desire to mobilize women as by a desire to liberate them, but it was a significant improvement over the hostility of earlier years.[80]

Of course, rank-and-file Communists did not necessarily share the attitudes of the leadership. Samoilova wrote in the fall of 1920 that many Bolsheviks referred to the Zhenotdel as the *babotdel*, from *baba*, a term commonly used to describe peasant women but carrying a note of derision that cannot be translated. This prejudice led to talk on the local level of abolishing the sections.[81] Female party members who worked in other jobs often shared the negative attitudes of their male comrades; Samoilova wrote of such women, "They do not work with women because they consider this work beneath their dignity and declare that the organization of women workers is 'feminism.' They talk this way only because they are absolutely unacquainted with work among the female proletariat and do not understand its goals and meaning."[82] A similar attitude prevailed in the trade unions, which considered organizing among the female membership to be their province, and therefore refused to work on joint programs with the Zhenotdel.[83]

Compounding this problem of resistance was the continuing organizational weakness of the Zhenotdel itself. The department did not have enough local sections or enough staff where sections existed. Many party committees refused them support, and therefore the ties between the

Zhenotdel and other departments were weak. The Zhenotdel workers in some areas were not even party members, so they could not have attended party meetings had they been welcome. Within the bureau, central, provincial, and local workers were out of touch with one another far too often. The Central Section did not know how many people were actually working on the local level, and it could not control their transfer to other jobs. That impotence was heightened by the fact that the Zhenotdel did not pay the salaries of their organizers. Those funds came from the party committees, which felt a right to assign people as they saw fit.[84]

The situation on the local level was also difficult because of confusion among the Zhenotdel workers themselves. Many of them were inexperienced young women who did not really understand the directives they received intermittently from Moscow.[85] In Simbirsk, for example, the workers in the provincial section concentrated on nonparty women because they thought the party committee was responsible for Bolshevik women.[86] To deal with these problems, Kollontai would have to improve the structure of the bureau itself, increase the number and training of its workers, and break down the hostility of other departments—all that in a period of continuing crisis in country and party as well.

Kollontai laid out her program in an article in *Kommunistka*, the Zhenotdel journal, in November 1920. The primary tasks facing the bureau were educating more personnel and "strengthening the communist consciousness" of those already involved in work among women. These people would then teach the female masses, drawing them into party membership and involving them in socialist construction. They would also pay particular attention to issues concerning women, for it was their responsibility to defend women's interests. With a directness Inessa had avoided, Kollontai declared that the Zhenotdel should serve as an advocate for women with party and government.

> In their work the sections should start from the premise that the organization and mobilization of female and male workers are one and indivisible. But the sections should keep their independence in bringing creative tasks to the party; they should set themselves the goal of genuine and full emancipation of women, while defending their interests as representatives of the sex that is largely responsible for the health and vitality of future generations.[87]

Many comrades, Kollontai wrote, thought of the Zhenotdel as a mere rallier of women to the cause, as a department that rewrote decrees in simple language for women. It was far more than that. True, it did call women to socialist construction, but it also should initiate programs on its own to increase production, such as helping women improve their job skills or organizing more communal facilities for them.[88] She saw the Zhenotdel not as a woman's auxiliary, but as a voice for women, an aid to their special needs, and a department generating new ideas. In so doing, she was operating from a conception of the party as pluralistic, composed of various interest groups vying for attention and free to speak their minds. Inessa had shared that vision, as did Samoilova to a lesser degree, but neither of them had ever proclaimed it quite as loudly as Kollontai. To implement her declaration of intent, she concentrated in the late fall on three projects—general improvement of the Zhenotdel's operation, the fight against prostitution, and a resolution for the Eighth Soviet Congress.

Carrying out the first objective, Kollontai presided over conferences of local Zhenotdel workers where resolutions were passed in favor of better communications between Moscow and the provinces, improved training in the party schools, and more full-time workers.[89] She supervised the daily operation of the Zhenotdel, spending time at the Orgburo to get approval for projects.[90] When a particular breakthrough in organizing on the local level occurred, she or Samoilova or another of the Central Women would leave Moscow to lend personal support to a provincial section.

Thus Kollontai traveled to Tula in the late fall of 1920 for a conference of peasant women. The Zhenotdel had always committed itself to reaching the rural poor, but in the countryside the barriers of misunderstanding were even greater than among city women, so the organizers had concentrated on the cities. In Tula, lying about one hundred miles due south of Moscow, a Bolshevik named N. S. Kokoreva had tried in the summer of 1918 to persuade peasant women to accept the new idea of public nurseries. She had received the reply: "Soviet power is our power. The land has been given to the peasant, his greatest joy. A deep bow [of thanks]. Thanks for caring for us mothers and children. Equal rights for us are also fine. But we won't give our child to a kindergarten or nursery."[91] Peasant women, if they did not perceive the Bolsheviks as a threat (which most clearly did), simply wanted to be left alone to get on with their lives. They had no time to go to meetings, nor did they see any particular reason to do so. They certainly had no intention of turning their children over to strangers. Of course, many factory women shared these same attitudes, due in no small measure to the fact that they were often only one generation away from the villages themselves, but city dwellers in general possessed higher levels of political awareness. The isolation of rural life and its community spirit sheltered the peasant, male and female alike, from the ideological ferment of the cities.

Therefore when Zhenotdel workers in Tula at last managed, with the help of a special organizer sent from Moscow, to set up a delegate conference of peasant women in 1920, Kollontai attended it as a gesture of congratulation and encouragement. She was elated to see the young women from the countryside gathered in the provincial capital, and she was pleased by the enthusiasm of the local Zhenotdel workers.[92] At the opening session, the first order of business was the election of a "presidium," or group of delegates to preside over the meeting. The Zhenotdel workers had drawn up a list of candidates which they presented to the conference. The nominees walked to the dais, and the audience began to grumble. Kollontai realized that they had made a crucial mistake in nominating one young women who, though she had grown up in the area, had also studied in Moscow, where she had adopted city ways. "She came to the platform with bobbed hair, in a short dress, with a cigarette in her lips. Not only did they turn her down for the presidium, but what was worse, they raised a din in the hall against all the rest of the list."[93]

Kollontai conferred with the local Zhenotdel women and persuaded them to drop the offender from the nominees. She argued that the conference delegates would never accept someone whose appearance seemed bawdy to them. Kollontai's young comrades finally agreed, but only under protest, for they resented having to bow to what they saw as the peasants' obnoxious conservatism. The rest of the conference then proceeded smoothly, but after Kollontai returned to Moscow she called a special meeting between provincial leaders and the Central Women. There instructions were drawn up on organizing peasants which urged local sections to study local customs, so that they would not alienate the masses with personal behavior that defied tradition.[94]

In addition to overseeing local Zhenotdel leaders and expanding the projects already underway, Kollontai sought to attack the problem of prostitution. Since the late nineteenth century the practice had concerned socialists, who saw it as symptomatic of women's degradation under capitalism. Kollontai had written a series of articles about it in 1910, when a conference on prostitution was held in Russia. Naturally she accepted the Social Democratic position that fundamental reform was impossible under capitalism, where low wages made the selling of one's body a necessity. Now, with capitalism officially vanquished in Russia, she found prostitution had not disappeared. The Provisional Government had out-lawed the legal prostitution of tsarist times, with its infamous "yellow tickets," which women obtained upon registering with the local police. Most of the red light districts in major cities had disappeared and open soliciting was less apparent, but prostitution continued, often among women who had not practiced it before. Female employees of government or party departments slept with their bosses for favors, such as ration coupons and higher wages. Working women offered themselves to the managers of state stores in return for a little extra food for their children.[95]

All of this seriously alarmed Kollontai, who considered the selling of one's body as the ultimate degradation. In 1919 she helped found a Commission to Fight Prostitution, under the Department for Social Wel-fare of the Commissariat of Labor.[96] In November 1920 she presented a program of reforms to that commission. She wrote that prostitution was an evil not only because it spread venereal disease, but also because it reduced a woman to "a simple instrument of pleasure." Prostitution con-tinued to exist in this time of transition, marked by economic hardship, and so long as it was present, true equality of the sexes was impossible.

To remedy the situation, the Zhenotdel proposed a set of reforms to the commission. The commission itself already recognized the need for improved living conditions for women, better maternity care, and training facilities to upgrade their job skills. It was very important also to find work for all women, Kollontai wrote, for "as long as we have an unem-ployed female population, existing by means of a husband or father, the buying and selling of female affection will exist."[97] Engels and Bebel had made this point years before: bourgeois marriage and prostitution both sprang from the economic dependence of woman on man and were the two major expressions of that dependence. Kollontai was arguing that until all women worked outside the home, they would continue to sell themselves into marriage or prostitution.

The Zhenotdel therefore proposed to fight prostitution by accelerating the emancipation of women. Kollontai also wanted the young to be taught to abhor prostitution. She did not want legal penalties, nor did she favor the local raids on brothels which had been organized from time to time. Such attacks interfered with women's privacy, she wrote, and made the women the scapegoats for society's failure to provide them with alternative means of feeding themselves. Prostitutes should have the same options as anyone else not engaged in socially productive labor; they should be educated to a useful job and then given employment. Women too ill to work should be admitted to state nursing homes for treatment.[98]

It was a humane proposal, enlightened by the progressive Marxist attitude toward prostitution and by Kollontai's faith in the liberating potential of work, but it yielded no immediate results. The commission drafted a resolution, then became embroiled in a jurisdictional dispute with another committee under the Commissariat of Health.[99] Nor was prostitution a problem of high priority in a country emerging from civil war and on the verge of famine. It was an issue which Kollontai had thought the revolution would solve, and which she now found lingering on, sustained by Russia's poverty and the chaos of the revolution itself. Prostitution continued to plague the Bolsheviks long after they could justly call it a product of capitalism, and Kollontai had struck at one of its essential causes—the material dependence of woman on man—which the revolution had not been able to alter fundamentally.

The third project consuming her attention in the fall of 1920 was a resolution "On Attracting Women to Economic Construction" for the Eighth All-Russian Congress of Soviets, scheduled for December. Superficially, the draft she prepared seemed no more controversial or important than the resolution on prostitution. It decreed that women must be enlisted in the reconstruction of the economy. To implement this objective, the congress was called upon to promote the involvement of women in all "economic institutions" and to aid them in organizing communal facilities that would free them for productive work.[100]

Kollontai presented the resolution to the meeting on December 28. She began with the mobilization argument: women could help rebuild the economy if services were organized to relieve them of the burdens of housekeeping and child care. Bluntly, Kollontai declared that not enough had been done. All the services for women had to be expanded, by encouraging women to become involved in such projects. "Great centralization is not needed now," she said, returning to her argument that women should emancipate themselves, "but it is necessary that the soviets support the initiative of women workers and peasants."[101]

Such facilities as nurseries and *stolovye* (public dining rooms) freed women for useful labor, but that labor itself had to interest them. Women would be fully committed to socialist construction only when they achieved full equality within it, so Kollontai proposed concerted efforts to include women on every decision-making body throughout the political and economic hierarchy.[102] The intent of the resolution was to put a Soviet congress on record as favoring positive steps to advance women into positions of authority. Kollontai wanted more than the benign approval of Lenin now; she wanted more than day care centers; she wanted the government to grant women access to political and economic power. She pointed out in closing that of the two hundred delegates sitting before her, only twenty were women.

> Remember, comrades, that without this [the involvement of women] we will not build our national economy. In spite of the fact that I see many skeptical faces, I must say flatly that the old petty-bourgeois attitudes are still strongly rooted in us; we brought our little resolution to the presidium only with difficulty. I strongly insist, therefore, that the whole conscious, revolutionary section of the congress, all conscious comrades, support our demands and translate them into reality.[103]

The crowd applauded and T. V. Sapronov, a prominent Bolshevik advocate of party democracy, recommended approving the resolution. Then one of the delegates called out from the floor: "I'm not at all against the involvement of women in labor for building the state, but not all of them." The congress delegates began to laugh. "There are some conditions that, if for example, they take my wife away from me . . . !" Other members of the audience yelled for recognition from the chair. They were gaveled into silence, and the man resumed: "I am saying that if, for example, they take my wife away from me, then I won't work myself."[104]

Kollontai rose to respond. No one was going to take his wife away from him, she said; women were already working outside the home. Now they had three jobs—wife, mother, and factory hand—and they needed facilities to relieve their burdens, so they could contribute more to society. "Only with the help of women will we really bring about the beginning of communist society," she declared, again to the sound of applause. The congress voted approval of the resolution. It was a paper victory in which Kollontai took great pride.[105]

By late December she had also begun work on a conference of women from the Muslim minorities, called the "Eastern women," although in fact many Muslims lived in the Ukraine and other areas that were not really eastern. Their enslavement, legitimized by the Koran, was even more brutal than that suffered by Russians. Polygamy, the veil, forced marriages, total exclusion from public life, made them slaves to men.[106]

The Central Section had managed to attract a few of these women to the December provincial workers' conference, and that conference voted to organize a meeting especially for them in February.[107] Kollontai was also working in the Woman's Secretariat of the Comintern with Clara Zetkin, giving talks to other departments, writing articles, and lobbying constantly. "Sometimes I was so tired," she wrote later of this period, "that I would come home, sit down on the sofa, and fall asleep right there for ten or fifteen minutes, and then back to work."[108]

The endless activity had yielded results. Kollontai could look back over the last two years and take pride in the fact that the woman's bureau she had sought for so long had been established. It was weak still, but it was growing. She could now stand up at a Soviet congress and demand special treatment for women, demand that they be promoted into positions of authority, without being shouted down as a feminist. In large part because of the compelling needs of the civil war, the party leadership had softened its opposition to organizing women. The sophisticated variant of Marxism which the leaders professed had always advocated true emancipation for women. The question among Bolsheviks had been one of priorities: when and how women would break free of hearth and home. Now crisis stilled the fears of separatism and roused the emancipating vision. Women should be freed so that they could join in the defense effort. Women were still pawns, their emancipation a means to a greater end, but the lessening of party resistance because of the war emergency offered Kollontai, and Inessa before her, an opportunity which they exploited skillfully. The Zhenotdel was established, and its leaders made socialist-feminist declarations that would have been unthinkable in 1917. When Kollontai temporarily suspended her work at the Zhenotdel in January 1921 to become involved in the Workers' Opposition, she could look with satisfaction on the advances the Central Women had made.

8

The Workers' Opposition

IN SEPTEMBER 1920 Kollontai had made her first public criticism
of the party leadership since her fight over the Brest-Litovsk Treaty.
She was responding to the death of John Reed, the American socialist
who had written a classic, though naive, history of the October Revolution, *Ten Days That Shook the World*, and had become a leader of the
nascent Communist Party of the United States. By 1920 Reed was beginning to criticize the bureaucratization of the Soviet government. His
erstwhile comrades among the Russians paid little attention to the complaints of a man whom they probably dismissed as an amateur revolutionary and professional romantic. In the late summer of 1920 Zinoviev
and Radek did take him to Baku to a conference of Asian Communists,
but this gesture only exposed Reed's weakened health to the difficulties
of travel. He returned to Moscow ill with typhus and in September he
died.

Although Louise Bryant wanted her husband's body returned to the
United States for burial, the Bolshevik leaders prevailed upon her to
allow a Moscow funeral. Bukharin, Radek, and Kollontai attended as
representatives of the party; foreign Communists who had been Reed's

friends were there, as were Emma Goldman and Alexander Berkman, the exiled American anarchists. When it was Kollontai's turn to eulogize Reed, she surprised Goldman by converting her address into a veiled attack on what she regarded as dangerous tendencies within the party: "We call ourselves Communists," she said, "but are we really that? Do we not rather draw the life essence from those who come to us, and when they are no longer of use, we let them fall by the wayside, neglected and forgotten? Our Communism and our comradeship are dead letters if we do not give out of ourselves to those who need us. Let us beware of such Communism. It slays the best in our ranks. Jack Reed was among the best."[1]

Kollontai did not usually criticize her own party in front of foreigners; indeed, she had irritated Goldman earlier by refusing to admit that the Soviet system had any important shortcomings.[2] To Reed, however, she felt an apology was owed, for ignoring him when he had asked embarrassing questions about the Russian party's high-handed treatment of foreign Communists and its growing bureaucracy. Reed had begun to wonder aloud whether the revolutionary government was degenerating into rule by a small elite; Kollontai was beginning to wonder, too.

Shortly after the funeral, the Ninth Conference of the party met in Moscow to discuss this very issue. The civil war was now all but won, though at enormous cost to the country. The economy lay devastated, the transportation and communications systems were disrupted, thousands were dead or dying from battle and the famine and disease that followed it. The industrial workers had been drawn away from the factories to government and party jobs, had fled back to the villages where food was still to be found, or were living on in misery in the cities. The country faced a long winter without adequate food, shelter, or heat.

Somehow the Bolsheviks were going to have to effect a transition from war to peace and begin the enormous tasks of reconstruction, while retaining the support of the population. This overwhelming challenge worried the party, as did the growing chorus of popular demands for improvements. Some of the Bolsheviks' most ardent supporters among the proletariat had begun to declare openly that the time had come for a real workers' democracy, with decent food, decent housing, and full representation in decision making. Mensheviks, anarchists, and various other political groups long since driven from positions of influence lent their voices to the chorus, thereby raising Bolshevik fears that the allegiance of the working class could be won away from them.

All of the calls for reform found advocates within the party itself. The regime was becoming highly centralized and bureaucratic, so much so that local officials now acted primarily as executors of decisions made in Moscow. Almost all the members of other parties had been ousted from the government. Bolsheviks who held government or trade union jobs were reminded repeatedly that they were Communists first, and that their loyalty lay with the party. Gradually, behind the myriad of governmental structures, power came to rest in the party, and within it, the leadership.

How had revolutionaries who hated autocratic bureaucracy come to build a comparable structure of their own? The answer lies in the principles and structure of their party, in the crisis they faced, and in their Russian heritage. The Bolsheviks had always professed a commitment to strong leadership and unity, as well as to the free exchange of opinion among party members, but in the days before 1917 they engaged in open discussion far more often than they practiced democratic centralism. Bolshevik and Menshevik leaders argued among themselves constantly over doctrine and strategy, and the lines between the factions were fluid enough to allow people who disagreed to switch sides, as Kollontai did in 1915, or to remain aloof from both groups, as Trotsky did throughout most of the prerevolutionary period. Among the party rank and file at work in the underground in Russia, factional loyalties were often less important than eluding the police, and that required Bolsheviks and Mensheviks to work together. Nor were local Social Democrats well informed about the ideological disputes of their leaders or overly concerned with Marxist exegesis. Their goals were the practical ones of avoiding arrest, holding their party organization together, and teaching the workers something about socialism. Rigid centralization and strict demarcation of factions not only contradicted the communal traditions of the revolutionary underground, they were almost impossible, given conditions in Russia. Thus before 1917 the Bolsheviks honored their democratic beliefs more consistently than their doctrines favoring unity. Only after they had a firm hold on the reins of power and had resolved as a group to retain it in the face of a challenge from their enemies did party leaders and the rank and file put the principles of democratic centralism into practice.

The Bolsheviks were motivated by a will to survive, but that alone does not explain the tenacity with which they clung to power. They believed that they were midwifing the birth of the proletarian revolution, because they had amended Marxism to make that revolution a realistic possibility. Despite Marx's determinism and their own professions of orthodoxy, the Bolsheviks accepted Lenin's and Trotsky's pronouncements that historical development could be advanced by a unified party. Unlike the Mensheviks in 1917, the Bolsheviks were not willing to wait; they wanted to shove Russia ahead to socialism by revising classical Marxism and forcing the revolution. This belief in their own ability to accelerate "normal" development through determined intervention was a key to their success, but it required honoring in practice the principles of unity and centralization. The same voluntarism led naturally to the conviction that the party must suppress alien social forces, fight the capitalists, and survive for the sake of world socialism. The Bolsheviks' promethean resolve intensified the emphasis on unified command which, although always part of their political culture, had been weakened before the revolution by the different imperatives of émigré and underground life.

With these ideological predilections, the Bolsheviks, inexperienced in the art of government, began to improvise strategies for the winning of Russia's civil war. They built on the bureaucratic tangle they had inherited from the tsar and the Provisional Government because they had had no time to restructure it. Nor did they have any plan for administering the dictatorship of the proletariat. Marx offered little help beyond suggesting the confiscation of private property by a temporary government of workers. Lenin, on the eve of the October Revolution, had written in his famous pamphlet *The State and Revolution* that any cook could be an administrator during the dictatorship of the proletariat. But cooks could not organize a new army or supply troops or keep industry going, so the Bolsheviks were obliged to bring back trained people, whom they denigrated as bourgeois but whose skills they desperately needed. As a stop-gap measure, they put party members at the top of inherited governmental structures, but kept the structures and many of the same personnel. These noncommunists influenced the formulation of policy, and their presence in the government provided still another impetus toward the consolidation of authority in the party Politburo. Thus the tendency toward centralization born of ideology and emergency was intensified by the dead weight of Russia's past.

The Bolsheviks continued to claim they were constructing a "proletarian democracy," but this declaration paled to hypocrisy in the light of their actions. When other political groups such as the Mensheviks and the SRs pointed out the Bolsheviks' failures, the party drove them out of the soviets, then imprisoned them, rather than listen. The leaders resolutely refused to allow anyone from the outside to question them. The greater their insecurity—and they were fighting for survival—the more they used force to crush opposition. Here again the Bolsheviks' ideology predisposed them to divide the world into enemies and friends, thus enabling them to explain criticism as the fabrication of hostile minds.

By the fall of 1920, some Bolsheviks had begun to worry about the increasing unwillingness of their comrades to listen to suggestions for reform, even from within their own ranks. Two groups had been demanding change for more than a year. The Democratic Centralists, led by former Left Oppositionists N. Osinskii, T. V. Sapronov, and V. M. Smirnov, called for reform in the party and government bureaucracy. Their demands struck a responsive chord, and the Bolshevik leadership established a commission to propose organizational changes; Sapronov was appointed a member. E. N. Ignatov was chosen to represent still another group of critics, the Workers' Opposition.[3]

Although also concerned over the erosion of party democracy, the Workers' Oppositionists differed from the Democratic Centralists in that their principal grievances arose out of a debate over trade union autonomy. The exact role of the trade unions in the Soviet system had never been clear. In the prerevolutionary period Mensheviks and Bolsheviks endorsed the unions as a means of propagandizing the working class, although they tended to feud over the extent of independence permissible for the unions.[4] After the February Revolution the Bolsheviks talked about granting power to the factory committees which the workers had organized. They promised worker control of industry, to be exercised through those organizations, without really agreeing among themselves on the meaning of the phrase "worker control."

When the Bolsheviks took power, the question of the trade unions' role in fomenting revolution became irrelevant, and the issue shifted to their part in building a new society. The Bolsheviks quickly merged the fragmented, chaotic factory committees into the more structured, more controllable unions, but they never formally disavowed the commitment to worker control nor did they systematically define the limits of trade union power. Instead the Bolshevik-dominated All-Russian Central Council of Trade Unions worked to mobilize, organize, and discipline labor, in the process creating friction between itself and the leaders of the individual unions. The council also vied for influence with the governmental departments that supervised the economy, the Commissariat of Labor and the Supreme Council of the National Economy.[5]

In the new party program approved by the Eighth Party Congress in 1919, the Bolsheviks attempted to define the relationship of the various institutions more clearly, but produced instead a document that clarified nothing and pleased no one. The final draft stated that "the trade unions should come to concentrate under their control the administration of the entire national economy,"[6] which sounded like a ringing endorsement of worker control. But the next sentence took away what the first had given: "Guaranteeing in that way an indissoluble tie between the central government administration, the national economy, and the broad masses of the toilers, the trade unions should involve the latter on a broad scale in the direct work of running the economy."[7] Here the unions were a link that brought people into contact with governmental departments. But what role were they to have in the formulation of these departments' policies? The program did not say, and other clauses in the document reaffirmed the need for "bourgeois specialists" in industry. Thus the problems had not been resolved. Rather than sort out the welter of ideological confusion and vested interests, the party increased its control over Bolshevik unionists, centralized union leadership, and purged non-Bolsheviks.[8]

Supporters of the Workers' Opposition came together to protest against the unions' diminishing autonomy and against the granting of a substantial decision-making role in industry to nonproletarians. In 1919 Shliapnikov, who had held a number of positions in the war effort since 1917 but who continued his leadership of the Metalworkers' Union, circulated a set of theses which called for trade unions to assume control over industry.[9] In September 1920 the Workers' Oppositionists joined the Democratic Centralists at the Ninth Party Conference to call for reform of the party bureaucracy. The Workers' Opposition wanted a greater number of workers in decision-making positions in the party and the government, an attack on bureaucratic abuses, and full freedom to criticize those abuses.

Kollontai supported the demand that Bolsheviks be allowed to speak their minds on party policies. "Comrades," she told the conference, "there should be a guarantee that if in fact we are going to criticize, and criticize thoroughly, what is wrong with us, then the one who criticizes should not be sent off to a nice sunny place to eat peaches. Now, comrades, this isn't a rare phenomenon."[10] She observed that currently "the Central Committee decrees [its will] and then it is put into practice through the provincial committees." Local officials, fearing to express their opinions, would simply change orders to suit local conditions without informing the center. Kollontai concluded, "Long live criticism, but without the necessity of eating peaches after it."[11]

Kollontai was not a Workers' Oppositionist in September 1920, nor, obviously, was she a trade unionist. She did share the unionists' concern about bureaucracy, which she had always abhorred, and she opposed the employment of bourgeois specialists, against whom she had protested in 1918 and 1919. She also disliked the stifling of inner-party criticism. Things were going wrong when men like John Reed could be snubbed for raising valid questions. Even more fundamentally, Kollontai shared the belief of the Workers' Opposition in proletarian democracy; she had, after all, always conceived of the revolution as democratic, spontaneous, and anti-authoritarian. Although she sympathized with both the Workers' Opposition and the Democratic Centralists, Kollontai avoided joining either of the groups, possibly because she feared being banished to "a nice, sunny place to eat peaches," but also because she wanted to concentrate on her work in the Zhenotdel. Throughout the fall Kollontai worked at the bureau, while the calls for reform in party and government were growing into a tumult of dissent.

The Ninth Conference passed a resolution vowing to fight the problem of bureaucracy by establishing new agencies, the control commissions, and promoting free discussion, but no fundamental improvements were immediately forthcoming. The control commissions themselves rapidly developed into nests of bureaucratic meddlers and spies. In November 1920 Trotsky shifted the focus of discussion from party reform to the role of the trade unions by proposing that all unions be restructured along military lines, so that they could become reliable executors of economic policy. He wanted to merge them fully into the government and replace their elected officials with appointed administrators. Trotsky had first tried out "militarization of the trade unions" in the *Tsektran*, or Central Transport Commission. There he had found that the military techniques of command which he had employed as head of the Red Army did bring some temporary improvement in Russia's communications network. It was logical, therefore, that he should advocate their application to the whole economy, but he made the tactical mistake of unveiling his plan at a national trade union conference. Predictably, the delegates responded angrily to this attack on union autonomy. The argument over the role of the trade unions in the Soviet system, provoked by Trotsky's proposal, continued through November and into December, despite Lenin's efforts to conciliate union leaders. On December 24, the Central Committee gave permission for a full debate among Bolsheviks on the issues involved. On January 3, 1921, the Petrograd party committee, led by Zinoviev, called for candidates to the Tenth Party Congress in March to be elected according to their stand on the trade union question. The party leaders accepted that proposal; factions were organized, drew up statements of belief, and began to choose delegates. For the first and last time, groups within the Russian Communist Party campaigned for election on platforms that acknowledged abuses and promised reforms.

In a speech before the Bolshevik delegates to the Eighth Congress of Soviets on December 30 Lenin laid out his position, a centrist one, which had the greatest appeal in the party. He said that the trade unions were important, for they represented the ruling class—by which he meant the proletariat—but that they were not governing institutions like the state. Instead they fulfilled an educational function; they were "schools of communism" for the masses and a "link" between the vanguard (the party) and the more backward workers. Within them the workers learned discipline and through them they could make reform proposals to correct bureaucratic abuses of the Soviet system. The unions should not be merged into the government, as Trotsky proposed, but neither were they capable of running industry. Lenin's position was summed up in the "Platform of the Ten," issued on January 14 and signed by him and nine other Central Committee members.[12]

Trotsky now decided to compromise with his earlier militancy. He still called for a gradual merger of the trade unions into the government, but he added that he favored "workers' democracy," a phrase from Bukharin which meant that the unions should be democratically organized. Trotsky's platform was also signed by a number of Central Committee members, most notably Bukharin. He had some support in Moscow and scattered throughout the Ukraine and the larger cities. So too did the Democratic Centralists, who published a platform criticizing party bureaucracy, but this faction campaigned very little.[13] Increasingly as January wore into February, Lenin turned his attention to the Workers' Opposition, which was emerging as the major challenge to his position.

Shliapnikov, the leader of the Workers' Opposition, had made the group's first public statement of the current debate in an article on December 13 and in a speech at the Soviet Congress on December 30. He recast this package of reform proposals into a platform, "The Tasks of the Trade Unions," which the other members of the faction signed on January 18. Here all the Workers' Opposition complaints of the past year were brought together. The faction accused the party of catering to the bourgeoisie at the proletariat's expense. They charged the party with not having faith in the proletariat and therefore deliberately stifling mass participation in the revolution. They said that the party could only correct these injustices by democratizing the unions and then allowing the unions a much greater role in running industry. To achieve the latter goal, the Workers' Opposition proposed the creation of an "All-Russian Congress of Producers," a national assembly elected by the trade unions. The assembly would set economic policy and choose administrators to handle the daily operation of industry. A similar group of congresses and executives on the local level would perform the same functions there. The government should also accelerate the communalization of proletarian life—of food supply, transportation, and housing. Shliapnikov even proposed organizing communal gardens at the factories. Not only would these measures immediately improve the workers' standard of living, but through them workers would learn to cooperate with one another in the re-education process that would eventually enable humankind to live together in harmony.[14]

The platform of the Workers' Opposition was signed by thirty-eight unionists, chiefly from among the munitions makers, the miners, and the metalworkers, whom Shliapnikov represented. All the signers were officers in their organizations, but none belonged to the main leadership group of the All-Russian Trade Union Council, and many were provincials. Thus while the Workers' Opposition did not spring from the rank and file directly, neither did its existence reflect a fight among the elite of the Central Committee. Furthermore it did have a following in the Ukraine, the Don Basin, Samara, and the industrial cities of central Russia.[15] Shliapnikov proposed specific reforms in the name of the ideal of worker control and he demanded democratization as a solution to the problem of bureaucracy. He suggested centralized planning within a federated structure that would promote initiative and provide incentives. He called for immediate improvements in the life of the proletariat.

Lenin knew this combination of Marxist idealism and practical reforms could win the Workers' Opposition substantial support in the party, and in late January he began to rebut their argument in detail. Primarily, Lenin charged that Shliapnikov's position was "syndicalism," "a complete break with communism" which ignored the role of the party in revolution. That was the crucial issue—the role of the party. In talking exclusively about the unions' role in building socialism, the Workers'

Opposition was guilty of seeing the unions, rather than the party, as the major vehicle of revolutionary change.[16]

There was some justice in Lenin's accusation. The Workers' Opposition's plans for the role of labor organizations in the period of socialist construction had a strongly syndicalist cast. The unions were to lay the economic foundations of socialism, and since orthodox Marxism asserted that economic foundations determined the entire structure of society, giving unions such power meant giving them the most important role in constructing a new society. In rebutting Lenin's charge, however, Shliapnikov could point to the series of Bolshevik proclamations espousing worker control of industry, particularly to the party program with its phrase "the trade unions should concentrate under their control the administration of the entire national economy as a single economic unit."[17] If the Workers' Opposition was syndicalist, Shliapnikov asserted, it was a syndicalism the party itself had endorsed. In fact, rather than work out the relationship between the unions, the government, and itself, the party had issued a series of contradictory declarations, from which both Lenin and Shliapnikov could draw support.

What Lenin did not admit, if he was aware of it himself, was that his vanguard theory of the party was changing. He, and not Shliapnikov, was the revisionist. His party had been developed to lead the overthrow of the enemy class, to spur the proletariat into action. He had never written clearly about its role after that victory, although he had acted consistently to increase its power. Even in 1921 he continued to refer vaguely to the party's mission of preparing the workers to run the economy and to the trade unions as "the source from which all our power flows," "a reservoir of state power."[18] He would not openly disavow the promises of worker control made in 1917, but he was transforming the vanguard theory from a means to revolutionary upheaval into a justification of one-party rule over the entire life of the postrevolutionary society. As usual, Lenin changed doctrine to meet his perceptions of current needs, while continuing to honor the old commitments verbally and cloaking himself in the mantle of orthodoxy.

The majority of Communists accepted this alteration of purpose without fully understanding that it had happened. The spokesmen of the Workers' Opposition barely mentioned the party in their initial statements, and the greatest shortcoming of their position throughout was that they did not systematically define the relationship between party, government, and unions, but instead chose to ask for an increase in the power of the unions. The Workers' Opposition realized that their plan would diminish the role of government institutions in economic management. Indeed they desired to do that, but they did not seem aware that the government was at the time losing power to the party.[19]

In election after election, the candidates of the Workers' Opposition lost to the Leninists, primarily because Lenin had seized the middle ground.[20] He promised reforms of the worst abuses without any major changes that might further unsettle an already difficult situation. He did not favor bureaucracy, as he claimed Trotsky did, or a weak party, as he said the Workers' Opposition did. Instead he was for careful, cautious improvements. The Bolsheviks felt embattled in the winter of 1920–21; their cohesion as a group was strengthened by the rising hostility of the vast Russian population and the enormity of the tasks before them. Lenin, more than anyone else, was the symbol of the success their common commitment had already brought them. They followed him instinctively in the best of times; their allegiance intensified when, as in this instance, he spoke to their own desire for stability, calm, and, within the boundaries of their radical socialism, moderation.

Lenin used more than personal prestige to persuade Communists. Party leaders such as Anatoli Lunacharskii, the commissar of education, and Mikhail Frunze, the Red Army commander, traveled around the country organizing a campaign in which Lenin's supporters vowed to make life better and threatened that a vote against the "Platform of the Ten" was a vote against Lenin.[21] They may also have used less savory tactics, such as the intimidation of subordinates by superior officials,[22] but coercion was not the primary reason for their success. The Leninists won because they represented the party majority from the outset, because Lenin led them, and because they could use the party machinery to their advantage.

In January 1921, precisely when the scope of Lenin's victory was becoming apparent, Kollontai joined the Workers' Opposition. She could no longer ignore the debates, nor was there a danger now of banishment to that "nice sunny place to eat peaches." The party leadership had proclaimed the right of Communists to speak out on the trade union question. Kollontai chose to align herself with the Workers' Opposition because in both general concerns and specific demands this group reflected her beliefs. She cherished the same concept of proletarian democracy as they, she was sympathetic to all their reform proposals, from trade union autonomy to communalization, and she shared their fear that the party was turning away from the workers toward the bourgeois specialists. When she informed Shliapnikov of her decision to join the faction is unknown, but her first public declaration of support for it came in a *Pravda* article on January 28. There Kollontai accused the party leadership of betraying the proletariat by relying on capitalist-trained managers and talking about a slow transition to worker control of industry. "If we had argued with similar wise caution and gradualness in 1917," she proclaimed, "our party would not have led us on that straight though rocky path that shortened the road to communism, but would have carried us along the more tested road to the swamps and forest wildernesses of history."[23]

Her oratorical skill made Kollontai a welcome addition to the Workers' Opposition. Exact information about where and when she spoke remains sequestered in closed Soviet files, but there is no doubt that her speeches increased the appeal of the faction. Shliapnikov formulated the ideas of the Workers' Opposition and acted as its leading advocate, but he was not as compelling a speaker as Kollontai.[24] Kollontai contributed more than speeches, however. Knowing that they would be a small minority at the Tenth Congress, the leaders of the Workers' Opposition decided to concentrate on winning over other delegates at the meeting itself. For this purpose they prepared two documents. The first was a set of theses on party reform. The second was a pamphlet by Kollontai, *The Workers' Opposition*. She wrote it sometime in February and then took it to a government press. The press refused to print it at government expense, and Kollontai had to pay the costs herself.

The Workers' Opposition, Kollontai argued in the pamphlet, had arisen as an expression of the discontent of the masses, from whom the revolution drew its life and on whom the government depended. The faction was composed of "workers, that part of the progressive vanguard of the Russian proletariat who carried all the difficulty of the revolutionary struggle on their shoulders and who have not been dispersed among Soviet institutions, losing their ties with the working masses."[25] All too many workers, drawn away from the factories into other jobs, had been corrupted by power, Kollontai wrote, and had become estranged from the proletariat. Only the unions retained their connections with the masses. The unions had given birth to the Workers' Opposition and therefore it followed that the Workers' Opposition reflected the aspirations of the proletariat. This argument was not quite accurate. The Workers' Oppositionists were leaders, if regional ones. Nor is there any evidence that the faction had a mass constituency, for the trade union membership from which they came and within which they were a minority, comprised a maximum of ten percent of the total nonagricultural labor force.[26] Nonetheless, Kollontai's assertion that the Workers' Opposition sprang from the people did point to the elite quality of the other factions and to the trade union origins of the Workers' Opposition. Using traditional Bolshevik notions about the proletariat and the unions' relationship to it, Kollontai began her pamphlet by staking out a special identity for her faction—democratic, uncorrupted, proletarian.

Why had the Workers' Opposition developed as an expression of popular discontent, she asked. Because the party leadership had failed the workers. The virtue of the Bolsheviks had always been in their ability to sense the needs of the proletariat and guide the satisfaction of those needs in such a way that historical development was advanced at the same time. During 1917 the party had performed that task brilliantly, but now Kollontai charged that "our party has not only slowed its headlong rush to the future, but more and more often 'prudently' looks backward."[27] The Bolsheviks had been corrupted by power and by the awesome task of governing an underdeveloped, war-ravaged country. They had compromised with nonproletarian elements, chiefly with the peasantry and the bourgeoisie. They had given bourgeois specialists power in industry, and since "production, its organization, is the essence of communism,"[28] to bring the bourgeoisie into decision-making positions in the economy was to reintroduce capitalist influences. All the present authoritarianism and bureaucracy sprang from this fundamental error. Furthermore, reliance on such people made the workers feel that their leaders no longer trusted them.

Kollontai went on to explain how the Workers' Opposition's proposals would correct present injustices. Most important was their package of economic reforms, for bureaucracy and autocracy in all other institutions sprang from the bureaucratization of industrial management by bourgeois elements. "The question is *who* will build a communist economy and how to build it," Kollontai wrote. "This is the essence of our program. This is its heart."[29] Obviously the workers should build the economy, for they were the only creative class in a socialist society. They alone could develop the new forms of production which socialism demanded. "The unions are not only *schools of communism*," Kollontai wrote in refutation of Lenin, "but *creators of communism*."[30] A federated structure such as that proposed by the Workers' Opposition would give full scope to the proletariat's collective efforts.

Here lay the crux of the confrontation between Lenin's majority and the Workers' Opposition. Both Kollontai and Lenin thought that the working class would build communism, so the issue at bottom was which institution, party or union, would best serve as a vehicle to channel proletarian energies into economic construction. For Kollontai the party should supervise the government and guard ideology, but it could not manage the development of an entirely new industrial system. She wrote that only the working class, through the unions, could accomplish the mammoth task of laying the economic base for communism. Clearly, Kollontai did not understand the transformation that was then molding the party into a manager of all Soviet life.

> The party can teach the Red Army soldier, the political worker, the person who performs any task that is already formulated. But the party cannot educate the builder of the communist economy, only the union gives scope for the construction of production.
> The task of the party is to create the conditions, that is, the scope for education of the broad working masses, united by economic production tasks; the worker is the *creator* of new types of labor, of a new system of using the workers' hands, of a new grouping of labor power.[31]

Kollontai claimed, with considerable justification, that her position followed the canons of Marxism more closely than did those of the other factions. The party might well represent the vanguard, but it could not substitute itself for the entire working class. The unions had to deal with production every day, so through them the workers would have the final control over the economy. Given that power in a decentralized system, they could promote *samodeiatel'nost'*, the spontaneity on which Kollontai believed socialist construction depended.

Just as the unions had to be democratized, so too did government and party. True to her notion that the party had gone astray in part because its proletarian essence had been corrupted by a flood of new members from the peasantry and the bourgeoisie, Kollontai proposed expelling everyone of nonproletarian origin who had joined since 1919. These people could appeal their expulsion within three months and could be readmitted, provided they did manual labor that would teach them about working-class life first hand, and provided they proved to the satisfaction of party officials that they were true Communists.

At the same time the party should honor its democratic principles. Workers should participate in all important party committees. Bolsheviks should be discouraged from holding both party and government jobs, and party officials should be elected rather than appointed. Free discussion should be honored at all levels of the hierarchy. Workers in power in a democratized party would ensure that the party acted as a guardian of revolutionary purity, of the "class line" of a government forced to rule a class-mixed country. The party committees would become "centers of ideological control over Soviet institutions." The Central Committee would be "the highest ideological center of our class politics, the organ of thought and control over the practical politics of the soviets, the spiritual embodiment of the fundamentals of our program."[32]

The pamphlet ended with an affirmation of the need for the Workers' Opposition. The group would continue to exist, within the party, because someone had to shock the Bolsheviks out of the numbing daily routine by demanding that they examine their failures. "Where there is criticism, analysis, there thought works, moves, and goes on, there is creativity, life, and that means movement forward, to the future." The Workers' Opposition had asked the party to honor its program, and it would continue to point out the correct course in the future. Eventually the leaders would acknowledge that the Workers' Opposition was right. "Il'ich will be with us yet," Kollontai predicted.[33]

The ideas expressed in *The Workers' Opposition* did not originate with Kollontai. Shliapnikov had formulated the economic proposals and was the first to charge that the party had lost faith in the proletariat. At the Ninth Party Conference, S. P. Medvedev had called for half of all party committees to be proletarian. The rest of the political reform notions and the arguments about the source of bureaucratization came out of the collaborative effort that had produced the "Resolutions on Party Construction" submitted to the Tenth Congress by the Workers' Opposition.[34] Kollontai may have drafted that document, since it follows *The Workers' Opposition* closely, but even there the ideas represent not an original formulation, but a fusion of many Democratic Centralist proposals with those of the Workers' Opposition.

What Kollontai did was to unite the demands of the faction into a coherent argument that was passionate, eloquent, and persuasive. She called for democracy and spontaneity rather than bureaucracy and coercion. If she did not demand democratic rights for Mensheviks or SRs (and she did not), at least she did ask such rights for Bolsheviks.

Furthermore, Kollontai advocated true power for the working class. She demanded complete, genuine worker control of industry in the belief that the masses would build a truly free society. Communism must develop out of the operation of social forces; it would not be coerced into being by party command. Perhaps that notion was naive in 1921, but Kollontai had always believed in the workers. Now that she saw her party heading toward autocracy, she demanded a return to a democracy that may have never existed within its ranks and a granting of full economic control to a class that had never proved itself capable of running industry. In a time of crisis she clung to the central beliefs of her Marxism—that collectivism as embodied in the proletariat was good, that communism came about through mass action, that authoritarianism was bad. She had joined the Workers' Opposition because they shared her wholehearted faith in the working class. Having joined, she produced for them a pamphlet that remains an eloquent statement of anarchistic Marxism and her finest political manifesto.

Kollontai managed to have 1,500 copies of *The Workers' Opposition* printed and distributed in time for the Tenth Congress. The prospects of any success for her group at the meeting were not bright, for of the 694 delegates with full voting rights accredited to the congress, only 45 to 50 came from the Workers' Opposition.[35] The faction's hopes of changing minds must have also been dimmed by an outbreak of unrest in Petrograd in February 1921. Strikes against the Bolsheviks culminated in an uprising of the naval garrison at Kronstadt, the island in the Gulf of Finland from which had come some of the most revolutionary sailors of 1917. Now Kronstadt exploded into riots over the sacrifices of the last three years, forcing Bolsheviks who had once gone to the troops with calls for militant action to return across the ice in violent repression. In all this unrest, Mensheviks, anarchists, SRs, and even defecting Bolsheviks were active, and the specter of the masses turning toward other socialists heightened the party's already considerable anxiety. When the delegates to the Tenth Party Congress assembled in Moscow in early March, therefore, they came more prepared than usual to follow Lenin and to overrule opposition. Even Trotsky and Bukharin had begun to swing over to support the "Platform of the Ten." The Democratic Centralists were not prepared for a concerted effort, so the Workers' Opposition stood virtually alone.

Kollontai's pamphlet achieved its objective of bringing the faction's demands to the attention of the congress, but it also turned the anger of

Lenin, Trotsky, and Bukharin against her. On March 8, the first day of the meeting, Angelica Balabanoff, a Bolshevik who had been a founder of the Zimmerwald Left, saw Kollontai talking to a French Communist in the foyer outside the auditorium.

> At that moment Lenin entered at a brisk pace. He looked very tense and did not stop to return greetings. Walking up to Alexandra Kollontai's interlocutor he said to him angrily, "What? You still speak to this individual?" He entered the assembly hall and became immediately engrossed in the reading of the pamphlet, entirely oblivious to his surroundings, even to greetings and words addressed to him directly. As he read on, his face darkened more and more.[36]

The confrontation with the Workers' Opposition began the next day, in the debate on the Central Committee report Lenin had presented to the congress. Shliapnikov rose to deplore the split between the leadership and the rank and file, which he said had been caused by the leadership's stifling of mass initiative. He concluded:

> Vladimir Il'ich, if we direct all our strength to the struggle here with these phenomena, and with elements not only abroad but here within our country, then the Workers' Opposition will be very solidly and unanimously with you. But don't go too far in fighting us. Perhaps you can suppress and divide us here, but you will only lose from it.[37]

Kollontai followed Shliapnikov's display of bravado with an equally challenging speech several hours later. She too said Lenin's report from the Central Committee had not dealt with the problem of "the managers and the governors" in the party. "It is most important, comrades, that the party recognize this crisis, recognize that whole ranks of alien elements are hanging onto us, that the resolutions on purging the party have been taken only on paper and not put into practice."[38]

The Central Committee, as the "ideological-political leading organ," must make positive efforts to prevent the split that was opening between the leadership and the proletariat. "The greatest misfortune, comrades, is that we feel a secret distrust of the broad masses, we feel the masses shrink from us," Kollontai warned. They could only conquer that feeling by improving the possibilities of *samodeiatel'nost'*, purging themselves of noncommunists, and turning their policies in the proper direction ideologically.[39]

In a final word that evening and again in a speech the next day, Lenin said that the time had come to end factionalism. In this dangerous period the party needed unity above all else. The factions themselves were a sign of the influence the Bolsheviks' enemies were exerting on the party, Lenin charged. The Workers' Opposition held anarcho-syndicalist ideas, the Kronstadt rebels held anarchist ideas, therefore there must be a "connection" between the Workers' Opposition and the Kronstadt uprising. Lenin stopped short of asserting that the Workers' Oppositionists had played any role in the rebellion; he knew they had not. He merely linked the faction's activities with the sailors' chronologically, charged that syndicalism and the anarchism of Kronstadt were the same, declared that the Workers' Opposition's ideas were syndicalist, and left the frightened delegates to draw their own conclusions. There were good Communists in the Workers' Opposition, and once they left the faction they should be welcomed back to full participation in the party, but for the leaders of the group Lenin had only scorn. Shliapnikov bragged about being a worker himself and Kollontai claimed that the faction was "class united and class conscious." "Well, thank God," Lenin said, "so we know that Comrade Kollontai and Comrade Shliapnikov are 'class united and class conscious.'" Those delegates who knew about the other unity that had existed between Kollontai and Shliapnikov snickered.[40]

Such were Lenin's tactics—sarcasm and slander, not serious debate. He had made up his mind, and he chose to denigrate his old friends rather than discuss the issues. He had the majority with him already, and the time had come to end this unnecessary squabbling and get on with the real problems that confronted the party. He knew Kollontai and Shliapnikov were not agents of the petty-bourgeoisie, leading honest communists astray, but he also knew the right course, so if he had to shout Bolshevik curses to defeat them, he would. He had to get his people together before he could rely on them to carry out the new programs he had formulated. Perhaps he even believed that the opposition had unwittingly aided the uprising at Kronstadt by revealing party disunity. He knew they had never intended that consequence, but he had warned the Bolsheviks in December about what would happen if the party made a public display of factionalism. Now two months had been wasted in a useless debate that may have encouraged rebellion as well. If Lenin was not quite fair in accusing the Workers' Opposition of falling under Menshevik or anarchist influence, he could believe that his condemnation was still a just punishment for the faction's obstinate utopianism. Besides, to characterize the Workers' Opposition as petty-bourgeois had the effect of frightening delegates too unsophisticated in Marxism to judge the validity of the charge.

Publicly, Lenin called for unity, and the delegates to the Tenth Congress followed him by approving all the reports and resolutions he submitted to them. Privately, Lenin held meetings with his supporters and with oppositionists in an effort to put together a Central Committee composed overwhelmingly of his people. He even succeeded in convincing four Workers' Oppositionists, including Shliapnikov, to serve, thereby co-opting them. In the future, as members of the Central Committee, they would be bound by the majority's decisions, and of course Lenin would hold the majority. When Kollontai rose to address the issue of party reform on the evening of March 13, therefore, Lenin had already secured the party endorsement and the Central Committee he wanted.[41]

She couched her speech as a response to Bukharin, who was supporting Lenin's proposals to democratize the party by means of the same resolutions and control commissions that had yielded no meaningful results before. Her real target was Lenin's theme that in this time of crisis the Bolsheviks must seek unity above all else. They did not need unity, Kollontai declared, as much as they needed a democratic party based on the proletariat.

> Our Workers' Opposition strongly insists that it is necessary not only to reorganize the whole apparatus. . . , but to say firmly and clearly that for all time and not only in a moment of respite a system of broadly developed democracy, of faith in the masses, and of guaranteed freedom of thought for comrades is necessary not only on paper but in fact.[42]

Kollontai referred to Lenin briefly, when she said that his angry response to her pamphlet showed that she must be right. By comparison with Lenin's speech, Kollontai's was a model of restraint; she did not even take on Lenin as her main antagonist, although the level of his attack on her must have angered her. Perhaps she believed the congress would react more favorably to a reasoned presentation than to sarcasm, and Angelica Balabanoff did remark much later on Kollontai's admirable "calm and self-control."[43] Whatever her goals, the delegates did not receive her warmly. When she concluded with the usual Workers' Opposition claim that the group was "connected with" the proletariat, someone yelled from the floor, "And with Kronstadt!" Kollontai responded angrily:

Comrades, you know that there was never a time when the Workers' Opposition refused work and did not go to work wherever it was sent. Who first responded to Kronstadt, who went there first, if not representatives of the Workers' Opposition? This time it wasn't the Red General Staff who went there; representatives of the Workers' Opposition went there. That's who went first. (Laughter in the hall.) And I repeat further, when we are needed we can support the party and do our duty in the name of communism, in the name of the international workers' revolution. We therefore demand the right, as a clearly working class party, to defend the interests of the proletarian revolution.[44]

The delegates muttered, some few probably applauded, but the speech won no friends in a congress already strongly organized behind Lenin. He had played on the danger they faced to argue for moderation and unity, because he believed moderation and unity were the only realistic ways to deal with that very real danger. Kollontai sensed the crisis, too, but she called for reliance on revolutionary principles, on the broadest kind of reform, because she felt Bolshevik survival depended on mass support. Mass support would come only through mass participation and mass participation would build communism. Kollontai had welcomed Lenin's determination to accelerate the revolution in 1917, but she would not accept his demand to govern the masses in 1921, even though both positions sprang from the same fundamentally Bolshevik, fundamentally Leninist, determination to control reality rather than let the natural forces they all professed to believe in develop naturally.

Lenin had never shared Kollontai's faith in the proletariat. She had realized that in 1903 when she sided with the Mensheviks, but she had forgotten it in 1915, or else had concluded then that Lenin had changed his attitudes. He had not. As deeply as she believed in unfettered mass action, he believed in disciplined, controlled mass action; while she reveled in the exuberance of 1917, he prodded his party to ride the unrest to power. Mass action was a force to be channeled, not trusted or allowed to run free. That was what Leninism was about—seizing control of history while professing determinism. And yet the difference between Kollontai and Lenin was not simply one of democracy versus dictatorship. Each drew on personal ideology to interpret reality; each ignored certain dangers while being obsessed with others. Lenin, who feared anarchy and the loss of control, who valued discipline and unified effort, who knew the Russian proletariat to be unskilled and unorganized, who had always accepted the necessity for coercion, thought the shortest route to a socialist economy lay through rapid industrial reconstruction. Only the party could lead this process; to grant a major initiative to the backward proletariat would sink Russia into a chaos like that of 1917. Surrounded by enemies at home and abroad, the Bolsheviks could not risk the disintegration of "the 'public meeting' democracy" with which he had felt uncomfortable as early as March 1918.[45] The party must build socialism now through a disciplined, unified effort, through granting concessions to the peasantry, through marshaling all their propaganda and power to make the Russian into a productive worker. Thereafter, when the economic base for communism had been laid, a true democracy would follow.

In 1918 Rosa Luxemburg had written, "Socialist democracy is not something which begins only in the promised land after the foundations of socialist economy are created; it does not come as some sort of Christmas present for the worthy people who, in the interim, have loyally supported a handful of socialist dictators."[46] For Luxemburg and for Kollontai, democracy was a process. It was the only medium in which to experiment with new types of organization. Democracy might sanction coercion to eradicate the forces of the past, but not to shape the future. These revolutionary women held to their populist principles because they both distrusted power and authority far more than did Lenin.

Rebellion against all forms of authority, not just tsarist autocracy, had initially brought Kollontai to Marxism. There is considerable merit in the charge of a Soviet historian that she held the anarchist view that governments were innately evil.[47] She distrusted the hierarchies of the German Social Democrats, the Soviet government, and her own party. She overlooked the proletariat's ignorance and fragmentation but she would not overlook the government's abuses, because she trusted the proletariat and distrusted governments. Kollontai cannot justly be called an anarchist, if only because she accepted, while anarchists denied, the necessity of government and party during the transition to communism; but there was a distinctly anarchist tinge in her fundamental distrust of power.

On the evening of March 14 the congress elected the Central Committee, approving Lenin's candidates with only minor revisions. Earlier that day Shliapnikov, Medvedev, and Kutuzov had spoken for the Workers' Opposition in the debate on the trade unions, but the position of the "Platform of the Ten" was adopted.[48] According to Anastas Mikoian, the delegates were tired of listening anyway, since all the issues had already been decided. "For more than two months," he wrote, "we had heard, read and talked so much about this subject that we were awfully bored."[49]

The next day Lenin introduced the first steps of the New Economic Policy (NEP), his plan for economic reconstruction, which would allow a partial return to private enterprise. Requisitioning of the peasants' grain was to be replaced by a tax low enough to encourage them to raise more food, then sell it for profit. Lenin had struck hard against the opposition, in part to insure unified party support for this concession to the peasantry. He expected many Bolsheviks to object to any return to a free market economy, but even the Workers' Oppositionists kept silent. Mikoian wrote that they did not seem to feel the proposal touched the issues under discussion.[50] Perhaps too they were weary with their losing battle.

Lenin had promised throughout the meeting that he would put an end to factionalism. On March 16, the last day of the congress, when some of the delegates had already left, he introduced two new documents, the "Resolution on Syndicalism and the Anarchist Deviation in our Party," and the "Resolution on Party Unity." The first condemned the Workers' Opposition as a petty-bourgeois group which had arisen because of the presence of Mensheviks and peasants in the party. The faction's ideas were un-Marxist and dangerous, and if the Workers' Opposition persisted in spreading them, they would be thrown out of the party. The "Resolution on Party Unity" gave the party the legal right, for the first time, to expel members for "factionalism." From now on, the Central Committee had the power to punish Communists for any "breach of discipline" or organized group dissent.[51]

Medvedev and Shliapnikov responded angrily to this attempt to throttle them. The Workers' Opposition, Medvedev said, knew that both resolutions were aimed at them, and that despite the pledges of freedom for inner-party criticism the resolutions would end all discussions in the future.[52] After Medvedev a furious Shliapnikov came to the podium and began, "I have not seen or heard anything more demagogic or slanderous than this resolution in my life, in a twenty-year tenure in the party." How dare Lenin accuse him and the other Bolsheviks in the Workers' Opposition of being petty-bourgeois? Almost all of them had been party members since well before the revolution. They were not calling for syndicalism; they advocated economic planning, the leadership of the party, and soviet government. If the congress passed Lenin's resolutions, the Workers' Oppositionists would resign from the Central Committee and their other posts and "take the discussion of the unworthy methods of struggle with the Workers' Opposition to the court of the international Communist proletariat." Still angry, Shliapnikov concluded sarcastically, "Of course, comrades, once you have stuck your label of anarchist-syndicalist on me here, although with that very big reservation about its being a deviation, I cannot be a competent member of the [Central Committee] and I tender my resignation."[53]

More debate followed, but the resolutions were passed. Lenin said a final comforting word to the effect that these were only temporary measures made necessary by the current crisis. He accepted none of the resignations. The delegates voted another resolution urging the Workers' Oppositionists to submit to party discipline by serving on the Central Committee. Lenin ended the meeting with a speech hailing all that the congress had accomplished.

Frightened by the tasks facing them and the world of enemies in which they lived, the Bolsheviks had now chosen to shut their ears to valid criticism, to cling to reforms that had not worked in the past, and to answer opposition with repression. No doubt many saw the resolutions as temporary measures, but as Trotsky later admitted, they had first outlawed all criticism by other political parties as a temporary measure, and now they moved against their own comrades.[54] They chose the easy route of intolerance, in the process rebuilding the autocracy that was the worst feature of their Russian heritage. Rather than reverse the wartime improvisations that had sustained the very bureaucratic authoritarianism they had once fought to destroy, the Bolsheviks refused to risk major reform.

Kollontai did not join the other Oppositionists in the protest of the last day's session, nor could she vote against the resolutions since she was accredited to the congress with "advisory" voting rights only. She may not have been in the hall; if she was, she kept silent. Almost all of her fears about the price of opposition had been confirmed. The attacks on her were to be expected, of course, and in her speeches she gave no evidence that Lenin had particularly wounded her. He probably had, however, as had Bukharin, for both men used personal insults that not only were unnecessary but also attacked her identity as a woman. Lenin made the remark about her relationship with Shliapnikov, and he knew she was still Dybenko's wife. If she and Shliapnikov had become lovers again (and there is no evidence that they had), Lenin did not need to bring it up in a debate at a party congress.

Bukharin struck harder in a speech on March 13 when he attacked an article, "The Cross of Motherhood," which Kollontai had published in January 1921. Kollontai had described the difficulties of being a mother in discussing a play entitled "The Miracle," which she had seen in Germany in 1914. The protagonists were three women—the Virgin Mary, the Mother Superior of a convent, and a young nun—and the message was that motherhood required a woman to sacrifice her child to the world.[55] The article was sentimental and muddled, and as Bukharin quoted it out of context, it sounded even stranger to the congress delegates. Obviously, he said, anyone who wrote such "disgusting, sentimental, Catholic banalities" about motherhood should not be taken seriously. He went on to criticize other oppositionists with equal fervor, but he did not attack their masculinity as he had subtly joked about Kollontai's femininity. Perhaps she would claim he did not understand her article because he was a man, Bukharin said, but if he could be turned into a woman he would still think it drivel, just like the "clear class line" she claimed in *The Workers' Opposition*.[56]

Lenin's reference to her sex life and Bukharin's attack on her article may have insulted Kollontai more than the other criticism because they seized on her womanhood in order to discredit her. The personal attack may have caused her to feel even more strongly the stinging rebuke that had been delivered to her faction. She had never liked party infighting, she had avoided it during emigration, and she feared its consequences in the fall of 1920. After the Tenth Congress she returned to the Zhenotdel to take up work that seemed less controversial. She did not renounce her principles; she simply retreated, as she had done after Brest-Litovsk.

9

The End of Opposition

THE WORKERS' OPPOSITION continued to exist as a faction after the Tenth Party Congress. Its members planned to keep in touch with one another and to criticize party policy, without violating the congress resolutions. They could not openly espouse the platform that had been condemned as "anarcho-syndicalist." Indeed, they could not advocate any platform at all, since such action was now illegal. Instead Shliapnikov and Medvedev shifted their attention to the NEP, which they saw as an open acknowledgement of the regime's preference for the petty-bourgeois peasantry over the proletariat. Lenin's cautious return to free trade, a concession which would prove a spur to economic recovery, was another compromise the Workers' Opposition could not accept, especially since no comparable steps toward helping the working class were taken at the same time.

The members of the faction soon found their worst fears about the stifling of inner-party criticism borne out. Not only were they forbidden from speaking freely, but the leadership also began removing them from their union and party positions. Throughout the spring, summer, and fall of 1921, the Workers' Opposition put up a good fight in party and union organizations in Samara, Nizhni-Novgorod, Omsk, Perm, and other cities, but they were no match for the powerful forces arrayed against them.[1]

For the most part Kollontai avoided this heroic but hopeless battle. Her lack of union affiliation excluded her from the campaign waged in the union and provincial party committees, and she had the Zhenotdel to attend to. There she could work for *samoideiatel'nost'*, for a party that allowed some small measure of pluralism, and for reforms for women. Still in touch with the Workers' Oppositionists throughout the spring, she applauded their efforts quietly from the sidelines.

Kollontai had not abandoned her work at the Zhenotdel during the days before the Tenth Congress. In January 1921 she persuaded Preobra-zhenskii, one of the party secretaries, to co-sign a Central Committee letter instructing provincial committees to improve their support of the woman's bureau.[2] After the congress she organized and then presided over a meeting of district workers, who discussed ways of following central guidelines in the provinces.[3] Toward the end of March she worked on drawing up instructions for paying the women workers assigned to training programs in government departments. Through negotiations with the Sovnarkom, Kollontai secured a decree supporting the programs and clarifying budget procedures, a decree soon made obsolete by the new conditions of the NEP but hailed in the spring as a major achievement.[4]

In addition to these administrative activities, Kollontai made her usual speaking appearances in the Moscow area and gave a series of lectures on the woman question at Sverdlov University.[5] She also chaired a meeting of organizers of Eastern women in early April; although the Zhenotdel had not been able to set up the conference for Muslim women she had initially planned for February, Kollontai was still hopeful that one could be held in June.[6] She was not in disgrace, as she had been after Brest-Litovsk; indeed, she seemed to have lost only her candidate membership on the Central Committee, a symbol of status in the party that was rather meaningless for Kollontai, since she had never participated in the internal politics of that group.

Nor did Kollontai feel as numb and defeated as she had in 1918. She plunged into the work of her department and published an article, "Theses on Communist Morality," which she knew would be controversial. In it Kollontai argued that the Bolsheviks must abolish the bourgeois family quickly, by accelerating the communalization of society. A "new morality" must be created, and with it a new marriage which would be based on emotional compatibility, common interests, and erotic attraction but would be devoid of the economic dependence and possessiveness that distorted the relations between the sexes in bourgeois society. Communism would not be built without a thoroughgoing change in human relations, without a "new morality," of which the rules governing the interaction between men and women were a part.[7]

Communalization, not power or industrialization, had always been the core of Kollontai's conception of socialism. By 1921, substantial progress had been made toward that goal. Large numbers of urban Russians ate in public dining rooms, had their clothes washed in public laundries, and lived in crowded apartments. They did so not out of choice, however, but largely because the civil war had robbed them of the means to feed and house themselves. Furthermore, the food was dreadful, and the laundries mutilated as many clothes as they cleaned; these conditions gave the masses cause for prejudice against communal, or rather governmental, services.

As she had for years, Kollontai was arguing for a major investment of resources in communal facilities, but she was doing so subtly now. The Workers' Opposition platform had advocated communalization, and she was careful in the spring of 1921 to avoid any statements that could be attacked as harkening back to the Workers' Opposition.[8] For three months, from mid-March to mid-June, her public behavior was irreproachable. Privately, Kollontai was growing increasingly alarmed by the NEP, for she too saw the policy as a capitulation to the peasantry. Finally in June she decided to take the Workers' Opposition's criticism of the NEP to the Communist International, which was scheduled to meet at the end of that month.

It was not an easy decision. Kollontai told Bernhard Reichenbach, a representative of the German Communist Labor Party (KAPD), that she feared the party leaders would order her arrest. That was not a realistic possibility at the time, since Kollontai had every right as an individual to express her opinions before the Comintern. Furthermore no Bolshevik leader had been jailed for dissent. Kollontai may have been apprehensive because she understood full well that none of her comrades would applaud her for criticizing them in front of foreign Communists. She felt she owed the workers and the Workers' Opposition this statement of principle, but she was not eager to make it.

For safekeeping, Kollontai gave Reichenbach a copy of her pamphlet, *The Workers' Opposition*; she thought it might be confiscated should she be arrested. She chose him as a confidant because the leftist KAPD had broken with the German Communist Party in 1920 in a center- versus left-Marxist split, similar to the feud between the majority Bolsheviks and the Workers' Opposition. Reichenbach promised to take care of the pamphlet, and a few days later he sent it to Berlin with a returning comrade.[9] Kollontai passed the middle week of June at the International Women Communists Conference, where she worked with Clara Zetkin and Lilina to draft resolutions for submission to the main Comintern Congress, chaired the general sessions, and talked enthusiastically about increasing work among women. The warmth of the delegates' response must have buoyed her flagging spirits.[10]

The Third Comintern Congress convened in the last week of June, with Lenin leading the Russians in speeches that counseled a retreat from expectations of world revolution and greater adherence to the proper line, the line of the Russian party. It was realistic to temper the always inflated hopes for rebellions in Europe, but highhanded and ultimately destructive to demand that foreign Communists sacrifice their independence just as the Bolsheviks were doing. Lenin held his party together in that demand until July 5, when Kollontai spoke.

Before her appearance she told Lenin she planned to criticize the Bolsheviks, which she knew would be taken as a breach of party discipline, regardless of its technical legality. He snapped back, "Are you asking my blessing for it? Then do it, but don't talk about it beforehand." "I'll take you at your word, Vladimir Il'ich," Kollontai replied. "I am not asking and I am putting my name down [to speak]." He said she should not, recommending instead that she visit a new hydroelectric project to see the progress Russia was making.[11] Kollontai remained unpersuaded.

She came to the podium after a speech by Radek, and the delegates, anticipating a stir, hurriedly returned to their seats. She spoke in German, the first language of the Comintern, then translated her remarks into French and Russian. Lenin, Trotsky, Zinoviev, Bukharin, Kamenev, Rykov and Radek sat in a row behind her. As they whispered to one another, Kollontai's face flushed, but she continued to address a silent audience.[12]

She began by announcing that she appeared as a representative of the Workers' Opposition, which was a minority group in the Bolshevik Party but which nevertheless felt a responsibility to report to the Comintern on the current, dangerous policies in Russia. There were several important questions that must be asked. First, would the NEP build a communist economy? No, Kollontai answered, it marked a return to private trade, hence to private property, and outdated capitalism. In taking these steps, the party was catering to the needs of the peasants, who wanted individual land ownership, and to the bourgeoisie working in the government, who were agents of foreign capital.

That last charge was patently false, but Kollontai clung tenaciously to her belief that the middle class was the cause of bureaucratization. The chief danger of the concessions to the peasantry lay, she said, in their effect on the revolutionary spirit of the proletariat. A retreat from communism as a goal would make the working class question communism as an ideology. The resulting crisis of confidence would strip the workers of "faith in their ability to achieve anything through *samodeiatel'nost'*, in their ability to create a new communist economic system." "I am seriously afraid," Kollontai warned, "that if we continue this policy of concession, we shall get to the point that when a social revolution breaks out in other countries it will be too late, for then we shall not have a genuine, solidly conscious revolutionary class on which a revolution can rely."[13] The bourgeoisie and the peasantry would have become so strong that the demoralized Russian proletariat would be unable to complete the final stages of communist construction.

Instead of catering to the enemy, the Bolsheviks should be building up the working class; but they refused to take substantive measures in that direction. There were no large-scale programs of worker education, no ideas about harnessing the people's creativity, nothing but paper resolutions. Thus, slowly, the Bolsheviks were squandering the revolutionary consciousness that had been awakened in 1917. No temporary gain in production achieved by the NEP could compensate for the stifling of mass initiative and the resultant loss of worker support for the party. She was speaking out now, Kollontai said, so that non-Russian communists would help the Bolsheviks by pointing out their errors. She defiantly affirmed her belief in world revolution and her resolve to continue to criticize.

> Genuine salvation for us consists in consolidating in our party a strong core which stands for our old, firm principles and which is able to show itself at the moment of the revolutionary outburst. If the deviation in all Soviet policy develops to the fullest and our Communist republic turns into simply a Soviet and not a Communist one, then this core of strong Communists will take into its hands the red banner of revolution to guarantee the victory of communism throughout the entire world.[14]

"The core of strong Communists" was presumably the Workers' Opposition, or perhaps a broader group of people committed to her notions of world revolution and proletarian democracy. Kollontai's claim of a redemptive mission for them—saving the revolution—was a bit arrogant, but the plea behind that bravado came through clearly. She was appealing to the international Communist community to rescue the ideals of 1917 now being compromised in Russia. She was calling again on her comrades to rely on the proletariat rather than the peasantry, and she warned that if they did not, the proletariat, already damaged by war, already wavering in its loyalty to the Bolsheviks, would lose its revolutionary spirit. Without a revolutionary class the party could not lead a revolution. The end result must inevitably be "a Soviet republic, but not a Communist one."

Kollontai's attack on the NEP displayed a characteristic left-Bolshevik hostility toward the peasantry. She clung to the Marxist dictum that the peasants were at base a petty-bourgeois class interested only in private property, and when she did mention them as people worthy of attention, she carefully noted that she was referring to the landless peasantry. That group, according to Bolshevik doctrine, could be rallied to oppose the richer peasants, the *kulaki*, and therefore support the Bolsheviks. Given Kollontai's childhood experience with the rural Finns, however, and the concern for them she manifested in her early writings, her outbursts against "the petty-bourgeoisie" in 1921 seem dogmatic and not a little cruel. The peasantry had suffered terribly during the civil war at the hands of both Reds and Whites, yet their greater hostility toward the Whites aided the Red victory considerably. They resisted the Bolshevik requisitioning squads that came from the cities to seize their grain, just as they avoided the early efforts to collectivize them, because they had learned over the centuries to rely on themselves and their neighbors. Why should a peasant trust outsiders, who must be either tax collectors or police? Why should he follow the Bolsheviks, except to rid himself of the landlord? That accomplished, the peasant wanted to be left alone to raise his crops and take care of his family. But although Kollontai was justified in viewing the peasants as less revolutionary than the proletariat, there was also reason to understand their attitudes, and even greater reason to compromise with them. Continued confrontation would further alienate the people of the countryside; far better to allow them to sell their grain than to risk more war by turning rural Russia into an armed camp.

Kollontai refused to admit the wisdom of the new tax law, and she decried the lack of comparable concessions to the working class. No programs were forthcoming that would cater to the proletariat's "healthy" desires for independence, no reforms had been launched to diminish the influence and prerogatives of bourgeois bureaucrats. To Kollontai, the relaxed official policies toward the peasantry seemed part of a pattern of disregard for the revolutionary class; that was the heart of her objection to them. If the Bolsheviks placated the enemy and alienated those who had made the October Revolution, they would lose not only their souls but their revolution as well.

Fear that the proletariat was turning away from them had plagued many Bolsheviks for months, and this fear had been one element causing them to react so strongly against the Workers' Opposition. When Kollontai made it the central charge of her speech, therefore, she spoke to an anxiety many felt, an anxiety justified by contemporary developments. Between June and September 1921, trade union membership dropped by six percent, a loss of 514,744 workers. Stories circulated among the Bolsheviks of long-time workers tearing up their party cards in disgust over the NEP; the representation of workers in the party fell by almost two percent during 1921.[15] Kollontai and her comrades saw this disillusionment as a major threat, for both ideology and history told them that the proletariat was their source of power. Kollontai attacked the NEP not because she was heartless where the peasantry was concerned, but primarily because she wanted measures equally supportive of the working class to be taken, and because she saw evidence all around her of a growth in proletarian disillusionment.

She was still fighting for her version of the ideals of 1917; now she appealed to foreign comrades for pressure on their Russian brothers. However, the international socialist community had disintegrated in August 1914, and her own party was busy stifling free criticism. When she gathered her notes together at the conclusion of the speech, she did not look at the audience, for she knew by the chilly reception that her plea had gone for nothing.[16]

Trotsky and Bukharin rebutted Kollontai's charges later in the day. First Trotsky asserted that the Russian party could make concessions to the peasantry, because the proletariat's rule in Russia was secure and therefore would not be threatened by dealing with the enemy. Bukharin brought up Kollontai's former Menshevism to explain her opposition to the NEP, accusing her of claiming to represent the Workers' Opposition when in fact she spoke only for herself. Bukharin's speech was an exercise in demagogy that resorted to slander and misrepresentation, but Trotsky, in attacking Kollontai's refusal to acknowledge the necessity for compromise with the peasantry, went straight to the weakness of the Workers' Opposition. The Bolsheviks must cope with a real world of miserable, inefficient, ignorant workers and hostile peasants, or they would perish. Still, Trotsky was unable to offer real improvement in the life of the proletariat. More fundamentally, he did not respond to Kollontai's demand that the workers be given a primary role in creating the new society. He simply declared that they already possessed it, which was not true.[17]

Not that Trotsky's evasions really mattered. The Comintern delegates ignored Kollontai and she felt isolated. "The speech ended," she wrote later. "I walked through the hall and left. No one noticed me. I had known it would be this way. But it was painful. Very painful. My soul was dark and heavy. Nothing is more terrible, more painful, than dissension with the party. Why had I spoken?"[18]

A day or two later, she asked Reichenbach to return the copy of *The Workers' Opposition* she had given him. (He later heard that Trotsky had convinced her that she should break off all contact with the KAPD.) But Reichenbach had already sent the pamphlet to Berlin. Upon his return to Germany in August, he published it, against Kollontai's wishes, and *The Workers' Opposition* began to circulate widely among socialists and Communists abroad.[19]

Kollontai's fears of party retaliation proved exaggerated. On July 8, she was back on the podium with Clara Zetkin to introduce the resolutions on Comintern work among women. If she felt subdued by Trotsky's pressure, she did not show it in a speech that chided the Russian party's attitudes toward women. She concluded with a ringing endorsement of an activist and independent Zhenotdel, and the delegates responded with "animated applause and approval." Three days later Kollontai and Zetkin spoke again at the session which passed the resolutions.[20] Thus despite the earlier rebukes, Kollontai continued to work at the congress and to receive a warm welcome. She had made her statement of principle without having Lenin's full wrath fall on her, although she later told Marcel Body, a French Communist and close friend, that Lenin had warned her not to participate in the opposition again.[21] She had suffered some humiliation and had consented to ask for the pamphlet back, but those were small penalties compared to the arrest she had feared.

Kollontai was determined now to avoid opposition activity and to attend to the mounting problems of the woman's bureau. The organizational weakness and the hostility of local Bolsheviks which had plagued the bureau since its creation were coming to a head in the summer of 1921. A resolution on agitation and propaganda passed by the Tenth Party Congress in March had included an innocuous sentence that read, "The Zhenotdely and the Sections for Work in the Country should be part of the regular agitation section of the given organization."[22] This brief reference was apparently designed to clarify accounting procedures, since the Zhenotdel still had no budget of its own, but some local party officials had taken the sentence as an order to merge the woman's bureau into *Agitprop*, the party's Agitation and Propaganda Department, and hence in effect abolish the Zhenotdel. Where sections were allowed to continue, their workers were often transferred to other jobs or ordered to restrict their activities. Provincial party conferences in Tver, Kostroma, and Astrakhan, among others, discussed abolishing the woman's bureau altogether.[23]

Word of these activities began to reach the Central Section in early summer, and on July 20 Kollontai issued a decree in the *Izvestiia* of the Central Committee, a biweekly newsletter, forbidding "the liquidation" of Zhenotdel sections on the local level.[24] Two weeks later a circular letter signed by Kollontai and Party Secretary Emelian Iaroslavskii reaffirmed Moscow's support for the bureau by clarifying its structure and functions. The letter noted carefully that in agitation campaigns the Zhenotdel sections should work "jointly" with Agitprop and that the party leaders should consider the sections' needs before transferring people. Both this decree and another addressed specifically to provincial officials stressed that the Zhenotdel must be included in general party work.[25]

In the September issue of *Kommunistka*, the journal for Zhenotdel workers, Kollontai lashed out at "the liquidators," those who wanted to abolish the bureau. Now the Zhenotdel must be strengthened, not weakened, she wrote, for there was much work to be done among peasant women and there was a growing unemployment problem for factory women. Yet some Communists still thought they did not need separate organizations for women.

Kollontai admitted that prejudice alone had not led to the misinterpretation of the Tenth Congress resolution. In many provinces the Zhenotdel sections had remained cut off from the party committees because party officials did not support their work. Thus the initial hostility between the activist women and the local leaders grew into separatism, which heightened the hostility. None of the Central Women had ever envisioned a hierarchy of independent women's bureaus working in isolation, because they knew the male majority would not tolerate it and because it would promote the notion that the Zhenotdel was a woman's auxiliary. If they wanted to do any work on the local level, however, the sections had to work apart, contributing to the very separatism they wanted to avoid.

The unintended autonomy of the Zhenotdel meant that the young, inexperienced women were on their own; consequently, they made mistakes that further irritated party officials and of course confirmed those officials' already low estimate of the worth of work among women. The Zhenotdel sections set up projects, such as famine relief, that duplicated the efforts of other departments or exceeded their authority, or both. When the leaders of one such section could not persuade factory women to attend meetings, they ordered them to hard labor as punishment. Such incompetent high-handedness reinforced the opinion of many Bolsheviks that the woman's bureau was a foolish waste of valuable resources.[26]

Kollontai did not spell out these shortcomings in detail in her September article; she did admit that the Zhenotdel sections had some problems which aggravated their relations with the party committees. But she could not resist adding that "the provincial committees' complete lack of information about the direction, principles, and methods of Zhenotdel work leads them with total naiveté to sanction these errors."[27] Furthermore, since provincial officials refused to help the women's sections, they bore some responsibility for the confusion. To correct it, Kollontai urged them to allow the Zhenotdel to work closely with the rest of the party apparatus, without sacrificing its special role as advocate for women or its special expertise where women were concerned.[28]

The problems in the bureau were not confined to the local level. Weaknesses existed also in Kollontai's Central Section, where there was a severe shortage of personnel. Without control over the budget or staffing, Kollontai could not prevent her workers from being transferred away from her. Between March 1921 and March 1922 she lost nineteen of the forty-two people assigned to the Central Section.[29] She did not have enough workers to answer the mail from the provinces. Staffers shifted from job to job without the time to concentrate on any one task effectively.[30] Encumbered by these organizational difficulties, the Zhenotdel workers had to participate in famine relief during the summer of 1921, formulate ways to deal with rising unemployment among women, reassign trainees to departments involved in NEP programs, and preserve the local sections at the same time.

To what extent was Kollontai herself responsible for the disorganization at the center? It is hard to say, since none of the available documents discusses individual performance. Kollontai had shown an interest in and an aptitude for administration as commissar of social welfare in 1917, and later she would run efficient embassies, but she could not have spent much time at the Zhenotdel in February and early March, or in late June and July. She was also devoting some attention to the Woman's Secretariat of the Comintern, and the absences caused by this other work may have hurt her supervision of the Central Section.

The bureau was further damaged by the loss of Samoilova, who had died of cholera while on an agitation tour in the spring of 1921. Samoilova had been a tireless worker who shared Kollontai's general view of female emancipation but who also possessed enough political realism to curb her colleague's tendency to rush ahead oblivious of party opposition. In May 1922 Kollontai wrote of her, "When the chances of putting through some Zhenotdel question at a bureau meeting were few, we brought up the heavy artillery—Comrade Samoilova."[31] Her death meant that of the initial three who pushed for the woman's bureau—Inessa, Samoilova, and Kollontai—only Kollontai was still alive, and of the small group active in 1917 only Lilina and Nikolaeva still worked with women. Most of the Central Women were young, inexperienced, and lacking status in the party.

Kollontai made some efforts to improve the functioning of the Zhenotdel in the fall of 1921, but they were not enough to prevent a serious loss of morale among Zhenotdel workers themselves. On November 2 a conference of provincial section leaders met in Moscow, and there Kollontai learned how disillusioned the local people had become. The conference began with the usual self-congratulatory speeches, including one by a Central Committee representative, L. S. Sosnovskii, who assured the assembly that the party leadership would support the Zhenotdel against all "liquidators." Later that day the real business of the meeting began with the reading of a Central Section report on Zhenotdel activity over the last six months, a report which included criticism of the provincial sections. The delegates responded angrily that the problems on the local level had arisen because the Central Section had failed to instruct local workers adequately. Defending Kollontai's staff, the two representatives of the Central Committee, Sosnovskii and P. A. Zalutskii, then admitted that the Central Committee had not given the Central Section of the Zhenotdel adequate personnel or guidance and at the same time had asked the Central Section to formulate new programs. The orders to the provinces, therefore, had become confused or communications had broken down altogether.[32]

Two speeches by Sosnovskii and one by Kollontai may have soothed the protest,[33] but there were still provincial leaders at the meeting who were so discouraged by the lack of help they received from Moscow and by the struggle with local Communists that they themselves thought the Zhenotdel should be abolished. Kollontai had been aware of this demoralization in October when she issued a directive ordering the local workers to speed up their preparations for the conference, but the full scope of the problem did not become apparent until the delegates poured out their frustration in Moscow.[34] Now Kollontai knew that the general party disbelief in the Zhenotdel's usefulness had permeated the bureau itself, in part because of failures in her own staff.

The provincial leaders concluded their conference with several resolutions aimed at improving their organization. They stressed the importance of ending "parallelism" between the work of the Zhenotdel and that of Agitprop, promised to bring the sections' activities under "the systematic leadership" of the party committees, and committed the sections to greater work in the protection of female labor, the trade unions, and the party schools. So serious was the demoralization, however, that representatives of four provinces—Ivanovo-Voznesensk, Kaluga, Vladimir, and Novo-Nikolaevsk—actually voted at the meeting to dissolve the Zhenotdel. After the delegates adjourned, the Central Women secured a Central Committee circular letter instructing the provincial and district party committees to support the Zhenotdely, not to do away with them.[35]

The Central Section concentrated in December and January on improving its organization. Kollontai had to retreat on the women's training programs and on work among ethnic minorities and peasants because there was no funding available. In general all the Zhenotdel's operations were hurt by smaller appropriations. At the same time the Central Women scored some success in a program allowing them to do more work among union women. The Central Trade Union Council had refused to permit such campaigns earlier, apparently because the union administrators did not want the Zhenotdel participating in union membership drives. They may also have resented Kollontai's demands to promote women within the unions. In their own defense the union leaders cited the fact that earlier in the year untutored Zhenotdel workers had made confused efforts which only interfered with the unions' programs. Finally, in late 1921, the Central Section and the Trade Union Council managed to draft a plan to cooperate in future agitation.[36]

The disorganization and demoralization of the bureau did not cause Kollontai to temper her conception of it as an advocate for women within the party. She continued her efforts to increase female participation at the higher levels of Soviet institutions. On November 9 she gave an interview to a reporter for the *Chicago Tribune* in which she declared, "I badgered the Government single-handed on the question of giving women representation in all economic institutions and won my point."[37] Just before the Ninth Congress of Soviets which convened in December, the Central Section sent out a letter instructing local Zhenotdel workers to campaign for the election of women delegates to the congress. The Central Women also drafted a slate of ten candidates to the Soviet Executive Committee, of whom four were elected, including Kollontai.[38] In an article in *Pravda* on December 27, the last day of the congress, Kollontai sternly criticized the lack of female representation at the meeting, and stressed, as she had so often before, the contribution women could make to economic reconstruction if they were only given a chance.[39]

Kollontai managed to hold the Zhenotdel together in the fall of 1921. She had to adjust some of the department's programs to aid economic reconstruction, and she had to cut back on most of the department's activities, but in the face of a crisis in organization and morale she was able to keep the Zhenotdel functioning. She also continued to demand attention to women, pushing particularly now on the question of granting women representation and therefore power in government and party. Meanwhile a few members of the Workers' Opposition, most notably Shliapnikov and Medvedev, were planning another protest.

In August 1921, at a party cell meeting, Shliapnikov had attacked the NEP, a move which was within the bounds of free inner-party criticism but which angered Lenin. Lenin demanded that the Central Committee expel the offender from the party for defying the Tenth Congress resolutions. Apparently Lenin was more upset than the rest of the leadership, however, for they refused to vote the two-thirds majority required to expel a Central Committee member, deciding instead to reprimand Shliapnikov and remove him from work in the party purge then underway.[40]

The purge itself took some toll among the Workers' Opposition, although its purpose was larger—to cleanse the party of the kind of non-revolutionaries against whom the Opposition itself protested. Lenin shared Kollontai's concern that alien elements were infiltrating the Bolsheviks, and he wanted the party purified so it could better meet the challenge of the NEP. At the same time he and his colleagues were still defining criticism as dangerous, so they used the purge mechanism to harry conscientious but independent Communists, as well as drunks and idlers. In addition to being threatened with expulsion, the Oppositionists were transferred, reminded that they must watch their tongues, and even spied on through intercepted mail and tapped telephones.[41]

Despite these pressures, Shliapnikov and Medvedev refused to face the fact that organized opposition had become impossible. They were still angry over the inadequacy of the party response to the workers' plight, and as famine spread through the countryside in the summer and unemployment began to rise in the fall, their concern grew. They finally decided after a brief consultation in January or early February 1922 that they must launch an open protest again, so Shliapnikov drew up a petition, the "Declaration of the Twenty-two," for submission to a plenary session of the Comintern Executive Committee scheduled for late February. In the declaration, the Workers' Opposition charged that the Russian party was using the trade unions to suppress the workers. Bureaucratic union officials worked closely with bureaucratic government officials and therefore the workers were growing ever more disillusioned with the Bolsheviks. The declaration called on the Comintern "to do away with all abnormalities" in the Russian party.[42]

Shliapnikov did not expect the foreign Communists to reprimand the Bolsheviks now, when they had been unwilling to do so during the preceding summer. Rather, he sought to force a new round of debate in his own party. He felt that the obstacles to inner-party criticism had grown so great that the leadership would not allow him to make a statement that would reach the rank and file. A plea to the Comintern, on the other hand, would be heard by his entire party.[43] Probably he also assumed that the leadership would have to respond to the protest at the Eleventh Party Congress in late March and therefore would also have to give its signers a chance to speak at that meeting. In presenting the "Declaration of the Twenty-two" to the Comintern Executive Committee in late February, Shliapnikov forced Lenin to discuss the Workers' Opposition at the party congress, rather than continue to coerce the faction into silence.

Kollontai did not sign the initial draft of the declaration. At the Eleventh Party Congress she denied playing any leading role in drawing up the petition, and her critics could produce no evidence that she had been involved in Workers' Opposition activities in the fall of 1921.[44] To all outward appearances she had avoided the faction. Keeping Zhenotdel afloat took all her time. She doubtless stayed informed of Shliapnikov's difficulties and shared his outrage at the continuing harassment of Oppositionists, but she confined her public criticism to demands for improvement in the status of women.

Then, some time in January or early February, Kollontai was dismissed from her post at the Zhenotdel, for reasons which are not altogether clear.[45] She had not distinguished herself by running the woman's bureau well, and she had vocally pointed out shortcomings in the party's work among women. She had even given a critical interview to a capitalist newspaper. Thus it is probable that in the view of party leaders such as Lenin, Stalin, and Zinoviev, her performance as head of the Zhenotdel had been unsatisfactory. She had proved to be just as flamboyant as they had feared when they passed over her for Inessa in 1919.

But Kollontai did not lose her position simply because the Zhenotdel had disintegrated or because she had given an interview to the *Chicago Tribune*. These events did not help her, but the decision to fire her was probably taken largely because of her association with the Workers' Opposition. The charge most often leveled against her at the Eleventh Party Congress was that she had sent her pamphlet, *The Workers' Opposition*, abroad.[46] There the German Communist Labor Party, now roundly critical of the Russian Communists, had spread Kollontai's views all over Europe and North America. In early 1922 the IWW published the pamphlet in Chicago, with an introduction that praised Kollontai for demonstrating all the errors of the Bolshevik dictatorship.[47] It was an embarrassment to Lenin and the other party leaders to have her words used against them by their critics abroad, and to have foreign socialists and Communists see a crack in the facade of Bolshevik unity. Thus it seems likely that Kollontai was dismissed from the Zhenotdel in early February because of the popularity of *The Workers' Opposition* abroad and because of reports that she was still in touch with the faction at home. Then, angry and defiant, she signed the "Declaration of the Twenty-two." With little left to lose, she flung herself back into open opposition, adding her name and that of her old friend Zoia Shadurskaia to the petition.

On February 24 Kollontai made a report to the Comintern Executive Committee on the activities of the Woman's Secretariat during the past six months. On February 26 she returned with Shliapnikov and A. G. Pravdin to present to the committee the "Declaration of the Twenty-two." The delegation demanded a hearing, which they got several days later, but the outcome was never in doubt. An investigative commission was chosen, composed of several members of the Executive Committee, including Kollontai's mentor Clara Zetkin. The commission held hearings, then issued a report which found the "Declaration of the Twenty-two" in violation of the resolutions of the Tenth Party Congress. The commission members agreed with Trotsky and Zinoviev, who had supplied them with copies of the resolutions and who accused the protestors of violating them.[48]

Shliapnikov and Kollontai must have expected this rebuke. The real arena they sought was the Eleventh Party Congress, and in the early weeks of March they made some efforts to rally their supporters in the lower ranks of the party.[49] They still met a sympathetic response in Nizhni-Novgorod and other cities of the central industrial area, but the general reaction was negative. When the Central Committee sent out an order that local party committees should condemn the "Declaration of the Twenty-two," most did so, including Samara, formerly a bastion of the Workers' Opposition. A high-powered delegation headed by Lenin and Zetkin went to a congress of Communist metalworkers in early March, and persuaded them to pass a resolution supporting the decision of the Comintern Executive Committee. Shliapnikov and Medvedev fought to elect their supporters to the governing board of the union, but were defeated.[50]

Shliapnikov, Medvedev, and Kollontai also had to appear before the Central Control Commission of the party to defend their appeal to the Comintern, and those hearings indicated that disciplinary action awaited them. When the congress convened, however, the Oppositionists could take heart from a rebellious mood among the delegates, some of whom questioned the form the NEP was taking, others of whom were planning a resolution to abolish the meddlesome control commissions. Furthermore Lenin, now in failing health, could not attend all the sessions; thus his overwhelming personal influence would be absent. Under those circumstances the Workers' Opposition could hope to convince discontented Communists to vote measures that would improve conditions for the workers and democratize the party.

Lenin was well enough to present the Central Committee's report on the first day of the congress. He admitted that the NEP was a retreat, and he said that in a period of retreat the Bolsheviks needed discipline. The Workers' Opposition had damaged discipline. "When such a retreat occurs in a real army," Lenin threatened with a typically heavy-handed metaphor, "the machine guns stand by, and when an orderly retreat becomes disorderly, the order 'Fire' is given. And rightly."[51]

Lenin did not plan to shoot Bolsheviks, but he did want Kollontai, Shliapnikov, and Medvedev expelled from the party. They had violated discipline repeatedly over the last year and he was through with them. On the evening of March 28, 1922, A. A. Sol'ts, a member of the Central Control Commission which had investigated the Workers' Opposition earlier in the month, accused the signers of the "Declaration of the Twenty-two" of factionalism in that they had written the petition without telling anyone else in the party. Factionalism was now a crime, the punishment for which was expulsion, and Sol'ts asked that this penalty be applied to Shliapnikov, Medvedev, and Kollontai, "who are the organizers of this business." He specifically accused Kollontai of having been a Menshevik until 1915, and of having allowed *The Workers' Opposition* to be published abroad. G. I. Petrovskii, a Ukrainian Bolshevik, then suggested that the congress should appoint a special committee to study the Workers' Opposition's protest "more precisely and objectively." The committee was duly elected, and a group of nineteen men, including Sol'ts, Zinoviev, Stalin, and Dzerzhinskii, began to deliberate the recommendations of the Control Commission.[52]

Shliapnikov and Medvedev defended themselves in eloquent speeches to the congress. Both men denied that they had formed a faction, but claimed instead that the people in their group were simply Old Bolshevik comrades who had become worried about the growing disaffection of the proletariat from the party and who had decided on the spur of the moment to present their worries to the Comintern. They had been unable to appeal to the Central Committee of the party because the leaders would not listen.[53]

When Kollontai spoke on March 29, she too denied that the petitioners were a faction. Responding to the specific charges Sol'ts had leveled against her, she said that she had, in good faith, asked the KAPD to stop publishing her pamphlet. If her former Menshevism was a crime, she could name a number of other Bolsheviks who had still been Mensheviks after she had joined the Zimmerwald Left. In any event, Sol'ts did not dispute the substance of the "Declaration of the Twenty-two," Kollontai declared, because he knew it to be true. She continued:

> The basic content of the appeal says: "The party is split off from the masses." The split exists, it is present, no one denies it. This is our misfortune, this is our pain. When you go to a factory where there are 900 workers, and where during a meeting on a party resolution 22 vote, 4 abstain, and the rest simply do not vote, this shows inertia, a split, that dark side of party life which we must fight against. And another thing shows the split; isn't it typical that here, at the congress, we do not hear a word in the political report about what the working class, strictly speaking, should do.[54]

The party had ruptured its relations with the proletariat because it had stifled free discussion and initiative among its rank and file, and not just because the war had taken its toll among the masses. Thus the link between people and party which existed in the factories had snapped, the Communist worker had lapsed into passivity, and the leaders had become increasingly unresponsive. Kollontai did not renew her attack on bourgeois influences as responsible for this degeneration, and the absence of that argument paradoxically made her charges all the more devastating. No broad social forces, no enemy agents explained the party's betrayal of the revolutionary class in this speech. The Bolshevik leaders' lack of faith in the workers and their intolerance toward the rank and file of their own party had led to the loss of proletarian support, which Kollontai had feared for over a year. Without party democracy, the revolution was in danger. She concluded with a strong call for the Bolsheviks to honor their principles.

> We stand by the resolutions of the Tenth Congress on workers' democracy and freedom of inner-party criticism, we want them to be put into practice, and we shall do everything so that workers' democracy will be firmly established not only on paper, not only in words, but in fact. We want a fundamental, principal, leading role for the workers in the party to be firmly established, recognized in reality. In the creativity of the working masses is our salvation![55]

It was a fine speech, worthy of Kollontai's oratorical skills and her revolutionary idealism, full not of demands for worker control of industry, which she could not advocate without breaking the Tenth Congress resolutions, but of calls for party reform, which were quite in line with other Tenth Congress resolutions. She, Medvedev, and Shliapnikov had gotten their forum at the Eleventh Congress, and perhaps they had even impressed some delegates. The Special Commission deliberating the fate of the Workers' Opposition recommended that Kollontai, Shliapnikov, Medvedev, and two other members of the group, F. A. Mitin and N. V. Kuznetsov, be expelled from the party. The congress delegates did expel the last two, who had joined the Bolsheviks recently. They refused, however, to inflict such drastic punishment on Old Bolsheviks such as Kollontai, Shliapnikov, and Medvedev. Instead the delegates instructed the Central Control Commission to expel the three, should they ever engage in "antiparty relations" in the future.[56]

Throughout the congress Kollontai retained her defiant mood. At a hearing of the Special Commission, she responded to the charge that the twenty-two had held factional meetings by declaring that they should have met more often than they did.[57] But after the congress her spirits fell. No reform was forthcoming, the trade unions lost even more autonomy and experienced further centralization of their internal structures.[58] Although the delegates refused to bow completely to Lenin's will, they did censure the protestors for a violation of party discipline and they refrained from dealing with the issues the opposition had raised. Kollontai had lost her position at the Zhenotdel and now felt the threat of expulsion hanging over her. She later described the spring and summer of 1922 as "months without fruitful work."[59]

Without Kollontai, the Zhenotdel struggled through 1922. It survived, but it never became the assertive advocate for women Kollontai had envisioned. Such a role would have been possible only in a relatively pluralistic party, where interest groups were free to operate openly. The Bolsheviks were not such a party; they institutionalized their distrust of separatism in general and feminist separatism in particular. Strong personalities such as Inessa and Kollontai had been able to overcome this resistance to establish a position of advocacy for the Zhenotdel, but by 1922 they were both gone from the bureau. Kollontai's successor was Sofia Smidovich, who had little status in the party. Nor did she share Inessa's and Kollontai's socialist feminism. Under Smidovich's leadership, the

Central Women toned down their demands for female representation in the government and party. They sought to achieve less controversial goals: full employment for women, maternity protection, child care, delegate conferences, liberation of Muslim women. The radical demands of the founders of the Zhenotdel for the abolition of the family and for female equality throughout the society were not pursued with the vigor accorded to more acceptable social welfare measures which helped women but did not alter their roles as wife, mother, and worker.

For Kollontai, the middle months of 1922 were a time of despair. She went to Odessa to be with Dybenko, who was stationed there, but their relationship had deteriorated beyond salvation. Now Kollontai discovered that he had taken her advice and found himself a younger woman. To the differences between them was also added a fear that her own political disgrace might impede his career. Kollontai wrote to him, "There was a time when our closeness helped you, made your way easier. Now, Pavel, you are grown, strengthened, I am proud of you. But now I not only do not help you, but our closeness is a positive hindrance to your future activity."[60]

The tension in her marriage, coming on the heels of the apparent end of her career, plunged Kollontai into depression. In the summer she wrote to Stalin, the party secretary, asking for a new assignment, and he responded that she should return to Moscow to await a diplomatic post abroad.[61] This was an offer of exile, but Kollontai accepted it. "I truly thought," she confessed later, "that this appointment was to be purely a formality and that I would also find time . . . to devote myself to my literary works."[62]

Georgii Chicherin, the commissar of foreign affairs who had sent her on speaking tours from Paris so many years before, now briefed Kollontai on her impending foreign service. He said she had been chosen because she possessed the necessary social graces, foreign languages, and experience abroad. Chicherin noted that there was resistance in the commissariat to appointing a woman diplomat, but he personally did not think her sex would be a problem. He told her that she was being proposed as envoy to Canada.[63]

While Kollontai waited through the late summer and early fall of 1922 she wrote several articles. One pamphlet, *Soon (In 48 Years)*, described a commune in the Soviet Russia of 1970. The people of that time were pictured as beautiful children who had never experienced capitalist injustice or, Kollontai added in reference to present injustice, known about the Cheka, the Communist secret police.[64] She also wrote the second in a series of articles for the journal for young people, *Molodaia gvardiia*. The first piece, published in January 1922, had been couched as an answer to a young Communist who had written to her asking about communist morality. What standards should a young person use to guide his or her behavior? Kollontai had answered that there were no hard and fast rules, no communist Ten Commandments. Moral norms had a purpose, she wrote, returning to her argument on ethics from 1905; they allowed people to live and work together peacefully. Therefore "right" behavior was behavior which prompted the harmony of the group.[65] Apparently the young Communist thought Kollontai's answer too vague, for he wrote back demanding more substantive rules to govern his behavior. In her second reply, written after the Eleventh Congress, Kollontai told him that she could not give specific guidelines. One learned how to be a communist by mastering Marxism and, she added in a subtle rebuke to the party leadership, by living with the workers.

These were themes Kollontai had been stressing for over a year, and her fundamental premise on the function of morality in furthering "social cohabitation" dated back to her writings of 1905. But now she began gently to add a note of disillusionment.

> So long as a member of a collective he loves (nation, class, *party*) depends on that collective, the commands of that collective will be compulsory for him. For if a member of a collective does not come to obey and support the orders of the collective, its morality, its rules of society, the collective will not tolerate him in its midst. Expulsion from the midst of the collective has always been and remains the harshest and most terrible punishment for a person.[66]

Kollontai steadfastly defended the right of the group to enforce its rules by disciplining its members, but she now showed a realization of the price of her earlier, blind espousal of total dedication to the collective. Before, when she praised the collective, she had meant the working class. Now she added to her list of collectives the nation, which she, the internationalist, had vowed to destroy, and the party, which was expelling her from her homeland for breaking its rules. Was she implying by this juxtaposition that the party, like the nation, was a bogus collective that endangered proletarian solidarity? Was she acknowledging here that the party had become a collective separate from and in some ways equivalent to an entire class? Perhaps, but the evidence for those associations is tenuous at best. What she was saying clearly was that the party was a collective that demanded the absolute loyalty of its members in the belief that only through unity could it survive.

In 1905 and in January 1922 Kollontai had written easily about the group's right to exact obedience to laws of its own creation. Now she had experienced the intolerance of comrades and the isolation of ostracism, and the rules were so strict that she could not express her anguish openly. She masked it with paragraphs that praised, and perhaps attempted to justify, the very "self-defense" of which she was a victim. She now understood the price of her collectivism. During the past year her individual opinions, the fundamentals of her ideology, had come into conflict with the will of the party majority. She had lost, and she was willing to submit to the group's decision. She did not admit that she had been wrong, but only that the party had the right to demand obedience and that she had a duty to obey, to accept the diplomatic exile she had been offered, to leave opposition politics for good. She had always been torn between independence and dependence, solitude and community. Now she chose community, she would subordinate herself to the party because it was the vehicle of the revolution to which she had dedicated herself so many years before. She still had some of the rebelliousness of her youth, she was still capable of fine explosions in the name of her anarchistic Marxism, but she was also fifty years old, and the party and the revolution were her life, however she might disagree with Lenin and Trotsky. In her middle age Kollontai resolved that obedience was preferable to isolation.

In September 1922 Canada refused to accept her because of her reputation as a fiery orator and probably also because of her sex. The Commissariat of Foreign Affairs then nominated Kollontai for a post in a Soviet trade delegation to Norway. The Norwegian authorities approved her quickly, and on October 9, 1922, she left Petrograd for Christiania, five and a half years after the jubilant day she had made the same trip in the other direction.

Kollontai's life at the center of Bolshevik politics had ended. The collective to which she belonged, the collective which had once shunned her friend John Reed, now shunned her. She had taken on her old comrades in open confrontation once too often. The *New York Times* reported, "One ungallant Communist remarked that Mme. Kollontai had constituted herself the official gadfly of the Communist Party, to sting it back into universal opposition."[67] The Bolsheviks had no more use for gadflies than did the ancient Athenians. When she was given the choice of remaining in opposition (as did Shliapnikov and Medvedev) or leaving her country, Kollontai chose to leave. She made a graceful exit to Norway, where she had been happy before. There she could write and see her old friends and perhaps even make something of a career for herself in diplomatic work.

The battle she had joined for the revolution as she defined it had been lost. The easy optimism of 1917 was gone. To industrialize Russia, the Bolsheviks were relying on hierarchy, persuasion, and coercion; they were seeking technological modernization through government fiat, a goal which they had inherited from the tsars but which they pursued with far greater dedication and organization. The world they inhabited was filled with enemies, Russia was a backward country, and the Bolsheviks had to temper their utopianism to hold power and build factories. One of the first ideals they sacrificed to a harsh reality was the notion of proletarian democracy for which Kollontai had spoken.

10

Winged Eros

WHEN SHE LEFT Russia, Kollontai had no intention of becoming a career diplomat. Rather she planned to avoid further
contact with opposition politics and to concentrate on writing about the
problems of women in Soviet society. In November 1922 and again in the
summer of 1923 when she returned to Moscow for brief visits, she was
questioned about her affiliation with the Workers' Opposition and, more
importantly, about her attitudes toward the power struggle among the
party leaders. By 1923 they knew Lenin was dying, and Zinoviev and
Kamenev had forged an alliance with Stalin to block Trotsky's succes-
sion. Bolshevik gossip said that Kollontai had been sent abroad not just
to punish her but to remove her from the new infighting.[1] This was a
dubious claim, since she had never been close to Trotsky politically. Now
however, she also avoided public association with Shliapnikov and Medvedev, who were continuing their criticism of the leadership. She did not
respond to overtures from various opposition members, and she refused
to answer when foreign Communists asked her opinions of the opposition.[2]

Kollontai used her exile to do her last writing on the woman question. In several articles she returned to her old theme of the psychological emancipation of women, but where once she had explored woman's position under capitalism, she now examined it in the emerging socialist society. She also tried her hand at fiction, producing short stories which examined woman's lot and also made frank political criticism. Kollontai probably believed that if she kept her distance from the opposition, she could write as she pleased.

The first of the articles was part of the series she had begun before leaving home, "Letters to Toiling Youth." In the third letter, "About 'The Dragon' and 'The White Bird,' " Kollontai discussed Anna Akhmatova, a lyrical poet distinguished by the introspective, individualistic quality of her work. Akhmatova could provide guidance to the young woman attempting to emancipate herself in the new, transitional society, Kollontai wrote, because she was deeply sensitive to the difficulties a woman experienced in reconciling love and work. Akhmatova understood and had examined in her poetry the conflict between woman's desire for a relationship with a man and her resentment of the sacrifices such a relationship often required.[3]

From discussing Akhmatova's sympathy for woman's dilemma, Kollontai moved in the next article to picturing the kind of erotic love that would not entrap and therefore not create that dilemma. "Make Way for the Winged Eros!" described the relations between men and women in the present and under communism. Kollontai wrote that during the civil war the party had been too busy to deal with the question of love, but now a respite had come in which Communists could think about how to live together. In the crisis of war they had time only for the "wingless Eros," hasty physical liaisons that satisfied sexual needs at the most primitive "biological level." Kollontai condemned such promiscuity as expressing merely "the reproductive instinct" and therefore lacking the "spiritual" interaction that should characterize love. She, like Engels and Bebel before her, believed erotic love should contain emotional commitment. It was understandable, Kollontai wrote, that in a period of upheaval people would concentrate on survival, thus having no energy left for long-term relationships, but now the crisis was over. Now the new society could cultivate the "winged Eros," love which would function as part of the building of communism by forging bonds of "comradely solidarity" between the members of the collective. This was the vision which Kollontai had created in her prewar articles on the new woman. The "winged Eros" was eroticism with the possessiveness removed, it was the attraction of equals that enhanced the harmony of the group rather than isolating the couple in self-absorption. Such love was based on three principles:

(1) Equality in mutual relations (without male self-centeredness and the slavish dissolution of personality in love on the part of the woman);

(2) Mutual recognition of the rights of the other, without a claim to rule the heart and soul of the other completely (the feeling of property developed by bourgeois culture);

(3) Comradely sensitivity, the capacity to listen and understand the work of a congenial soul and beloved person (bourgeois society demands this sensitivity in love only on the part of the woman).[4]

Kollontai saw the development of such love as an integral part of the building of communism. For a collective to prosper, its members must care for one another. All must learn to work together in mutual respect and forebearance, and those men and women who loved one another erotically must learn to live that love without separating themselves from the group or attempting to possess one another. To achieve this transformation, communist society must increase the human being's ability to care for his fellow creatures, must civilize, or rather perfect, human nature. People must learn to express all of the varieties of love freely, and to do that they had to escape the bourgeois notion that the only form of erotic love permissible was the "love of the legally married, conjugal pair."[5]

Kollontai did not declare that marriage should be abolished. She merely said that bourgeois monogamy was not the only form in which heterosexual love should be permitted. Often a woman was drawn to one man by his spirit, to another by his physical appeal, and she should not be barred from pursuing both loves. So long as love was based on the "higher," less carnal human emotions, Kollontai welcomed it. She did not recommend that everyone should have multiple affairs. She said that the proletariat must release eroticism from its bourgeois fetters and allow people to express their love for one another freely. Then whatever happened would be part of the proletariat's new morality and therefore progressive. Kollontai, like Engels, refused to prophesy the exact form of relations between women and men in the future. She knew only that isolation would end.

Collectivism of will and spirit will conquer individualistic self-sufficiency. The coldness of spiritual solitude, from which people in bourgeois culture often seek salvation in love and marriage, will disappear; a multitude of ties binding people to one another in emotional and spiritual union will grow. The feelings of people will change in the sense of a growth of community, and the inequality between the sexes and every kind of dependence of woman on man will disappear without a trace, lost in the memory of past centuries.[6]

In the present Kollontai asserted that the proletariat was working out its morality as part of building the new society. Already the "winged Eros," the coupling of women and men who were equals, was emerging. It should be "free love," that is, it should be unbound by convention. This was a liberal view of sexuality, but not a libertine one; it was very close to Engels and Bebel and to Kollontai's articles on the new woman. Erotic love remained for her what it had always been—an expression of the human search for community.

Kollontai continued to conjure up this vision in six works of fiction also published in 1923. In the fiction she added criticism of the unemployment that was rising among women and she railed against the material need that still made women sell themselves to men. For example, "Sisters," a short story, painted a sympathetic portrait of a woman who had been driven to prostitution because she had no job. Kollontai wrote that the prostitute and the wife of the party official who bought the prostitute were "sisters," because the oppression of woman by man created a bond between them.[7] She made this argument repeatedly in the fiction, and she also explored the difficulties women faced in choosing between love and work in the new society.

In a collection of short stories published early in 1923 under the title *Woman at the Turning Point*, Kollontai presented women torn between men who did not want them to work and the work which was their means to independence. The unnamed heroine of "Thirty-two Pages" finally chooses to leave her husband, but only after much agonizing over the loneliness that such a choice entails. Walking alone along a foggy street at night, she examines her love for a man and for her work as a scientist, which she has had to curtail in order to live in the provincial town where her husband is employed.

She will go her own way, she won't let herself be shackled by the chains of love. Not thinking about him, not looking back. Going ahead all the time, toward her goal. Alone, so that no one will delay her on the way, deflect her to the side. Going, as now, through the fog, but knowing that ahead there is a light, her goal, her scientific work. It doesn't matter that it's difficult, that her feet stick in the sand, that the package of books and provisions weighs down her arms, that the hem of her skirt beats around her legs unmercifully. Isn't it difficult to be alone? In return, you gain freedom, in return you belong to your beloved work—scientific work. Herself and her work! And no more misunderstanding, no resentment that there are differences with him, that he doesn't listen to her soul, doesn't value her cherished work. Living and not suffering. Living and not loving anymore with a feeling of despair. Well, so what? Let him not understand. Let him not listen. But being together, seeing him, reassuring herself over and over again that he still loves her. And work, her work, well conceived, stands still, doesn't progress. All these months. Oh, that waking up with the sharp thought that burns the consciousness like a pain until it hurts: five months, and only thirty-two pages written.[8]

The third and longest story in *Woman at the Turning Point*, "A Great Love," describes Kollontai's affair with Maslov in the same terms, reaching the embittered conclusion that relationships with men always end in mutual recrimination, that women must pursue their own careers, that no man will allow them to do that. With an anger she had not shown in "Make Way for the Winged Eros!" Kollontai declared that marriage was doomed because people did not know how to love. Perhaps she was still suffering over her divorce from Dybenko, or perhaps she was simply expressing the disillusionment of a lifetime spent pursuing a lasting relationship she never found. Her condemnation of marriage did not limit her faith in the possibility of a purified erotic love, however. That faith had endured all her disappointments. Kollontai had always believed in love, but she had never believed that it could be successfully institutionalized in marriage.

There has been speculation that "A Great Love" was actually a portrait of Lenin's relationship with Inessa, and that Stalin forced Kollontai to publish it in 1927 because he wanted to humiliate Krupskaia. Thereby he dissuaded Krupskaia from joining the United Opposition led by Trotsky, Zinoviev, and Kamenev.[9] In fact, however, Kollontai was writing about herself, and the story first appeared in 1923, not 1927. It is doubtful that Stalin would have tried to threaten Krupskaia with such a weak reed, when he could have used more persuasive weapons against her.[10]

The present economic difficulties women faced and the love-work conflict were also Kollontai's central concern in a second set of short stories published in 1923, *The Love of the Worker Bees*. The heroine of the first story, Vasilisa Malygina, is a dedicated Communist who chooses to put her career ahead of her marriage to her comrade husband, who has been corrupted by the NEP. She leaves him, after coming to pity his mistress, a bourgeois woman unable to live without a male to support her. When Vasilisa returns to Moscow from the provincial town where her husband works, she finds that she is pregnant, but rather than go back to the father of her child she decides to rear the baby herself and continue her career as a party member alone.[11] Once again Kollontai sees solitude as the price women must pay for independence.

In this story Kollontai added to her portrait of the emancipated woman direct criticism of Soviet society under the NEP. She pictured party officials as overly fond of power and material possessions, and in one particularly scathing characterization she presented a police agent as a fop with carefully waxed mustache and fine leather boots. The compromise tactics of the party had led now, Kollontai said in no uncertain terms, to the corruption of weak-willed communists and to a widening of the already dangerous rift between party and proletariat.

The Love of the Worker Bees also contained a story entitled "The Love of Three Generations," which was destined to become well known in Europe and to brand Kollontai as an advocate of promiscuity. Its heroine, a young woman named Zhenia, is caught up in the civil war and has no time for commitment to anything but revolution. Desiring to satisfy herself physically, yet unwilling to divert herself with a real love affair, Zhenia sleeps with many men, including her mother's husband. She becomes pregnant but plans to have an abortion and go back to party work. Kollontai appears in the story as an older Communist to whom Zhenia tells her story; she listens bemused and tolerant, understanding the girl's amorality as a product of her dedication to communism and her inability to establish long-term relationships in a time of crisis. Kollontai does not approve of Zhenia's promiscuity, but neither does she condemn it. It is presented as a phase through which society is passing, a symptom of the genesis of a new morality.[12]

Through her fiction Kollontai's ideas on erotic love spread around the world, becoming known by the end of the twenties even in China. This was unfortunate, because the stories do not contain as full a statement of her views as articles such as "Make Way for the Winged Eros!" A reader unaware that Kollontai disapproved of promiscuity could see Zhenia as a model, and even young, middle-class Chinese cited Kollontai as advocating casual sex.[13] In Soviet Russia, her name was widely identified with "the glass of water theory," a defense of promiscuity on the grounds that one should satisfy the sex drive as simply as one satisfies thirst. Kollontai did not originate or even favor "the glass of water theory," but one could draw that conclusion from reading only "The Love of Three Generations."

Kollontai's fiction is thus an incomplete guide to her views on erotic love. It is also bad literature. It lacks the strength of her sometimes overwritten but generally lucid and well-organized nonfiction. The characters are one-dimensional, the females all saintly, maternal, and committed to the cause and to other women, the men childish, demanding, selfish, and not a little stupid. The men are also easily corrupted by the NEP, while the women remain untarnished, unless they are bourgeois in origin. The prose is florid, and the ideas are hammered home with a lack of subtlety suited more to an agitational harangue than to fiction. Kollontai made major points—that women were still having to choose between love and work, that they still had to contend with economic insecurity, unsympathetic husbands, and pregnancy, that Soviet society should permit a variety of relationships between women and men. When she discussed the same issues in nonfiction, she produced work which suffered less from her didactic tendencies and which presented her ideas in more complete form.

The publications of 1923 were the last in which Kollontai spoke for women, for party reform, and for communalization. Her socialism was based on those three elements—community, revolutionary purity, and female emancipation. The uniqueness of her voice within Bolshevism came from her eloquent defense of her ideals and from the way those ideals intermingled and were strengthened by their mutual dependence. The emancipation of women and the emancipation of all people would proceed from the creation of a harmonious society, built by the working class and by a party of revolutionaries who refused to compromise their principles. It was a fine vision, unsullied by realism. Factories, electrification, uneducated workers, military power, foreign policy, nuts and bolts —none of these concerned Kollontai. She demanded communes, revolutionary purity, and the emancipation of women. And 1923 was the last year she was allowed to do so.

A Soviet reviewer in that year pointed out the deficiencies of *Woman at the Turning Point*. The style was poor, he wrote, and the subject matter reminiscent of prewar ladies' magazines. The reviews of *The Love of the Worker Bees* were more mixed; one commentator said the book was "lively and fascinating," but another advised Kollontai to confine herself to nonfiction.[14] These notices in relatively nonpolitical journals, however, were not the ones that mattered, and by the fall of 1923 Kollontai found herself under attack in the party press.

The new criticism of her work began with a hint in midsummer. On July 26 Polina Vinogradskaia, one of Kollontai's former colleagues at the Zhenotdel, published an attack on recent articles by Trotsky. She said he was wasting his time writing about literature when the workers were struggling with the practical problems of daily life. In fact, Trotsky had been taking a rest from political squabbling to explore serious questions of art in the new society, and Vinogradskaia was picking at his ruminations.[15] She went on to lay out her own thoughts about abolishing the bourgeois family, but in a footnote she included a gibe at Kollontai. "Comrade Kollontai, in the journal *Molodaia gvardiia*, occupies herself now with purely intellectual literary exercises about the 'winged, wingless, etc., Eros.'" The average woman cared far more about feeding her children than about reforming love.[16] Vinogradskaia was probably correct in that assertion, but her criticism of Trotsky and Kollontai was gratuitous. The reforms she discussed in the article were those Kollontai had always championed, and she did not need to attack either Kollontai or Trotsky in order to argue for better communal facilities.

The attack on Kollontai became more intense in the fall. In *Molodaia gvardiia* a Communist named Arvatov criticized her theories on sexuality. Arvatov took issue with Kollontai's praise of Anna Akhmatova, whom he condemned as a bourgeois poet. He did not want young people reading Akhmatova, and he advised them not to accept Kollontai's positive appraisal of her. Furthermore he did not approve of Kollontai's concentration on female personality. The problem under socialism, he wrote, was the development of a new human personality, not just a new woman. Kollontai's special emphasis on women was feministic. After he made that charge, Arvatov added in parentheses, "I personally beg the author's pardon."[17]

Arvatov did not care for Kollontai's stress on the difficulties of reconciling love and work. Like many Communists, he did not understand her assertion that women had to overcome the tendency to put their lover's needs ahead of their own. Kollontai felt that the psychological development of women under socialism would be somewhat different from men's, because female bondage was deeply ingrained in the psyches of both sexes; Arvatov rejected that notion because he felt it was not "scientific," but "feministic." In so charging, he was expressing the fundamental Marxist reluctance to see woman's position as determined by elements different from those determining man's. Such criticism might not be original, but it was genuine, in that it was part of the ideological argument over female oppression which Marxists had been engaged in for years.

In her second, direct attack on Kollontai, which may have been approved in advance by Krupskaia,[18] Polina Vinogradskaia did not debate issues so much as she attempted to demolish Kollontai's writing in order to discredit her politically. Vinogradskaia began by saying that now was indeed a good time to discuss questions of secondary importance, such as sex and family, but that one must be careful to keep the discussions thoroughly Marxist. Kollontai's articles in *Molodaia gvardiia* did not do that; they wandered off into "metaphysics." "Comrade Kollontai takes off with great zest on trips to the communist future, filling the sails of the socialist boat with the wind of sexual problems."[19] Vinogradskaia accused Kollontai of not grounding her speculations in materialism, of ignoring the practical problems of daily life, and of claiming the development of socialism depended on relations between the sexes. The article was laced with slander and half-truths: Kollontai had always been petty-bourgeois, she was guilty of "George Sandism," she had been influenced by the anarchists Kropotkin and Tolstoi. She was "a woman Communist with a solid dose of feminist trash." Almost at the end of the article, Vinogradskaia came to the crux of the matter. "How could she have been considered for so long one of the leaders not only of the Russian, but of the international Communist women's movement?"[20]

Like Arvatov, Vinogradskaia stood on solid ideological ground when she charged that Kollontai wanted sexual relations changed independently of the material substructure. The dispute among Marxists over how much purposive effort would be required to alter social relations was longstanding; Kollontai had always believed in morality as a tool in the change, not as a simple concomitant of it, and in that belief she differed significantly from many Bolsheviks. Vinogradskaia went beyond intellectual debate, however. She threw every slander she could summon into the fight, with the purpose of destroying Kollontai's influence. Her goal was more political than intellectual: she wanted to be certain that young Communists would wonder why this woman, with her "petty-bourgeois" notions, had ever been considered a leader.

Kollontai took these articles as a sign from the party leadership, and after 1923 she published nothing more about female personality and never ventured a public word of political criticism. Marcel Body, a French Communist who had worked with Inessa and who was Kollontai's friend and colleague in the trade mission to Norway, said many years later that Kollontai had at the time protested strongly against the attacks on her. She may even have returned to Moscow for a hearing before the Control Commission on her association with the Workers' Opposition. Body's memory was not always reliable, but he wrote that after Kollontai convinced Stalin that she had severed her connection with her former comrades, the press campaign stopped. An apology for the Vinogradskaia article was published in December.[21]

Although the exact details of Kollontai's response to Vinogradskaia are uncertain, the motives for the attacks of 1923 and their effect are relatively clear. The accusations that Kollontai was a feminist, made by Krupskaia and Natalia Sedova (Trotsky's wife) to the *New York Times* early in the year,[22] and repeated by Arvatov and Vinogradskaia in the fall, were at least in part politically motivated. No doubt the accusers also disliked Kollontai's articles for their content, but Kollontai's theories on erotic love had been well known for years, and she had been attacked publicly for her writing about women only in 1921, during the Tenth Party and Comintern congresses. Even then Bukharin and Trotsky joked about her opinions on the woman question, without directly charging feminism. Now, in 1923, worry lingered that she would return to opposition, and she herself may have increased that concern with the criticism of NEP society that appeared in the fiction. Thus a few Communists attacked her ideas on female emancipation, which had always been controversial, as a way to diminish the influence of a woman who had once been "one of the leaders not only of the Russian but of the international Communist women's movement."

Again, it is true that many party members found Kollontai's articles unacceptable because they thought her "winged Eros" a grand name for old-fashioned promiscuity. Vinogradskaia wrote much later that she and Krupskaia had discussed Kollontai's writings on erotic love, and that Krupskaia had said such ideas should not appear in party publications.[23]

Nor did the majority of Communists understand Kollontai's talk about woman's complete psychological emancipation. Rarefied notions of the perfecting of human personality through communalization had never appealed to the more traditional Marxists, who saw revolution primarily as a process of political and economic change; now the party contained more people than ever who had few intellectual predilections and an overwhelming interest in practical matters—personal improvement, decent housing, bureaucratic management. To them Kollontai's ideas really did seem bourgeois, the ramblings of a George Sand, sanctioning immorality.

Furthermore, these Communists considered promiscuity to be a problem in Soviet Russia. In the early twenties, there really were thousands of Zhenias who preached that the revolution meant sexual freedom; complaints circulated in the party that young Bolsheviks were pressuring each other into bed by accusing anyone who resisted of petty-bourgeois morality. Given the primitive quality of birth control methods then available, many girls found themselves pregnant and abandoned by their once ardent comrades. Without sufficient day care, without decent jobs, these young women were burdened by liberal sexual mores. How to protect them from the new freedom was becoming a heated point of debate among Communists just when Kollontai published "The Love of Three Generations." Some favored increasing maternity and child care and other communal facilities.[24] Others, advocates of traditional marital relations, wanted to diminish sexual experimentation and make fathers responsible for supporting their children.[25] By 1926 the party leadership had swung toward the more traditional position, because they disliked the instability produced by the new morality, because they had never accepted the liberal attitude toward sexuality of Engels, Bebel, and Kollontai, and because they did not think they had the funds to pay for the maternity care and nurseries that would support the offspring of unregulated sexuality. This renewed stress on traditional morality was beginning in 1923, and the criticism of Kollontai reflected a growing feeling against the Zhenias.

When Kollontai left Russia in 1922, she had thought that if she avoided contact with the opposition she could write. She had sought to retreat to Norway, from which she could continue to examine the position of women and vent her spleen over the effects of the NEP. That had been a realistic hope, for the twenties were a period of experimentation in Soviet Russia, and the press teemed with debate about the daily life of the new society. Kollontai found, however, that the role of writer in exile was not open to her. She was expected to cease her feministic musings and behave herself.

After 1923 she concentrated on diplomatic notes and her memoirs. In 1924 she published *Fragments from a Diary*, which described her experience in Germany in August 1914. As she had done in *Around Workers' Europe* so many years before, Kollontai shaped her diaries into a good journalistic narrative, in which she controlled her sentimentality and allowed herself to be an observer. It was an unusual accomplishment, since autobiography is such a personal medium, so conducive to egocentricity, but Kollontai was adept at it. In the *Fragments* and a later book, *In Kerensky's Prison* (1927), she recorded personal images of events that are far more successful as literary works than was the fiction she loved but had not the temperament to master.[26]

Kollontai did allow her work to be published abroad in translation, so that at the very time she was being condemned at home she was reaching a new audience in Western Europe. Feminists and socialists accepted her as one of a number of writers on the new sexual freedom of the twenties, and some students of the status of women read the lectures she had given in 1921, published as *The Labor of Woman in the Evolution of the Economy*. In the thirties, when the interest in feminism waned, Kollontai's writing also went into eclipse, to be rediscovered with the woman's movement that began in the 1960s. This development has been confined to those countries where feminism has reappeared. In the Communist nations of Eastern Europe and Asia, only Kollontai's proposals for social services such as day-care centers remain known, for those governments consider sexual liberation libertine and irrelevant.[27]

No longer able to write about the psychological emancipation of women, Kollontai thought she could continue to make suggestions for reforms that would improve women's daily lives. In 1926, therefore, when she returned to Moscow after completing her assignment in Norway, she joined in a debate over revision of the Soviet marriage code. Since 1918, evidence had been growing that the law enacted with such fanfare during the early days of the revolution had actually increased women's burdens. Community property had been abolished, allowing men to walk out on their wives and take all the family's assets with them. The lack of a clear statement of the father's financial responsibility for his children meant that he could abandon them, and the wife could receive restitution only through litigation. Women who had not registered their marriages with the government—and there were many such women—were in even greater difficulty, for they had no legal recourse. A marriage code that had been designed to liberate was thus enabling some men to victimize dependent women. By 1925 the government had decided that the law had to be rewritten to reinstitute alimony. If men could be forced to support their families, it was believed they might not abandon so many women or father so many unwanted children. The proposed law also recognized common law marriages, that is, those that had not been registered, as legal and the spouses in such marriages as entitled to alimony. Furthermore it asserted the right of the wife to share in property which the couple had acquired during their marriage.[28]

However circumspect she had now become, Kollontai could not ignore the marriage law debate. It was so much a part of her life's work. In a speech to a group of Soviet workers in January 1926, she suggested dealing with the problem of woman's dependence on the father of her children by broadening public funding of child care. She dismissed as petty-bourgeois the proposed law which reinstituted the legal responsibility of men. Equally mistaken were those people who claimed that easy divorce encouraged licentiousness. Society had moved to a new stage, Kollontai said; its marital relations now must perforce be new, and therefore difficult for people nurtured in old values to understand.

Kollontai urged Communists to innovate, not to cling to the morality of the past. The proposed law code required the payment of alimony in both common law and registered marriage, which seemed a great advance, superficially. Suppose, however, a man had several common-law wives? Suppose a woman had one "registered" husband and one common-law husband? Suppose the man was too poor to support his wife? Above all, what would happen to the unmarried woman with a child to rear?

Rather than alimony, Kollontai proposed marriage contracts which would spell out the division of family property. The peasants were greatly concerned about the ambiguity of present laws as they applied to land and household goods. Kollontai believed that a clear contract drawn up between the spouses when they married would resolve that problem. She also wanted marriage contracts among the proletariat, but for a different reason.

These contracts . . . are important for women workers, who in this way can know that their housework also counts for something and is recognized to be just as important as work in factories and plants. For as long as we have the consumer cell in the person of the working family we must understand that the woman's labor in this cell should be taken into account in some way and valued. This would lead to a real equality of the members of the cell, not in words but in deeds.[29]

Kollontai was making an extraordinary proposal. She had backed away from her calls for the immediate construction of collectives, had accepted the nuclear family as inevitable in the present, and was suggesting written agreements which took into account the full economic contributions of the woman. One Soviet economist estimated very conservatively in 1923 that the Russian woman spent ten percent more time working than her husband, chiefly because five hours of her day were taken up with housework.[30] To remedy this situation Kollontai wanted marriage contracts, a solution that would be suggested by feminists in the United States forty years later.

For unmarried women she proposed the creation of maternity benefits funded by payroll deductions of about two rubles per year per worker. Single women could draw payments for obstetrical care and child support, as could divorced women. The obligation for bearing those expenses among the married would be spelled out in their marriage contracts. Privately paid alimony and the complicated laws regulating it would then be unnecessary. Nor would the new system encourage immorality; Kollontai sensed strongly that much of the pressure for more conservative measures came from people reacting against the freer sexual mores of the young. Communists must fight excesses by teaching their children to work for the collective, not retreat into "petty-bourgeois family illusions."[31]

There was support for Kollontai's proposals among youthful party members, but the leadership felt the conservative peasantry would not accept the contract notion. Nor was it feasible in a nation of high illiteracy. The leaders themselves did not give serious consideration to Kollontai's plan, because she was too discredited for her ideas to count for much. After a few critics accused her of feminism, her suggestions were ignored. The new marriage law attempted to protect women in marital relationships with a clear statement of the responsibilities of the partners. Irritated at what she saw as another compromise of socialist principle, Kollontai wrote shortly thereafter that the Soviet Union's code was little better than those of the most progressive Western democracies.[32]

Her contribution to the marriage law debate was the last echo of the work for women Kollontai had begun in 1905. She recognized that a great deal had been accomplished in the Soviet Union since the revolution. Women had made substantial advances toward political equality. They were equal to men in the eyes of Soviet law. Education was now fully open to them. They could claim generous maternity benefits. The government still had not provided substantial day care; it would not do so for decades, but a start had been made. These were major gains, achieved very rapidly by a regime that had also been struggling to survive, and Kollontai accepted them as laying the foundation for female emancipation. Her disappointment over the marriage law did not diminish her awareness of the enormous significance of her government's dedicating itself to emancipating women. None of the Western democracies had made even such a verbal commitment.

Yet Kollontai wanted more. She could propose a plan as impractical and visionary as marriage contracts in 1926, when peasant men still considered it their right to beat their wives and when in Central Asia outraged Muslims murdered Zhenotdel workers for attempting to unveil Muslim women.[33] Kollontai had always envisioned a far more thoroughgoing emancipation than did other Bolsheviks and the people of her country. Over the years she had encountered resistance to her most controversial proposals from women as well as men, resistance which meant that the full scope of her vision—women working equally with men, their children cared for collectively and their household duties taken over by communal facilities—could not have been realized. There simply was not enough support among the population, and the party could not be induced to push the people into Kollontai's conception of full emancipation when the party itself gave it only lukewarm support. The Bolshevik leadership made pledges to communalize "housework," but they were considerably less enthusiastic about the communalization of child rearing, which would have meant a genuine alteration in the assignment of roles within the nuclear family. Had they been wholly committed to that change, they would have lacked the resources to realize it and they would have faced enormous public resistance.

More feasible was Kollontai's demand that the party promote women into positions of authority throughout the Soviet system. Here the male leadership balked. They had always resented calls for special treatment for women, but by the early twenties they could no longer defend that resistance on ideological grounds. There were already too many reforms that took account of women's burdens, and there existed the Zhenotdel. The party leaders believed, however, that granting women equality of opportunity was enough; special efforts to encourage their progress, such as instructing middle-echelon managers to promote them, were unnecessary. Soviet women did in fact make great strides in subsequent decades, rising to prominent positions in industry, education, and the arts, far outstripping the women of Europe and North America. They did not gain access to political power, however. The upper echelons of the Communist Party remained almost exclusively male, because women were still tied down by marriage and family responsibilities and because men did not want to grant them access to power. Kollontai, seeing that the party leadership was making no effort to bring women into the inner sanctums of the Soviet hierarchy, called for deliberate efforts to advance women. She did not win her case, and the reason seems largely to have been male prejudice, reinforced by the ideological resistance to separatism.

Kollontai's party, impelled by the commitments to women in its platform and by the prodding of Kollontai, Inessa, Samoilova, and the Zhenotdel, accomplished more reform for women between 1917 and 1929 than any other European political movement. In so doing, the Bolsheviks overcame significant opposition within Russia but they stopped short of abolishing women's traditional roles and eliminating traditional discrimination. Thus women continued to work as wives and mothers, and added work outside the home to their duties. This triple responsibility meant they could not function as men's full equals in Soviet society. They lacked the time and the mobility of men and they still had to battle discrimination.

Furthermore, the Bolsheviks persisted, before and after they took power, in tempering their commitment to women with their fears of separatism and their unexamined prejudice. Thus they screamed "feminism" far too often, and on these grounds, resisted Kollontai's demands for the enactment of reforms to which they were already committed on paper. When Stalin came to power, he openly embraced the nuclear family as the basic unit of Soviet society, and woman remained wife, mother, and factory worker. Thereafter the Soviet Union proudly and complacently claimed to have emancipated women completely. But as Lenin had said:

The chief thing is to get women to take part in socially productive labor, to liberate them from "domestic slavery," to free them from their stupefying and humiliating subjugation to the eternal drudgery of the kitchen and the nursery.

This struggle will be a long one, and it demands a radical reconstruction both of social technique and of morals. But it will end in the complete triumph of communism.[34]

The party had never sought female emancipation to the extent that it preached it, and this difference between professed goals and actual performance was the source of Kollontai's anger. The communism of which Lenin spoke, of which women's equality was so integral a part, had been postponed to an indefinite future, and Kollontai's socialist feminism was once again unacceptable to Bolsheviks. She turned to her work as a diplomat. When she wrote about the position of women again, it was to praise Soviet achievements in the docile prose that became characteristic of her chastened middle age.

11

Diplomat

FROM 1924 UNTIL 1945 Kollontai devoted herself to her work as a diplomat. When she left Russia, she did not intend to spend the rest of her life in this new career. She thought she could write and wait until the attitude toward her in Moscow had softened. That never happened, and Kollontai remained abroad. She made of her banishment a graceful exile, learned to hold her tongue, and managed to survive the purge of the 1930s, in which most of the Old Bolsheviks died. The last twenty-five years of Kollontai's life were a retreat from which she was never to come back.

In Norway, Kollontai managed to play her role as obedient Communist by working in the trade delegation. When she arrived in Christiania, her colleagues did not know what her duties were to be within the mission, because the Commissariat of Foreign Affairs was still making futile efforts to place her in Canada but also because her assignment had been arranged so hastily.[1] Apparently Kollontai set to work with an industry that impressed Chicherin, the commissar of foreign affairs, for in February 1923 the commissariat announced that she would become head of the trade delegation. In late May she received that appointment. Kollontai spent the rest of the year negotiating trade agreements and testing the Norwegian attitude toward *de jure* recognition of the Soviet Union.[2] In February 1924 Norway extended recognition, taking its cue from Great Britain, which had broken the diplomatic ostracism of the Bolsheviks shortly before. By December 1925 a trade treaty was signed, as a result of talks held primarily in Moscow, and Kollontai considered her mission to Oslo complete.[3]

She seemed to be adjusting to the demands of her new career. Occasionally she broke strict protocol; she once wrote directly to the Norwegian Ministries of Agriculture, Education, and Trade asking for interviews and received a polite message from the Ministry of Foreign Affairs that in the future she should contact other departments only through them.[4] Kollontai soon mastered the fine points of diplomatic etiquette, however. As Chicherin had predicted, the social graces she had learned in her childhood stood her in good stead, and she quickly developed her own style, compounded of charm and the caution she was coming to in middle age.

Still she chafed under the restriction of carrying out orders from home, and sometimes, when the endless negotiations slowed, she seized the initiative. One minor sale of fish bogged down over a 50 øre difference (equivalent to 10¢ in U.S. currency) in the price the Norwegians were asking and the Soviets were willing to pay. Exasperated, Kollontai told the exporters, "You take off 25 øre per barrel and we shall add 25 øre. If my government finds that I have acted without authorization, I am ready to pay this sum out of my salary for the rest of my life."[5] The ploy moved the Norwegians to split the difference and the sale was made.

Many newspapers in Europe and the United States printed exaggerated stories about Kollontai, the wild-eyed woman revolutionary now turned diplomat. One French paper declared that the feathers of her hat were red with the blood of the Bolsheviks' innocent victims. A president of the National Association of Manufacturers charged in 1923 that a child labor law, proposed for the United States, was inspired by "the communist work of a mysterious Soviet bureaucrat named Madame Kollontai," and for the next three years American organizations opposed to reforms in child labor practices claimed that social feminists in the United States were part of an international feminist conspiracy masterminded by Kollontai. There were also stories that she secretly bought high-fashion clothes in Paris with embassy funds, and that she was smuggling Soviet spies into Norway by arranging marriages to Norwegian citizens. None of these fabrications bothered the Norwegian Foreign Ministry, and Kollontai did not encounter resistance from the government because of her gender.[6] She had always loved Norway, she was busy, she was among friends, and she was even learning to ski. In her spare moments she took pleasure from the beauty of the country. A letter to Zoia Shadurskaia described a trip from Bergen to Oslo:

> I got on the train, spent the night there, and to the astonishment of the conductor, rushed out of the sleeping car at the highest point we went through, Finse station. On the tracks the eternal snows. A clean mountain hotel. Today a marvellous sky. The sun is hot but there is snow on the mountains and in the crevasses of the hotel itself. A mountain lake. Steel blue and cold, as if made of ice. A glacier has crept into it.[7]

The moods of euphoria were short-lived, however, for in addition to feeling the sting of the attacks on her writing, Kollontai did not like the confinement of diplomatic life. In the summer of 1925 she wrote Maksim Litvinov, then deputy commissar of foreign affairs, that she was going to ask the Central Committee and the Commissariat of Foreign Affairs to relieve her of her duties. "I am morally and physically tired of the eternal 'full dress coat' which this work demands," she explained.[8] The party leaders had no desire for her to return from exile. By 1925 Stalin had begun to turn against Zinoviev and Kamenev, his former allies, Trotsky had lost virtually all his power, and the old leadership was beginning to realize the threat posed by Stalin, who now controlled job assignments. In that atmosphere Stalin wanted former troublemakers such as Kollontai to remain abroad.

According to Marcel Body, Kollontai's friend and co-worker in Norway, she did not intend to join the anti-Stalin group. She could not quite forgive Zinoviev and Trotsky their earlier attacks on her, but, more important, she thought their cause was lost and she was tired of fighting against overwhelming odds. When she heard that the party had denounced Angelica Balabanoff, she lamented to Body, "How can one fight, how can one defend oneself against injury? They have at their command too many means to diffuse it." Apparently what she wanted was party permission to leave diplomatic service so that she could rest and write her memoirs. Although she sent messages of support to Zeth Höglund and Fredrik Ström when they were expelled from the Swedish Communist Party, and although she admitted to them that she still heard from Shliapnikov occasionally, Kollontai had no heart for combat now. More than once she said that she just wanted to be free.[9]

In the winter of 1925–26 she returned to Moscow to plead her case. There she attended the Fourteenth Party Congress, where Kamenev openly accused Stalin of assuming one-man rule over the party, and she wrote to Ström afterward that the approval of Stalin's and Bukharin's leadership meant "carrying out the peasants' policy." She still thought the government was allowing the peasantry too much economic autonomy, at the price of delaying communalization of agriculture. Her opinions of Stalin she kept to herself.[10] Publicly she participated in the marriage law debate, and the criticism of her proposals as feministic indicated that Stalin's supporters still considered Kollontai suspect politically. In the fall when she was offered the post of Soviet representative to Mexico, she accepted it and left Moscow.

Kollontai went to Berlin, where Marcel Body met her, and she confided to him that she still wanted to leave government work. Perhaps the Central Committee would give her permission to go to France, to write her memoirs. Body replied that such permission would never come; she would have to break with the party altogether. Did she have the strength for it? he asked. Could she face a life cut off from Russia, engaged in émigré politics? She replied that she could not. She had once again rejected the overtures of opposition members such as Kristian Rakovskii while in Moscow, and the German Communist Ruth Fischer, who saw Kollontai in Berlin, found her "depressed and unwilling to continue 'the hopeless struggle.' "[11]

These were the components of Kollontai's despair. Stalin would win, she could become an émigré or stay in the party away from the center, as a diplomat. She did not like diplomacy because of its personal and political restrictions; she had to move carefully, cultivate patience, and take orders. Yet her only alternative to diplomacy was a useless life among the exiles in Paris. She loved work and she still believed in the Soviet experiment. Thus she decided that serving from a distance was preferable to writing her memoirs.

Kollontai arrived in Mexico on December 7, 1926, but her appointment had stirred a controversy even before she came. In October she had requested permission to cross the United States en route to Mexico City, and Secretary of State Frank B. Kellogg had wired back that she was "inadmissible" on the grounds that, in the words of a State Department press release, "she has been actively associated with the International Communist subversive movement."[12] Kellogg was not so much worried about allowing a dangerous Red to enter the United States, however, as he was intent on expressing his displeasure over her appointment to Mexico, a country considered vital to American political and economic interests. Many U.S. newspapers and some congressmen criticized Kellogg's decision as unnecessary harassment,[13] but the secretary of state stood fast. He did not look kindly on the arrival in Mexico City of a prominent Bolshevik.

Nor was Mexican President Plutarco Elías Calles overjoyed, for he had to contend with strongly anticommunist forces within his own country. Mexico's communist party, the Partido Communista de Mexico (PCM), was led by the American Bertram Wolfe until his expulsion from the country in 1925. It was opposed by an active, socialist trade union organization, the Confederación Regional de Obreros Mexicanos (CROM), which had successfully fought off the infiltration of the Communists because its leaders considered them too closely tied to Moscow.[14] The Soviet ambassador who preceded Kollontai, S. S. Pestkovskii, had supported both the PCM and Wolfe's contacts with the Communist Party of the United States. He had therefore been asked to leave Mexico, as Calles attempted to placate Washington and Mexican anticommunists, while establishing a modicum of foreign policy independence.[15]

Kollontai entered Mexico at Vera Cruz, where she received a warm reception from a crowd of leftist students and workers. The governor of the state asked her to stay for a visit, and the newspapers were friendly. When she wrote home to Maksim Litvinov at the Commissariat of Foreign Affairs on December 16, 1926, Kollontai was optimistic that she could improve Soviet-Mexican trade, while countering the impression that she was just a revolutionary propagandist.[16] Despite her best efforts, however, she achieved very little. Kellogg continued to be worried by Soviet activity in Mexico, and he was further annoyed by Calles's criticism of American intervention in civil unrest in Nicaragua. In testimony in January 1927 before the Senate Foreign Relations Committee he accused the Soviet Union of attempting to use Latin America, specifically Mexico, as a base for propaganda against the United States.[17] Kollontai repeatedly denied that she had any goal other than improving diplomatic relations between the two countries, but she could not deny the obvious connection between the Mexican communist party and Moscow. She herself may have played a part in that contact, although there is no solid evidence that she did.[18] With this cloud of suspicion hanging over her work and under pressure from Kellogg, Kollontai found it extremely difficult to negotiate trade agreements. The most she achieved was a small exchange of films and the maintenance of commerce between the two countries which had been established by her predecessor.[19]

Kollontai's health was not good during most of her stay in Mexico City. The altitude irritated her chronic angina. She found breathing difficult in the thin air, and she did not like the arid climate. "Everyone has skin like a crocodile from the dryness," she wrote to an old friend, N. N. Iakimov. "And creams do not help. I am a denizen of the Leningrad marshes. I miss the moisture. I long for the water."[20] She enjoyed the colors of Mexican folk art and the paintings of Diego Rivera, but these small joys did not compensate for the frustrations of ill health and the political situation.

In March, a strike provoked a confrontation between the Mexican Communists and the trade unionists of the CROM. When the Railway Workers Union of the Soviet Union openly gave money to striking Mexican railway workers, a group with close ties to the Communists, the CROM protested against Soviet interference in Mexico's internal affairs. President Calles asked Kollontai to transmit his government's displeasure to Moscow, and the showing of several Russian films was cancelled. Kollontai escaped the fight by retreating to Cuernavaca, a lovely town of lower altitude where her heart was under less strain. A band of local outlaws was rampaging through the area robbing everyone they met, however, and she soon had to flee her refuge in a rickety bus.[21]

By April the CROM was loudly criticizing Kollontai.[22] When in May she requested a vacation for health reasons, the Mexican government recognized the ploy as a graceful way of leaving an unsuccessful mission. In June Kollontai sailed back to Europe, and from France she wrote mournfully to her old friend Tatiana Shchepkina-Kupernik, "Again I am almost home, although actually I don't have a home."[23]

Kollontai returned to Moscow. In late December 1927 she was named Soviet representative to Norway, succeeding the man who took her place in Mexico, Aleksandr Makar. While in the Soviet Union she offered her sympathy privately to Trotsky, who was soon to be exiled to Alma Ata.[24] By now the oppositionists had been defeated. Trotsky, Zinoviev, and Kamenev had attempted to forge an alliance, once they realized that Stalin threatened to consolidate power in his hands. They had moved too late, however, and by 1927 they had been condemned under the resolutions against factionalism which they had once applied to Kollontai. She had known that there was no hope of winning support with a campaign for party democracy; that hope had died for her years before. Now, in 1927, Kollontai made her disillusionment public in an article in *Pravda*.

Entitled "The Opposition and the Party Masses," it appeared on October 30, and was seen by socialists in the Soviet Union and abroad as Kollontai's farewell to revolutionary idealism.[25] Denying that the opposition to Stalin had any support among the party rank and file, she wrote:

> In the party, as in every collective, in a given moment and under definite conditions there always prevails some kind of mental attitude, there is always a "spirit." However strong the apparatus leading the collective is, if there is discord between the policies and direction of the apparatus and the attitude prevailing among the broad, lower strata of the collective, this discord will show up above all in the way the masses react, respond to events.[26]

The masses had greeted the opposition with "bitterness, hostility, and irritation." They were far too busy building "collectives" to listen to criticism; they were pioneering a new way of life.

> And all this work is concentrated in innumerable collectives: in soviets, unions, commissions, committees. Nowhere in the world does the collectivist foundation of work have such clear prevalence over the initiative of the person [*edinitsa*], of the individual, as in our unions. Often these collective organs block things up, making individual initiative difficult, but this is another question; it is an important fact that all these collective beginnings are creating a new approach to the life of the masses, a new ideology.[27]

The collective—a union or other institution—was shunting the old "bosses" aside, generating its own leadership, making its own decisions. Once its priorities were set, it demanded obedience, thus its hostility to the opposition. "This is now a period of construction and above all unity is needed, not only in action but also in thought," Kollontai declared, defending the Leninist principle which she had once attacked. The opposition violated unity and diverted the people from their important tasks.

> The masses do not believe in the opposition. They greet every statement of the opposition with smiles. Is it possible that the opposition thinks the masses' memory is so short? If they come across defects in the party, in the political line, who, if not the famous members of the opposition, established them and built them? It seems that the policy of the party and the structure of the apparatus become unfit only from the day that a group of oppositionists breaks with the party.[28]

Here was her anger, her disappointment, and her hopelessness. The party machine they had set working was rolling remorselessly over the Old Bolsheviks, and now they were saying it had a dreadful defect—Stalin. Now, years after they had trampled her into silence, Trotsky and Zinoviev talked about the problems of authoritarianism. Why had they been so unconcerned before, when they mouthed slogans about democratization while making no reform? She had not spent her life in revolutionary politics so that she could celebrate her fifty-fifth year with an article that praised the "collective" for taking "such clear prevalence over the initiative of the individual." Perhaps that development had always been implicit in her collectivism, perhaps she had been naive to hope that a communal society could give freedom to the individual. She had never been able to reconcile those contradictory impulses—the human needs for dependence and independence—in her own soul. But if she had been naive before in believing the socialist vision of a free spirit in a communal society, she was naive no longer. Thus she lashed out at the men who had once refused to listen to her and at the same time gave voice to her own depression. She told them what she had learned: that the party, their collective, would not tolerate deviation from its will as defined by the Central Committee and that most Communists approved of that policy.

> The masses consider that the living spirit of "collectivist democratism," in contradiction to the petty-bourgeois understanding of democratism, will become apparent to the opposition only when the opposition wants to understand that the decision of the Central Committee plenum is a reflection of the will of the masses of the party collective. And understanding this, the opposition will cease violating the unity of the party and cease being in conflict with the attitudes and the will of the millions of the party collective.[29]

Kollontai's criticism of the men who had once accused her of damaging party unity is quite clear here, as is her picture of the party rank and file as a great hive buzzing with activity and resentful of anyone who disrupted the natural harmony. What is less clear is her attitude toward the leaders of that hive. Did she approve of the squashing of Zinoviev, Kamenev, and Trotsky? She left only a few clues: she visited Natalia Sedova, Trotsky's wife, she wrote subdued but critical letters to Fredrik Ström and Zeth Höglund.[30] The impression that emerges from this fragmentary evidence is that she did not like Stalin, and she did not like the authoritarianism of the party, but she did still think the revolution had been a great victory. She sang of the collective with confidence in the long-range rightness of its purpose but sorrow over the victims it was taking, and she could not resist giving those victims the same advice they had once given her: do not violate the will of the party as enshrined in the Central Committee.

Kollontai's obedience earned her the appointment to Norway, and in November 1927 she returned to Oslo. For the next two years she concentrated on trade agreements, fishing rights in the Arctic, and tedious negotiations for a nonaggression treaty between Norway and the Soviet Union.[31] At times Litvinov was irritated by her tendency to soften the Soviet position a bit on her own initiative, if she thought this would improve the likelihood of agreement.[32] Such conciliatory behavior became characteristic of her style as a diplomat, and it earned her high praise in Scandinavia. It was the only sign of Kollontai's former independence. Outwardly, she had become a quiet, docile ambassador. In 1929 she told Body sadly: "Outside of a half-dozen comrades, I no longer know anyone in Moscow. Everything has changed completely. But what can I do? One cannot oppose the apparatus. For my part I have put my principles away in a corner of my conscience and I have carried out as well as possible the policies that have been dictated to me."[33]

In 1930 the Soviet ambassador to Sweden, Victor Kopp, became terminally ill with cancer. Kollontai was named his replacement in July, but before she accepted the post she went to Stockholm to sample the reception she would get. On July 3 she wrote to Litvinov that the government officials she had seen welcomed her appointment.[34] She moved to the new position in October. In mid-November Kollontai presented her credentials of accreditation to King Gustav. A gilded coach with liveried attendants called for her; she arrived at the palace, climbed a long marble staircase, and made her formal speech to the king. After the ceremony, she and Gustav had a brief conversation in French, then she returned to the embassy. The next day the Foreign Ministry quietly cancelled the 1914 order that had declared her *persona non grata*.[35]

Thus began Kollontai's last and most pleasant assignment, a fifteen-year period in which she became the dean of the diplomatic corps in Stockholm. In the thirties she dealt primarily with trade agreements and with the delicate task of improving Swedish opinion of the Soviet Union. Both proved difficult, but she did facilitate the exchange of commodities such as timber and fish.[36] To cultivate Swedish public opinion she made contacts among leftist intellectuals and brought in exhibits, films, and speakers to inform Stockholm about her country. Her most important means of raising the reputation of the Soviet Union, however, was her own personality. Swedes of all political persuasions praised Kollontai's concern and respect for Scandinavia, her charm, and her restraint. As the decade wore on, the increasing tension in foreign relations and the grisly news of Stalin's purges and the Nazi-Soviet Pact did not diminish the Swedish leaders' admiration for Kollontai, although those events did affect their attitude toward her country. Repeatedly they wrote that she was a friend to Sweden.[37]

She was living in refuge. She had made for herself a comfortable life: she got up every day at seven, did calisthenics to an old record of military marches, had coffee and read the newspapers and mail. Then she began a round of conferences with embassy personnel and official visitors.[38] Often she held dinner parties for other members of the diplomatic corps, or for Höglund or Ström, with whom she was still friendly. Her son Misha, now in his forties, was working in the United States as an engineer; through his mother's efforts and his own he spent most of his time outside the Soviet Union. His son, Vladimir Mikhailovich, lived in Sweden with his grandmother. Kollontai watched over him and the families of the mission, arranging plays in the evening and sending presents to the children.

In a strange way she had found her much sought communal family —the embassy staff, Swedish friends, her grandson. Surrounded by people who cared for her, she could live out her life in useful work at which she had become skilled, withdrawn from the contradictions of the situation at home. She returned to Moscow yearly for visits, but her life was in Stockholm. The genteel origins of this revolutionary had rounded into a genteel old age.

Yet she had lost much in accepting a graceful exile. Ivan Maiskii, in 1932 the Soviet ambassador to Finland, had become friends with Kollontai when she went to London in 1911. There he had seen her as joyously full of life. When he visited her in Stockholm in 1932, he found her changed. "Externally," Maiskii wrote, "she still looked very youthful, but inside she had become much more serious, deeper, more thoughtful, more cultivated."[39] A perceptive Swedish writer, Anna Elgstrom, found her "a human being like everyone else, only a little more experienced, but also wearier and more disillusioned."[40] Kollontai chose her words carefully, rarely letting down her guard; she made it a practice to discuss controversial subjects only with her closest friends. The Turkish ambassador to Sweden, Ragip Raif Bey, a kind man who first introduced her to the diplomatic circles of Stockholm, used to take guests aside during crisis periods in the thirties and whisper, "Please don't talk politics with Madame Kollontai."[41]

She had learned to be silent about the passions of her life. As the decade wore on, she did react publicly to the growing tension in Europe. In 1936 she went to Geneva as a member of the Soviet delegation to the League of Nations. There she participated in the debates on opium traffic and nutrition, but her concern lay with the League's taking action to resolve the Spanish civil war.[42] On October 4 she wrote to Ada Nilsson, a Swedish physician and friend, "We work and work, but what are the results? No practical results on all the big questions: Spain, the revision of treaties, disarmament. 'Passivity' is the leading mood here."[43]

She was alarmed by Hitler's successes in Europe; in 1938 she told Carl Gerhard, a Swedish theatrical director, that France and Britain were giving Czechoslovakia away to Germany without consulting the Soviet Union.[44] There was considerable truth in the charge, and Kollontai was repeating Moscow's official position, but she was also horrified by fascism. Appeasement by the Great Powers and their refusal to act in concert with the Soviet Union so alarmed Kollontai that she dropped her customary reserve and made her anger public.[45]

At the same time she was living through another crisis, about which she kept silent. In 1936 Stalin initiated the purges which killed millions of Soviet citizens, including most of the Old Bolshevik leadership. Many diplomats were called home, only to disappear. Kollontai watched the terror from Stockholm, wondered when her time would come, and kept up the daily round of meetings with her usual poise, knowing that there were police spies among her own staff. Swedish friends who were aware of the purges tactfully avoided the subject.[46]

How did she feel? In 1937 when Body visited her, she broke her protective silence and talked about the new mood in her embassy.

Dear Marcel Iakovlevich, our romantic epoch is completely finished. With us, we could take the initiative, stimulate the administration, make suggestions. Now we must be content with executing what we are ordered. Between my colleagues and me there is neither camaraderie nor friendship. Moreover the activity of each of us is strictly compartmentalized. Our relations are cold and distrust is everywhere.[47]

Body asked her about Shliapnikov and Dybenko; Kollontai said they were dead.[48] He named other Bolsheviks, her answer remained the same;

they were dead. Then, feeling that she owed Body some sort of explanation for the terror sweeping the Soviet Union, she said lamely that democracy was not yet possible in Russia.

> I, I have understood that Russia could not pass from absolutism to liberty in a few years. The dictatorship of Stalin or another which would have been put together by Trotsky was inevitable. This dictatorship has made waves of blood flow, but blood flowed before, under Lenin, and undoubtedly too much innocent blood. Remember the massacres of hostages that Zinoviev ordered in Petrograd to stop the terrorists. How many dozen years will it take for Russia to arrive at a regime of liberty? I can't say. Historically, Russia, with her numberless uncultured, undisciplined masses, is not mature enough for democracy.

Kollontai had never liked the violence her own people committed, although she had countenanced it, while seeking to reduce it. Now a great horror had come out of the revolution and she was trying to explain it by saying that Stalin's dictatorship had been inevitable. It was not. Stalin and his subordinates initiated the purges because they were afraid of the turmoil of the thirties and determined to establish absolute control over their nation by hunting down imaginary enemies and terrorizing everyone else into submission. Having chosen to attack their own people, they mobilized the apparatus of the Soviet state to shed blood, which it did, remorselessly, capriciously, probably beyond the intentions of those who had set it going. This was not of the same order as Zinoviev's sometimes excessive repression in Petrograd, nor had Zinoviev's brutality led to this. Between Zinoviev's policies in 1919 and Zinoviev's execution in 1936 lay a series of choices by the party leadership, each choice increasing the power of that leadership and of Stalin. The terror had its roots in earlier Bolshevik actions, in qualities of the party Lenin had built, and in Russia's autocratic heritage, but it was not, as Kollontai implied, inevitable.

She would not admit this, in part because she was a determinist, uncomfortable with granting such fearful coercive power to any individual or group of individuals, but also because linking Stalin's terror to Lenin's gave hope that Stalin's violence would not thwart the revolution, as Lenin's had not. She clung to her belief in the future, in the eventual success of the Soviet experiment, which she repeatedly declared was also inevitable. In the meantime she waited for the terror to pass. Again she chose to remain at her job, although she could have defected, because to defect would require renouncing the revolution as betrayed, and this Kollontai would not do.

She mourned the dead so privately that even Body could not see it. The party expelled Shliapnikov in 1933 on the grounds that he was "a degenerate"; he was jailed in 1935 and probably died in 1937, refusing with his customary dignity to make a public confession.[49] Dybenko had a successful military career which ended in his serving on the tribunal that ordered the execution of Army Commander-in-chief M. N. Tukhachevskii in June 1937. Several months later the NKVD arrested Dybenko. He was shot in 1938.[50] Kollontai must have cried for him, for Shliapnikov, and for the many hundreds of others who disappeared. She may not have known the full extent of the purges, but she did not deceive herself about the fact that people were being killed, and that she herself was vulnerable. In fact, she expected to die. On July 4, 1937, she wrote to Ada Nilsson that she would soon have to return to Moscow.

> Dear, dear Ada, my friend. Kindly keep the notes, diaries, and all personal material you have until 1947 (that is, if I shall fall victim to a misfortune).
>
> Ten years after my death I ask you to hand over all this material to the Marx-Engels Institute in Moscow. It can be published when it is suitable in the Soviet Union.
>
> Thank you for everything. Your friendship is a great happiness and a support for me. I embrace you with warm friendship and affection.
>
> Your Alexandra Kollontay[51]

She did not expect to return from the trip to Moscow, or even to survive it. The odds were against her. Of the original Council of People's Commissars, only Kollontai and Stalin lived through the purges, and she was one of the very few former oppositionists, a one-time Menshevik at that, who did not at least experience arrest. The death toll among the diplomatic corps alone was high.[52] Yet this terror was capricious, and a combination of circumstances—Kollontai's long absence from the political infighting in the Soviet Union, her visibility in Europe, her sex—probably account for her survival. It may also be that she proved her loyalty to the authorities when she went back in 1937, although it is difficult to know how she could establish innocence at a time when everyone was innocent, except the police.

Kollontai may have implicated others, but there is no evidence that she did so. There is only one incriminating article from 1937, a piece first published in 1927 and then reissued to commemorate the twentieth anniversary of the revolution. In the original version Kollontai described the meeting where the Central Committee voted for an armed uprising in October 1917. She discussed Zinoviev's and Kamenev's opposition to precipitous action and Lenin's argument that their fears were unfounded.

She presented Dybenko as impatient to proceed, Trotsky as calm and impressive, the gathering as tense but harmonious. After they had made their historic decision, the committee members adjourned to the dining room for tea and sausages.[53]

The 1937 version of this article was considerably different. Kollontai did not mention Dybenko now, but she did praise Stalin, whom she had ignored in 1927. Stalin energetically supported Lenin, she declared. Stalin had led the Bolsheviks while Lenin was hiding in Finland, and he had provided the revolutionary spark necessary to fire the party into action. Zinoviev, Kamenev, and Trotsky, on the other hand, malevolently plotted to thwart Lenin. In the vituperative prose required during the purge period, Kollontai wrote: "The two base figures of the malicious enemies and traitors to the party sat separate from us on the divan, not at the table. They sat side by side, they whispered to one another, Zinoviev and Kamenev came out against Lenin, against the C.C., with foully cowardly objections, with criminal, disorganizing arguments."

She said that Zinoviev and Kamenev wanted the Bolsheviks to seize power by parliamentary means, which was true, in a sense. They had favored delaying until the Constituent Assembly convened, in the belief that the party would be stronger then. Lenin and Trotsky responded by arguing instead for an armed uprising, but Trotsky wanted to wait until the Congress of Soviets in early November. That is in fact what the Bolsheviks did, but Kollontai pictured Trotsky's general agreement with Lenin as even more deceitful than Zinoviev's and Kamenev's open opposition. Trotsky was hiding his true desire to subvert the revolution. "Here the Judas Trotsky, future agent of the Gestapo, fawned. He was for the uprising, 'for legality,' and 'for delay.' He was for waiting until the Congress of Soviets. Also treachery, only in a hidden form. The Judas told everything on himself in this decisive hour."[54] When the vote was taken, "the two hands of the traitors" showed their "treachery," but the wisdom of Lenin and his great disciple Stalin prevailed.[55]

Kollontai had been forced out of her refuge in Sweden and into the nightmare. She paid abject homage to Stalin, she lied about the past, she edited out all references to Dybenko, whom she had loved. Once again she was willing to meet the party's requirements for membership, on which now depended not only the meaning of her life, but her physical survival as well.

The article may have been the final element that proved Kollontai's loyalty in 1937 and saved her. She returned to Sweden to resume her work. She had always read history in her leisure time, and now she cast about in the story of the past for reassurance that present atrocities would end. In 1938 in a letter to Tatiana Shchepkina-Kupernik, she testified to her faith in the future, which she was trying to buttress by reminding herself of the brutality of other ages.

> Now I value and understand that epoch [the Renaissance] in a different way. An epoch when thought moved and the search for everything new went on. . . . What persecution of thought! And what a will to defend one's beliefs. It has much in common with our epoch. . . . Those who made discoveries about the universe were considered more heretical than those who tried to reform social relations. Now there is a battle of moribund capitalism with the builders of new social relations and economics. The battle is carried on according to a different plan, but then the transition from one stage to another was accompanied by wars, political intrigues, terror—everything. And time passes. And in the squares where John Hus and Giordano Bruno were burned, their monuments now stand![56]

She was looking ahead, ten or twenty years, when the NKVD would be restrained and the Old Bolsheviks honored again. Until then she chose to wait out the present, serving the revolution she still believed in, making the sacrifices it demanded.

The reprieve of 1937 seemed to be rescinded in the summer of 1938, when Kollontai was again called home. Her friend Ada Nilsson had been instructed to burn all of Kollontai's letters if Kollontai gave her the signal that she was about to be arrested by one of the spies on her staff. That had not happened, but Kollontai took the order to return to Moscow for consultations as an ominous sign, and she sent Nilsson what she again believed was a farewell letter.

> I have written this letter in Saltsjöbaden the 21st of July 1938, 11 o'clock in the morning. A. K.
>
> My dear, dear friend Ada,
>
> You have asked me to collect my articles, letters, and notes so that you can write a biography of me. Accordingly I have fulfilled your desire: I am sending you two bags with material of different kinds, photographs, notes, biographies, letters, etc. In the event of my death (for something can always happen on a trip), I ask you to keep all these *purely personal* papers.
>
> My life has been rich and exciting. I have lived through many great events. But also great pain. The great part is the fulfillment of my entire life's struggle, dreams, and endeavors: the socialist state a reality, woman's emancipation, for which I have fought so hard and for which I laid the foundation in the Soviet Union.

Pain? I hate brutality, intolerance, wrong, and human suffering. At certain times humanity finds itself in a period when all these apparitions are enormous. It always happens that way in times of revolution in the socio-political and economic systems. It is historically required. But that makes it no less painful.

I thank you Ada, my great and dear friend, for your friendship and for many years, beautiful times, and spiritual harmony.

I embrace you and thank you again.

Your Alexandra Kollontay[57]

She won another reprieve in 1938. Now the arrests began to taper off, and Kollontai returned to Stockholm to watch the leaders of Europe attempt to fashion one more compromise that would prevent Adolf Hitler from launching a continental war.

Kollontai looked in horror at the thirties not only because of the excesses of Stalin's regime but also because of the naked brutality of nazism. Many Communists justified remaining in the party through the purges because fascism and the weakness of the Western democracies during the Great Depression offered a grim alternative to the authoritarian socialism of the Soviet Union. Kollontai gave vent to similar feelings in her lamentations that the times had gone mad. Less than a year after she had been spared arrest at home, in late August 1939, Kollontai learned that her government had made a nonaggression treaty with the Nazis.

Her Swedish friends were so shocked by the news that some of them broke off communications with Kollontai.[58] She was obliged to play hostess to the German ambassador, Prince Victor von Wied, whom she had hitherto snubbed. Refugees from Hitler's attack on Poland wrote her a threatening note. Kollontai sent another letter to Ada Nilsson, affirming her faith that the current crises were an aberration. Justifying the Nazi-Soviet Pact, she added lamely, "And isn't this an absolutely new method of solving conflicts that the Soviet Union is practicing now? Isn't it wiser and more humane to seek to solve problems through treaty and negotiations instead of taking up arms?"[59]

That pathetic optimism was little warranted by events in the black fall of 1939. At the time Kollontai wrote the letter, the Soviet Union, emboldened by its new diplomatic "methods," began to put pressure on Finland, Poland, and the Baltic states of Estonia, Latvia, and Lithuania. Stalin was seeking to expand his borders through aggression against his weak neighbors, with Hitler's blessing. From Finland he wanted the land adjacent to Leningrad, in exchange for a barren northern stretch of

Karelia, and he wanted leases for military bases on Finnish soil, all to guard the sea approaches to Leningrad.[60]

When the Soviet demands for territorial concessions reached Helsinki in October 1939, the Finns sent a delegation headed by Social Democrat Väinö Tanner to Moscow, but the negotiations broke down quickly. Relations between Finland and the Soviet Union had never been cordial. It was Kollontai who had voiced the Bolshevik pledge to allow Finland autonomy in 1917, but when that nation actually broke away from Russia, it became a haven for anti-Bolshevik elements, both Finnish and Russian. Although during the twenties Finland was ruled by moderate regimes, the political right, connected through educational background and philosophy to conservatives in Germany, wielded significant power. The right remained resolutely anticommunist. In the early thirties a semifascist group called the Lapua movement gained notoriety for its vociferous demands for a hard line toward the Soviet Union, and the existence of such extremists bore witness to the continuation of the strong anti-Soviet and pro-German element in Finnish politics, particularly in the military.[61]

Once Hitler came to power, foreign policy makers in Moscow watched Finland's relations with Germany and the Scandinavian countries closely. Kollontai received frequent orders to report on the Swedish attitude toward Finland. The Finnish governments were actually trying to strengthen their neutrality by aligning with the neutral Scandinavians, thereby hoping to soothe Soviet fears, but they were unsuccessful. Both Maksim Litvinov and B. S. Stomoniakov, a specialist on Scandinavia in the Commissariat of Foreign Affairs, suspected their neighbor of trying to move Sweden and Norway into the German orbit and of aiming at an anti-Soviet, Scandinavian military alliance. They also referred occasionally to a small group, the Academic Karelia Society, which demanded annexation of large amounts of Soviet territory on the specious claim that the land was historically Finnish. Moscow saw the society as symptomatic of Finland's aggressive aspirations.[62]

In 1938 and 1939 Moscow made overtures toward an anti-German alliance with Finland, but the Finns put off the proposal out of a fear that such a treaty would violate their neutrality.[63] Neither government came to the negotiations in October 1939 prepared to compromise significantly, therefore: the Soviets distrusted their adversary and were bent on moving their vulnerable frontier westward; the Finns were determined to resist their aggressive neighbor. The result was a stalemate that raised hostility on both sides. On December 1 the Soviet Union declared a group of Finnish Communists headed by Otto Kuusinen to be the legitimate government of Finland, a fiction that allowed them to claim they were commencing military action in response to a request from the Finns. On November 30 the Soviet army had launched the initial attacks of the Winter War.

At first, Finnish forces defeated the ill-prepared Soviet troops in a display of courage that stirred worldwide admiration. Here at last was a small nation that could stand against the attack of the dictators. Finland could not survive alone, however, and her leaders hoped that they could either win Western aid or negotiate a reasonable peace with the Soviet Union. The existence of the puppet Kuusinen regime made the process more difficult, for as long as Moscow recognized an illegitimate government, they could not negotiate with Finland's real leaders—Prime Minister Risto Ryti and Foreign Minister Väinö Tanner. Yet Stalin could not afford to wait for a military triumph and dictated peace. The Nazis were openly scornful of the poor Russian showing in the war; a prolonged conflict would seriously weaken the Soviet relationship with Germany. Furthermore, a beleaguered Finland might well get British and French aid, thus pulling the Soviet Union into World War II on the side of the Axis.[64] For both the Finns and the Soviets, then, there were incentives to end the fighting, if a way could be found to negotiate.

Meanwhile, Sweden's foreign office was watching with alarm. The guiding principle of Swedish foreign policy was neutrality; Sweden saw it as her means of survival in a world of larger powers. Quietly throughout the thirties, Swedish foreign ministers had reassured the Soviet Union that Finland sought no anti-Soviet bloc in Scandinavia, that Scandinavia would always remain neutral. When the Winter War began, however, there was a great outpouring of sympathy in Sweden for Finland. "Finland's cause is ours" became the cry of public opinion,[65] and the government had to find a course between popular demands to support the Finns and its own determination to remain uninvolved. Foreign Minister Christian Günther believed that Finland should not be pushed into major concessions, but that everything must be done to facilitate communications between the combatants. Thus Sweden chose the role of mediator.[66]

What of Kollontai? She had apparently decided she now had to help the country in which she had spent so much of her childhood. If she felt any despair over the fact that her second home had been attacked by her government, she never revealed it. Instead she went to work, traveling back to Moscow during the fall negotiations. She was there ostensibly to report on Swedish public opinion, but Väinö Tanner, who was heading the Finnish delegation to Moscow, heard that she had spent her evenings in long meetings on the Finnish question. Her efforts yielded no conciliation, and she returned to Stockholm expecting war.[67]

Once the combat began, Kollontai broached the subject of peace negotiations to Swedish leaders. She had long since mastered the art of diplomacy, and now she had set herself a task that would test all her skills. She wanted to do everything she could to restore peace. This required opening communications between Helsinki and Moscow, which in turn required Swedish help. She would also have to deal gently with Viacheslav Molotov, the recently appointed commissar of foreign affairs. Kollontai was less suspicious of the Finns than he, more willing to negotiate, and above all, more anxious to end the war. Thus she set out to bring her government to a peace conference by conciliating not only the Finns but her own superiors. To achieve that objective she would have to make maximum use of the freedom she was allowed, without alienating Molotov and Stalin and thereby jeopardizing her own position as well as the negotiations.

Kollontai began her efforts with several exploratory talks with Swedish officials in late December 1939. On December 25 she cancelled an invitation to Christmas dinner with friends so that she could discuss the war with Gustav Möller, a Social Democrat and friend who was minister of social welfare.[68] Möller had worked with Shliapnikov during World War I, and throughout the thirties Kollontai consulted with him. On December 27, she talked directly with Foreign Minister Christian Günther, telling him that because of her special affection for Finland she wanted to find a way to peace. She said she had not checked with Moscow before she saw him, an admission which Günther received skeptically. It might be true, he thought, or it might be a means of explaining later policy changes as a result of her exceeding her authority. As the weeks wore on, Günther would learn how often Kollontai was acting on her own initiative. She told him the Soviet Union wanted to begin negotiations, but that their battlefield defeats had so humiliated Soviet leaders that they had to rebuild their prestige. Günther replied soothingly that the Soviets need not fear a loss of face; no one believed that they had sent their full military might against the Finns. Kollontai agreed that the opinions of other nations should not be a prime consideration in ending a war, but she cautioned Günther that domestic policy was also involved here. The Soviet government had to explain its failures in Finland to its own people. Günther said he hoped the resolution of the war did not hang on the Soviet Union's internal politics.[69]

This talk was the first of several between Kollontai and Günther or his deputy Erik Boheman. The Swedes told her that the Kuusinen regime would have to be abandoned, that the Finns might compromise on territorial concessions in Karelia and on leases on the Baltic islands, where the Soviets wanted to build military bases, but they would never cede the Cape of Hangö. That peninsula, which guards the entrance to the Gulf of Finland, lies seventy-five miles from Helsinki. Granting it to the Soviet Union would give the Soviets a foothold in the western part of the country as well as the potential to cut off access to Helsinki by sea. Gently Günther and Boheman reminded Kollontai that Britain and France were considering intervention. She responded that she wanted peace, but that Moscow would insist on Hangö.[70]

At the same time secret contacts had begun between Kollontai and the Finns through the unlikely agency of Hella Murrik Wuolijoki, a Finnish playwright and Communist who was an old friend of Kollontai's. On New Year's Day 1940 Wuolijoki wrote to Väinö Tanner, the Finnish foreign minister, and volunteered to go to Stockholm to see the Soviet ambassador. Tanner thought Wuolijoki a foolish woman, but he approved her trip after conferring with his colleagues. Wuolijoki then went to Sweden on January 10 and met with Kollontai in great secrecy. Kollontai volunteered to send another dispatch to Molotov requesting a clarification of what the Soviet Union now sought in a peace treaty. She included in her message a glowing report on Finland's desire to negotiate, but Molotov was skeptical. He thought, quite rightly, that Kollontai was exaggerating the willingness of the Ryti government to grant the territory the Soviet Union demanded. Molotov therefore sent two envoys to Stockholm to verify what Kollontai had written by talking with Swedish officials.[71]

Apparently the report he received from these men satisfied him, for Molotov sent Kollontai a telegram soon thereafter spelling out the Soviet demands. It was a stern message: Moscow would abandon the puppet Kuusinen regime and negotiate with the Ryti-Tanner government, they would demand stricter "guarantees" of their borders than they had in October, and they inquired what concessions the Finns were prepared to make. Günther forwarded this message to Helsinki, with his advice that the government there should seize the opportunity to establish direct contact with the Soviets.[72]

Tanner was pleased by Moscow's willingness to drop the Kuusinen regime and deal directly with the real leaders of Finland, but he was worried by the fact that the Soviet Union was raising its territorial demands. Through Wuolijoki he sent several messages to Kollontai, asking her assessment of Molotov's willingness to compromise, and she replied evasively that the Finns must begin negotiations. She believed that once the process was underway the two governments could bargain over the land involved. Her first imperative was to get them talking to one another, by using her role as intermediary to soften the position of each side when reporting it to the other. She did state clearly that there could be no compromise on Hangö, but she implied that all else was negotiable.

In the course of these exchanges over the last days of January and early February 1940, Tanner began to realize that Kollontai was being more conciliatory than Moscow, and he learned that on at least one occasion she had received an order from home to temper her encouragement of Finnish overtures.[73] Tanner also gathered from telephone conversations with Wuolijoki that Kollontai was not informing Moscow of the Finnish refusal to cede Hangö. Disturbed by the thought that she might be misrepresenting her government's intentions, Tanner decided to go to Stockholm to see her himself and possibly to begin those direct communications with Moscow which Günther advised.

He met her twice, on February 5 and 6. Kollontai stressed that peace must be made to save Finland from further devastation. When Tanner suggested that an island in the Gulf of Finland and additional land along the inland frontier could be substituted for Hangö, she said her superiors might accept that compromise. On the sixth, however, she came back to him with a telegram from Moscow that declared that the Finnish proposals did not offer sufficient basis for negotiations. Tanner left Stockholm convinced that the contact between the two countries was at an end for the time being; Kollontai's encouragement had not been able to sway Molotov and Stalin.[74]

The Finns switched their efforts now to gaining military aid from Britain, France, and Sweden, while keeping the link to Kollontai open.[75] Despite rising public pressure, the Swedish government still wanted accommodation between the combatants, and Günther gently urged the Finns to compromise. He, Boheman, and the prime minister, Per Albin Hansson, knew the Soviet demands were severe, but they also knew that Finland had very few choices. Only massive foreign intervention would save them, at the risk of involving all Scandinavia in World War II.

That prospect horrified Günther, who sought to pressure both sides into concessions that would enable negotiations to begin. On February 21 he thought he detected a new willingness from the Finns to consider ceding Hangö, and he encouraged Tanner to come back to Stockholm for talks with Kollontai.[76]

Kollontai was just as anxious as Günther that the Finns compromise. She told Eljas Erkko, the Finnish chargé d'affaires in Sweden, that his government must accept the Soviet demands immediately. To the Swedish ambassador to Moscow, Vilhelm Assarsson, she confided that the peace terms would be difficult for the Finns. However, there must be peace. She too feared British involvement that might spread the war over Scandinavia. She also worried about the possibility that when the Soviet forces began to win, as they must by virtue of their numerical superiority, the Finns would be forced to sign away even more of their land.

When Tanner came to see Kollontai in Stockholm on February 27, she was close to tears. As she had feared, Molotov had sent her a new set of demands, the harshest yet.[77] She had warned the Finns, Kollontai said sadly, to accept the proposals of early February. In a communiqué on February 12, Molotov had declared that the Soviet Union was seeking a lease on Hangö and the cession of the Karelian Isthmus and the eastern shore of Lake Ladoga. Now his latest message had made those demands preconditions for negotiations; the Finns must grant them before talks could even begin. Tanner said that such a peace would permanently damage Soviet-Finnish relations, but he promised to keep contacts open. He left a troubled Kollontai and returned to Helsinki.[78]

However they loathed the idea of surrender, the Finns had few options left now, for the tide of combat had turned against them. To prevent further Finnish delay which might give the Allies time to intervene, the Soviet Union delivered an ultimatum to Ryti's government on February 28. The Finns must respond to their terms within two days. There followed a hectic round of talks in which the British and French offered help, but not enough, the Swedes refused to allow foreign troops to cross their soil, and the Finns debated their alternatives. Tanner tried to stall by requesting a clarification of the Soviet ultimatum. Meanwhile the conditions at the front continued to deteriorate. On March 5 the Finns gave up and accepted the Soviet demands "on principle."[79] Within a few days a negotiating team went to Moscow. There Molotov presented them with terms that were more severe than they had hoped but which were not significantly worse than those of the preceding fall. The Soviet Union took the land north and west of Leningrad, the Isthmus of Karelia, Hangö, and some territory along the inland frontier. Considering their military advantage in March, they could have demanded more, but their fear of Germany and of Allied intervention made them anxious to settle. They now had the land necessary to guard the approaches to Leningrad.[80]

For their part the Finns found little comfort in Soviet "leniency." They had lost their fourth largest city, Viipuri, one-tenth of their farm-land, and an important part of their timber industry. Some 23,000 men had been killed and 43,000 wounded; 42,000 refugees flooded across the new border, fleeing the Russians. The Finns considered themselves the victims of aggression, and their anger made them more anti-Soviet than before.[81]

The war was over. Kollontai had achieved her objective. She had cajoled the two governments into dealing with one another, occasionally delaying communiqués that might shatter the negotiations, occasionally glossing over Molotov's intransigence with her assurances that the Soviet Union really wanted peace. In the words of the diplomat and historian Max Jakobson, "She acted more like an advocate of peace than an imper-sonal intermediary."[82] After all the years of obedience to Moscow, she had finally been able to help one of Stalin's victims. She had not saved Finland from aggression nor could she ameliorate the terms of the settle-ment, but she had opened communications between the two countries and she had worked with the Swedes to convince the Finns to abandon their heroic but doomed defense. Kollontai, the Old Bolshevik who had grown up in Finland, who once called for Finnish autonomy and de-manded revolutionary war, now gently, tactfully, sadly helped persuade the Finns to capitulate before more of them died. She had come to a strange, mournful realism in her old age.

For the next year Kollontai worked again on improving Soviet rela-tions with Sweden. Under orders from Moscow she discouraged overtures toward a Swedish-Finnish military alliance, and thereby encouraged Fin-land to strengthen its ties to Germany.[83] Meanwhile relations between Berlin and Moscow deteriorated. At a luncheon in March 1941 Kollontai asked Swedish diplomat Gunnar Hagglof his opinion of German attitudes toward her country. Hagglof had just returned from Berlin, and he told Kollontai he expected Hitler to make war on the Soviet Union. "I saw tears in her eyes as she sat for a moment in silence, then she tapped my hand mildly and said, 'Be quiet, my dear Mr. Hagglof. You have no right to tell me this and I have no right to listen to you.' "[84]

In June 1941 Germany invaded the Soviet Union and Kollontai's mission abruptly changed. She was charged now with watching Swedish foreign policy for "favoritism" toward the Nazis. Kollontai had never been comfortable with the Nazi-Soviet Pact, of course, and the Germans had complained to Moscow in June 1940 that she was "hostile" toward them.[85] Once the war began, she could set about helping her country, now besieged by the enemy she had always hated. From June 1941 to August 1942 she pursued a gruelling schedule, performing her diplomatic duties, nursing her son who had come to Sweden ill with heart disease, and acting as grandmother to the Soviet colony in Stockholm. In June 1942 she wrote to Isabel de Palencia, the former Spanish ambassador to Sweden, "One lives on tenterhooks here and my nerves are beginning to go, but I try to work on with courage and energy."[86]

In August 1942, after five days with little sleep, Kollontai collapsed from a stroke. She was seventy years old now, and the attack was almost fatal. Nanna Svartz, a prominent Swedish physician who treated her, was pessimistic at first, but slowly Kollontai recovered. By Christmas she could speak clearly and work from a wheelchair, but she remained partially paralyzed on her left side. She could never again walk without help or write easily.[87] She returned to a regular schedule only in 1943, when she gave herself once again to negotiating an end to a war between the Soviet Union and Finland.

After Hitler attacked the Soviet Union, Finland had entered World War II on the side of the Axis, hoping to regain what had been lost in the Winter War. At first the Finns defeated the Soviet army, and emboldened conservatives talked about moving Finland's borders eastward through Karelia into historically Russian territory. In 1942, however, the Soviets began to turn the Germans back, and by 1943 Finnish officials realized that the Allies would win the war. Finland had to settle with a victorious Soviet Union.[88] Again Sweden was anxious to mediate, although its leadership never supported the Finns in this second war—the so-called Continuation War. They were repelled by the alliance with Germany, and some newspapers even advised abandoning Finland to defeat by the Soviet Union. Foreign Minister Günther and his deputy Boheman felt, however, that they must work to keep their neighbor from falling under Soviet occupation.[89]

In the summer of 1943, when Kollontai was well enough to return to work, she took up her old role of urging the Finns to open negotiations. She told de Croy, the Belgian ambassador to Stockholm, that her country was interested in peace, but when the Finnish envoy to Sweden, Georg Gripenberg, pursued the overture it led nowhere, possibly because she had again exceeded her authority. Throughout the fall Kollontai continued to push for contacts by telling members of the diplomatic corps that negotiations could begin.[90] Then, on November 13, she came to see Erik Boheman to tell him she hoped the Continuation War would not damage relations between Sweden and the Soviet Union. Boheman was alarmed by the Allies' recent decision to require "unconditional surrender" from the Axis. Would Stalin demand that of Finland? he asked. Kollontai promised to seek instructions on the subject from Moscow.[91]

On November 20 she called Boheman to come to see her. "Her excitement was strong when I arrived," he wrote, "she had a message that she gave alternatively in French, German, and her broken Swedish-Norwegian." Moscow had responded to her request with an invitation for Finland to send negotiators to Moscow. First, however, the Finnish government must specify what concessions they were willing to make. Smiling, Kollontai noted that there was nothing in the statement about unconditional surrender.

Boheman observed that Finland would have a difficult time breaking free of Germany. He was deeply concerned, as were the Finns, that the Nazis would retaliate mercilessly, should the Finns conclude a separate peace. There were German troops on Finnish soil, close contacts between the German and Finnish High Commands, and Nazi agents in the Finnish government. The Germans had no desire to see the Soviet units that were fighting in Karelia loosed against them. Thus Boheman feared that a Nazi occupation of Finland similar to the occupation of Italy was a distinct possibility, and he warned Kollontai of the difficulties the Finns faced. Kollontai said she hoped that since Finland had not formally joined the Axis it might be able to ease free of the Germans without paying Italy's penalty of bloody reprisals. She told Boheman that the two of them must work secretly to "save Finland" and he went away encouraged. Moscow, with Kollontai's prodding, had shown a willingness to talk.[92]

The next several months were a time of messages between Kollontai, Boheman and Günther in the Swedish government, and Gripenberg at the Finnish Embassy in Stockholm. They kept their meetings a secret, lest news of the negotiations reach the press. Public disclosure at this point might end the contacts and provoke the Nazis stationed all over Finland. "Gripenberg and I talked in code on the telephone," Boheman wrote. "When I visited Madame Kollontai I did it in the evening; at twilight I cycled to her house with a peaked cap on my head."[93] The Finns balked at the Soviet demand for a return to the borders of March 1940, and they feared that the Russians might make peace, wait until the Finnish army was demobilized, and then occupy the entire country. The Finns also were receiving veiled threats of German retaliation, timed to coincide with every new message from Stockholm. They stalled, awaiting the out-come of the fierce battles for the Baltic then in progress, and weighing the prospects of increased German aid against the growing likelihood of German defeat. They even nursed a remote hope that Anglo-American occupation of Europe would force Moscow to be lenient. Meanwhile Kollontai and the Swedes pressed the Finns to accept the 1940 borders as a means to negotiation. As she had during the Winter War, Kollontai feared that if the Finns delayed, Soviet victories would make the peace terms all the more severe. Finally in late March Helsinki agreed to send negotiators to Moscow, but when they arrived, Molotov was in no mood for conciliation.[94]

The conditions he had laid down for a cease fire, not a final peace, were rigorous—internment or expulsion of German troops by April 30, return of Soviet POWs, an immediate retreat within the 1940 borders, and a reduction of the Finnish army to one-half its present size by the end of May, to peacetime status before August 1. Furthermore, Finland had to pay $600 million in reparations in kind over the next five years and cede more land. If these terms were met, the Soviet Union would consider renouncing the lease on Hangö. The Finnish government re-fused the exorbitant demands; Kollontai's and Boheman's efforts had come to nothing. When the negotiations collapsed, she was so disap-pointed that her health failed her and she was forced to spend several weeks in bed.[95]

In June a Soviet offensive began smashing through Karelia, and Kollontai, Günther, and Boheman renewed their efforts to induce the Finns to settle. Late in the month the Finns offered to send a delegation to Moscow. Kollontai again felt optimistic, but then Molotov demanded that President Ryti sign a statement of "capitulation" to the Soviet Union.

Kollontai assured an anxious Boheman and the Finns that this did not mean unconditional surrender, but given Molotov's past performance she could not have been sure herself.[96]

At the same time Joachim von Ribbentrop, the German foreign minister, flew into Helsinki. His trip was the climax of growing German pressure, which had included the cutting down of arms shipments to a bare minimum. The Finns were almost wholly dependent on German supplies, so to mollify the Nazis President Ryti wrote a letter to Hitler assuring him that Finland would not give up any of its territory without German approval. In return the Germans promised more aid. On July 27 that letter became public, and Boheman, Gripenberg, and Kollontai thought they were seeing their latest hopes for peace die in a reassertion of the Nazi-Finnish alliance.[97] Kollontai was becoming increasingly impatient with Finnish delaying tactics, however sympathetic she might be to the government's difficulties. Again she was pressing for a settlement now, rather than later, when it might be still more onerous. And in the summer of 1944, pressure from the Allies was added to the growing reverses at the front.

Throughout the abortive deliberations Britain and the United States had been urging the Finns to make peace. Roosevelt and Churchill believed that they had reliable Soviet pledges not to occupy the country, and the Finnish alliance with Nazi Germany made them unsympathetic to Finland's search for security. For their part the Finns now realized that the Anglo-American Allies were not going to save them from the Russians, an unpleasant fact that became even clearer when the United States broke off diplomatic relations in the wake of the Ryti letter. That step, and more importantly the worsening conditions at the front, persuaded the Finns to reorganize their government in early August. Kollontai welcomed that action as the prelude to Finnish acceptance of Soviet demands.[98]

When the overture did not come, therefore, she became "all the more impatient"[99] and she did not keep her anger a secret. She bluntly told another diplomat that Moscow was tired of Finland's insincerity.[100] Finally, in late August, the new Finnish president, Marshall Carl Gustaf Mannerheim, requested in writing that the Soviet Union receive a delegation from Finland. He also said that he had informed Germany he did not consider himself bound by the declarations of his predecessor, that is, by the Ryti message to Hitler. There followed more secret night-time meetings between Kollontai, her aide Vladimir Semenov, Gripenberg, and Boheman, in which the Finns continued to balk over the question of interning German troops, but by the evening of September 3 the negotiators in Stockholm had finally worked out an armistice acceptable to both sides.

On September 7, 1944, a Finnish delegation went to Moscow to accept terms more severe than those they had earlier refused. Molotov demanded less in reparations, but he continued to call for a return to the 1940 borders, demobilization of the Finnish army in two and a half months, the dissolution of all pro-German groups within Finland, trial of war criminals, and the disarmament of German forces beginning September 15. In return the Soviet Union received a lease on the Porkkala peninsula near Helsinki rather than Hangö. The Nazis almost immediately began to take reprisals, ushering in a new war that lasted until April 1945. Väinö Tanner described September 1944 as "the bitterest time in our people's life."[101]

"I cannot say that I was particularly surprised by the severity of the peace," wrote Erik Boheman, "even though I was more optimistic for awhile, perhaps too much encouraged by Madame Kollontai's gentle voice."[102] Again she had carefully played the role of intermediary, aided by the Swedes and by Finns such as Gripenberg who accepted the necessity for concession. She used the same tactics she developed during the Winter War—liberal interpretation of Soviet intentions, editing of messages from both sides, cajolery, and impatient statements to other diplomats when progress slowed. Both the Swedes and the Finns were well aware that she was more generous than Molotov, and therefore unreliable as a gauge to Moscow's real goals; but they accepted her zeal as motivated by a genuine desire to help Finland.[103]

Perhaps in some small way, Boheman thought, she helped spare the Finns the kind of Soviet occupation meted out to Romania and Hungary.[104] Of course, Churchill and Roosevelt had pressed Stalin to respect Finland's sovereignty. Furthermore Finland had never been a central concern of Soviet foreign policy. With its demands for strategically important territory achieved, the Soviet Union could turn its attention to Central and Eastern Europe, areas far more important to its objectives.

Yet Kollontai had been able to contribute to the peacemaking, and she told both Boheman and Gripenberg that she was happy with the success of their mutual endeavor.[105] On September 30 she held a luncheon for members of the Swedish Foreign Office and the Finnish embassy. At the end of a short speech praising the peace they had finally made, she proposed a toast: "I wish Finland's people happiness and success, and I drink a toast to your Marshall [Mannerheim]; *je bois à la santé de votre Maréchal*."[106]

Kollontai spent the rest of 1944 in the less hectic work of managing Soviet relations with Sweden. In February 1945 she contracted pneumonia, which her physician Nanna Svartz attributed to her being overtired. After three weeks she could sit up and begin working again. Shortly afterward Molotov called her back to Moscow for consultations. Svartz advised her that she should postpone the trip until she was stronger, but Kollontai replied that she had to obey orders. She did ask that Svartz go with her, and on a freezing morning in March the two women boarded a Soviet military aircraft for the flight to Moscow.

When they arrived, the temperature was thirty degrees below zero, the airport waiting room was icy, and there was no one to meet them. Svartz was worried about Kollontai, who was chilled, so she found an army officer to drive them to the city. On the way they came upon the welcoming committee, Semenov and Petrov, formerly Kollontai's subordinates in Stockholm, waving frantically from the roadside, having driven their car into a snowbank.[107]

Kollontai settled into a large apartment in the center of Moscow. Although she probably had been summoned home for consultations, her health was now so poor that she, or her superiors, decided it was time for her to retire.[108] She was made an adviser to the Commissariat of Foreign Affairs and she began to renew acquaintances in Moscow and complete the memoirs she had been writing since 1939.[109]

She lived for seven years as a pensioner, in an apartment decorated with the bright colors of Mexico. Her companions were Emy Lorentsson, her secretary, and Aleksandr, her cat. She had been richly honored—she received the Order of Lenin, two Orders of the Laboring Red Banner, a silver-framed picture of the Swedish King Gustav V, and in 1946 a nomination for the Nobel Peace Prize for her work in ending the Russo-Finnish wars. Some of her oldest friends came to see her—Ivan Maiskii, the Litvinovs, visiting Scandinavians—and Misha's family was living nearby; he had died during the war. Kollontai still dressed well, her eyes were still bright, although her face was marked by the stroke.[110]

Her life settled into a pattern. She did her correspondence with Lorentsson, then worked on preparing her archive. True to her historian's temperament, she had saved copies of her diaries, letters, and writings.

She dictated the final version of her memoirs, sitting at a desk next to a window where she also watched birds come to feed. Occasionally, Lorentsson read history aloud. Then, if Kollontai felt strong enough, she saw visitors or even went out to a diplomatic reception. In the summer she spent time in a rest home on the outskirts of the city; there she could sit on the porch in a wheelchair and look at the forest.[111]

Her health bothered her. She could not write or read easily because she could only use one hand. It took her a long time to dress every morning. She felt she had gotten too fat, but primarily she disliked being dependent on the people around her. She found it curious to be old and sick and working so little.[112] As she gathered the written record of her life, she made notes about its meaning.

She had made three contributions, she wrote. First, she had worked for full female emancipation. After all the years, she still put that first. "Hence my struggle for the new morality (brochure *The New Morality and the Working Class*, 1918). Although this brochure was written in the years of emigration, that is, before October, there are many valid ideas and Marxist positions in it." She also still took pride in *The Labor of Woman in the Evolution of the Economy, The Family and Communism*, the articles in *Kommunistka*, and her proposals in the 1926 marriage law debate. "My short stories had the same goal," she wrote, "struggle with bourgeois morality for the emancipation of women."[113]

Her second contribution was her "international work, agitation and propaganda in many countries" and the third was her diplomatic career. "Strictly speaking I lived not one, but many lives, the separate periods of my life so differed from one another. This was not an easy life, 'no walk through the roses,' as the Swedes say. There was everything in my life—achievement and great work, recognition, popularity among the broad masses, persecution, hatred, prison, failure and misunderstanding of my basic thoughts (on the woman [question] and on the way the marriage question was stated), many painful breaks with comrades, divergences from them, but long years of friendly, harmonious work in the party (under Lenin's leadership)."[114]

On March 8, 1952, the forty-first anniversary of International Woman's Day, Kollontai suffered severe chest pains. At 4:10 the next morning she died of heart failure.[115] She was buried in Novodevichii Cemetery in Moscow. Above her grave was erected a white marble statue, bearing the inscription "Revolutionary, Tribune, Diplomat." No obituary appeared in *Pravda*, for Kollontai had not been popular among Stalin's men. A small tribute was sent to *Izvestiia* signed by "a group of friends and associates."[116]

She was almost eighty when she died. Before her death she was still cheerful, still convinced that her country was building a great society, and, finally, willing to admit in writing that she had abandoned none of her feminism, and that she resented the price she had paid. She could have left the service of her country, but she stayed on, to be stained by her association with brutality and then redeemed by her work for Finland. She said she had survived by putting her faith in the future.

> This childlike ability to dream helped me all my life; I not only saw what was real, but I could easily imagine how it would be if life were changed. This ability to dream helped me to look into the future when our Soviet state would begin to be built. I can tell myself that I lived intensely, that by my nature and persuasion I was very active, and widely and greedily seized life, and my imagination made life even more interesting.[117]

She was a dreamer at the end, as she had been in the beginning; the utopian vision which had made her a revolutionary sustained her. She was a human being of beauty and hope and compromise and despair and vanity and dignity and belief. She outlived her illusions, but she remained faithful to her dream, even though its earthly manifestation took too much blood. She never found the reconciliation she sought between independence and community. To the women who continue that search after her, she left an epitaph.

> One must write not only for oneself. But for others. For those far-away, unknown women who will live then. Let them see that we were not heroines or heroes at all. But we believed passionately and ardently. We believed in our goals and we pursued them. We were sometimes strong, and sometimes we were very weak.

Notes

PREFACE

1. See Bibliography, Note on Sources.
2. Aleksandra Mikhailovna Kollontai, *Den första etappen* (Stockholm: Bonniers, 1945), p. 177. I am using the definition of the intelligentsia developed by Martin Malia in "What Is the Intelligentsia?" *The Russian Intelligentsia*, Richard Pipes, ed. (New York: Columbia University Press, 1961), pp. 1–18.

1. GIRLHOOD

1. Kollontai, "Iz vospominanii," *Oktiabr'*, no. 9 (1945), p. 60; "Mikhail Alekseevich Domontovich," *Voennaia entsiklopediia* (St. Petersburg, 1912), 9:178.
2. In Kollontai's memoirs the nanny's name is given in Russian as Godzheon. I have chosen Hodgson as the likely English original.
3. Kollontai, *Den första etappen*, p. 140.
4. Gustav Johansson [Carsten Halvorsen], *Revolutionens ambassadör: Alexandra Kollontays liv och gärning, åren 1892–1917* (Stockholm: Arbetarkulturs-förlag, 1945), p. 52.
5. Kollontai, "Iz vospominanii," p. 80.
6. Ibid., p. 61.
7. Ibid., p. 68.
8. Ibid., p. 65.
9. Ibid., p. 75.
10. Kollontai maintained that Mravinskii did not know he was working for the police. Ariadne Tyrkova-Williams, a Kadet and an opponent of Kollontai's, wrote that he was a police agent (Tyrkova-Vil'iams, *Na putiakh k svobodu* [New York: Izd-vo. im. Chekhova, 1952], p. 401). Neither woman was unbiased; therefore Mravinskii's relationship to the police remains a mystery.
11. Kollontai, *Den första etappen*, pp. 80–84.
12. Ibid., pp. 83–84.
13. Ibid., p. 72.

14. Ibid., p. 117.

15. Halvorsen, p. 26.

16. Kollontai, *Den första etappen*, p. 156.

17. Ibid., p. 209.

18. Ibid., p. 211.

19. Kollontai, *Iz moei zhizni i raboty* (Moscow: Sovetskaia Rossiia, 1974), pp. 60–61.

20. Kollontai, *Den första etappen*, p. 217.

21. Kollontai, "Avtobiograficheskii ocherk," *Proletarskaia revoliutsiia*, no. 1 (1921), p. 261.

22. Kollontai, *Den första etappen*, pp. 218–19.

23. Ibid., pp. 7, 218–20.

24. Ibid., p. 226.

25. Ibid., pp. 226, 227–28.

26. Kollontai, *Iz moei zhizni*, p. 73.

27. Kollontai, *Den första etappen*, p. 234.

28. Ibid., pp. 176–77.

29. Ibid., p. 185.

30. Kollontai, *Iz moei zhizni i raboty*, p. 85; Kollontai, *Den första etappen*, pp. 238–42.

31. Kollontai, *Den första etappen*, pp. 244, 245.

32. Ibid., p. 246.

33. Ibid., pp. 255–56.

34. Ibid., p. 257.

35. Ibid., p. 78, 258.

36. Kollontai, "Osnovy vospitaniia po vzgliadam Dobroliubova," *Obrazovanie*, no. 9 (September 1898), p. 2.

37. Ibid., no. 10 (October 1898), p. 3.

38. Ibid., pp. 17, 14.

2. SOCIAL DEMOCRAT

1. George Lichtheim, *Marxism: An Historical and Critical Study*, 2d ed. (New York: Praeger, 1965), pp. 286–89; Peter Gay, *The Dilemma of Democratic Socialism: Eduard Bernstein's Challenge to Marx* (New York: Collier, 1962), pp. 110–30, 146–51, 166–74.

2. Adam Ulam, *The Bolsheviks* (New York: Collier, 1965), pp. 150–51; John L. H. Keep, *The Rise of Social Democracy in Russia* (Oxford: Clarendon Press, 1963), pp. 58–59.

3. Samuel Baron, *Plekhanov, the Father of Russian Marxism* (Stanford: Stanford University Press, 1963), p. 200; Ulam, *The Bolsheviks*, p. 151; Keep, *The Rise of Social Democracy in Russia*, pp. 59–65.

4. Kollontai, "Avtobiograficheskii ocherk," p. 263.

5. See below, p. 33.

6. George Lichtheim has written that there are strong elements of liberalism in Bernstein, and naturally nonrevisionists perceived that. (*Marxism*, pp. 287–89.)

7. Halvorsen, p. 93; Erkki Salomaa, "Pervoe nauchnoe issledovanie o zhizni finskikh rabochikh," *Skandinavskii sbornik* 7 (1963):300.

8. Salomaa, p. 299.

9. Kollontai, "Avtobiograficheskii ocherk," p. 265; Kollontai, "Kollontai, Aleksandra Mikhailovna," *Deiateli SSSR i Oktiabr'skoi Revoliutsii: Entsiklopedicheskii slovar'*, 3 parts (Moscow and Leningrad: Granat, 1925–28), part 1, p. 199.

10. Halvorsen, p. 95.

11. Ibid., p. 94.

12. Ibid., p. 93.

13. Anna Markovna Itkina, *Revoliutsioner, tribun, diplomat: Stranitsi zhizni Aleksandry Mikhailovny Kollontai*, 2d ed., enlarged (Moscow: Politizdat, 1970), pp. 35–36.

14. Kollontai, *Den första etappen*, p. 110.

15. Kollontai, "Promyshlennost' i torgovlia Velikogo Kniazhestva Finliandskogo," *Nauchnoe obozrenie*, no. 1 (1901), p. 9.

16. Ibid., pp. 24–36; Kollontai, *Zhizn' finliandskikh rabochikh* (St. Petersburg: Khudozhestvennyi pechat, 1903), pp. 5, 71–106, 124, 221.

17. Kollontai, "Zemelyni vopros v Finliandii," *Nauchnoe obozrenie*, no. 4 (1902), p. 136.

18. Ibid., pp. 134–36.

19. See Akselrod's request for a copy of one of her articles in P. B. Aksel'rod, *Pis'ma Aksel'roda i Iu. O. Martova*, Russian Reprint Series, Alexandre V. Soloviev and Alan Kimball, eds. (The Hague: Mouton, 1967), p. 168.

20. Kollontai, "Avtobiograficheskii ocherk," pp. 265–66.

21. Halvorsen, p. 100.

22. E. D. Stasova, *Vospominaniia* (Moscow: Mysl, 1969), pp. 113–14.

23. Halvorsen, p. 104.

24. Ibid.

25. Vladimir Il'ich Lenin, *Polnoe sobranie sochinenii*, 5th ed. in 56 volumes (Moscow: Politizdat, 1958–66), 47:6.

26. Keep, *The Rise of Social Democracy*, pp. 190, 281.

27. See her attack on the German trade unions for their compromise tactics in Kollontai, "Itogi mangeimskogo s"ezda (sotsial'demokraticheskaia partiia i professional'nye soiuzy)," *Sovremennyi mir* 1 (November 1906):1–19.

28. Kollontai, "Kollontai," p. 200; Halvorsen, p. 112.

29. Kollontai, *K voprosu o klassovoi bor'be* (St. Petersburg: Malykh, 1905), p. 7, 12.

30. Ibid., p. 31.

31. Kollontai, "Kto takie sotsial-demokraty i chego oni khotiat?" *Rabochii ezhegodnik* 1 (1906):79, 82.

32. Ibid., pp. 78, 85.

33. I am adapting here the analysis of Philip Converse ("The Nature of Belief Systems in Mass Publics," *Ideology and Discontent*, David E. Apter, ed. [New York: The Free Press, 1964], p. 208). He uses the concept "idea-element" to designate components of belief systems, and he asserts that "idea-elements in

a belief system vary in a property we shall call *centrality* according to the role that they play in the belief system as a whole." (Ibid.) The greater its centrality the more fundamental an idea-element is to a belief system. It is therefore less likely to change either over time or under stress than the more peripheral premises. I would add that the central idea-elements are tightly tied to the intellectual and emotional needs of which the ideology is an expression. Not only are they logically necessary to the belief system, but they are also psychologically necessary. The presence of psychological need will reinforce the tendency to defend these idea-elements from change. It also follows that individuals within a movement ostensibly sharing one ideology will differ in the centrality of idea-elements to their own individual belief systems, and that those differences spring from psychological as well as intellectual causes. Thus an ostensibly like-minded group like the Bolsheviks is actually an amalgam of individuals, bound together by certain shared idea-elements but differing in the importance they attach to those components of their belief systems. They are far more like a mixture than a compound, hence their volatility.

34. Gay, *Bernstein*, pp. 151–60.

35. Kollontai, "Problema nravstvennosti s positivnoi tochki zreniia," *Obrazovanie* 14 (September 1905):80.

36. Kollontai, "Etika i sotsial-demokratiia (po povodu stat'e g. Pokrovskogo v No. 4 'Poliarnoi zvezdy,')" *Obrazovanie*, 15, no. 2 (February 1906), pp. 24, 25, 26, 27. Emphasis Kollontai's.

37. Kollontai, "Problema nravstvennosti," *Obrazovanie*, (September 1905):94.

38. Ibid.

39. Ibid., (October 1905):97.

40. Ibid., p. 96.

41. Kollontai, "Etika," p. 30.

42. Kollontai, "Problema nravstvennosti," no. 10, pp. 106, 106–7.

3. SOCIALIST FEMINIST

1. Marie Zebrikoff, "Russia," in *The Woman Question in Europe*, Theodore Stanton, ed., unabridged republication of the 1884 New York edition (New York: Source Book Press, 1970), p. 400; Käthe Schirmacher, *The Modern Woman's Rights Movement*, Carl Conrad Eckhardt, trans. (New York: Macmillan, 1912), pp. 226–27.

2. Richard Stites, "M. L. Mikhailov and the Emergence of the Woman Question in Russia," *Canadian Slavic Studies* 3 (Summer 1969):180–81, 187–95.

3. Robert H. McNeal, "Women in the Russian Radical Movement," *Journal of Social History* (Winter 1971–72), p. 144.

4. See Barbara Alpern Engel and Clifford N. Rosenthal, eds. and trans., *Five Sisters: Women Against the Tsar* (New York: Alfred A. Knopf, 1975).

5. See Richard Stites, "Women's Liberation Movements in Russia, 1900–1930," *Canadian-American Slavic Studies* 7, no. 4 (Winter 1973):460–74.

6. Kollontai, "Avtobiograficheskii ocherk," pp. 267–68, 270.

7. See Rose Glickman, "The Russian Factory Woman, 1880–1914," *Women in Russia*, Dorothy Atkinson, Alexander Dallin, and Gail Warshofsky Lapidus, eds. (Stanford: Stanford University Press, 1977), pp. 64–73.

8. Kollontai, "Avtobiograficheskii ocherk," p. 271. It is not altogether accurate to refer to the German organization as a "Woman's Bureau" until 1908; before that the agitators who worked with women were called *Vertrauenspersonen*, their leader in Berlin was the *Zentralvertrauensperson*. In 1908, when the German government legalized female participation in political parties, the SPD established a *Frauenbureau*.

9. Ibid., p. 272. Emphasis Kollontai's.

10. Kollontai, "K istorii dvizheniia rabotnits v Rossii," *Kommunisticheskaia partiia i organizatsiia rabotnits* (Moscow and Petrograd: Kommunist, 1919), p. 75; S. N. Serditova, *Bol'sheviki v bor'be za zhenskie proletarskie massy* (Moscow: Politizdat, 1959), p. 55n.

11. Kollontai, "K istorii," p. 76; Kollontai, "Na puti k kommunizmu i polnomu raskreposhcheniiu zhenshchiny," Kommunisticheskaia partiia Sovetskogo Soiuza, *Tri goda diktatury proletariata (Itogi raboty sredi zhenshchin Moskovskoi Organizatsii RKP)* (Moscow: Izd. Moskovskogo komiteta RKP, [1921]), pp. 13–14. According to one Soviet source women workers were already attending the clubs organized predominantly for men. He estimates the figure for female participation at 15–20 percent. The men did not really welcome them, however, and when asked why they did not bring their wives, they often replied, "Why, what would she do here?" (I. D. Levin, "Rabochie kluby v Peterburge," Vserossiiskii tsentral'nyi sovet professional'nykh soiuzov, Komissia po izucheniiu istorii professional'nogo dvizheniia v SSSR, *Materialy po istorii professional'nogo dvizheniia v Rossii* [Moscow: VTsSPS, n.d.], p. 99.)

12. Kollontai, "Avtobiograficheskii ocherk," pp. 274–75. Elsewhere Kollontai charged that party comrades had "broken up" the club, but she did not say who or how. (Kollontai, "Zhenskoe rabochee dvizhenie," *Nasha zaria*, no. 2 [1913], p. 16.)

13. Kollontai, *Sotsial'nye osnovy zhenskogo voprosa* (St. Petersburg: Znanie, 1909), pp. 314–15.

14. *Vörwarts*, 18 August, 21 August 1907. For Zetkin's proposals see International Socialist Congress, 7th, Stuttgart, 1907, *Compte rendu analytique* (Brussels: Brismee, 1908), p. 261, 329–43.

15. Kollontai, "Dva techeniia (po povodu pervoi mezhdunarodnoi zhenskoi sotsialisticheskoi konferentsii v Shtutgarte)," *Obrazovanie* 16 (October 1907): 54.

16. Friedrich Engels, *The Origin of the Family, Private Property, and the State* (New York: International Publishers, 1940), p. 5.

17. Ibid., p. 6. Emphasis Engels's.

18. H. Kent Geiger, *The Family in Soviet Russia* (Cambridge: Harvard University Press, 1968), pp. 29–32, 39. Engels was criticized on this point by contemporaries Heinrich Cunow and Karl Kautsky. See Werner Thönnessen,

The Emancipation of Women: The Rise and Decline of the Women's Movement in German Social Democracy 1863–1933, Joris de Bres, trans. (London: Pluto Press, 1973), p. 38.

19. Engels, *Origin*, p. 47. Emphasis Engels's.

20. Ibid., pp. 54, 56.

21. Ibid., pp. 61, 62.

22. Ibid., pp. 68, 63, 68.

23. Ibid., p. 68.

24. August Bebel, *Woman Under Socialism*, trans. from the 33rd edition by Daniel De Leon (New York: New York Labor News, 1904), p. 65. I am discussing Bebel after Engels, even though his book was published earlier, because his later editions, which I am summarizing, drew on Engels.

25. Ibid., p. 150. Emphasis Bebel's.

26. Ibid., p. 180.

27. Ibid., pp. 115, 116.

28. Ibid., p. 86.

29. Ibid., p. 349.

30. For an analysis of these attitudes see Alfred Meyer, "Marxism and the Women's Movement," *Women in Russia*, pp. 98–102.

31. Kollontai, *Sotsial'nye osnovy*, p. 45.

32. Ibid., p. 56.

33. Ibid., p. 89. The program is repeated in greater detail on pp. 227–29.

34. Ibid., p. 111.

35. Ibid., pp. 114, 135.

36. Ibid., pp. 196–97.

37. Ibid., pp. 241–430.

38. Ibid., p. 286. Emphasis Kollontai's.

39. Ibid., pp. 287, 298–99, 388.

40. Ibid., p. 110.

41. Kollontai, "K istorii dvizheniia rabotnits," p. 79.

42. Kollontai, "Avtobiograficheskii ocherk," p. 279.

43. Kollontai, "K istorii dvizheniia rabotnits," p. 79.

44. This account of the preparations for the Woman's Congress is based on Kollontai, "Avtobiograficheskii ocherk," pp. 276–79; Kollontai, "K istorii dvizheniia rabotnits," pp. 77–79; Kollontai, "Zhenshchina-rabotnitsa na pervom feministskom s"ezde v Rossii," *Golos sotsial-demokrata* 2 (March 1909):6–7.

45. Linda Edmondson, "Russian Feminists and the First All-Russian Congress of Women," *Russian History* 3, part 2 (1976), p. 131.

46. Kollontai, "Zhenskoe rabochee dvizhenie," p. 6.

47. Kollontai, "Zhenshchina-rabotnitsa v sovremennom obshchestve," *Trudy I vserossiiskogo zhenskogo s"ezda* (St. Petersburg: 1908), pp. 800–801.

48. Ibid.

49. Edmondson, "The Russian Feminists and the First All-Russian Congress of Women," p. 147.

50. Kollontai, "Zhenskoe rabochee dvizhenie," p. 7.

51. A. Ermanskii, "Vserossiiskii zhenskii s"ezd," *Sovremennyi mir*, no. 1–2 (January 1909), pp. 108–12; W., "Zhenskii s"ezd i rabochaia gruppa (Pis'mo iz Peterburga)," *Golos sotsial'demokrata* 2 (March 1909):7–8. A Soviet scholar, V. N. Smirnova, has written that this advocacy of cooperation with "democratic elements" was a Menshevik, "liquidationist" approach not shared by the Bolsheviks. Smirnova also attempts to show that throughout 1908 the Bolsheviks supported the congress work, while the Mensheviks opposed it. There is no contemporary evidence that the Petersburg Committee members of the two factions differed significantly on the issue, however. Furthermore, the Bolsheviks seem to have held the majority on the committee at that point, and Slutskaia, the delegate sent to head the delegation at the last minute, was a Bolshevik. Thus the argument that the pro-congress Bolsheviks were thwarted by the anti-congress Mensheviks seems inaccurate. (V. N. Smirnova, "Iz istorii bor'by za razoblachenie burzhuaznogo feminizma v Rossii," *Voprosy istorii, filologii, i pedagogiki* 2 [1967]:34–35.) Despite these shortcomings, Smirnova is franker than most Soviet scholars who have written about the congress. Several attempt to present the delegation as purely Bolshevik and write as if Kollontai were a Bolshevik. See, for example, E. I. Bochkareva and S. Liubimova, *Svetlyi put'* (Moscow: Politizdat, 1967), p. 29; I. M. Dazhina, "Predislovie," in Kollontai, *Izbrannye stat'i i rechi* (Moscow: Politizdat, 1972), pp. 6–8; Itkina, pp. 47–53.

52. Kollontai, "Avtobiograficheskii ocherk," p. 280.

53. Karen Honeycutt, "Clara Zetkin: A Socialist Attempt to Combat Woman's Oppression," paper presented at the Second Berkshire Conference on the History of Women, Cambridge, Mass., October 1974, pp. 13–21.

54. Kollontai, *Po rabochei Evrope* (St. Petersburg: Semenov, 1912), p. 116.

55. G. D. Petrov, "Aleksandra Kollontai nakanune i v gody pervoi mirovoi voiny," *Novaia i noveishaia istoriia* 13 (1969):70.

56. International Socialist Congress, 8th, Copenhagen, 1910, *Compte rendu analytique* (n.p.: "Volksdrukkerij," 1911), pp. 492–95; *Vörwarts*, 28 August 1910.

57. Kollontai, "Itogi vtoroi mezhdunarodnoi zhenskoi sotsialisticheskoi konferentsii," *Nasha zaria* 1 (September 1910):93–94.

58. For the Braun-Zetkin disagreement over insurance funding see Jacqueline Strain, "Feminism and Political Radicalism in the German Social-Democratic Movement, 1890–1914" (Ph.D. dissertation, University of California, Berkeley, 1964), pp. 183–86.

59. Ibid., p. 95.

60. I. M. Maiskii, "A. M. Kollontai," *Oktiabr'*, no. 7 (1962), pp. 107–8.

61. Ibid.

62. *Arbetet*, 5 September 1910. For Kollontai's record of the congress see also *Po rabochei Evrope*, pp. 260–68.

63. Kollontai said that prostitution could be eradicated only by fundamentally improving the lives of working women, not by giving them charity. See Kollontai, "Zadachi s"ezda po bor'be s prostitutsiei," *Vozrozhdenie* 2 (30 March 1910):8–17; "Zadachi rabotnits v bor'be s prostitutsiei," *Golos' sotsial-*

demokrata 3 (April 1910):3–4; "Proletariat i burzhuaziia v bor'be s prostitut-siei," *Pravda* (Vienna), 24 June (7 July) 1910, p. 3; "Itogi s"ezda po bor'be s prostitutsiei," *Sotsial' demokrata*, 22 July (5 July), 1910, pp. 5–6. Kollontai's letters to Russia on this subject attracted the attention of the Okhrana, or tsarist police, in Paris, and it prepared a report listing Kollontai as "one of the most prominent and active" of the Russian Social Democrats in Berlin. See Paris Okhrana Files, XVIIn, folder 26, Hoover Institution on War, Revolution and Peace, Stanford.

64. Kollontai, "K istorii dvizheniia rabotnits," p. 84.

65. Savva Dangulov, *Dvenadtsat' dorog na Egl* (Moscow: Sovetskaia Rossiia, 1970), pp. 321–22.

66. Kollontai, "Avtobiograficheskii ocherk" pp. 283–84. See also the articles for this period listed in the Bibliography.

67. I. M. Dazhina, one of the few scholars given access to Kollontai's archive at the Marx-Lenin Institute in Moscow, has confirmed that Kollontai wrote her reminiscences from diaries. See Dazhina, "Aleksandra Kollontai o sebe i svoei epokhe," in Kollontai, *Iz moei zhizni*, p. 7.

68. Kollontai, *Po rabochei Evrope*, p. 32.

69. Ibid., p. 35.

70. Ibid., p. 16.

71. Halvorsen, p. 176. The sources on this episode are complex. Kollontai referred in print to Maslov as a colleague, once in a review of his books ("Sud'ba chelovechestva v voprose narodnogo naseleniia," *Zhizn'* [September 1910], pp. 10–24) and many years later in a memoir article ("Avtobiograficheskii ocherk," p. 274). She described the affair in a 1923 novelette, *Bol'shaia liubov'* [A Great Love], but she named the man Senia. The first contemporary of hers to write about the subject was Gustav Johansson, but he did not identify her lover. Much later he and Kollontai's secretary Emy Lorentsson told Kaare Hauge that the man was Maslov. See Kaare Hauge, "Alexandra Mikhailovna Kollontai: The Scandinavian Period, 1922–1945" (Ph.D. dissertation, University of Minnesota, 1971), p. 28; Halvorsen, pp. 173–76.

72. Kollontai, "Bol'shaia liubov'," *Zhenshchina na perelome* (Moscow and Petrograd: Gosizdat, 1923), p. 91.

73. Kollontai reissued all three virtually without editing in 1918 under the title *Novaia moral' i rabochii klass* (Moscow: Izd. VTsIK, 1918). References below are to this edition because it is more easily available. I have compared it sentence by sentence to the original articles and Kollontai changed only the phrase "progressive class" to "working class." The following discussion is also based on two less important, but related articles, "Dve pravdy," *Novaia zhizn',* no. 8 (1912), pp. 166–75, and "Soiuz zashchity materinstva i reforma seksual'-noi morali," *Novaia zhizn',* no. 11 (1912), pp. 239–54.

74. Kollontai, *Novaia moral',* pp. 40–41.

75. Ibid., p. 51.

76. Ibid., p. 57.

77. Ibid., p. 12.

78. This theme is developed particularly in "Dve pravdy."

79. Kollontai, *Novaia moral,'* p. 15.

80. Ibid., pp. 60–61. Emphasis mine.

81. Kollontai's 1905–6 articles also show traces of Bogdanov's influence in their similar, though more muted stress on proletarian ideology. See above, pp. 35–38. According to Bogdanov, "Custom, law, morality are a special series of adaptation-mechanisms directed towards achieving the most harmonious relations between people in the social-labor process." Quoted by S. V. Utechin, "Philosophy and Science: Alexander Bogdanov," in *Revisionism, Essays on the History of Marxist Ideas,* Leopold Labedz, ed. (New York: Praeger, 1962), p. 121.

82. Kollontai, *Novaia moral,'* p. 59.

83. Ibid., p. 6.

84. Ibid., pp. 7, 35.

85. Ibid., p. 9.

86. Ibid., p. 20.

87. Ibid., p. 45.

88. For the testimony to this process see Inessa Armand, *Rabotnitsy v Internatsionale* (Moscow: n.p., 1920), p. 20; Vera Dridzo, "Slovo iasnoe, prostoe i glubkoe: Nadezhda Konstantinovna Krupskaia i zhurnal 'Rabotnitsa,'" *Vsegda s vami: Sbornik posviashchennyi 50-letiiu "Rabotnitsa"* (Moscow: Rabotnitsa, 1965), p. 31; A. I. Elizarova, "Rozhdenie 'Rabotnitsy,'" *Vsegda s vami,* p. 23; A. Grigor'eva-Alekseeva, "Vpervye v Rossii," *Zhenshchiny v russkoi revoliutsii* (Moscow: Politizdat, 1959), p. 95; Kollontai "I v Rossii budet zhenskii den'," *Izbrannye stat'i,* pp. 126–27; Kollontai, "K istorii zhenskogo dvizhenii," pp. 84–85; Lenin, *PSS,* 55:448; S. T. Liubimova, "Raznostoronnii um i bol'shoe serdtse," *Riadom s Leninym: Vospominaniia o N. K. Krupskoi* (Moscow: Politizdat, 1969), p. 295. See also Anne Bobroff, "The Bolsheviks and Working Women, 1905–30," *Soviet Studies* 26 (1974):549–55; Rose Glickman, "The Russian Factory Woman, 1880–1914," *Women in Russia,* pp. 79–83. Both of these historians question 1912 as a time of new female participation. Possibly the Bolsheviks thought they saw an awareness which was not actually different from earlier years.

89. "Samoilova, Konkordiia Nikolaevna," *Deiateli SSSR i Oktiabr'skoi Revoliutsii,* part 3, pp. 1–2.

90. Bertram Wolfe, "Lenin and Inessa Armand," *Slavic Review* 22 (March 1963): 98–99.

91. Ibid., pp. 99–102.

92. Jean Fréville, *Inessa Armand: Une Grande Figure de la Révolution Russe* (Paris: Éditions sociales, 1957), p. 72.

93. G. I. Petrovskii, "Zhizn' polnaia blagorodstva i predannosti idee kommunizma," *Riadom s Leninym,* p. 85.

94. "Krupskaia Nadezhda Konstantinovna," *Deiateli SSSR i Oktiabr'skoi Revoliutsii,* part 1, p. 237.

95. Grigor'eva-Alekseeva, pp. 96–98; Samoilova, *V ob"edinenii zalog pobedu* (*K mezhdunarodnomu sotsialisticheskomu dniu rabotnits 8 marta 1921*) (Moscow: Gosizdat, 1921), p. 10.

96. Armand, *Rabotnitsy v Internatsionale*, p. 22; Liudmilla Stal', "Istoriia zhurnala 'Rabotnitsa'," *Zhenshchiny v russkoi revoliutsii*, p. 108; *Vsegda s vami*, pp. 48, 50, 55, 58, 59; Fréville, *Inessa Armand*, pp. 80–81.

97. Kollontai, "Zhenskoe rabochee dvizhenie," p. 6; Kollontai, "Zashchita materinstva," *Nasha zaria*, no. 9 (1913), p. 21. See also Kollontai, "Zhenskii den'," *Pravda*, 17 February 1913, as reprinted in *Izbrannye stat'i*, pp. 109–12; Kollontai, "Zhenskii den' priblizhaetsia," *Novaia rabochaia gazeta*, 21 January 1914, p. 2; Kollontai, "I v Rossii budet zhenskii den'," pp. 125–27. All these articles call for a woman's bureau and maternity insurance.

98. As quoted in Dridzo, "Slovo iasnoe," p. 32. The article never appeared in *Rabotnitsa* because the police confiscated it.

99. S-va, "K mezhdunarodnomu dniu zhenshchin-rabotnits," *Put' pravdy*, 29 January 1914, p. 2.

100. Dridzo, "Slovo iasnoe," pp. 25–26; Z. P. Igumnova, *Zhenshchiny Moskvy v gody grazhdanskoi voine* (Moscow: Moskovskii rabochii, 1958), p. 8.

101. Lenin, *PSS*, 48:336.

102. Ibid., pp. 303–4. Emphasis Lenin's.

103. Kollontai, "Avtobiograficheskii ocherk," p. 290; Akademiia nauk SSSR, Institut istorii, *Istoriia vtorogo Internatsionala*, 2 v (Moscow: Nauka, 1965–66), 2:380. See also two of Kollontai's letters in the Nicolaevsky Archive, N. 119, Box 2, Item 28, Hoover Institution on War, Revolution and Peace.

4. INTERNATIONALIST

1. G. D. Petrov, "Meridiany druzhby," *Moskva*, no. 1 (1967), pp. 163–64; Akademiia nauk, *Istoriia vtorogo Internatsionala*, 2:243.

2. Itkina, pp. 82–83.

3. Kollontai, *Otryvki iz dnevnika 1914 g.* (Leningrad: Gosizdat, 1925), p. 5.

4. Ibid., p. 24.

5. Kollontai, "Golos Lenina," *Oktiabr'* 40 (1963):5.

6. Kollontai, *Otryvki*, p. 42.

7. Kollontai, "Golos Lenina," p. 5.

8. Kollontai, *Autobiographie einer sexuell emanzipierten Kommunistin*, Iring Fetscher, ed. (Munich: Rogner and Bernhard, 1970), p. 32.

9. Kollontai, "Till de socialistiska kvinnorna i alla länder," *Stormklockan*, 15 November 1914, p. 2.

10. Michael Futrell, *Northern Underground* (New York: Praeger, 1963), p. 86; A. G. Shliapnikov, "Shliapnikov, Aleksandr Gavrilovich," *Deiateli SSSR i Oktiabr'skoi Revoliutsii*, part 3, p. 245.

11. Ibid., pp. 246–49; G. Shklovskii, "Vladimir Il'ich nakanune Bernskoi konferentsii," *Proletarskaia revoliutsiia*, no. 5 (40) (May 1925), p. 142.

12. Futrell, p. 106.

13. Lenin, *PSS*, 49:20–21.

14. Itkina, p. 96.

15. Lenin, *PSS*, 49:39; *Leninskii sbornik*, 3rd edition in 35 vols. (Moscow and Leningrad: Gosizdat, 1925), 2:221, 222–23; G. D. Petrov, "A. M. Kollontai v gody pervoi mirovoi voiny," *Istoriia SSSR*, no. 3 (1968), p. 86.

16. Kollontai, "Avtobiograficheskii ocherk," p. 291; *Riksdagens protokoll vid lagtima riksmötet år 1915: Andra kammaren* (Stockholm: Norstedt, 1915), 1:54–55.

17. Kollontai, "Kriget och våra närmaste uppgifter," *Forsvarsnihilisten*, no. 11 (1914), as reprinted in *Izbrannye stat'i*, pp. 128–32.

18. Hjalmar Branting, "Alexandra Kollontay utvisad!" *Socialdemokraten*, 21 November 1914, p. 3.

19. Dangulov, *Dvenadtsat' dorog na Egl*, pp. 300–301.

20. Zeth Höglund, "Den skamliga utvisningen," *Stormklockan*, 28 November 1914, p. 1; Halvorsen, pp. 214, 211; Dangulov, *Dvenadtsat' dorog na Egl*, p. 301. For the parliamentary debate see *Riksdagens protokoll*, 1915, 1:47–48, 54–56, 60–61, 64–66.

21. Kollontai, "Avtobiograficheskii ocherk," p. 38; Kollontai, *Iz moei zhizni*, p. 173.

22. Kollontai, "Chto delat'? Otvet sotsialistkam," *Nashe slovo*, 19 February 1915, p. 1; "K vozrozhdeniiu," *Nashe slovo*, 28 April 1915, p. 1; "Kopengagenskaia konferentsiia," *Nashe slovo*, 29 January 1915, p. 2; "Kopengagenskaia konferentsiia," *Nashe slovo*, 2 February 1915, p. 1; "V Germanii," *Nashe slovo*, 8 April 1915, p. 1; "Vmesto 'zhenskogo dnia,'—internatsional'naia demonstratsiia sotsialistok," *Nashe slovo*, 25 February 1915, p. 2; "Zhenskii den'," *Nashe slovo*, 18 March 1915, p. 2; "Zhenskii sotsialisticheskoi Internatsional i voina," *Nashe slovo*, 7 March 1915, pp. 3–4; "Fosterlandsförsvar eller internationell solidaritet," *Stormklockan*, 26 December 1914, pp. 6–7.

23. V. S. Nevolina and N. V. Orlova, eds., "O mezhdunarodnoi zhenskoi sotsialisticheskoi konferentsii v 1915 g.," *Istoricheskii arkhiv*, no. 3 (1960), p. 113.

24. Ibid., p. 117.

25. Kollontai, "Germanskaia sotsialdemokratiia v pervye dni voiny," *Nashe slovo*, 4 April 1915, p. 2; 9 April 1915, pp. 1–2; 10 April 1915, p. 1.

26. Nevolina and Orlova, "O mezhdunarodnoi zhenskoi konferentsii," p. 123.

27. Kollontai, "Pochemu molchal proletariat Germanii v iiul'skie dni," *Kommunist*, no. 1–2 (1915), pp. 159–61.

28. Trotsky was attempting the same task. See Isaac Deutscher, *The Prophet Armed: Trotsky, 1879–1921* (New York: Vintage, 1954), pp. 216–26.

29. Kollontai, "Avtobiograficheskii ocherk," p. 293; Kollontai, *Autobiographie*, p. 36; Lenin, *PSS*, 49:76–77, 94–95. In the second letter Lenin's tone was friendly and informal, and he signed it "Yours, Lenin." As the year progressed he became surer of Kollontai and his letters became friendlier.

30. I. M. Dazhina and P. Tsivlina, eds., "Iz arkhiva A. M. Kollontai," *Inostrannaia literatura*, no. 1 (1970), p. 227.

31. Ibid., p. 228. See also Kollontai, *Iz moei zhizni*, pp. 181–85. Although she now criticized *Nashe slovo* for indecision, Kollontai continued to contribute

to it. On one article in April 1916 the editors (Trotsky?) politely noted that the writer's views were those of a Leninist (Kollontai, "Vesti iz Rossii: Interv'iu s 'obyvatelem,'" *Nashe slovo*, 18 April 1916, p. 1). See Bibliography for a list of her other articles in *Nashe slovo*.

32. Kollontai, *Komu nuzhna voina?* (Bern: TsK RSDRP, 1916); Lenin, *PSS*, 49:106–7, 118.

33. Stephen F. Cohen, *Bukharin and the Bolshevik Revolution* (New York: Alfred A. Knopf, 1973), pp. 24–25, 36–37; Kollontai, "Avtobiograficheskii ocherk," p. 293; Kollontai, "'Belyi' i 'zheltyi' kapitalizm," *Nashe slovo*, 20 June 1915, pp. 1–2. See also an earlier article which argued against the validity of "national culture" in an international era; "Fosterlandsförsvar eller internationell solidaritet," *Stormklockan*, 26 December 1914, pp. 6–7. For further evidence on her position in the summer of 1915 see *Iz moei zhizni*, p. 186.

34. G. D. Petrov, "O broshiure A. M. Kollontai 'Komu nuzhna voina,'" *Sovetskie arkhivy*, no. 5 (1968), p. 110.

35. L. D. Trotskii, *Nashe slovo*, no. 10, 10 May 1916, as quoted in Deutscher, *The Prophet Armed*, p. 225.

36. Shliapnikov had come to Norway in 1915, because, he said, life was cheaper there and police surveillance lighter. One suspects Kollontai also had something to do with his decision. He remained in Sweden until April, when he went to Britain, then back to Russia in midsummer. He passed through Christiania en route. In early 1916 he returned to Scandinavia. A. G. Shliapnikov, *Nakanune 1917 goda*, 2 vols. (Moscow: Gosizdat, 1920), 1:62–71, 188.

37. Petrov, "A. M. Kollontai v gody mirovoi voiny," p. 92; Dazhina and Tsivlina, "Iz arkhiva A. M. Kollontai," no. 2, p. 227; Kollontai, *Iz moei zhizni*, p. 175. Höglund did not discuss these talks in his articles about Kollontai, beyond saying in his memoirs that she and Shliapnikov presented Lenin's views to him. (*Minnen i fackelsen*, 3 vols. [Stockholm: Tiden, 1951–60], 2:178.) Nerman also gave no details in his later writing about Kollontai (*I vilda östern* [Stockholm: Ljungbergs förlag, 1930]; "Lika vacker som klok," *Röster i radio*, no. 20 [1967], pp. 14–15).

38. Kollontai, *Iz moei zhizni*, p. 188; Lenin, *PSS*, 49:138.

39. Ibid., p. 193.

40. Kollontai, "Amerikanskie dnevniki A. M. Kollontai, 1915–1916," *Istoricheskii arkhiv* 1 (January 1962): 133.

41. Theodore Draper, *The Roots of American Communism* (New York: Viking, 1957), p. 57.

42. Ibid., pp. 66–67.

43. Ludwig Lore, "Leon Trotsky," *One Year of Revolution* (Brooklyn: Socialist Publication Society, 1918), p. 7.

44. Horst Lademacher, ed., *Die Zimmerwalder Bewegung*, 2 vols. (The Hague: Mouton, 1967), 2:176–78; Kollontai, "Amerikanskie dnevniki," p. 135; D. Baevskii, "Bol'sheviki v Tsimmerval'de," *Proletarskaia revoliutsiia*, no. 5 (1935), pp. 38–39.

45. Kollontai, "Amerikanskie dnevniki," pp. 135, 138, 143.

46. Ibid., p. 138. For representative interviews see "Says Kaiser and Czar Fear Revolt at Home," *New York Times,* 11 October 1915, sec. 1, p. 3; *Cleveland Plain Dealer,* 15 December 1915, sec. 1, p. 1.

47. Kollontai, "Amerikanskie dnevniki," p. 149. The italicized portions are in English in the original.

48. Ibid., p. 146; Tyrkova-Vil'iams, *Na putiakh k svobode,* pp. 78–79; "A. Kolontai [sic] protiv samooborony (pis'mo iz Detroita)," *Svobodonoe slovo,* no. 5 (February 1916), pp. 309–11. A Soviet historian wrote that Kollontai sought to unite the various Russian communities and bolshevize them, but nothing in her diary bears that out. (Petrov, "A. M. Kollontai v gody pervoi mirovoi voiny," p. 94; Petrov, "Aleksandra Kollontai v SShA," *Novaia i noveishaia istoriia,* no. 3 [1972], pp. 130, 134.) Lenin told her to put Bolsheviks everywhere in touch with him, which she may have attempted to do with limited success. (*Leninskii sbornik,* 2:354.) For some reason, the paragraph telling her to contact Bolsheviks was left out of this letter as published in *PSS,* 49:163–64.

49. Kollontai, "Amerikanskie dnevniki," p. 149. The italicized portions are in English in the original.

50. Kollontai, "The Attitude of the Russian Socialists," *New Review* 4 (March 1916):60–61; Kollontai, "Do Internationalists Want a Split?" *International Socialist Review* 16 (January 1916):394–96; Kollontai, "The Third International," *The American Socialist,* 23 October 1915, p. 2.

51. Draper, *Roots of American Communism,* pp. 75–76.

52. Kollontai, "Amerikanskie dnevniki," pp. 155–56.

53. He found to his dismay that the people he was to contact in New York were all on vacation. Shliapnikov, *Nakanune 1917 goda,* pp. 188–94.

54. Merle Fainsod, *International Socialism and the World War* (New York: Octagon Books, 1973), p. 118; N. E. Korolev, *Lenin i mezhdunarodnoe rabochee dvizhenie 1914–1918* (Moscow: Politizdat, 1968), pp. 138–39; Lademacher, *Zimmerwalder Bewegung,* 2:560–62, 570–71, 578–79; A. P. Iakushina, "Iz istorii antivoennoi deiatel'nosti bol'shevikov pod rukovodstvom V. I. Lenina," *Voprosy istorii KPSS,* no. 2 (1962), p. 159; Lenin, *PSS,* 49:237.

55. Kollontai, *Obshchestvo i materinstvo* (Petrograd: Zhizn' i znanie, 1916), p. 9.

56. For the earlier articles see "Groznyi prizrak," *Sovremennyi mir,* no. 3 (1914), pp. 65–84; "Krest materinstva," *Sovremennyi mir,* no. 1 (1914), pp. 42–54; "Novye zakony strakhovaniia materinstva," *Rabotnitsa-mat'* (St. Petersburg: Bib. Rabotnitsy, 1914); " 'Soiuz zashchity materinstva' i reforma seksual'-noi morali"; "Zashchita materinstva"; "Staatliche Mütterschaftsversicherung," *Die Neue Zeit,* 1, no. 10 (December 1914), pp. 363–71.

57. Kollontai, *Iz moei zhizni,* p. 180.

58. Sir Bernard Pares met Vladimir Kollontai at the front in 1915 and found him "cool headed" and "practical." (*My Russian Memoirs* [London: Jonathan Cape, 1931], p. 303.) Kollontai had remarried; he died in 1918 in the civil war.

59. Dazhina and Tsivlina, "Iz arkhivy," no. 2, p. 236.

60. Petrov, "Meridiany druzhby," pp. 164–65.

61. Dazhina and Tsivlina, "Iz arkhivy," no. 2, p. 238.

62. Ibid., p. 239.

63. Ibid., p. 240; Lenin, *PSS*, 49:387.

64. Cohen, *Bukharin*, p. 43; Dazhina and Tsivlina, "Iz arkhivy," no. 2, p. 242.

65. Ia. G. Temkin, *Lenin i mezhdunarodnaia sotsial-demokratiia 1914–1917* (Moscow: Nauka, 1968), p. 499; Dazhina and Tsivlina, "Iz arkhivy," no. 2, pp. 242–43.

66. Lore, "Trotsky," p. 7.

67. Draper, *Roots of American Communism*, pp. 80–81; Dazhina and Tsivlina, "Iz arkhivy," no. 2, p. 242.

68. Ibid., no. 2, pp. 242–43, 240; Draper, *Roots of American Communism*, p. 82. See Lademacher, *Zimmerwalder Bewegung*, 2:688, for a letter from Kollontai to Grimm asking him to pay more attention to the United States. Kollontai was not aware that Lenin and Grimm had quarrelled.

69. Lenin, *PSS*, 49:387–89.

70. Ibid., pp. 393–96.

71. Kollontai, *Iz moei zhizni*, p. 230.

72. Kollontai, "Komu nuzhen tsar?" *Izbrannye stat'i*, pp. 195–204.

73. Kollontai, *Iz moei zhizni*, pp. 231–32.

5. REVOLUTION

1. Kollontai, "Skoree v Rossiiu," *Sovetskie arkhivy*, no. 2 [1967], p. 24.

2. Lenin, *PSS*, 49:399.

3. Ibid., pp. 399–401.

4. Kollontai, *Izbrannye stat'i,* pp. 235–36, 238; Halvorsen, p. 251.

5. Kollontai, *V tiur'me Kerenskogo* (Moscow: Izd. vsesoiuznogo obshchestva, 1928), p. 6.

6. Kollontai, *Iz moei zhizni*, pp. 240–41.

7. Kollontai met Stalin for the first time on March 20 ("Molodomu pokoleniiu," *Rabotnitsa* 23 [April–May 1946]:17).

8. For studies of the attitudes of various groups in the early days of the revolution see Oskar Anweiler, "The Political Ideology of the Leaders of the Petrograd Soviet in the Spring of 1917," *Revolutionary Russia*, Richard Pipes, ed. (Cambridge: Harvard University Press, 1968), pp. 114–28; Marc Ferro, "The Aspirations of Russian Society," ibid., pp. 143–63, especially p. 146.

9. For evidence about Kollontai's position see Shliapnikov, *Semnadtsatyi god*, 3 vols. (Moscow: Gosizdat, 1923–27), 3:209–10; Kollontai, *Iz moei zhizni*, p. 249; Kollontai, "Nash pamiatnik bortsam za svobodu," *Pravda*, 23 March 1917, p. 1; Kollontai, "Kuda vedet revoliutsionnoe oboronchestvo?" *Pravda*, 5 April 1917, p. 1.

10. Kollontai, *Iz moei zhizni*, pp. 244–45.

11. Ibid., p. 245.

12. The complete story is in ibid., pp. 244–47.

13. Itkina, pp. 136–37.

14. Kollontai, *Iz moei zhizni*, p. 255.

15. N. N. Sukhanov, *The Russian Revolution 1917*, edited, abridged, and translated by Joel Carmichael (London: Oxford University Press, 1955), p. 288; Kollontai, "Avtobiograficheskii ocherk," p. 296; Kollontai, *Iz moei zhizni*, p. 257; Itkina, p. 142; Kollontai, *Autobiographie*, pp. 42, 44.

16. Itkina, pp. 143–44.

17. I. G. Tsereteli, *Vospominaniia o fevral'skoi revoliutsii*, 2 vols. (Paris: Mouton, 1963), 1:33.

18. Kollontai, *Iz moei zhizni*, p. 262.

19. Bobroff, "The Bolsheviks and Working Women," p. 527; Carol Shelly, "The Bolshevik Party and Work Among Women, 1917–1925," paper presented at Stanford Conference on Women in Russia, June 1975, p. 3; N. D. Karpetskaia, "Vovlechenie trudiashchikhsia zhenshchin Petrograda v revoliutsionnoe dvizhenie (mart-iiul' 1917 g.)," *Vestnik Leningradskogo universiteta* 21 (1966): 45–46; Rossiiskaia sotsial-demokraticheskaia rabochaia partiia, 7th Conference, Leningrad, 1917, *Petrogradskaia obshchegorodskaia vserossiiskaia konferentsiia RSDRP v aprele 1917 g.* (Moscow: Gosizdat, 1925), p. 26; Liudmilla Stal', "Rabotnitsa v Okt'iabre," *Proletarskaia revoliutsiia* 10 (1922):299.

20. Karpetskaia, "Vovlechenie trudiashchikhsia zhenshchin Petrograda," pp. 45–46; Kollontai, *Iz moei zhizni*, p. 267; Kollontai, *Rabotnitsa za god revoliutsii* (Moscow: Kommunist, 1918), p. 9.

21. Nina N. Selivanova, *Russia's Women* (New York: E. P. Dutton, 1923), p. 198; Kollontai, *Iz moei zhizni*, p. 268.

22. *Pravda*, 12 April 1917.

23. Kollontai, *Iz moei zhizni*, p. 268.

24. Ibid., pp. 267–69; Kollontai, "Avtobiograficheskii ocherk," pp. 296–97; Stal', "Rabotnitsa v Okt'iabre," p. 299; R. Kovnator, "The Press as a Means of Organizing the Proletarian Women," in Communist Party of Great Britain, *Work Among Women* (London: Communist Party of Great Britain, 1923), p. 38.

25. Marc Ferro, *The Russian Revolution of February 1917*, J. L. Richards, trans. (Englewood Cliffs: Prentice-Hall, 1972), p. 324; Edward A. Ross, *The Russian Bolshevik Revolution* (New York: Century, 1921), pp. 130–31; Trotsky, *The History of the Russian Revolution*, Max Eastman, trans., 3 vols. (New York: Simon and Schuster, 1932), 1:349; Akademiia nauk SSSR, *Khronika sobytii* in *Velikaia oktiabr'skaia sotsialisticheskaia revoliutsiia,* 5 vols. (Moscow: Izd. Akademii nauk SSSR, 1957), 1:618.

26. Kollontai, "Avtobiograficheskii ocherk," p. 297; Sukhanov, *Zapiski o revoliutsii*, 7 vols. (Berlin: Grzhebin, 1922) 4:143–44; Sovet rabochikh i krasnoarmeiskikh deputatov, *Protokoly zasedanii* (Moscow: Gosizdat, 1925), p. 137; Kollontai, "Na nashe 'linii ognia,'" *Pravda*, 22 May 1917, p. 3; A. Anskii, ed., *Professional'noe dvizhenie v Petrograde v 1917 g.* (Leningrad: Leningrad. oblastoi sovet profsoiuzov, 1928), p. 93.

27. Kollontai, "Rech' na IX s"ezde sotsial-demokraticheskoi partii Finliandii," *Izbrannye stat'i*, pp. 214–16.

28. RSFSR, S"ezd sovetov, 1st, Leningrad, 1917, *Pervyi vserossiiskii s"ezd sovetov R. i S.D.: Stenograficheskii otchet*, 2 vols. (Moscow and Leningrad: Gos. sotsialno-ekonomicheskoe izdatel'stvo, 1931), 2:171–73, 180, 185–89, 194. The first resolution called for a general commitment to self-determination, the second for autonomy for Finland.

29. Vserossiiskaia konferentsiia professional'nykh soiuzov, 3d, Leningrad, 1917, *Tretii vserossiiskaia konferentsiia professional'nykh soiuzov: Rezoliutsii* ... (Petrograd, 1917), pp. 23–24; *Bol'sheviki v period podgotovki i provedeniia velikoi oktiabr'skoi sotsialisticheskoi revoliutsii* (Leningrad, 1947), pp. 132–33.

30. Angelica Balabanoff, *Die Zimmerwalder Bewegung 1914–1919* (Frankfurt: Verlag Neue Kritik, 1928; reprint edition 1969), pp. 74–75; Shliapnikov, "Fevral'skaia revoliutsiia i evropeiskie sotsialisty," *Krasnyi arkhiv*, no. 2 (15) (1926), pp. 32–33; Kollontai, *Iz moei zhizni*, pp. 273–74; Warren Lerner, *Karl Radek, The Last Internationalist* (Stanford: Stanford University Press, 1970), pp. 61–62.

31. Kollontai, *V tiur'me Kerenskogo*, p. 4.

32. Lademacher, *Zimmerwalder Bewegung*, 2:538.

33. Kollontai, *V tiur'me Kerenskogo*, p. 19.

34. This account of Kollontai's arrest is drawn from ibid., pp. 7–22.

35. Quoted from the statement of the public prosecutor, 22 July, by A. I. Spiridovich, *Istoriia bol'shevizma v Rossii ot vozniknoveniia do zakhvata vlasti 1883–1903–1917* (Paris: Société anonyme de presse, 1922), p. 356. See also Robert Paul Browder and Alexander F. Kerensky, eds., *The Russian Provisional Government 1917*, 3 vols. (Stanford: Stanford University Press, 1961), 3:1370–76.

36. Spiridovich, *Istoriia bol'shevizma*, p. 355.

37. See also Alexander Rabinowitch, *Prelude to Revolution: The Petrograd Bolsheviks and the July 1917 Uprising* (Bloomington: Indiana University Press, 1968), pp. 191–93.

38. Kollontai, *V tiur'me Kerenskogo*, p. 26.

39. "Plenniki russkikh imperialistov," *Pravda*, 16 June 1917, pp. 2–3.

40. Kollontai, *V tiur'me Kerenskogo*, p. 45.

41. Ibid., p. 47; Trotskii, *Sochinenii* (Moscow: Gosizdat, 1927), 3:277–79; Vera Vladmirova, *Revoliutsiia 1917 goda*, 4 vols. (Leningrad: Gosizdat, 1924), 4:188–89.

42. Trotsky, *Stalin: An Appraisal of the Man and His Influence*, Charles Malamuth, ed. and trans. (New York: Harper and Bros., 1941), p. 221; Rossiiskaia sotsial-demokraticheskaia rabochaia partiia, *Shestoi s"ezd RSDRP (bol'shevikov): Protokoly* (Moscow: Politizdat, 1958), p. 251.

43. *Proletarii*, 19 August 1917.

44. V. V. Anikeev, *Deiatel'nost TsK RSDRP(b) v 1917 godu (Khronika sobytii)* (Moscow: Mysl, 1969), p. 383; Trotskii, *Sochinenii*, 3:176, 200, 201; G. Zinov'ev, *God revoliutsii* (Leningrad: Gosizdat, 1925), p. 656.

45. Pitirim Sorokin, *Leaves From a Russian Diary* (Boston: Beacon Press, 1950), p. 59.

46. Kollontai, "Oktiabr'skaia revoliutsiia i massy," *Molodaia gvardiia*, no. 6–7 (October 1922), p. 213. For a statement of Kollontai's interpretation of the October revolution in the fall of 1917 see "Varför Bolsjevikerna bör segra," *Revolt,* 1 May 1918, pp. 5–6, reprinted in *Izbrannye stat'i*, pp. 232–36. The editor of *Izbrannye stat'i*, Dazhina, dates the article as having been written in December 1917.

47. Kollontai, *Autobiographie*, p. 49; Kollontai, "Sistema izdevatel'stva prodolzhaetsia," *Rabochii put',* 15 September 1918, p. 4; *Profsoiuzy v bor'be za pobedu Oktiabr'skoi sotsialisticheskoi revoliutsii* (Moscow: Profizdat, 1957), p. 52; Vladimirova, *Revoliutsiia 1917 g.*, p. 269; Kollontai, "Kogda konchitsia voina?" *Izbrannye stat'i*, p. 255; Akademiia nauk, *Khronika sobytii*, 4:175, 234; Akademiia nauk, *Revoliutsionnoe dvizhenie v Rossii v sentiabre 1917 g.* (Moscow: Izd. Akademii nauk SSSR, 1961), p. 65.

48. Kollontai, "Tvorcheskoe v rabote K. N. Samoilovoi," *Kommunistka*, no. 3–5 (May 1922), p. 9; Shelly, "The Bolshevik Party and Work Among Women," pp. 5–6; A. V. Krasnikova, *Na zare sovetskoi vlasti* (Leningrad: Lenizdat, 1963), p. 18; Kollontai, "Avtobiograficheskii ocherk," p. 299. For a list of Kollontai's articles on the conference at the time see the Bibliography.

49. Kollontai, "Ruka istorii, Vospominanii A. Kollontai," *Krasnoarmeets*, no. 10–15 (November 1927), p. 68.

50. Ibid., p. 69.

51. Robert V. Daniels, *Red October* (New York: Scribners, 1967), pp. 95, 106–8, 216.

52. Kollontai, "Ruka istorii," p. 69; *Rabochii put'*, 11 October 1917; Stanislav Pestkovskii, "Ob oktiabr'skikh dniakh v Pitere," *Ob Oktiabr'skoi revoliutsii: Vospominaniia zarubezhnikh uchastnikov i ochevidtsev* (Moscow: Politizdat, 1967), p. 155.

53. John Reed, *Ten Days That Shook the World* (New York: Vintage, 1960), pp. 177–78.

54. Kollontai, "Lenin v Smol'nom," *Utro novogo mira: Sbornik vospominanii i dokumentov o II Vserossiiskom s"ezde sovetov* (Moscow: Politizdat, 1962), p. 29.

6. PEOPLE'S COMMISSAR

1. Ada Nilsson, "Det stora uppdraget," *Vi*, no. 35 (1961), p. 9.

2. Bessie Beatty, *The Red Heart of Russia* (New York: The Century Company, 1918), p. 380.

3. Jacques Sadoul, *Notes sur la révolution bolchévique* (Paris: Editions de la Sirène, 1920), pp. 95–96; Louise Bryant, *Six Red Months in Russia* (New York: Doran, 1918), p. 128.

4. K. Riabinskii, *Revoliutsiia 1917 goda*, 6 vols. in 4 ([Moscow]: Gosizdat, 1926), 4:82; Kollontai, "Lenin i rabotnitsy v 1917 godu," *Rabotnitsa*, no. 1 (October 1947), p. 6; Stal', "Rabotnitsa v Okt'iabre," p. 300; Akademiia

nauk, *Sovety v pervyi god proletarskoi diktatury, oktiabr' 1917–noiabr' 1918 g.* (Moscow: Izd. Akademii nauk), p. 75. Another petition to the Military Revolutionary Committee is recorded in I. I. Mints, ed., *Dokumenty Velikoi proletarskoi revoliutsii* ([Moscow]: Ogiz, 1938), p. 193. The tone of the Sovnarkom response quoted above implies that there had been additional instances, the records of which have not been published.

5. Kollontai, "Pochemu bol'sheviki dolzhen pobedit'," p. 234.

6. Kollontai, *Autobiographie*, p. 49. Kollontai struck the words "splendid illusions" from the galley proofs in 1926, but Iring Fetscher restored them in his 1970 edition of the essay.

7. Kollontai, *Vospominaniia ob Il'iche* (Moscow: Politizdat, 1959), p. 3.

8. Ibid., pp. 3–4.

9. Kollontai, "Pervoe posobie iz Sosbesa," *Krasnaia niva*, no. 45 (1927), p. 39.

10. Kollontai, "Pervye dni Narkomsobesa," *Nemerknushchie gody* (Leningrad: Politizdat, 1957), pp. 267–68.

11. Ibid., pp. 268–69.

12. Ibid., p. 269.

13. Ibid., p. 270.

14. Browder and Kerensky, *Russian Provisional Government*, 2:800; Itkina, p. 167.

15. Kollontai, "Pervye dni Narkomsobesa," p. 271.

16. Ibid., pp. 271–72; Kollontai, "Oktiabr'skaia revoliutsiia i massy," pp. 216–17.

17. Kollontai, "Oktiabr'skaia revoliutsiia i massy," p. 217. Minutes of a meeting of Kollontai's employee soviet are recorded in Akademiia nauk, *Khronika sobytii*, 5:174–75.

18. Akademiia nauk, *Petrogradskii voenno-revoliutsionnyi komitet: Dokumenty i materialy*, 3 vols. (Moscow: Nauka, 1966), 2:494. John Reed (*Ten Days*, p. 347) and Albert Rhys Williams (*Through the Russian Revolution* [New York: Boni and Liveright, 1921], p. 161) said that Sofia Panina, a Kadet and former official of the ministry, was tried for taking the money. A later edition of Williams's book is corrected to note that Panina was actually charged with absconding with the funds of the Ministry of Education (*Journey into Revolution, Petrograd 1917–1918,* Lucita Williams, ed. [Chicago: Quadrangle, 1969], p. 163). See also William G. Rosenberg, *Liberals in the Russian Revolution* (Princeton: Princeton University Press, 1974), p. 279. Kollontai probably thought Panina had taken some of the money from her commissariat and told Williams and Reed so.

19. *Izvestiia*, 2 December, 21 December 1917; Akademiia nauk, *Petrogradskii voenno-revoliutsionnyi komitet*, 3:584.

20. From the text of the resolution reprinted in Kommunisticheskaia partiia Sovetskogo Soiuza, *Kommunisticheskaia partiia i organizatsiia rabotnits* (Moscow and Petrograd: Kommunist, 1919), p. 113.

21. Ibid., pp. 112–18; Akademiia nauk, *Triumfal'noe shestvie sovetskoi vlasti*, 4 vols. (Moscow: Izd. Akademii nauk, 1963), 4:176–77.

22. Samoilova, "Konferentsiia rabotnits i organizatsionnaia rabota," *Pravda*, 9 December 1917, p. 3. The contents of the foregoing paragraphs are also based on Riabinskii, *Revoliutsiia 1917 goda*, 6:192, and Shelly, "The Bolshevik Party and Work Among Women," pp. 6–7.

23. Kollontai, *Autobiographie*, p. 50.

24. *Izvestiia*, 12 November, 22 November 1917; Kollontai, "Avtobiograficheskii ocherk," p. 330.

25. Bryant, *Six Red Months*, p. 131.

26. Kollontai, *Autobiographie*, pp. 50–51; *Izvestiia*, 30 November, 2 December 1917.

27. Beatty, *Red Heart*, pp. 380–81.

28. Kollontai, *Autobiographie*, pp. 52–53; Kollontai, "Avtobiograficheskii ocherk," pp. 299–300; Akademiia nauk, *Petrogradskii voenno-revoliutsionnyi komitet*, 4:161; Henri Niessel, *Le triomphe des bolchéviks et la paix de Brest-Litovsk: Souvenirs, 1917–1918* (Paris: Pron, 1940), pp. 193–94; Bryant, *Six Red Months*, pp. 133–34; *Izvestiia*, 10 December, 21 December 1917, 21 January, 28 January 1918.

29. Bryant, *Six Red Months*, p. 134.

30. *Izvestiia*, 4 January 1918; Kollontai, *Autobiographie*, p. 53; Kollontai, "Pervye shagi," *Izbrannye stat'i*, pp. 337–38; *Pravda*, 11 January 1918.

31. Kollontai, "Pervye shagi," pp. 338–39.

32. *Izvestiia*, 6 February, 8 February 1918.

33. Kollontai, *Autobiographie*, p. 53; Kollontai, "Pervye shagi," p. 338.

34. Kollontai, "Iz vospominanii," p. 87; Kollontai, *Autobiographie*, p. 54.

35. E. Fortunato, "Nash drug Aleksandra Kollontai," *Neva*, no. 3 (1959), p. 184; Kollontai, "Iz vospominanii," p. 87; Kollontai, *Den första etappen*, p. 133.

36. Kollontai, "Iz vospominanii," p. 88; Fortunato, "Nash drug," p. 184; Kollontai, *Den första etappen*, p. 131.

37. Kollontai, "Iz vospominanii," pp. 88–89.

38. Kollontai, *Den första etappen*, pp. 136–37.

39. Shliapnikov, "K oktiabriu," *Proletarskaia revoliutsiia*, no. 10 (1922), p. 26.

40. Bryant, *Six Red Months*, p. 132.

41. *Vestnik otdela mestnogo upravlenia*, 18 January 1918, p. 3; *Izvestiia*, 23 December 1917, 4 January, 13 February 1918.

42. Kollontai, *Iz moei zhizni*, p. 333–34; John Shelton Curtiss, *The Russian Church and the Soviet State, 1917–1950* (Boston: Little, Brown, 1953), p. 48. The order for seizure is reprinted in James Bunyan and H. H. Fisher, eds., *The Bolshevik Revolution, 1917–1918* (Stanford: Stanford University Press, 1934), p. 587. Kollontai presented herself in her memoirs as acting reluctantly, but that seems a bit disingenuous, given her earlier decrees reducing the Church's role in education and her admission to Beatty that she favored the confiscation of church property. (*Red Heart*, p. 383). Ariadne Tyrkova-Williams saw the whole episode as part of a Bolshevik campaign against the

Church in which Kollontai participated willingly, and she may well be right. (*From Liberty to Brest-Litovsk* [London: Macmillan, 1919], pp. 410–11.)

43. Kollontai, *Iz moei zhizni*, pp. 334–35; Tyrkova-Williams, *From Liberty to Brest-Litovsk*, pp. 408–9.

44. Kollontai, *Iz moei zhizni*, p. 235; Itkina, p. 173. Tyrkova-Williams also thought the two events were connected; she did not know Kollontai acted without authorization in the monastery incident. (*From Liberty to Brest-Litovsk*, pp. 410–11.)

45. Tyrkova-Williams, *From Liberty to Brest-Litovsk*, p. 409; Curtiss, *Russian Church and Soviet State*, pp. 48–49.

46. Kollontai, *Iz moei zhizni*, p. 335.

47. Kollontai, "Lenin v Smol'nom," pp. 31–32.

48. Williams, *Journey Into Revolution*, p. 185; Zeth Höglund, "Den lyckliga trons lotusblossom," *Morgon-Tidningen*, 18 April 1954; Carl Lindhagen, *I revolutions land* (Stockholm: Åhlen and Åkerlund, 1918), pp. 62–63; N. F. Izmailov and A. G. Pukhov, *Tsentrobalt* (Moscow: Politizdat, 1963), pp. 200–201; Kollontai, "Zvezdy," *Vospominaniia o V. I. Lenine*, 3 vols. (Moscow: Gosizdat, 1969), 3:186–87.

49. P. E. Dybenko, "Dybenko, Pavel Efimovich," *Deiateli SSSR i Oktiabr'skoi revoliutsii*, part 1, pp. 128–29.

50. Ibid., pp. 129–31.

51. Reed, *Ten Days*, p. 88.

52. Georges Haupt and Jean-Jacques Marie, *Makers of the Russian Revolution*, C. I. P. Ferdinand and D. M. Bellos, trans. (Ithaca: Cornell University Press, 1974), p. 122.

53. Trotsky, *Stalin*, pp. 243–44.

54. Kollontai, *V tiur'me Kerenskogo*, p. 29; Kollontai, *Iz moei zhizni*, p. 265.

55. Itkina, p. 190.

56. Ibid., p. 191.

57. Isabel de Palencia, *Alexandra Kollontai: Ambassadress from Russia* (New York: Longmans Green, 1947), pp. 163–64.

58. Höglund, "Den lyckliga trons"; Albert Rhys Williams, *Lenin, the Man and His Work* (New York: Scott and Seltzer, 1919), pp. 58–59; Niessel, *Le triomphe des Bolchéviks*, p. 199.

59. Trotsky, *Stalin*, pp. 243–44.

60. Kollontai, *Novaia moral' i rabochii klass*, p. 55.

61. KPSS, *Sed'moi ekstrennyi s"ezd RKP(b): Stenograficheskii otchet* (Moscow: Politizdat, 1962), p. 250; Richard Kent Debo, "Litvinov and Kamenev—Ambassadors Extraordinary: The Problem of Soviet Representation Abroad," *Slavic Review* 34 (September 1975):470.

62. Kollontai, *Autobiographie*, p. 55; Kollontai, "Avtobiograficheskii ocherk," p. 300; Itkina, pp. 177–78.

63. Palencia, *Kollontai*, p. 173.

64. Cohen, *Bukharin*, pp. 64–69.

65. Sadoul, *Notes*, pp. 96–97.

66. Ibid., pp. 180–81, 215.

67. Max Hoffman, *Die Aufzeichningen des Generalmajors Max Hoffman*, 2 vols. (Berlin, 1929); 1:187, as quoted in Deutscher, *The Prophet Armed*, p. 383.

68. Lenin, *PSS*, 35:369.

69. Morgan Philips Price, *My Reminiscences of the Russian Revolution* (London: G. Allen and Unwin, 1921), p. 247.

70. Lenin, *PSS*, 35:345.

71. Vsevolod Eichenbaum, *Nineteen-Seventeen: The Russian Revolution Betrayed*, Holley Cantine, trans. (New York: Libertarian Book Club, 1954), p. 98. See also Cohen, *Bukharin*, p. 65.

72. KPSS, *Sed'moi s"ezd*, p. 88.

73. Ibid., p. 89.

74. Ibid., pp. 241–71.

75. Ibid., pp. 294–97.

76. Lenin, *PSS*, 36:18.

77. Ibid., p. 203. Emphasis Lenin's. The speeches from which this summary are drawn are in ibid., pp. 3–36, 92–111, 127–64, 167–208.

78. *Kommunist*, 20 April, 27 April, June 1918. She was not listed in the first Moscow edition of 29 April 1918.

79. V. A. Nelaev, *Pavel Dybenko* (Moscow: Politizdat, 1965), pp. 54–55.

80. Ibid., p. 57.

81. Ibid., pp. 56–57; *Pravda*, 16 May 1918.

82. "Korniloff's Capture Near," *New York Times*, 28 March 1918, sec. 1, p. 6; Sadoul, *Notes*, p. 271; U.S. Department of State, *Russia*, 2:124.

83. Sadoul, *Notes*, p. 270; *New York Times*, 24 March 1918. One of his acquaintances, Isaac Steinberg, a Left SR and Commissar of Justice, claimed that Dybenko had gone further than threats, that he had actually made plans for a rising when in the South in January. (Haupt and Marie, *Makers of the Russian Revolution*, pp. 122–23.) In fact, Dybenko spent January in the Petrograd area. Nor would it have made sense to plan to wreck the treaty in January, before it had been negotiated.

84. Kollontai, "Avtobiograficheskii ocherk," p. 300.

85. "Germans Provoke Revolt in Ukraine," *New York Times*, 29 March 1918, sec. 3, p. 1.

86. Sadoul, *Notes*, p. 316.

87. "Dybenko Missing, Mme. Kollontai, Too," *New York Times*, 19 April 1918, sec. 1, p. 1; Sadoul, *Notes*, p. 315; "Reports Korniloff and Semenov Dead," *New York Times*, 22 April 1918, sec. 1, p. 1 and 6.

88. Bryant, *Mirrors of Moscow* (New York: Thomas Seltzer, 1923), p. 115.

89. Walter Duranty, *I Write as I Please* (New York: Simon and Schuster, 1935), p. 240; Williams, *Journey*, p. 200. Williams heard the story from Iakov Peters, an assistant to Feliks Dzerzhinskii, head of the revolutionary police, the Cheka.

90. William Henry Chamberlin, *The Russian Revolution 1917–1921*, 2 vols. (New York: Macmillan, 1960), 1:332; Dybenko, "Dybenko," *Deiateli SSSR i Oktiabr'skoi revoliutsii*, p. 132.

91. Nelaev, *Dybenko*, p. 57; *Pravda*, 12 May, 16 May, 19 May 1918.
92. Kollontai, *Autobiographie*, p. 56. She also said she withdrew from politics in *Den första etappen*, p. 138.
93. Kollontai, *Den första etappen*, pp. 123–24.

7. WORK AMONG WOMEN

1. Stasova, *Vospominaniia*, p. 173.
2. Angelica Balabanoff, *My Life as a Rebel* (New York: Harper, 1938), pp. 98–99. Kollontai hints in her *Autobiographie* that she was ostracized (p. 56, quoted above, p. 147).
3. Kollontai, *Iz moei zhizni*, pp. 351–54; Kollontai, "Kak my sozvali Pervyi Vserossiiskii s"ezd rabotnits i krestianok," *Kommunistka*, no. 11 (November 1923), p. 4; Kollontai, "Kak i dlia chego sozvan byl Pervyi Vserossiiskii s"ezd rabotnits," *Kommunisticheskaia partiia i organizatsiia rabotnits*, p. 8. When the editors of *Izbrannye stat'i* reprinted this article, they omitted the sentences, italicized in the original, that charged the party with failure to work among women (p. 258). No ellipsis indicates the deletion, which changes the meaning of two paragraphs and much of the thrust of Kollontai's article.
4. Kollontai, *Rabotnitsa za god revoliutsii*, pp. 18–19.
5. Carol Eubanks Hayden, "The *Zhenotdel* and the Bolshevik Party," *Russian History*, 3, part 2 (1976):150.
6. Women constituted 7.5 percent of party members in 1917, a figure that remained constant throughout the civil war years. See Gayle Durham Hannah, "Political Equality for Russian Women: An Unfulfilled Promise of the Revolution," paper presented at the Midwest Slavic Conference, Cleveland, Ohio, May 1975, p. 27.
7. This *Pravda* article is reprinted in *Izbrannye stat'i*, pp. 237–42. See the same themes in "Kak my sozvali," p. 4, and *Rabotnitsa za god revoliutsii*, pp. 20–29.
8. Kollontai, *Rabotnitsa za god revoliutsii*, p. 21; *Kommunisticheskaia partiia i organizatsiia rabotnits*, p. 98; *Pravda*, 26 April 1918.
9. Zinaida Chalaia, "V pervykh riadakh (V. A. Moirova)," *Zhenshchiny russkoi revoliutsii* (Moscow: Politizdat, 1968), p. 267.
10. N. K. Krupskaia, *Sobranie sochinenii* (Moscow and Leningrad: Politizdat, n.d.), p. 112; N. Sazonova, "Konferentsii rabotnits i krestianok," Moscow, Institut istorii partii, *V edinom stroiu* (Moscow: Moskovskii rabochii, 1960), p. 178.
11. Kollontai, "Kak my sozvali," p. 5.
12. It is always difficult to determine from Soviet historiography which individual is responsible for what policy, because actions tend to be presented as the product of group effort. Thus, although both Krupskaia and Kollontai acknowledged that the delegate conferences were Inessa's idea, neither clearly said when she proposed them. See Kollontai, "Zhenshchiny-bortsy v dni veli-

kogo oktiabria," *Izbrannye stat'i,* p. 373; N. K. Krupskaia, ed., *Pamiati Inessy Armand* (Moscow, 1926), p. 53. Kollontai did imply strongly in one article written five years later that Inessa suggested it during discussions prior to the November conference ("Kak my sozvali," p. 6).

13. Kollontai, "Kak my sozvali," p. 6.
14. Ibid.; Kollontai, *Iz moei zhizni,* p. 355.
15. Kollontai, "Kak my sozvali," p. 7; Itkina, p. 197.
16. *Pervyi vserossiiskii s"ezd rabotnits 16–21 noiabria 1918 g. i ego rezoliutsii* (Kharkov: Vseukrainskoe izdatel'stvo, 1920), pp. 10–11; *Pravda,* 17 November, 19 November, 21 November 1918.
17. *Kommunisticheskaia partiia i organizatsiia rabotnits,* p. 41. I refer to Armand as "Inessa" because the Bolsheviks called her that, using the first name alone or "Comrade Inessa."
18. *Pervyi s"ezd,* pp. 12–14.
19. N. Sukhareva-Klochkova, "Nash pervyi s"ezd," *V edinom stroiu,* p. 108.
20. *Kommunisticheskaia partiia i organizatsiia rabotnits,* pp. 108–109; Sukhareva-Klochkova, "Nash pervyi s"ezd," p. 109.
21. Itkina, p. 197. For a brief and eloquent evaluation of this congress see Richard Stites, *"Zhenotdel:* Bolshevism and Russian Women, 1917–1930," *Russian History,* 3, part 2 (1976):176–78.
22. Lenin, *PSS,* 50:197.
23. The decree begins with praise for the conference. Kollontai gave Sverdlov credit for helping them obtain the final resolution in an obituary she wrote for him. (Kollontai, "Kogo poteriali rabotnitsy," *Izbrannye stat'i,* p. 266).
24. *Kommunisticheskaia partiia i organizatsiia rabotnits,* pp. 100–101.
25. Ibid., pp. 101–4.
26. See, for example, *Kommunar,* November 1918–April 1919; *Krasnaia gazeta,* December 1918; *Petrogradskaia pravda,* March–May 1919; *Pravda,* December 1918.
27. *Perepiska sekretariata TsK RKP(b) s mestnymi partiinymi organizatsiiami (avgust–oktiabr' 1918 g.),* 6 vols. (Moscow: Politizdat, 1969), 6:210; Sazonova, "Konferentsii rabotnits i krestianok," p. 178.
28. Shelly, "The Bolshevik Party and Work Among Women," p. 11; E. I. Pismannikh, "Stupeni rosta," *Bez nikh my ne pobedili by: Vospominaniia zhenshchin-uchastnitsy Oktiabr'skoi revoliutsii, grazhdanskoi voiny i sotsialisticheskogo stroitel'stva* (Moscow: Politizdat, 1975), p. 369.
29. A. Unskova, "Za tri goda," *Tri goda diktatury,* p. 19; Inessa Armand [pseud. Elena Blonina], "Vseros. soveshchanie organizatorov otdelov po rabote sredi zhenshchin," *Pravda,* 24 October 1919, p. 4.
30. Arthur Ransome, *Russia in 1919* (New York: Heubsch, 1919), pp. 30, 41, 42; Sorokin, *Leaves from a Russian Diary,* p. 231.
31. Kollontai, *Iz moei zhizni,* pp. 356–57.
32. Ibid., p. 357.
33. Ibid.
34. Ibid., p. 358.

35. Ibid.

36. Communist International, 1st Congress, Moscow, 1919, *Pervyi kongress Kominterna, mart 1919 g.* (Moscow: Partizdat, 1933), pp. 166, 214.

37. Kollontai, "Avtobiograficheskii ocherk," pp. 300–301; Itkina, p. 208.

38. KPSS, *Vos'moi s"ezd RKP(b): Protokoly* (Moscow: Gosizdat, 1959), p. 225.

39. Ibid., p. 298.

40. Ibid.

41. The entire speech is in ibid., pp. 296–300. For the resolution see p. 435.

42. Itkina, p. 181; Kollontai, "Avtobiograficheskii ocherk," p. 301.

43. Itkina, pp. 181–82.

44. Kollontai, "Avtobiograficheskii ocherk," p. 301; Itkina, p. 185.

45. Itkina, p. 187.

46. Ibid., p. 194; Kollontai, "Avtobiograficheskii ocherk," p. 301.

47. Polina Vinogradskaia, *Pamiatnye vstrechi,* 2d ed. (Moscow: Sovetskaia Rossiia, 1972), pp. 196–97.

48. Z. N. Gagarina, "Zhenshchiny v bor'be za sotsializm i mir," *Bez nikh my ne pobedili by,* p. 425. For a list of the pamphlets see Bibliography.

49. Kollontai, "Avtobiograficheskii ocherk," p. 301. For several get-well messages from groups of women workers see *Pravda,* 6 December, 14 December, 28 December 1919. That Kollontai was really ill at this time and not in political disgrace again is testified to by contemporary sources, among them Krupskaia, "Inessa Armand," *Kommunistka,* no. 5 (October 1920), p. 19; Emma Goldman, *Living My Life,* 2 vols. (New York: Alfred A. Knopf, 1941), 2:756; Margaret Elton Harrison, *Marooned in Moscow* (New York: Doran, 1921), p. 78.

50. KPSS, *Vos'maia konferentsiia: Protokoly* (Moscow: Gosizdat, 1961), pp. 223–25.

51. Ibid., p. 170.

52. KPSS, Tsentral'nyi komitet, Otdel po rabote sredi zhenshchin, *Sbornik instruktsii Otdela TsK RKP po rabote sredi zhenshchin* (Moscow: Gosizdat, 1920), pp. 3–7. Hereafter abbreviated as *Sbornik zhenotdela.*

53. Ibid., pp. 30–76.

54. For references to this aspect of the work see ibid., pp. 22–24, 74.

55. Ibid., p. 13, 65, 28.

56. Ibid., pp. 11–18, 79–81, 15.

57. Moirova, "Women's Delegate Meetings and Their Role in the Work of the Party Among Working and Peasant Women," Communist Party of Great Britain, *Work Among Women,* p. 20.

58. V. P. Tachalova and N. I. Troitskaia, "Varia, ona zhe Elena Ivanovna," *Bez nikh my ne pobedili by,* p. 280.

59. Inessa Armand [pseud. Elena Blonina], *Ocherednye zadachi po rabote sredi zhenshchin (Doklad na Vserossiiskom soveshchanii organizatorov otdelov po rabote sredi zhenshchin 28 marta 1920 v Moskve)* (Moscow, 1920), pp. 6–13. For the resolutions of the March conference see KPSS, *Sbornik zhenotdela,* pp. 18–22, 27–30, 83–88.

60. Kollontai gave Samoilova credit for getting the resolution passed; see "Tvorcheskoe v rabote K. N. Samoilovoi," p. 10. For the resolution see KPSS, *Kommunisticheskaia partiia Sovetskogo Soiuza v rezoliutsiiakh i resheniiakh s"ezdov, konferentsii i plenumov TsK,* 8th ed., vol. 2, 1917–24 (Moscow: Politizdat, 1970):178.

61. "Otchet o deiatel'nosti otdela TsK RKP po rabote sredi zhenshchin," *Izvestiia TsK RKP,* 18 September 1920, pp. 20–22; KPSS, *Sbornik zhenotdela,* pp. 32–35; V. I. Bil'shai, "Shtab zhenskogo dvizheniia," *Bez nikh my ne pobedili by,* p. 251; Levikova, "Po zovu gudka," ibid., p. 302; P. Vinogradskaia, "Pamiati Inessy Armand," Krupskaia, *Pamiati,* p. 65; N. K. Krupskaia, *O rabote sredi zhenshchin* (Moscow, 1926), p. 19.

62. K. Samoilova, *Organizatsionnye zadachi otdelov rabotnits* (Moscow: Gosizdat, 1920), p. 6; "Rabotnitsa na sovetskoi rabote," KPSS, *Tri goda diktatury,* p. 31; Poriadochnova, "Rabote pri otdele okhrany truda," ibid., pp. 36–37; Gagarina, "Zhenshchiny v bor'be," p. 425; Pismannikh, "Stupeni rosta," p. 370. A leader of the Kharkov provincial party organization called the women there "the barefoot Zhenotdelki," which indeed they often were. (G. D. Zlobinskaia, "Bosoi zhenotdel," *Bez nikh my ne pobedili by,* p. 307.)

63. N. S. Kokoreva, "Okhrana materinstva," *Bez nikh my ne pobedili by,* pp. 220–21; M. Petrova, "Moia rabota v mediko-sanitarnom otdele," KPSS, *Tri goda diktatury,* p. 35.

64. Kollontai, "Eshche odno oruzhie v bor'be protiv dezorganizatsii," *Izvestiia,* 17 March 1920, quoted in full in Jerome Landfield, "Kollontai and the New Morality," *The Weekly Review,* July 1920, pp. 85–86.

65. Alexander Berkman, *The Bolshevik Myth (Diary 1920–1922)* (London: Hutchinson, [c. 1925]), p. 137.

66. Itkina, p. 193. It is difficult to date these brief excerpts from letters. Itkina does not give their dates but includes them after her description of Kollontai's and Dybenko's trip in May 1920. She strongly implies that strain had developed in the relationship by then.

67. This speculation is based on the fragments in Itkina.

68. Krupskaia, *Pamiati Inessy Armand,* pp. 32–33; Kollontai, "Pervaia mezhdunarodnaia konferentsiia kommunistok," *Kommunistka,* no. 1–2 (June–July 1920), pp. 3–4; Kollontai, "Mezhdunarodnaia solidarnost' i den' rabotnits," International Conference of Women Communists, 1st Congress, Moscow, 1920, *Otchet o pervoi mezhdunarodnoi konferentsii kommunistok* (Moscow: Gosizdat, 1921), pp. 5–12.

69. For the congress resolutions see Communist International, 2d Congress, *Vtoroi kongress Kominterna iiul'–avgust 1920 g.* (Moscow: Partizdat, 1934), pp. 673–86, 692–95. Zetkin did manage to put her stamp on the theses in a way that must have irritated Kollontai. She wrote that when women became economically independent of men, they would be able to harmonize housework, motherhood, and a career. Zetkin was never willing to embrace Kollontai's wholehearted assault on the traditional family. See Honeycutt, "Clara Zetkin," pp. 10–11.

70. *Izvestiia*, 14 July 1920; *Kommunistka*, no. 1–2, p. 40; R. Kovnator, "Pervaia posle ob'edineniia," *V edinom stroiu*, p. 189.

71. This speculation comes from Kollontai via Marcel Body, a French Communist and close friend of hers in the twenties. When Kollontai died, *Pravda* did not publish an obituary, which so angered Body that he wrote one himself, revealing in print for the first time the gossip about Lenin and Inessa. (Marcel Body, "Alexandra Kollontai," *Preuves*, no. 14 [April 1952], p. 17.) Naturally his testimony is not wholly reliable, both because of his own emotion and Kollontai's tendency to gossip. Armed with Body's revelations, however, Bertram Wolfe had an interview on the subject with Angelica Balabanoff, who did agree that Lenin was grief-stricken at Inessa's funeral. (Wolfe, "Lenin and Inessa Armand," p. 112.)

72. "Otchet o rabote otdela TsK RKP po rabote sredi zhenshchin s marta 1920 g. do fevralia 1921 g.," *Izvestiia TsK*, March 1921, pp. 26–31; P. M. Schimchenko-Ksendzova, "K novoi zhizni," *Bez nikh my ne pobedili by*, p. 288.

73. "Otchet o deiatel'nosti otdela TsK RKP po rabote sredi zhenshchin," *Izvestiia TsK*, 18 September 1920, p. 21; "Otchet," *Izvestiia TsK*, 5 March 1921, p. 26.

74. *Sbornik instruktsii*, p. 76.

75. Ibid., pp. 76–77.

76. "Otchet," *Izvestiia TsK*, 18 September 1920, p. 21; Hayden, "The Zhenotdel and the Bolshevik Party," p. 159. Kollontai claimed that the resolution reflected the Zhenotdel position on the question. ("Otchet," *Izvestiia TsK*, 5 March 1921, p. 28.)

77. Klara Zetkin, *Lenin on the Woman Question* (New York: International Publishers, 1934), pp. 16, 19.

78. Ibid., p. 19.

79. Ibid., pp. 62, 67.

80. For samples of two Bolshevik leaders' statements, see N. I. Bukharin, *Rabotnitsa, k tebe nashe slovo!* (Moscow: Gosizdat, 1919); Grigorii Zinov'ev, *Rabotnitsa, krest'ianka, i Sovetskaia vlast'* . . . (Petrograd: Petrogradskii sovet rabochikh i krasnoarmeiskikh deputatov, 1919).

81. Samoilova, *Organizatsionnye zadachi*, p. 4.

82. Ibid., p. 12.

83. Ibid., pp. 13–19.

84. Ibid., pp. 5–10.

85. Ibid., p. 8; E. N. Gribova, "Klara Tsetkin v Ivanove," *Bez nikh my ne pobedili by*, p. 212; Shimchenko-Ksendzova, "Novoi zhizni," p. 288; V. M. Tarantaeva, "Podnialis' ugnetennye iz ugnetennykh," *Bez nikh my ne pobedili by*, pp. 352–53; Gagarina, "Zhenshchiny v bor'be," p. 425.

86. Samoilova, *Organizatsionnye zadachi*, p. 11.

87. Kollontai, "Zadachi otdelov po rabote sredi zhenshchin," *Kommunistka*, no. 6 (November 1920), p. 3.

88. Ibid., pp. 3–4.

89. A. Itkina, "O rabote sredi zhenshchin," *Izvestiia TsK*, 12 October 1920, p. 11; *Izvestiia*, 28 November 1920.

90. Itkina, p. 202.

91. Kokoreva, "Okhrana materinstva," p. 221.

92. Kollontai, *Iz moei zhizni*, p. 362.

93. Ibid.

94. Ibid., pp. 362–63.

95. Bryant, *Mirrors of Moscow*, pp. 125–26.

96. Kollontai, "Avtobiograficheskii ocherk," p. 302.

97. Kollontai, "Trudovaia respublika i prostitutsiia," *Kommunistka*, no. 6 (November 1920), p. 16.

98. Ibid., p. 17.

99. KPSS, Tsentral'nyi komitet, Otdel po rabote sredi zhenshchin, *Otchet otdela TsK RKP po rabote sredi zhenshchin za god raboty* (Moscow: Gosizdat, 1921), p. 8.

100. RSFSR, *Vserossiiskii s"ezd sovetov, 4–6, 9: Stenograficheskii otchet* (Moscow, 1918–1935), p. 266.

101. Ibid., p. 205.

102. Ibid.

103. Ibid., p. 206.

104. Ibid.

105. Kollontai, "Avtobiograficheskii ocherk," p. 302; Kollontai, "Na puti k kommunizmu," p. 15.

106. See Gregory Massell, *The Surrogate Proletariat* (Princeton: Princeton University Press, 1974).

107. Kollontai, "Posledniaia rabynia," *Kommunistka*, no. 7 (December 1920), pp. 24–26; "Otchet," *Izvestiia TsK*, 5 March 1921, pp. 27–28.

108. Itkina, p. 202.

8. THE WORKERS' OPPOSITION

1. Emma Goldman, *My Further Disillusionment in Russia* (New York: Doubleday, Page, 1924), pp. 27–28. See also Berkman, *The Bolshevik Myth*, p. 278; Richard O'Connor and Dale L. Walker, *The Lost Revolutionary: A Biography of John Reed* (New York: Harcourt, Brace and World, 1967), p. 302.

2. Goldman, *Further Disillusionment*, p. 28; Goldman, *Living My Life*, 2: 757.

3. Robert Daniels, *Conscience of the Revolution* (Cambridge: Harvard University Press, 1960), p. 116.

4. See above, p. 31.

5. Paul Avrich, "Russian Factory Committees in 1917," *Jahrbücher für Geschichte Osteuropas* 11 (1963):161–82; Isaac Deutscher, *Soviet Trade Unions* (London: Royal Institute of International Affairs, 1956), pp. 13–28.

6. KPSS, *Vos'moi s"ezd*, p. 403.

7. Ibid.

8. Ibid., pp. 402–4; Deutscher, *Trade Unions*, pp. 31–33; Leonard Schapiro, *The Origin of the Communist Autocracy: Political Opposition in the Soviet*

State. First Phase, 1917–1922 (London: The London School of Economics and Political Science, 1955), pp. 232–33.

9. Schapiro, *Origin*, pp. 321–32; Daniels, *Conscience*, pp. 125–26.

10. KPSS, *Deviataia konferentsiia RKP(b): Protokoly* (Moscow: Politizdat, 1972), p. 188.

11. Ibid.

12. Lenin, *PSS*, 42:202–26; KPSS, *Desiatyi s"ezd RKP(b): Stenograficheskii otchet* (Moscow: Politizdat, 1963), pp. 663–74.

13. For the text of the Trotsky-Bukharin platform see ibid., pp. 674–85. For the platform of the Democratic Centralists see ibid., pp. 656–62.

14. For the text of the speech introducing Shliapnikov's theses in December see Vserossiiskii tsentral'nyi sovet professional'nykh soiuzov, *O roli professional'nykh soiuzov v proizvodstve* (Moscow: [Pervaia Obraztsovaia tip. MSNKh], 1921), pp. 54–59. For his fall theses, "The Organization of the National Economy and the Tasks of the Trade Unions," see KPSS, *Desiatyi s"ezd*, pp. 819–23. The December article is reproduced in G. Zinov'ev, *Partiia i soiuzy* (Petersburg: Gosizdat, 1921), pp. 287–304. The text of "The Tasks of the Trade Unions," the Workers' Opposition platform, is in KPSS, *Desiatyi s"ezd*, pp. 685–91. Initially it was published in *Pravda*, 26 January 1921, pp. 2–3.

15. Anastas Mikoian said that Lenin took the Workers' Opposition more seriously than the Trotsky supporters because of their mass following. (*Mysli i vospominaniia o Lenine* [Moscow: Politizdat, 1970], p. 163.) Obviously such generalizations must be approached with care, for the writer had an interest in diminishing the influence of the Trotskyites.

16. Lenin, *PSS*, 42:241.

17. KPSS, *Vos'moi s"ezd*, p. 403.

18. Lenin, *PSS*, 42:241, 249, 294.

19. Soviet historians have continued to accuse the Workers' Opposition of seeking to weaken the party, an unfair charge because it is an intention the faction does not seem to have had. All Soviet commentators write that the group's ideas were an important challenge, although they do not admit the justness of any of the criticism or the power of the reform proposals. For a survey of Soviet treatment of the Workers' Opposition over the years see: Ia. Bronin, "K kharakteristike platformy rabochii oppozitsii," *Proletarskaia revoliutsiia*, no. 11/94 (November 1929), pp. 3–25; *Bol'shaia sovetskaia entsiklopediia*, 1st ed., s.v. "VKP(b)" by A. Bubnov; S. L. Dmitrienko, "X s"ezd RKP(b) o edinstve partii," *Vestnik Moskovskogo universiteta, Istoriia*, no. 3 (1971), pp. 27–44; M. G. Gaisinskii, *Bor'ba s uklonami ot general'noi linii partii: Istoricheskii ocherk vnutripartiinoi bor'by posleoktiabr'skogo perioda* (Moscow and Leningrad, 1931), pp. 56–76; E. Iaroslavskii, *Protiv oppozitsii* (Moscow: Gosizdat, 1928), pp. 3–26; S. N. Kanev, "Bor'ba V. I. Lenina protiv anarcho-sindikalistskogo uklona v RKP(b)," *Voprosy istorii KPSS*, no. 3 (1971), pp. 93–102; V. V. Kuzin, *Bor'ba kommunisticheskoi partii s anarkho-sindikalisticheskim uklonom s 1920–1922 gg.* (Moscow: Znanie, 1958); N. N. Popov, *Ocherk istorii RKP(b)*, 2 vols. (Petrograd: Gosizdat, 1934), 2:79–82; K. Shelavin, *Rabochaia oppozitsiia* (Moscow: Molodaia gvardiia, 1930); M. M.

Vasser, "Razgrom anarkho-sindikalistskogo uklonom v partii," *Voprosy istorii KPSS*, no. 3 (1962), pp. 62–78.

20. For example, the vote in Moscow went 76 for Lenin, 27 for Trotsky, 4 for the Workers' Opposition, 25 for the Ignatovtsy, who in February allied with the Workers' Opposition. (Mikoian, *Mysli*, p. 115.) The Communist fraction of the miners' union: 137 for Lenin, 62 for the Workers' Opposition. (Lenin, *PSS*, 42:304.) Petrograd party organization: 95 percent for Lenin. (L. I. Petrova, *Sovetskie profsoiuzy v vosstanovitel'nyi period 1921–1925 gg.* [Moscow: Profizdat, 1962], p. 15.)

21. Petrova, *Sovetskie profsoiuzy*, p. 14. For a detailed discussion of the Leninists' campaign in Nizhni Novgorod see Mikoian, *Mysli*, pp. 124–27.

22. Ibid., p. 124; Victor Serge, *Memoirs of a Revolutionary, 1901–41*, Peter Sedgwick, ed. and trans. (London: Oxford University Press, 1963), p. 123; Gaisinskii, *Bor'ba s uklonami*, pp. 74–75; Goldman, *Further Disillusionment*, p. 52; Daniels, *Conscience*, pp. 139–42.

23. Kollontai, "Pora proanalizirovat'," *Pravda*, 28 January 1921, p. 1.

24. For a description of her talk at the Red Army War College in Moscow see Alexander Barmine, *One Who Survived* (New York: G. P. Putnam's, 1945), pp. 91–92.

25. Kollontai, *Rabochaia oppozitsiia* (Moscow: 81a Gos. tip., 1921), p. 3.

26. Schapiro, *Origin*, pp. 224–25.

27. Kollontai, *Rabochaia oppozitsiia*, p. 10.

28. Ibid., p. 13.

29. Ibid., p. 21. Emphasis Kollontai's.

30. Ibid., p. 27. Emphasis Kollontai's.

31. Ibid., p. 32. Emphasis Kollontai's.

32. Ibid., p. 43.

33. Ibid., pp. 47, 48.

34. KPSS, *Desiatyi s"ezd*, pp. 651–56.

35. Schapiro, *Origins*, p. 314.

36. Angelica Balabanoff, *Impressions of Lenin*, Isotta Cesari, trans. (Ann Arbor: University of Michigan Press, [1964]), pp. 97–98.

37. KPSS, *Desiatyi s"ezd*, p. 76.

38. Ibid., p. 101.

39. Ibid., pp. 102–3.

40. Lenin, *PSS*, 43:34–50; Balabanoff, *Life*, p. 252.

41. For Lenin's politicking for the Central Committee see Mikoian, *Mysli*, pp. 136–44.

42. Ibid., p. 300.

43. Balabanoff, *Life*, p. 252.

44. KPSS, *Desiatyi s"ezd*, pp. 300–301.

45. Lenin, *PSS*, 36:203.

46. Rosa Luxemburg, *Rosa Luxemburg Speaks*, ed. with an Introduction by Mary-Alice Waters (New York: Pathfinder, 1970), pp. 393–94.

47. Bronin, "K kharakteristike platformy rabochei oppozitsii," p. 15.

48. Mikoian, *Mysli*, p. 161; KPSS, *Desiatyi s"ezd*, pp. 359–67, 373–75, 383–89.

49. Mikoian, *Mysli*, p. 161.

50. Ibid., p. 156.

51. KPSS, *Desiatyi s"ezd*, pp. 571–76.

52. Ibid., pp. 526–30.

53. Ibid., pp. 530–32.

54. Trotsky, *The Revolution Betrayed*, Max Eastman, trans. (Garden City, N.J.: Doubleday, Doran, 1937), p. 96.

55. Ibid., pp. 104–5.

56. KPSS, *Desiatyi s"ezd*, p. 325.

9. THE END OF OPPOSITION

1. For information on the Workers' Opposition after the Tenth Congress see KPSS, 11th Congress, *Materialy po voprosu o gruppe Rabochei oppozitsii na XI s"ezde RKP* (Moscow: Izd-vo. TsK RKP[b], 1922); Mikoian, *Mysli*, pp. 207–10; Moscow, Institut Marksizma-Leninizma, *Kommunisticheskaia partiia v bor'be za postroenie sotsializma v SSSR, 1921–1937*, vol. 4 of *Istoriia kommunisticheskoi partii Sovetskogo Soiuza*, 6 vols. (Moscow: Politizdat, 1966–70), 1970, part 1, p. 83; Vasser, "Razgrom anarkho-sindikalistskogo uklonom," pp. 69–72.

2. *Izvestiia TsK*, 27 January 1921, pp. 22–23.

3. KPSS, *Otchet zhenotdela*, p. 5.

4. Ibid., p. 6; *Pravda*, 24 April 1921; Kollontai, "Na puti k kommunizmu," p. 18; Bil'shai, "Shtab zhenskogo dvizheniia," pp. 255–56.

5. *Pravda*, 10 April 1921. According to the editors of *Izbrannye stat'i*, the lectures ran from February to July (p. 424). Isabel de Palencia places them in 1920, and there is internal evidence that they were written then. Furthermore, one chapter was published as an article in 1920. ("Trudovaia povinnost' i okhrana zhenskogo truda," *Kommunistka*, no. 1–2 [June–July 1920], pp. 25–27.) Probably, therefore, the lectures were written in 1920 and delivered in 1921. They were later published together as *Polozhenie zhenshchiny v sviazi s evoliutsiei khoziaistva* (Moscow: Gosizdat, 1921).

6. *Pravda*, 19 April 1921.

7. For two earlier articles which began Kollontai's discussion of the abolition of the bourgeois family see Kollontai, *Prostitutsiia i mery bor'by s nei* (Moscow: Gosizdat, 1921), and Kollontai, "Sem'ia i kommunizm," *Kommunistka*, no. 7 (December 1920), pp. 16–17. Kollontai later wrote that the "Theses" ("Tezisy o kommunisticheskoi morali v oblasti brachnikh otnoshenii," *Kommunistka*, no. 13–14 [May–June 1921], pp. 28–34) provoked a "heated discussion." (*Autobiographie*, p. 60; "Avtobiograficheskii ocherk," p. 302.) Krupskaia, the editor of *Kommunistka*, did append a note to the article, requesting letters that debated the issues Kollontai had raised, but if they came in they were never printed in that journal. Subsequent editions of *Kommunistka* were devoted to famine relief and then to the NEP.

8. For two other articles that stress communalization but avoid reference to the Workers' Opposition see Kollontai, "Proizvodstvo i byt," *Kommunistka*, no. 10–11 (March–April 1921), pp. 6–9; Kollontai, "Profsoiuzy i rabotnitsa," *Pravda*, 22 May 1921, p. 2.

9. Bernhard Reichenbach, "Moscow 1921," *Survey* (October 1964), pp. 20–21; Daniels, *Conscience*, p. 162.

10. *Pravda,* 11 June, 12 June, 14 June, 15 June, 16 June, 17 June 1921.

11. Itkina, p. 214. Body also says Lenin asked her not to speak. ("Kollontai," p. 12.)

12. Body, "Kollontai," pp. 12–13; Reichenbach, "Moscow," p. 21.

13. Communist International, 3d congress, Moscow, 1921, *Tretii vsemirnyi kongress Kommunisticheskogo Internatsionala: Stenograficheskii otchet* (Petrograd: Gosizdat, 1922), p. 369.

14. Ibid., pp. 367–70.

15. A. A. Andreev, *Professional'nye soiuzy v Rossii v 1921–1922 godu* (Petrograd: Izd. redaktsionno-izdatel'stvennogo otdela VTSPS, 1922), p. 52; T. H. Rigby, *Communist Party Membership in the U.S.S.R., 1917–1967* (Princeton: Princeton University Press, 1968), p. 85.

16. Body, "Kollontai," p. 13.

17. Communist International, *Tretii kongress*, pp. 371–74, 379–81.

18. Itkina, p. 214.

19. Reichenbach, "Moscow," p. 21.

20. Communist International, *Tretii s"ezd*, pp. 435–36, 437.

21. Body, "Kollontai," p. 13.

22. KPSS, *Desiatyi s"ezd*, p. 597.

23. KPSS, *Otchet zhenotdela*, pp. 18–19.

24. *Izvestiia TsK*, 20 July 1921, p. 11.

25. Ibid., 6 August 1921, pp. 15, 15–16.

26. KPSS, *Otchet zhenotdela*, pp. 5–7, 20; M. O. Levkovich, "Kto-kogo?" *Bez nikh my ne pobedili by*, p. 262; Tarantaeva, "Podnialis," p. 353.

27. Kollontai, "Ne uprazdnenie, a ukreplenie," *Kommunistka*, no. 16–17 (September–October 1921), p. 26.

28. Ibid., pp. 25–27.

29. *Izvestiia TsK*, March 1922, p. 45.

30. R. Kovnator, "Rabotnitsa v pechat," *Tri goda diktatury*, p. 56.

31. Kollontai, "Tvorcheskoe v rabote K. N. Samoilovoi," p. 10.

32. *Pravda*, 5 November 1921.

33. *Pravda* did not report the contents of Sosnovskii's speech. For a very brief summary of Kollontai's, see "Itogi vserossiiskogo Soveshchaniia Zagubzhenotdelami," *Kommunistka*, no. 1 (January 1922), p. 2.

34. *Izvestiia TsK*, 15 November 1921, p. 16; 15 December 1921, p. 26.

35. Ibid., 15 December 1921, pp. 26–27; January 1922, p. 22; "Itogi vserossiiskogo Soveshchaniia Zagubzhenotdelami," pp. 2–3.

36. *Izvestiia TsK*, March 1922, pp. 45–46, 49–51; KPSS, *Otchet zhenotdela*, pp. 5, 6, 10–11, 24; Smidovich, "The Russian Communist Party at Work

Among Women," CPGB, *Work Among Women*, pp. 23–24; O. Chernisheva, "Methods of Approaching the Working Women Through the Unions," ibid., p. 46; Bil'shai, "Shtab zhenskogo dvizheniia," pp. 253–54; Petrova, *Sovetskie profsoiuzy*, p. 38.

37. "Kollontai in Russia Fights for Her Sex; First Woman Commissar Heckles Government Till She Gets Action," *New York Times*, 21 November 1921, sec. 1, p. 5.

38. *Izvestiia TsK*, January 1922, p. 23; S"ezd sovetov, *Vserossiiskii s"ezd sovetov*, 9:265.

39. Kollontai, "Eshche odin perezhitok," *Pravda*, 27 December 1921, p. 1.

40. KPSS, *Odinnadtsatyi s"ezd RKP(b): Stenograficheskii otchet* (Moscow: Politizdat, 1961), p. 748; Schapiro, *Origins*, p. 326.

41. Schapiro, *Origins*, pp. 329–30; Rigby, *Communist Party Membership*, pp. 98–100; M. S. Zorkii, *Rabochaia oppozitsiia* (Moscow: Gosizdat, 1926), pp. 59–61.

42. Zorkii, *Rabochaia oppozitsiia*, pp. 59–60. This group was not the faction of the year before. Only eight of the present twenty-two had signed the "Theses" then, although at least two others, A. G. Pravdin and N. V. Kutuzov, had been identified with the faction throughout 1921. Two of the spokesmen at the Tenth Congress, A. S. Kiselev and I. I. Kutuzov, had left the Workers' Opposition. Lutovinov had fallen away during the summer. Included in the group now were F. A. Mitin and V. P. Bekrenev, who had only recently joined the Bolsheviks, having been Mensheviks or anarchists, and G. I. Miasnikov, who advocated peasant unions.

43. Shliapnikov and Kollontai said as much in their statements to the party congress. (KPSS, *Odinnadtsatyi s"ezd*, p. 187, 198.)

44. Ibid., p. 196, 177, 702–10.

45. The exact date she was fired is not clear, either. A Zhenotdel decree of 16 February bears the signature of Sofia Smidovich as department head, so Kollontai was definitely out by then. (*Izvestiia TsK*, May 1922, p. 35.) Since her deputy Golubeva signed the decrees issued in January by the bureau, however, it is impossible to tell exactly when she was removed. She did not mention it in her memoirs.

46. KPSS, *Odinnadtsatyi s"ezd*, pp. 132, 177.

47. Kollontai, *The Workers Opposition in Russia* (Chicago: Industrial Workers of the World, 1921), pp. 1–2.

48. Communist International, Executive Committee, 1st plenum, 1922, *Compte rendu de la conférence de l'exécutif élargi de l'Internationale Communiste* (Paris: "L'Humanité," 1922), pp. 59, 170–71; Zorkii, *Rabochaia oppozitsiia*, pp. 60–64.

49. Schapiro, *Origins*, p. 334; Mikoian, *Mysli*, p. 210; KPSS, *Odinnadtsatyi s"ezd*, p. 195.

50. Vasser, "Razgrom anarkho-sindikalistskogo uklonom," pp. 73–74.

51. Lenin, *PSS*, 45:88–89.

52. KPSS, *Odinnadtsatyi s"ezd*, pp. 166–79.

53. Ibid., pp. 186–89, 191–96.

54. Ibid., p. 199.

55. Ibid., pp. 200–201.

56. Ibid., pp. 702–10, 577–80; Schapiro, *Origins*, p. 336.

57. KPSS, *Odinnadtsatyi s"ezd*, p. 577.

58. Deutscher, *Trade Unions*, pp. 61–65.

59. Kollontai, *Autobiographie*, p. 61.

60. Itkina, p. 193. Palencia (p. 176) and Hauge (pp. 50–51) assert that the two broke up in 1922. Emy Lorentsson, Kollontai's secretary in the thirties and forties, told Hauge that the short story "Vasilisa Malygina" described Dybenko's suicide attempt on learning that Kollontai planned to leave him for good. She then stayed to nurse him back to health, only to hear him call deliriously for his mistress. Lorentsson did not know Kollontai in 1922, and it seems likely that she is assuming Kollontai's melodramatic story was true in all its details. Without less gossipy corroboration, that is a dubious assumption. Anna Itkina, who did know Kollontai at the time, says also that Dybenko had a mistress, but she shows far more convincingly that the couple decided on a final separation only in early 1923 (p. 194). The editors of Kollontai's memoirs also accept that date (*Iz moei zhizni*, p. 408, n. 1.). There is some evidence that the woman pictured as the mistress in "Vasilisa Malygina," a bourgeoise unable to support herself without a man, is drawn from Dybenko's new love. In the September issue of *Kommunistka* Kollontai attacked the "doll-parasite" woman who had begun to flourish under the NEP by latching on to Soviet officials. ("Novaia ugroza," *Kommunistka*, no. 8–9 [August–September 1922], pp. 5–9.)

61. Palencia, *Kollontai*, p. 176.

62. Kollontai, *Autobiographie*, p. 61.

63. Itkina, p. 216.

64. Kollontai, *Skoro (cherez 48 let)* (Omsk, 1922).

65. Kollontai, "Pis'ma k triudiashcheisia molodezhi. Pis'mo pervoe: Kakim dolzhen byt' kommunist?" *Molodaia gvardiia*, no. 1–2 (1922), pp. 136–44.

66. Kollontai, "Pis'ma k triudiashcheisia molodezhi. Pis'mo vtoroe: Moral kak orudie klassovogo gospodstva i klassovoi bor'by," *Molodaia gvardiia*, no. 6–7 (September–October 1922), p. 132. Italics mine.

67. "Soviet Names Woman for Diplomatic Post," *New York Times*, 28 September 1922, sec. 1, p. 3.

10. WINGED EROS

1. Body, "Kollontai," p. 13; Isaac Deutscher, *The Prophet Unarmed: Trotsky, 1921–1929* (New York: Vintage, 1959), pp. 95–96. The same rumors usually said Zinoviev was her chief persecutor. See also Ellen Michelsen, *Sju kvinnor ur den ryska revolutionens historia* (Stockholm: Axel Holmströms, 1932), p.163.

2. Alfred Rosmer, *Lenin's Moscow*, Ian H. Birchall, trans. (London: Pluto, 1971), p. 168; Body, "Kollontai," p. 14.

3. Kollontai, "Pis'ma k triudiashcheisia molodezhi. Pis'mo tret'e: O 'drakone' i 'beloi ptitse,'" *Molodaia gvardiia*, no. 2 (February–March 1923), pp. 162–74.

4. Kollontai, "Pis'ma k triudiashcheisia molodezhi. Dorogu krylatomu Erosu!" *Molodaia gvardiia*, no. 3 (May 1923), p. 122.

5. Ibid., p. 121.

6. Ibid., p. 123.

7. Kollontai, "Sestry," *Kommunistka,* no. 3–4 (March–April 1923), pp. 23–26.

8. Kollontai [pseud. A. Domontovich], "Tridtsat'-dve stranitsy," *Zhenshchina na perelome*, p. 5.

9. Kendall E. Bailes, "Alexandra Kollontai et la nouvelle morale," *Cahiers du monde russe et soviétique* 6 (October–December 1965):489–96.

10. Though he accepts Bailes's hypothesis, Robert McNeal sees Krupskaia as avoiding the Opposition primarily because she wished to remain in useful work. (*Bride of the Revolution: Krupskaya and Lenin* [Ann Arbor: University of Michigan Press, 1972], pp. 252–56.)

11. Kollontai, *Svobodnaia liubov' (Liubov' pchel trudovikh)* (Riga: Knigoizd. O. D. Strok, 1925).

12. Kollontai, "Liubov' trekh pokolenii," *Liubov' pchel trudovikh* (Petrograd: Gosizdat, 1923), pp. 3–74.

13. I thank my colleague Guy Alitto for bringing the influence of Kollontai in China to my attention.

14. *Biulleten' knigi*, no. 3 (1923), p. 45; *Novaia kniga*, no. 3–4 (1924), p. 27; *Russkii sovremennik*, no. 1 (1924), pp. 339–40.

15. For a discussion of Trotsky's ideas see Deutscher, *The Prophet Unarmed*, pp. 164–200.

16. Polina Vinogradskaia, "Voprosy byta," *Pravda*, 26 July 1923, pp. 4–5.

17. B. Arvatov, "Grazhdanka Akhmatova i tov. Kollontai," *Molodaia gvardiia*, no. 4–5 (1923), p. 148.

18. Vinogradskaia wrote that Krupskaia approved it. (Vinogradskaia, *Pamiatnye vstrechi*, p. 53.)

19. P. Vinogradskaia, "Voprosy morali, pola, byta, i tovarishch Kollontai," *Krasnaia nov*, no. 6 (16) (November 1923), p. 181.

20. Ibid., pp. 210, 213.

21. Body, "Kollontai," p. 14; *Krasnaia nov,*' no. 7 (1923), p. 306. Body says Kollontai was protesting against a series of articles published in *Pravda* which carried exaggerated versions of her ideas over her initials. A thorough search of the newspaper for 1923 has not turned up any such articles, however. It seems likely, therefore, that Body was confused about the Vinogradskaia articles, which certainly did exaggerate Kollontai's views.

22. "Soviet Envoy a Feminist," *New York Times*, 13 February 1923, sec. 1, p. 2.

23. Vinogradskaia, *Pamiatnye vstrechi*, p. 53.

24. S. I. Kaplun, *Sovremennye problemy zhenskogo truda i byta* (Moscow: Voprosy truda, 1924).

25. See A. Zalkind, "Polovoi vopros s kommunisticheskoi tochki zreniia," in *Polovoi vopros*, S. M. Kalmanson, ed. (Moscow: Molodaia gvardiia, 1924), pp. 5–38. This article is especially interesting because Professor Zalkind later became the advocate of a puritanical sexual code popular during the thirties.

See Jessica Smith, *Women in Soviet Russia* (New York: Vanguard, 1928), pp. 129–30. For a good discussion of the early Soviet debate on sexuality, see Geiger, *The Family in Soviet Russia*, pp. 61–75. For a fascinating collection of letters by women Communists discussing the effect of freer sexuality see L. S. Sosnovskii, *Bol'nye voprosy (zhenshchina, sem'ia i deti)* (Leningrad: Priboi, 1926).

26. For a discussion of these and later memoir articles see Note on Sources in the Bibliography.

27. I base these conclusions on an interview with Bertram Wolfe, Stanford, California, 1973, and on one with Alva Myrdal conducted by Britta Stövling, Stockholm, February 1976; on the dossier of press clippings at the Bibliothèque Marguerite Durand; and on a number of articles, books, and book reviews. See Katharine Anthony, "Alexandra Kollontay," *The North American Review* 230 (September 1930):277–82; Alexandra Kollontai, *Marxisme et révolution sexuelle*, Judith Stora-Sandor, ed. (Paris: François Maspero, 1973); Anna Louise Strong, *I Change Worlds* (New York: Henry Holt, 1935); and reviews in *Die Frau*, no. 33 (1925), p. 432; *The Times Literary Supplement*, 29 April 1926, p. 310; *Weltbühne*, 10 August 1926, p. 230; *Schweiz Rundschau*, no. 30 (1929), p. 260.

28. Geiger, *Family in Soviet Russia*, pp. 50, 59; Smith, *Women in Soviet Russia*, pp. 96–110. For a detailed account of this debate see Beatrice Farnsworth, "Bolshevik Alternatives and the Soviet Family: The 1926 Marriage Law Debate," in *Women in Russia*, pp. 139–65, and *Brak i byt: Sbornik statei i materialov* (Moscow: Molodaia gvardiia, 1926). Kollontai pointed out that the reformers were motivated as much by their concern over "depravity" as by a desire to provide regular alimony, and her observation seems to be borne out by the evidence. See E. Lavrov, "Polovoi vopros i molodezh'," *Molodaia gvardiia*, no. 2 (March 1926), pp. 136–48. Emelian Iaroslavskii, an Old Bolshevik, said he had spent nine years in prison without sex and suffered no ill effects, but that now he often met young men worn out by "leading a life that many of us old men have not led." "Continence," he assured the young, was not harmful. He could not quite bring himself to say it was desirable. (E. Iaroslavskii, "Moral' i byt proletariata v perekhodnyi period," *Molodaia gvardiia*, no. 3 [May 1926], pp. 138–53.)

29. Kollontai, "Brak i byt," *Rabochii sud'*, no. 5 (1926), p. 372.

30. Kaplun, *Sovremennye problemy*, pp. 75–76.

31. Kollontai, "Brak i byt," p. 376.

32. Kollontai, *Autobiographie*, p. 60.

33. See Massell, *The Surrogate Proletariat*.

34. V. I. Lenin, *The Emancipation of Women* (New York: International Publishers, 1966), p. 81.

11. DIPLOMAT

1. Body, "Kollontai," p. 13; Hauge, p. 54. Kaare Hauge based his study of Kollontai's activities in the twenties on research in the foreign ministry archives

of Norway and Sweden, and on oral interviews. I am indebted to him here and elsewhere.

2. Hauge, pp. 67–76; *Dokumenty vneshnei politiki SSSR*, 19 vols. (Moscow: Politizdat, 1960–74), 6 (1962): 456–66; Kollontai, *Izbrannye stat'i*, pp. 353–56.

3. Kollontai, *Autobiographie*, pp. 65–66; Itkina, pp. 223–33; *Dokumenty vneshnei politiki*, 7 (1963):107–9, 704, n. 24; 8 (1963):463–64; Hauge, pp. 77–94.

4. Itkina, p. 222.

5. Ibid., p. 224.

6. The treatment of the French and Scandinavian press is preserved in a collection of clippings at the Marguerite Durand Library in Paris. My generalizations are drawn from their "Dossier" in addition to surveys of the *London Times, New York Times,* and various magazines listed in the Bibliography. See also J. Stanley Lemons, *The Woman Citizen: Social Feminism in the 1920's* (Urbana: University of Illinois Press, 1973), pp. 193, 212–13, 216–18. The charge that American feminists were linked to Bolsheviks and especially to Kollontai was first made during the "Red Scare" in the United States in 1919–20. See Richard J. Evans, *The Feminists: Women's Emancipation Movements in Europe, America, and Australasia 1840–1920* (New York: Barnes & Noble, 1977), p. 207.

7. Itkina, p. 226.

8. Ibid., pp. 233–34.

9. Body, "Kollontai," pp. 17, 18; Hauge, pp. 97–101, 104; Futrell, *Northern Underground*, pp. 113–14. Kollontai's attempt to resign from diplomatic work may have been the source of rumors in 1925 that Bukharin was planning to remove her from her post because she had spent too much money on high-fashion Parisian clothes. There was a soberer report that the party was angry at her for communications with the Norwegian Communist Party. Here again Bukharin was said to be in Oslo in disguise for the purpose of firing her. This latter story may be true, although it is not clear why Bukharin would have been the official involved. If there is truth in it, the evidence is lost, and all we have are rumors so wildly exaggerated that we cannot determine with any certainty what actual events gave rise to them. They were reported by moderate to conservative papers always prone to see the Soviet ambassador up to her neck in conspiracy. For representative newspaper articles see Dossier, Bibliothèque Marguerite Durand; *Social-Demokraten*, 14 May 1925.

10. Hauge, p. 108.

11. Body, "Kollontai," pp. 19–22; Ruth Fischer, *Stalin and German Communism* (Cambridge: Harvard University Press, 1948), pp. 159–60n.

12. Stanley S. Jados, ed., *Documents on Russian-American Relations* (Washington: The Catholic University of America Press, 1965), p. 62.

13. "The Case for Madame Kollontay," *The Literary Digest,* 20 November 1926, p. 15; "Kollontai Rebuff Condemned by Borah," *New York Times,* 6 November 1926, sec. 1, p. 19; "Cuba Bars Mme. Kollontai," *New York Times,* 4 December 1926, sec. 1, p. 5; "Mme Kollontai at Havana," *New York Times,* 5 December 1926, sec. 1, p. 7; *Dokumenty vneshnei politiki,* 9 (1964):586–89.

14. Karl M. Schmitt, *Communism in Mexico: A Study in Political Frustra-*

tion (Austin: University of Texas Press, 1965), pp. 9–12; J. Gregory Oswald, "An Introduction to Soviet Diplomatic Relations with Mexico, Uruguay, and Cuba," *The Communist Tide in Latin America,* Donald L. Herman, ed. (Austin: University of Texas Press, 1973), p. 75.

15. Oswald, "Introduction," pp. 77–78; Bertram Wolfe, interview at the Hoover Institution on War, Revolution and Peace, Stanford, California, July, 1973.

16. *Dokumenty vneshnei politiki,* 9:588.

17. "Kellogg Offers Evidence of Red Plots in Nicaragua and Aid from Calles; Mexico Looks for Recall of Sheffield," *New York Times,* 13 January 1927, p. 1; U.S. Department of State, *Papers Relating to the Foreign Relations of the United States, 1927,* 3 vols. (Washington: Government Printing Office, 1942), 1:356–63.

18. For Kollontai's denials that she was bent on revolutionary propaganda see "Woman Envoy Hits Intrigue," *New York Times,* 19 October 1926, sec. 1, p. 26; "Reds of Mexico City Hail Mme. Kollontay," *New York Times,* 9 December 1926, sec. 1, p. 5; "Woman Envoy's Books Far Outnumber Gowns," *New York Times,* 10 December 1926, sec. 1, p. 3; A. I. Sizonenko, "Polgoda v Meksike," *V strane atstekskogo orla* (Moscow: Mezh. otnosheniia, 1969), p. 49; Oswald, "Introduction," p. 77.

19. Sizonenko, "Polgoda," pp. 48–49; Oswald, "Introduction," p. 78; *Dokumenty vneshnei politiki,* 10 (1965):625, n11.

20. Itkina, p. 240.

21. Sizonenko, "Polgoda," p. 49; Itkina, pp. 241–44.

22. "Want Mme. Kollontai Expelled from Mexico," *New York Times,* 12 April 1927, sec. 1, p. 23; Alfonso Taracena, *La verdadera revolución mexicana* (Mexico City: Editorial jus, 1963), p. 180.

23. Itkina, p. 246. Kollontai's successor as Soviet ambassador to Mexico, Aleksandr Makar, was expelled in 1930 for conspiratorial associations with the PCM. Diplomatic relations between the Soviet Union and Mexico were not restored until 1942. See Oswald, "Introduction," p. 79.

24. Victor Serge and Natalia Sedova Trotsky, *The Life and Death of Leon Trotsky,* Arnold J. Pomerans, trans. (New York: Basic Books, 1975), p. 155.

25. Ibid.; Susanne Leonhard, "Alexandra Kollontaj," *Aktion,* 2 June 1952, p. 48.

26. Kollontai, "Oppozitsiia i partiinaia massa," *Pravda,* 30 October 1927, p. 3.

27. Ibid.

28. Ibid.

29. Ibid.

30. Hauge, pp. 121–22.

31. *Dokumenty vneshnei politiki,* 11 (1966):116–18, 150–51, 501–3, 565–66, 602–3, 614–16; 12 (1967):62, 72–73, 99–100, 330–33, 476–78; 13 (1967):11–13, 29–30, 40–42, 75, 80–81, 133–36, 143–44, 171–73, 452–53, 502–3, 528–29; Hauge, pp. 127–50; Itkina, pp. 246–55.

32. Ibid., 11:614–16; 12:99–100; 13:133–36, 463–65.

33. Body, "Kollontai," p. 23.

34. Hauge, p. 151; E. G. Lorenson, "A. M. Kollontai v Shvetsii," *Novaia i noveishaia istoriia,* no. 1 (1966), p. 106; *Dokumenty vneshnei politiki,* 13:377.

35. "Kollontay i Finland, på stormigt Ålands hav, i fängelse och sjuglasvagan," *Folket i bild,* no. 51–52 (1944), p. 81.

36. *Dokumenty vneshnei politiki,* 13:720–21; 14(1968):449–50; 15 (1969): 53–55, 571–72, 633–34; 16 (1970):91–93; 17 (1971):46–48, 237–38, 298, 318–20; 18(1973):618, 110–11; Hauge, pp. 167–77; Lorenson, p. 109; Kollontai, "Iz vospominanii," pp. 81–82.

37. For a sample of government and nongovernment impressions see Vilhelm Assarsson, *I Skuggan av Stalin* ([Stockholm]: Bonniers, 1963), pp. 25–26; Erik Boheman, *På vakt: Kabinettssekreterare under Andra Världskriget* (Stockholm: Norstedt, 1964), p. 51; Karl Gerhard, *Om jag inte minns fel* (Stockholm: Bonniers, 1952), p. 207; "Alexandra Kollontay—75 år," *Morgon-Tidningen,* 1 April 1947, p. 5; Per Nyström, "Alexandra Kollontay," *Afton-Tidningen,* 30 July 1945, p. 5; "Madame Kollontai—den sista puritanen," *Stockholms-Tidningen,* 26 July 1945, p. 7; Nanna Svartz, *Steg för steg* (Stockholm: Bonniers, 1968), p. 134. This conclusion is also based on interviews conducted by Sonya Baevsky and Britta Stövling with Erik Boheman, Margit Palmaer-Waldén, Alva Myrdal, Nanna Svartz, Eva Palmaer, and Agneta Pleijel, in Stockholm in February and March 1976.

38. E. Voskresenskaia, "Sovetskii polpred," *Ogonek,* no. 15 (April 1962), p. 5.

39. Maiskii, "Kollontai," p. 109.

40. Anna Lenah Elgström, "Alexandra Kollontay, Sovjets ambassadör," *Tidens kvinnor* (Stockholm: Steinvicks bokförlag, 1944), p. 13.

41. Gerhard, *Om jag inte minns fel,* p. 207.

42. League of Nations, *Official Journal,* Special Supplement #157, Records of the 17th Ordinary Session of the Assembly, Meetings of the Committees (Geneva: League of Nations, 1936), pp. 12–13, 32–34. Kollontai also attended in 1935 and 1937. See League of Nations, *Official Journal,* Special Supplement #139, Records of the 16th Ordinary Session of the Assembly, Meetings of Committees (Geneva: League of Nations, 1935), pp. 13–31, 37, 51; *Official Journal,* Special Supplement #170, Records of the 18th Ordinary Session of the Assembly, Meetings of the Committees (Geneva: League of Nations, 1937), pp. 20–21; *Official Journal,* Special Supplement #174, Records of the 18th Ordinary Session of the Assembly, Meetings of the Fifth Committee (Geneva: League of Nations, 1937), pp. 63–64.

43. Nilsson, "Det stora uppdraget," no. 35, p. 11.

44. Gerhard, *Om jag inte minns fel,* p. 208.

45. See also Nilsson, no. 36, p. 17.

46. Ibid., no. 37, p. 40. Nilsson said that Kollontai thought she was being watched. (Ibid., p. 16.) This was common practice in Soviet embassies. One NKVD agent who spied on her in 1943 and 1944 later defected and described his activity. See Vladimir M. and Evdokia Petrov, *Empire of Fear* (New York: Praeger, 1956), pp. 160, 173–75, 189–93.

47. Body, "Kollontai," p. 24.

48. Ibid. Either Kollontai or Body errs slightly here; Dybenko was not killed until 1938, although he was arrested in 1937.

49. Haupt and Marie, *Makers of the Revolution*, p. 221.

50. Ibid., p. 125; Robert Conquest, *The Great Terror* (New York: Macmillan, 1968), pp. 222–23. In memoirs written between 1939 and 1944 she said that she did not believe Dybenko to be guilty. (Petrov, *Empire of Fear*, p. 192.) Although he was rehabilitated in 1964, that portion of her memoirs has never been published. For the rehabilitation see "Vernyi syn Leninskoi partii," *Pravda*, 17 February 1964, p. 4.

51. Nilsson, "Det stora uppdraget," no. 37, p. 40.

52. Conquest, *The Great Terror*, p. 454.

53. Kollontai, "Ruka istorii," pp. 68–70.

54. I have taken some liberties here in translating *iudushka* as "Judas." It literally means "little Judas," and figuratively means dissembling hypocrite. Lenin originally applied it to Trotsky in 1912 and 1913, thereby likening Trotsky's attempt to mediate between the Bolsheviks and Mensheviks to the hypocrisy of Iudushka Golovlev, a character in *The Golovlevs*, a novel by the nineteenth-century writer M. E. Saltykov-Shchedrin.

55. Kollontai, "V V," *Izvestiia*, 24 October 1937, n.p. Later versions of this article have relied on the 1927 original. See "Na istoricheskom zasedanii," *Ob Il'iche: Vospominaniia pitertsev* (Leningrad: Lenizdat, 1970), pp. 351–54; *Iz moei zhizni*, pp. 311–13. Another article published in November 1937 praises Stalin, but does not criticize the defeated Bolsheviks. (Kollontai, "Zhenshchiny v semnadtsatom godu," *Rabotnitsa*, no. 31 [November 1937], pp. 12–13.)

56. Petrov, "Meridiany druzhby," pp. 165–66.

57. Nilsson, "Det stora uppdraget," no. 37, p. 40.

58. Gerhard, *Om jag inte minns fel*, p. 209.

59. Nilsson, "Det stora uppdraget," no. 36, p. 17.

60. Adam Ulam, *Expansion and Coexistence: The History of Soviet Foreign Policy 1917–67* (New York: Praeger, 1968), p. 290; C. Leonard Lundin, *Finland in the Second World War* (Bloomington: Indiana University Press, 1957), pp. 51–52.

61. Lundin, *Finland in the Second World War*, pp. 10–11, 35–42.

62. For the Soviet attitude see *Dokumenty vneshnei politiki*, 17:64–65, 636–38, 644–46, 699–700; 18:467–68, 473, 521–23, 543–44, 559–60, 575–76; 19 (1974): 80–86, 114. For the Finns see Lundin, *Finland in the Second World War*, pp. 28–29, 35–36.

63. Ibid., pp. 42–49.

64. Ulam, *Expansion and Coexistence*, pp. 290–94.

65. Assarsson, *I Skuggan av Stalin*, p. 13.

66. Boheman, *På vakt*, p. 98. Boheman was a deputy foreign minister who served as Günther's assistant during the Winter War and as chief mediator in 1943–44.

67. Krister Wahlbäck, *Finlands frägan i svensk politik 1937–1940* (Stockholm: Stockholm Universitet, 1964), p. 193; Väinö Tanner, *The Winter War* (Stanford: Stanford University Press, 1957), p. 62; "U.S. to Demand Soviet

Release Ship," *New York Times*, 25 October 1939, p. 1; Nilsson, "Det stora uppdraget," no. 35, p. 10.

68. Gerhard, *Om jag inte minns fel*, p. 214.

69. Boheman, *På vakt*, pp. 98–99.

70. Ibid., pp. 99–100; Gerhard, *Om jag inte minns fel*, pp. 214–16.

71. Tanner, *The Winter War*, pp. 123–24.

72. Boheman, *På vakt*, p. 100; Tanner, *The Winter War*, pp. 124–26.

73. Tanner, *The Winter War*, pp. 125–30.

74. Ibid., pp. 130–50.

75. Ibid., pp. 151–70.

76. Boheman, *På vakt*, pp. 100–102, 104; Tanner, *The Winter War*, pp. 170–74; Lundin, *Finland in the Second World War*, pp. 64–65.

77. Tanner, *The Winter War*, p. 179, 185; Assarsson, *I Skuggan av Stalin*, pp. 13–14.

78. Tanner, *The Winter War*, p. 185.

79. Ibid., pp. 188–213; Boheman, *På vakt*, pp. 101–5; Lundin, *Finland in the Second World War*, pp. 73–77.

80. Ulam, *Expansion and Coexistence*, p. 294.

81. Boheman, *På vakt*, pp. 106–8; Tanner, *The Winter War*, pp. 219–40; Lundin, *Finland in the Second World War*, pp. 78–79.

82. Max Jakobson, *The Diplomacy of the Winter War* (Cambridge: Harvard University Press, 1961), p. 210.

83. Assarsson, *I Skuggan av Stalin*, pp. 22–27; Itkina, p. 27; A. S. Kan, *Vneshnaia politika skandinavskikh stran v gody vtoroi mirovoi voiny* (Moscow: Nauka, 1967), p. 144; J. K. Paasikivi, *President J. K. Paasikivis minnen*, 2 vols. (Stockholm: Bonner, 1958), 2:70.

84. Gunnar Hagglof, *Diplomat* (London: Bodley Head, 1971), p. 162.

85. Itkina, pp. 270–73; *Documents on German Foreign Policy*, Series D (1937–45), 13 vols. (Washington: Government Printing Office, 1956), 9:567.

86. Palencia, *Kollontai*, p. 18.

87. Svartz, *Steg för steg*, pp. 120–25; Nilsson, "Det stora uppdraget," no. 37, pp. 18–19.

88. Lundin, *Finland in the Second World War*, pp. 82–189; John H. Wuorinen, ed., *Finland and World War II, 1939–1944* (New York: Ronald Press, 1948), pp. 81–144. Professor Wuorinen was the editor of this book, smuggled out of Finland in 1945. He thought it was written by several Finnish government officials. It is a statement of the Finnish position, and although it contains valuable material, it attempts to prove that the Soviet Union started the Continuation War. This contention is not borne out by the facts. The study generally represents the attitudes of the conservative to moderate elements in the Ryti cabinet.

89. Boheman, *På vakt*, pp. 245–47; Samuel Abrahamsen, *Sweden's Foreign Policy* (Washington: Public Affairs Press, 1957), p. 47.

90. G. A. Gripenberg, *En beskickningschefs minnen*, 2 vols. (Stockholm: Natur och kultur, 1960), 2:153–67; Väinö Tanner, *Vägen till fred, 1943–1944*

(Stockholm: Holger Schildt, 1952), p. 174; Wuorinen, *Finland and World War II*, p. 156. Tanner was now finance minister.

91. Boheman, *På vakt*, p. 248.

92. Ibid., p. 249–51: Lundin, *Finland in the Second World War*, p. 146; Tanner, *Vägen*, p. 119.

93. Boheman, *På vakt*, p. 255.

94. Ibid., pp. 251–55; Gripenberg, *Minnen*, pp. 175–207; Tanner, *Vägen*, pp. 93–141; Wuorinen, *Finland and World War II*, pp. 145–65, 162–63; Lundin, *Finland in the Second World War*, pp. 193–98.

95. Boheman, *På vakt*, pp. 255–56; Gripenberg, *Minnen*, pp. 210–18; Tanner, *Vägen*, pp. 147–64; Lundin, *Finland in the Second World War*, pp. 199–200: "Mme. Kollontay is Ill," *New York Times*, 3 April 1944, sec. 1, p. 9.

96. Boheman, *På vakt*, pp. 256–57; Tanner, *Vägen*, pp. 162–228; Gripenberg, *Minnen*, pp. 219–37; Wuorinen, *Finland and World War II*, pp. 172–73.

97. Boheman, *På vakt*, pp. 257–58; Gripenberg, *Minnen*, pp. 239–43; Lundin, *Finland in the Second World War*, pp. 206–21; Wuorinen, *Finland and World War II*, pp. 173–74.

98. Boheman, *På vakt*, pp. 258–59; Gripenberg, *Minnen*, pp. 249–55.

99. Boheman, *På vakt*, p. 259.

100. Gripenberg, *Minnen*, p. 259.

101. Tanner, *Vägen*, pp. 251–82; Boheman, *På vakt*, pp. 259–62; Gripenberg, *Minnen*, pp. 257–94; Lundin, *Finland in the Second World War*, pp. 224–49.

102. Boheman, *På vakt*, p. 262.

103. Ibid.; Gripenberg, *Minnen*, pp. 296–97; Wuorinen, *Finland and World War II*, p. 167; *Morgon-Tidningen*, 26 July 1945.

104. Boheman, *På vakt*, p. 262.

105. Ibid.; Gripenberg, *Minnen*, p. 284.

106. Ibid., p. 295.

107. Svartz, *Steg för steg*, pp. 125–27.

108. Nilsson, "Det stora uppdraget," no. 38, p. 16; *Stockholms-Tidningen*, 26 July 1945.

109. For notes on these memoirs see Note on Sources in the Bibliography.

110. Itkina, pp. 278–84; Bertil Wagner, "Alexandra Kollontay—världens första kvinnliga ambassadör," *Arbetartidning*, 13 March 1962, p. 9; "Nobel Prize May Go to Madame Kollontay," *New York Times*, 31 October 1946, sec. 1, p. 4; Nilsson, "Det stora uppdraget," no. 38, p. 16.

111. Kollontai, *Iz moei zhizni*, p. 368; Dangulov, *Dvenadtsat' dorog na Egl*, p. 288.

112. Kollontai, *Iz moei zhizni*, pp. 367–68; Wagner, "Kollontay," p. 9.

113. Kollontai, *Iz moei zhizni*, pp. 365–66.

114. Ibid., p. 367.

115. Itkina, p. 285.

116. *Izvestiia*, 11 March 1952, p. 4. The foreign press was kinder. *Time* and *Newsweek* described Kollontai as "the red rose of the Revolution." (24 March

1952, p. 79; 24 March 1952, p. 98.) The *London Times* saw her as an "impetuous" radical in her youth, but a competent diplomat in later life. (12 March 1952, p. 8). For Swedish newspapers see *Arbetaren*, 13 March 1952, p. 2, and *Social-Demokraten*, 12 March 1952, pp. 1 and 8. The latter observed, "It is certainly no exaggeration to say that passionate struggle was fundamental in her nature, and that it did not always live in peace and harmony with the quick and clear intellect, which was another of her many gifts."

117. Kollontai, "Iz vospominanii," p. 85.

Bibliography

NOTE ON SOURCES

Kollontai is unusual among Bolsheviks in the amount of autobiographical writing she produced. So many and varied are these materials that a word needs to be said about them. Complete citations for each of the items referred to in this note are given in the bibliography that follows.

First, Kollontai wrote the journalistic narratives based on her diaries, which have been discussed in the text. Her initial such effort was *Po rabochei Evrope* [Around Workers' Europe] in 1912; then in the twenties she produced *Otryvki iz dnevnika 1914 g.* [Fragments from a Diary] and *V tiur'me Kerenskogo* [In Kerensky's Prison]. In addition to these long reminiscences about relatively short periods (1909–10, August 1914, August 1917), a few snippets of Kollontai's diaries, on which the books were based, have appeared. They are most revealing about her daily moods, although they have been carefully edited to remove any disagreements with Lenin.

During the twenties Kollontai wrote a second type of autobiographical work, the memoir article. The first article, "Avtobiograficheskii ocherk" [An Autobiographical Sketch], published in 1921, covered her life up to that year, in the stiff, impersonal prose that was considered good taste among Bolsheviks. She told what she had done but glossed over both her own feelings and her opposition activity.

Kollontai made another attempt to recount her life in an article for the Soviet Granat encyclopedia collection of short sketches of the leading Bolsheviks, published between 1925 and 1927. Here she added a few details to the 1921 outline, but again provided only delicate clues to the more controversial aspects of her life. In 1926 or early 1927 she wrote a more revealing piece, "Ziel und Wert meines Lebens" [The Goal and Worth of My Life], which was published in a German collection of articles on the lives of leading European women. Iring Fetscher, the German editor who reissued this article in 1970, has restored the deletions Kollontai made from the original galleys.

All of these sketches and memoirs provide a survey of the events of Kollontai's life. Generally they avoid her feuds with the party, play down her Menshevik affiliation before 1915, and ignore her private life. In 1939 she began

315

writing a memoir revealing the whole woman. Only a portion of this final, multi-volume work has been published; it appeared in Swedish as *Den första etappen* [The First Steps] in 1945. That same year a slightly expurgated version was published in the Soviet magazine *Oktiabr'*. It is here that the best picture of Kollontai's parents and the young Shura emerges, and the life, humor, and grace of the book make one wish the Soviet government would publish it in its entirety.

After she retired Kollontai continued to write and rewrite her memoirs. She assembled a voluminous archive, which is now in the Marx-Lenin Institute in Moscow, seen only by a few Soviet scholars. Bits of her writing on the revolutionary years have appeared, most recently in a collection entitled *Iz moei zhizni i raboty* [From My Life and Work], but the Workers' Opposition and her theories on erotic love remain too controversial to discuss. Soviet authors present a sanitized Kollontai—obedient servant of Lenin, life-long Bolshevik, advocate of day-care centers.

The biographical material on Kollontai is of very uneven quality. The most important sources are referred to frequently in the text, but a word on several studies is in order here. The worshipful biography by Isabel de Palencia is generally of little use. The book by Gustav Johansson, a Swedish Communist who used the pseudonym Carsten Halvorsen, also suffers from his admiration for Kollontai, and from the fact that it stops with the outbreak of the revolution; he and Kollontai agreed that he should not deal with the later, more controversial years. Nevertheless, Johansson supplies useful information obtained directly from Kollontai.

Margaret Pertzoff made the first effort at a scholarly biography in a doctoral dissertation, "Lady in Red: A Study of the Early Career of Alexandra Mikhailovna Kollontai." The bibliography she amassed was most useful, although it has since been superseded by the impressive lists compiled by Henryk Lenczyc and by Kaare Hauge. Professor Hauge's dissertation is an important work, covering the diplomatic period of Kollontai's life and based on extensive research in Scandinavia.

Four Soviet historians deserve mention. Anna Itkina, a young Zhenotdel worker during the civil war, has written the only full-length Soviet biography of Kollontai, the second edition of which is most useful. Emelian Mindlin has produced a fictionalized account of her life, *Ne dom, no mir*, which I have not used because its content—including whole conversations derived from unnamed sources—is unreliable. I. M. Dazhina, the editor of two recent collections of Kollontai's writings, has provided valuable chronological and biographical details. Finally, Grigorii Petrov has published a number of informative articles on Kollontai during World War I.

The following bibliography, based on the bibliographies compiled by Pertzoff, Lenczyc, and Hauge combined with the results of my own burrowing through periodicals, represents an attempt to list all editions of Kollontai's writings. Although probably not complete, since Kollontai was so prolific and since her work appeared in so many editions, it is the fullest list to date. Other sources given below are among those consulted in the preparation of this book.

KOLLONTAI'S WRITINGS

Each piece is listed according to its first published version; later editions are noted after the initial citation. An asterisk (*) marks articles reprinted in *Izbrannye stat'i i rechi* (Moscow: Politizdat, 1972); a dagger (†) indicates those reprinted in *Iz moei zhizni i raboty* (Moscow: Sovetskaia Rossiia, 1974).

1898

"Osnovy vospitaniia po vzgliadam Dobroliubova." *Obrazovanie*, no. 9 (September 1898), pp. 1–15; no. 10 (October 1898), pp. 1–19; no. 11 (November 1898), pp. 1–16. "A. M. Kollontai o N. A. Dobroliubove." *Narodnoe obrazovanie*, no. 4 (1972), pp. 77–85.

1900

"Die Arbeiterfrage in Finnland." *Soziale Praxis, Centralblatt für Sozial Politik*, no. 9 (1900), pp. 50ff. *International Review* (Dresden), no. 49 (1900).

1901

"Promyshlennost' i torgovlia Velikogo Kniazhestva Finliandskogo." *Nauchnoe obozrenie*, no. 7 (1901), pp. 8–40.
"Protest' Finliandskogo naroda." *Iskra*, 20 November 1901, p. 1.

1902

"Promyshlennost' i zemel'nye voprosy v Finliandii." *Nauchnoe obozrenie* (1902).
"Sotsializm v Finliandii." *Zaria*, no. 4 (1902), pp. 71–79. In *Finliandiia i sotsializm: Sbornik statei*, pp. 6–18. St. Petersburg: Malykh, 1906.
"Splavshchiki lesa v Finliandii." *Nauchnoe obozrenie*, no. 9 (1902), pp. 69–78.
"Zemel'nyi vopros v Finliandii." *Nauchnoe obozrenie*, no. 2 (1902), pp. 45–54; no. 3 (1902), pp. 202–10; no. 4 (1902), pp. 124–36.
"Zhilishcha finliandskikh rabochikh." *Russkoe bogatstvo*, no. 7 (July 1902), pp. 126–44.

1903

"Rabochee dvizhenie v Finliandii." *Iskra*, 1 April 1903.
"Russkie bonapartisty v Finliandii." *Iskra*, 1 April 1903, p. 1.
Zhizn' finliandskikh rabochikh. St. Petersburg: Khudozhestvennoi pechati, 1903.

1904

"Die Arbeiterbewegung in Finnland und die russische Regierung." *Die Neue Zeit*, no. 22 (1903–4), pp. 749–57. In *Finliandiia i sotsializm*, pp. 19–34.
"Osnovniia agrarniia tendentsii (Sravnitel'nyi razbor trudov: E. David'a—'Socialismus und Landwirtschaft' i P. Maslova—'Usloviia razvitiia sel'skogo khoziaistva v Rossii')." *Pravda* 1 (November 1904):197–211.

1905

*K voprosu o klassovoi bor'be. St. Petersburg: Malykh, 1905. 2d edition, 1912, confiscated.
"Problema nravstvennosty s pozitivnoi tochki zreniia." Obrazovanie 14, no. 9 (September 1905), pp. 77–95; no. 10 (October 1905), pp. 92–107.

1906

"Etika i sotsial-demokratiia (po povodu stat'e g. Pokrovskogo v no. 4 'Polarnoi zvezdy')." Obrazovanie 15 (February 1906):22–32.
*Finliandiia i sotsializm: Sbornik statei. St. Petersburg: Malykh, 1906.
"Itogi mangeimskogo s"ezda (sotsial'demokraticheskaia partiia i professional'-nye soiuzy)." Sovremennyi mir 1 (November 1906):1–19.
*"Kto takie sotsial-demokraty i chego oni khotiat?" Rabochii ezhegodnik 1 (1906):74–87. St. Petersburg: Kniga, 1906. Petrograd: Kniga, 1917. Minsk: Zvezda, [1918?]. New York: Pervoi russkii otdel Amerikanskoi sotsialisticheskoi partii, 1918.
O sobeshcheinom predstavitel'stve. St. Petersburg: Molot, 1906.
"Pis'mo k redaktsiiu." Obrazovanie, 1906.

1907

"Dva techeniia (po povodu pervoi mezhdunarodnoi zhenskoi sotsialisticheskoi konferentsii v Shtutgarte)." Obrazovanie 16 (October 1907):46–62. In Mezhdunarodnye sotsialisticheskie soveshchaniia rabotnits. (Moscow: Izd. VTsIK Sovet RS i K deputatov, 1918), pp. 46–62.
"Izbiratel'naia kampaniia v Finliandii." Otgoloski, no. 3 (1907), pp. 46–61.
"Novyi finliandskii Parlament." Obrazovanie 16, no. 4 (April 1907), pp. 72–90; no. 5 (May 1907), pp. 54–69; no. 7 (July 1907), pp. 20–47.

1908

"Aleksei Remizov: Chasy roman." Sovremennyi mir, no. 1 (1908), pp. 125–27.
"Zhenshchina-rabotnitsa v sovremennom obshchestve." Trudy I vserossiiskogo zhenskogo s"ezda, pp. 792–801. St. Petersburg, 1908.

1909

*Sotsial'nye osnovy zhenskogo voprosa. St. Petersburg: Znanie, 1909. St. Petersburg: Znanie, 1916. Excerpted in Alexandra Kollontai, Marxisme et révolution sexuelle, edited by Judith Stora-Sandor, pp. 52–96. Paris: Maspero, 1973.
"Zhenshchina-rabotnitsa na pervom feministskom s"ezde v Rossii." Golos sotsial-demokrata 2 (March 1909):6–7.

1910

"Itogi s"ezda po bor'be s prostitutsiei." Sotsial'demokrat, no. 14 (July 1910), pp. 5–6.
"Itogi vtoroi mezhdunarodnoi zhenskoi sotsialisticheskoi konferentsii." Nasha zaria 1 (September 1910):89–95. Obrazovanie, 1910. "Vtoraia mezhdunarod-

naia zhenskaia konferentsiia," in *Mezhdunarodnye sotsialisticheskie soveshchanie rabotnits*, pp. 24–33. Moscow: Izd. VTsIK, 1918.

"Die ökonomishche Lage der russischen Arbeiterinnen." *Die Gleichheit*, nos. 24, 25, 26 (1910).

"Proletariat i burzhuaziia v bor'be s prostitutsiei." *Pravda* (Vienna), 7 July 1910, p. 3.

"Die russische Arbeiter-bewegung in den Zeiten der Reaction." *Die Neue Zeit*, 8 July 1910, pp. 484–92.

"Sud'ba chelovechestva v voprose narodnogo naseleniia." *Zhizn'* (September 1910), pp. 10–24.

"Vtoraia mezhdunarodnaia zhenskaia sotsialisticheskaia konferentsiia." *Sotsial'-demokrat*, no. 7 (1910), n.p.

"Zadachi rabotnits v bor'be s prostitutsiei." *Golos sotsial'demokrata* 3 (April 1910):3–4.

"Zadachi s"ezda po bor'be s prostitutsiei." *Vozrozhdenie* 2 (30 March 1910): 8–17. *Sotsial'demokrat*, no. 17 (1910).

"Zhenskoe rabochee dvizhenie na Zapade." *Zhizn'*, no. 2 (1910), pp. 47–52.

1 9 1 1

"Aus der Bewegung." *Die Gleichheit*, no. 17 (1911), pp. 265–66.

"Aus der Gewerkschaftsbewegung Russlands." *Die Gleichheit*, no. 19 (1911), p. 302.

"Dvizhenie menazherok (khoziaek) vo Frantsii." *Nasha zaria* 2 (September 1911):75–80.

"Der erste Mai im Zarenreich." *Die Gleichheit*, no. 15 (1911), pp. 228–29.

"Formy organizatsii rabotnits na zapade." *Delo zhizni*, no. 1 (22 January 1911), pp. 79–88. Moscow: Izd. VTsIK, 1918.

"Iz zapisok zagranichnogo agitatora." *Russkoe bogatstvo*, no. 11 (November 1911), pp. 167–83.

"Na staruiu temu." *Novaia zhizn'* (1911), pp. 174–96. "Liubov' i novaia moral'," in *Novaia moral' i rabochii klass*, pp. 36–47. Moscow: Izd. VTsIK, 1918. "L'amour et la morale nouvelle," in *Marxisme et révolution sexuelle*, pp. 156–68.

"Polovaia moral' i sotsial'naia bor'ba." *Novaia zhizn'*, no. 9 (1911), pp. 155–82. "Otnoshenie mezhdu polami i klassovaia bor'ba," in *Novaia moral' i rabochii klass*, pp. 48–61. "Les rapports entre les sexes et la lutte des classes," in *Marxisme et révolution sexuelle*, pp. 168–82.

"Zhenskii den'." *Nasha zaria* 2 (March 1911):39–43.

1 9 1 2

"Dve pravdy." *Novaia zhizn'*, no. 8 (1912), pp. 166–75.

"Den internationella arbetarklassen och kriget." *Social-Demokraten*, 2 May 1912, p. 1.

"Novaia Angliia." *Nasha zaria*, no. 11–12 (1912), pp. 89–99.

"Novye zakony strakhovaniia materinstva." *Sovremennyi mir*, no. 10 (1912), pp. 221–30.

"Obshchestvennoe dvizhenie v Finliandii." *Obshchestvennoe dvizhenie v Rossii.* L. Martov, P. Maslov, and A. Potresov, eds. St. Petersburg: Obshchestvennaia pol'za, 1912.

"Po rabatschei Jewrgse." *Korrespondenzblatt der General-kommission der Gewerkschaft Deutschlands,* no. 69 (1912).

†*Po rabochei Evrope.* St. Petersburg: Semenov, 1912. *Bei den europäischen Arbeitern.* Dresden: Kaden, 1912. *Po burzhuaznoi Evrope.* Kazan': Gosizdat, 1921.

"Soiuz zashchity materinstva i reforma seksual'noi morali." *Novaia zhizn',* no. 11 (1912), pp. 239–54.

"Zhenskii den' v Germanii i Avstrii." *Delo zhizni,* no. 4 (1912), pp. 67–72.

"Zhenskoe izbiratel'noe pravo v shvedskom parlament." *Nasha zaria* 3 (July 1912), pp. 55–60.

1913

"Novaia zhenshchina." *Sovremennyi mir,* no. 9 (1913), pp. 151–85. *Novaia moral' i rabochii klass,* pp. 3–35. "Femmes célibataires," *Marxisme et révolution sexuelle,* pp. 100–34.

"Organizatsiia rabotnits i partiinoe stroitel'stvo." *Luch',* no. 127 (1913).

*"Veliki borets za pravo i svobod zhenshchiny (Pamiati Avg. Bebelia)." *Nasha zaria,* no. 7–8 (1913), pp. 15–24. *Suuri Esitaistelija.* Porvos, 1914. In Avgust Bebel, *Zhenshchina i sotsializm.* Petrograd: Izd. Petro. soveta rab. i krasno. deputatov, 1919.

"Zapiski agitatora." *Sovremennyi mir,* no. 2 (1913), pp. 1–14.

"Zashchita materinstva." *Nasha zaria,* no. 9 (1913), pp. 10–21.

*"Zhenskii den'." *Pravda,* 17 February 1913.

"Zhenskoe rabochee dvizhenie." *Nasha zaria,* no. 2 (1913), pp. 3–16.

1914

"Fosterlandsförsvar eller internationell solidaritet." *Stormklockan,* 26 December 1914, pp. 6–7.

"Gosudarstvennoe stremlenie materinstva." *Strakhovanie rabochikh,* no. 3 (1914).

"Grosnyi prizrak." *Sovremennyi mir,* no. 3 (1914), pp. 65–84.

*"Jean Jaurès." *Julfacklan,* supplement to *Social-Demokraten* 12 (1914):n.p.

"Krest' materinstva." *Sovremennyi mir,* no. 1 (November 1914), pp. 42–54.

*"Kriget och våra närmaste uppgifter." *Forsvarsnihilisten,* no. 11 (1914).

"Mezhdunarod. sotsial. konferentsiia." *Golos,* 30 December 1914, p. 1.

"Otechestvo ili rabochii internatsional." *Golos,* 19 December 1914, pp. 1–2.

Rabotnitsa-mat'. St. Petersburg: Bib. Rabotnitsy, 1914. St. Petersburg: Nauchnoe delo, 1917. St. Petersburg: Zhizn' i znanie, 1917. Moscow, 1918. Petrograd, 1918. *A dolgozo anya; forditotta.* Budapest, 1919.

"Staatliche Mutterschaftsversicherung." *Die Neue Zeit,* 11 December 1914, pp. 363–71.

"Till de socialistiska kvinnorna i alla länder." *Stormklockan,* 15 November 1914, p. 2.

"Tipy i formy strakhovaniia materinstva." *Novaia zhizn'*, no. 2 (1914), pp. 20–31. *Nasha zaria*, no. 2 (1914).

*"Und in der Russie eine Frauen Tagen gewesen." *Die Gleichheit*, no. 12 (1914).

"Zhenskii den' priblizhaetsia." *Novaia rabochaia gazeta*, 21 January 1914, p. 2.

1915

" 'Belyi' i 'zheltyi' kapitalizm." *Nashe slovo*, 20 June 1915, pp. 1–2.

"Chto delat'? Otvet sotsialistkam." *Nashe slovo*, 19 February 1915, p. 1.

"Dve pobedy norvezhskikh rabochikh." *Nashe slovo*, 23 May 1915, p. 2.

"Germanskaia sotsialdemokratiia v pervye dni voiny (Lichnaia nabliudeniia)." *Nashe slovo*, 4 April 1915, pp. 1–2; 9 April 1915, pp. 1–2; 10 April 1915, p. 1.

"K vozrozhdeniiu." *Nashe slovo*, 28 April 1915, p. 1.

"Kongress norvezhskoi sots-dem." *Nashe slovo*, 13 June 1915, pp. 1–2.

"Kopengagenskaia konferentsiia." *Nashe slovo*, 29 January 1915, p. 2.

"Kopengagenskaia konferentsiia." *Nashe slovo*, 2 February 1915, p. 1.

"Krizis v Shvedskoi partii." *Nashe slovo*, 13 May 1915, p. 1.

"Den nye ungdomsinternationale og arbeiderungdommen." *Ungdomsinternationalen* (Zurich, Scandinavian edition), no. 1 (3 October 1915), pp. 6–7.

"O linii mezhevaniia." *Nashe slovo*, 7 September 1915, p. 2.

"Pochemu molchal proletariat Germanii v iiul'skie dni." *Kommunist*, no. 1–2 (1915), pp. 159–61.

"Rabochaia zhizn' v Norvegii." *Nashe slovo*, 15 May 1915, p. 1.

"Den socialistiska kvinnointernationalen och kriget." *Morgonbris*, no. 1 (1915), pp. 3–5.

"Sotsial-demokraticheskii deputat Finliandskogo seima soslan v Sibir." *Golos*, 9 January 1915, p. 1.

"Statlig moderskapsförsäkring." *Morgonbris*, no. 6 (1915), pp. 2–3; no. 7 (1915), p. 2.

"The Third International." *The American Socialist*, 23 October 1915, p. 2.

"V Germanii." *Nashe slovo*, 8 April 1915, p. 1.

"Verdenkrigens følger set fra sociale, politiske og økonomiske synpunkter." *Klassenkampen*, 13 November 1915, pp. 559–61.

"Vesti iz Finliandii." *Nashe slovo*, 5 August 1915, pp. 1–2; 6 August 1915, pp. 1–2.

"Vesti iz Rossii." *Nashe slovo*, 16 June 1915, pp. 1–2.

"Vmesto 'Zhenskogo dnia'—internatsional'naia demonstratsiia sotsialistok." *Nashe slovo*, 25 February 1915, p. 2.

"Zhenskii den'." *Nashe slovo*, 18 March 1915, p. 2.

"Zhenskii sotsialisticheskii Internatsional i voina." *Nashe slovo*, 7 March 1915, pp. 3–4.

1916

"Antimilitarizm rabochikh v Amerike." *Nashe slovo*, 30 April–1 May 1916, pp. 2–3.

"The Attitude of the Russian Socialists." *New Review* 4 (March 1916):60–61.

"Do Internationalists Want a Split?" *International Socialist Review* 16 (January 1916):394–96.

"Finskie sotsialisty v Amerike." *Nashe slovo*, 6 May 1916, pp. 1–2; 7 May 1916, p. 2.

"Gotoviatsia k voine." *Nashe slovo*, 6 January 1916, p. 1.

*_Komu nuzhna voina?_ Bern: TsK RSDRP, 1916. 2d ed. St. Petersburg: Priboi, 1917. St. Petersburg, 1918. *Arbeiterpolitik* (Bremen), 7 December 1918, pp. 297–98; 21 December 1918, pp. 308–10; 28 December 1918, pp. 314–16; 4 January 1919, pp. 320–22. *Wem nützt der Krieg?* Moscow, 1918. *Qui veut la guerre?* Switzerland, n.d.

†"My Agitational Tour Around the United States." *New Yorker Volkszeitung*, March 1916.

Obshchestvo i materinstvo. Petrograd: Zhizn' i znanie, 1916. *Gesellschaft und Mutterschaft.* 1916. Moscow: Gosizdat, 1921, 1923.

"Vesti iz Rossii: Interv'iu s 'obyvatelem.'" *Nashe slovo*, 15 April 1916, p. 1; 18 April 1916, p. 1.

"Vseobshchaia zabastovka v Norvegii." *Nashe slovo*, 23 June 1916, p. 1; 24 June 1916, p. 1.

1917

*"Bankrotstvo lozunga 'grazhdanskogo mira.'" *Rabochii put'*, 13 October 1917, p. 2.

"Demonstratsiia soldatok." *Pravda*, 12 April 1917, p. 2.

"Dorogovizna i voina." *Rabotnitsa*, 1917.

"Durch Bürgerkrieg zur Gleichberechtigung der Frauen." *Jugend-Internationale*, no. 8 (May 1917), pp. 9–10.

"Das fremde Kollektiv." *Jugend-Internationale*, no. 10 (1 October 1917), pp. 5–6.

"Genom krig mot de bestående samhället fram till kvinnornas likaberättigande med männen!" *Morgonbris*, no. 5 (1917), pp. 6–7.

"Informatsiia." *Pravda*, 11 April 1917, p. 1.

"Itogi izbiratel'noi kampanii v Soedinennykh Shtatakh." *Letopis'* (January 1917), pp. 223–36.

"K tovarishcham vsekh Petrogradskikh raionov." *Pravda*, 16 November 1917, p. 4.

"Kak nado rabotnitsam gotovitsiia k Uch. Sobranie?" *Rabochii put'*, 27 October 1917, p. 2.

"Ko vsem rabotnitsam." *Pravda*, 17 November 1917, p. 4.

*"Kogda konchitsia voina?" *Izbrannye stat'i*, pp. 225–27.

"Konferentsiia rabotnits i partiinie raioni." *Rabochii put'*, 3 November 1917, p. 2.

*"Kuda vedet revoliutsionnoe oboronchestvo?" *Pravda*, 5 April 1917, p. 1.

"Na nashe 'linii ognia.'" *Pravda*, 22 May 1917, p. 3.

*"Nash pamiatnik bortsam za svobodu." *Pravda*, 23 March 1917, p. 1.

*"Nashi zadachi." *Rabotnitsa*, no. 1–2 (1917), pp. 3–4.

"Die Opposition in der 'American Socialist Party.'" *Die Arbeiterpolitik* (Bremen), no. 14 (7 April 1917), pp. 108–10.

"Paa havet i blokadezonen." *Lordagskvelden* (Oslo), 3 March 1917, pp. 1–2; 10 March 1917, p. 1; 17 March 1917, pp. 1–2.

"Pervaia konferentsiia rabotnits." *Rabochii put'*, 8 November 1917, p. 4.

"Pervye shagi k sozyvu konferentsii rabotnits." *Pravda*, 23 October 1917, p. 2.

"Pis'ma iz Ameriki." *Letopis'* (May–June 1917).

"Plenniki russkikh imperialistov." *Pravda*, 16 June 1917, pp. 2–3.

"Prikaz narodnogo komisara po gosudarstvennomu prizreniiu." *Pravda*, 8 December 1917, p. 3.

"Rabotnitsy i Raionnyi Duma." *Pravda*, 8 June 1917, pp. 2–3.

"Rabotnitsy i uchreditel'noe sobranie." *Pravda*, 21 March 1917, pp. 1–2. Petrograd: Priboi, 1917.

"Rabotnitsy, zanimaite svoi revoliutsionnye posti!" *Pravda*, 10 November 1917, p. 4.

*"Varför bolsjevikerna bör segra." *Revolt*, no. 12 (1917). *Revolt*, 1 May 1918, pp. 5–6.

"La vie politique et sociale Amérique." *Demain* (Geneva), no. 13 (May 1917), pp. 34–39.

"La vie politique et sociale Suède." *Demain*, no. 13 (May 1917), pp. 46–48.

*"Vosstanovlenie administratsionnogo proizvola." *Rabochii put'*, 20 September 1917, p. 2.

1918

"Amerikanskii proletariat." *Pravda*, 12 October 1918, p. 2.

"Dekret." *Izvestiia*, 4 January 1918, p. 2.

†"Gorod pervykh 'buntarei.' " *Pravda*, 3 October 1918.

"K pervomu vserossiiskomu soveshchaniiu rabotnits." *Pravda*, 30 October 1918, p. 3.

"K 1-mu vserossiiskomu soveshchaniiu 'rabotnits.' " *Pravda*, 2 November 1918, p. 3.

*"Krest materinstva i Sovetskaia respublika." *Pravda*, 1 October 1918.

Mezhdunarodnye sotsialisticheskie soveshchaniia rabotnits. Moscow: Izd. VTsIK Sovetov RSK i K Deputatov, 1918.

Novaia moral' i rabochii klass. Moscow: Izd. VTsIK, 1918. *La femme nouvelle et la classe ouvrier.* Paris and Brussels, 1932. *Die neue moral und die arbeiterklass.* Berlin: A. Seehof, 1920. *La mujer nueva y la moral sexual.* Madrid, n.d. *Den nya moralen och arbetarklassen.* Stockholm: Framsförlag, 1932.

"Pervoe vserossiiskoe soveshchanie rabotnits." *Pravda*, 5 October 1918, p. 2.

"Pis'mo k rabotnitsam Krasnogo Petrograda." *Izbrannye stat'i*, pp. 246–47.

*"Popy eshche rabotaiut." *Pravda*, 19 December 1918.

*"Pora pokonchit' s 'Chernymi gnezdami.' " *Pravda*, 10 November 1918.

Rabotnitsa za god revoliutsii. Moscow: Kommunist, 1918.

Sem'ia i kommunisticheskoe gosudarstvo. Moscow: Kommunist, 1918. Samara: VSIK, 1919. Kharkov, 1920. Moscow: Gosizdat, 1920. Ekaterinoslav and Kharkov: Vseukrizdat, n.d. *Communism and the Family.* London: The Workers' Socialist Federation, [1918]. "Die Familie und der Kommunistische Staat." *Sowjet* (Vienna), no. 8/9, 10/11 (1920). *La famille et l'Etat com-*

muniste. Paris: Bib. communiste, 1920. Brussels: Ed. communiste, 1921. "La famiglia e lo Stato comunista." *Communismo; Rivista della III Internazionale*, 1919–20, pp. 617–30. *Communism and the Family*. Sydney: D. B. Young, 1971. *Women Workers Struggle for Their Rights*. Bristol, England: Falling Water Press, 1971. Excerpted in *Marxisme et révolution sexuelle*, pp. 210–13.

"Sistema izdevatel'stva prodolzhaetsia." *Rabochii put'*, 28 September 1918, p. 4.

*"Starost'—ne proklait'e, a zasluzhennyi otdykh." *Vechernie izvestiia*, 30 October 1918.

1919

*"Bor'ba s tsarem-golodom." *Izvestiia Khar'kovskogo Soveta i gubernskogo ispolnitel'nogo komiteta Sovetov rab., kres. i krasnoarmeiskikh deputatov*, 13 May 1919.

Bud' stoikim bortsom. Moscow: Gosizdat, 1919.

*"Chei budet zolotoi urozhai?" *Krasnyi ofitser* (Kiev), no. 3 (July 1919).

*"K istorii dvizheniia rabotnits v Rossii." *Kommunisticheskaia partiia i organizatsiia rabotnits*, pp. 51–90. Moscow: Izd. RKP, 1919. Kharkov: Vseukrainskoe izd., 1920.

Kak boriutsia rabotnitsy za svoi prava. Moscow: Izd. VTsIK, 1919. *Kommunisticheskaia partiia i organizatsiia rabotnits. Pervyi Vserossiiskii s"ezd rabotnits 16–21 noiabria 1918 g. i ego rezoliutsii*, pp. 3–9. Kharkov, 1920.

*"Karl Libknekht i Rosa Liuksemburg—Bortsy, geroi, i mucheniki." *Rabochii mir*, no. 2–3 (February 1919), pp. 14–15.

*"Kogo poteriali rabotnitsy?" *Kommunar*, 21 March 1919.

"Krasnyi garnizon i zadachi rabotnits." *Pravda*, 25 October 1919, p. 1.

"Letter." *Revolutionary Age*, 22 February 1919, p. 4.

Mezhdunarodnaia konferentsiia sotsialistok. Moscow: Izd. TIK, 1919.

Ne bud' dezertirom! Kiev: Izd. Vseukrainskoe pri TsKIK Sov. RK i K Deputatov, 1919. Moscow: Gosizdat, 1919.

"O rabote voennikh organizatorov." *Pravda*, 26 October 1919, p. 3.

*"Perelom v derevne." *Izvestiia*, 23 November 1919.

"Po Rossii." *Pravda*, 13 July 1919, p. 4.

"Prava rabotnits v Sovetskoi Rossii." *Kommunisticheskaia partiia i organizatsiia rabotnits*, pp. 20–23.

Rabotnitsy, krest'ianki i krasnyi front. Moscow: Izd. VTsIK, 1919. In *Puti sovetskogo stroitel'stva, 1917–1919*. P. K. Kudriashev, ed. Moscow: Gosizdat, 1919. Moscow: Gosizdat, 1920.

"Rabotnitsy v Oktiabr'skoi revoliutsii." *Pravda*, 6 November 1919, p. 3.

Staryi vrag bednoty-kholod. Moscow: Gosizdat, 1919.

"Vse na bor'bu s kholodom!" *Pravda*, 28 November 1919, p. 2.

*"Za chto my voiuem?" *Izvestiia Khar'kovskogo soveta*, 7 May 1919.

1920

Bor'ba rabotnits v poslednie gody. Kharkov: Vseukrizdat, 1920.

"Eshche odna pobeda kommunistok." *Izvestiia*, 14 July 1920, p. 1.

"Eshche odno oruzhie v bor'be protiv dezorganizatsii." *Izvestiia*, 17 March 1920.

"Gigant dukha i vol'i." *Krasnoarmeets,* no. 21–22 (April 1920), p. 14. In *Oktiabr'* 40, no. 1 (1963), pp. 4–5.

"Klassovaia voina i rabotnitsy." *Kommunistka,* no. 5 (October 1920), pp. 6–9.

Mezhdunarodnyi den' rabotnits. Moscow: Gosizdat, 1920.

*"Pervaia mezhdunarodnaia konferentsiia kommunistok." *Kommunistka,* no. 1–2 (June–July 1920), pp. 3–5. Moscow: Gosizdat, 1921.

"Posledniaia rabynia." *Kommunistka,* no. 7 (December 1920), pp. 24–26.

"Rabochii filosof F. I. Kalinin." *Sbornik pamiati F. I. Kalinina.* 1920.

Rabotnitsy i Krasnaia armiia. Moscow, 1920.

"Radostnyi itog." *Izvestiia,* 10 December 1920, p. 1.

"Sem'ia i kommunizm." *Kommunistka,* no. 7 (December 1920), pp. 16–19.

"Trudovaia povinnost' i okhrana zhenskogo truda." *Kommunistka,* no. 1–2 (June–July 1920), pp. 25–27.

"Trudovaia Respublika i prostitutsiia." *Kommunistka,* no. 6 (November 1920), pp. 15–17.

"V te dni." *Krasnaia gazeta,* 1920.

"Vozhd' proletarskoi revoliutsii." *Krasnoarmeets,* no. 21–22 (1920), p. 14.

"Vserossiiskoe soveshchanie kommunistok." *Izvestiia,* 28 November 1920, p. 1.

Za tri goda: Rechi i besedy agitatora. Moscow: Gosizdat, 1920.

*"Zadachi otdelov po rabote sredi zhenshchin." *Kommunistka,* no. 6 (November 1920), pp. 2–4.

1921

†"Avtobiograficheskii ocherk." *Proletarskaia revoliutsiia,* no. 1 (1921), pp. 261–302. *Iz moei zhizni i raboty.* Odessa: Vseukgosizdat, 1921. "Souvenirs et memoirs revolutionnaires." *Bulletin communiste,* no. 4 (December 1925), pp. 110–12.

"Eshche odin perezhitok." *Pravda,* 27 December 1921, p. 1.

"Geschlechtsbeziehung und die klassenkampf." *Forum,* no. 1–7 (1921), pp. 186–204.

"Komintern i II mezhdunarodnaia konferentsiia kommunistok." *Kommunistka,* no. 12–13 (May–June 1921), pp. 2–4.

"Kommunistka pervoi revoliutsii." *Kommunistka,* no. 16–17 (September–October 1921), pp. 5–7.

"Krest materinstva." *Kommunistka,* no. 8–9 (January–February 1921), pp. 22–29.

"Mezhdunarodnaia konferentsiia kommunistok." *Pravda,* 11 June 1921, p. 1.

"Mezhdunarodnaia solidarnost' i den' rabotnits." *Otchet o pervoi mezhdunarodnoi konferentsii kommunistok,* pp. 5–12. Moscow: Gosizdat, 1921.

"Na puti k kommunizmu i polnomu raskreposhcheniiu zhenshchiny." *Tri goda diktatury proletariata,* pp. 11–18. Moscow: Izd. Moskovskogo komiteta RKP, [1921].

"Ne uprazdenie, a ukreplenie." *Kommunistka,* no. 16–17 (September–October 1921), pp. 25–27.

"Nedelia Kominterna." *Pravda,* 13 November 1921, p. 1.

"O rabote mezhdunarodnogo zhenskogo sekretariata." *Kommunisticheskii internatsional,* no. 19 (1921), pp. 5097–5100.

Otchet o deiatel'nosti otdela Ts.K. RKP po rabote sredi zhenshchin. Moscow: Gosizdat, 1921.

"Pervoe maia i rabotnitsa." *Pravda,* 1 May 1921, p. 4.

"Pis'ma Rozy Liuksemburg." *Kommunistka,* no. 8–9 (January–February 1921), pp. 36–38.

"Pora proanalizirovat'." *Pravda,* 28 January 1921, p. 1.

*"Profsoiuzy i rabotnitsa." *Pravda,* 22 May 1921, p. 2.

"Proizvodstvo i byt." *Kommunistka,* no. 10–11 (March–April 1921), pp. 6–9.

Prostitutsiia i mery bor'by s nei. Moscow: Gosizdat, 1921. *Borba protiv prostitucije.* Chicago: Nakladom Jugoslavenske radničke knjižare, 1921.

Rabochaia oppozitsiia. Moscow: Gos. tip., 1921. *The Workers Opposition in Russia.* Chicago: IWW, 1921. *Tyoväen oppositsioni.* Duluth: Workers Socialist Publishing Co., n.d. *Was bedeutet die Arbeiter-Opposition?* Berlin: Kommunistische Arbeiterpartei Deutschlands, 1922. *The Workers Opposition.* London: Dreadnought, 1923. *L'opposizione operaia.* Milan: Azione, 1952. "L'Opposition ouvrière." *Socialisme ou Barbarie,* no. 6 (1964), pp. 57–107. *The Workers Opposition.* Reading: E. Morse, 1962. "Arbetaroppositionen." *Zenit,* no. 4 (1967), pp. 45–60.

Rabotnitsa i krest'ianka v sovetskoi Rossii. Moscow: Gosizdat, 1921. Petrograd: Kominterna, 1921. *The Peasant and Working Woman in Soviet Russia.* Moscow: Comintern, n.d. *L'ouvrière et la paysanne dans la République Soviétique.* Paris: "L'Humanité," 1921. *Die Arbeiterin und Bauerin in Sowjetrusslands.* Leipzig: Frankes, 1921.

†*"Soveshchanie kommunistok—organizatorov zhenshchin vostoka." *Pravda,* 19 April 1921, p. 4.

"Tezisy o kommunisticheskoi morali v oblasti brachnikh otnoshenii." *Kommunistka,* no. 12–13 (May–June 1921), pp. 28–34.

*"Tretii Internatsional i rabotnitsa." *Pravda,* 13 November 1921, p. 3.

*"Tsar'-golod i Krasnaia armiia." *Voin revoliutsii,* no. 2 (1921), p. 3.

*"Vtoraia mezhdunarodnaia konferentsiia." *Pravda,* 5 June 1921, p. 2.

"Zhizn' bortsa: Pamiati tov. A. S. Vedernikov-Sibirak." *Proletarskaia revoliutsiia,* no. 2 (1921), pp. 129–38.

1922

"Edinym frontom na zashchitu rabotnits." Supplement to *Pravda,* 8 March 1922, p. 1.

"Mezhdunarodnyi den' rabotnits." *Kommunistka,* no. 2 (1922).

"Novaia ugroza." *Kommunistka,* no. 8–9 (1922), pp. 5–9.

†"Oktiabr'skaia revoliutsiia i massy." *Molodaia gvardiia,* no. 6–7 (October 1922), pp. 211–18.

"Pis'ma k triudiashcheisia molodezhi. Pis'mo pervoe: Kakim dolzhen byt' kommunist?" *Molodaia gvardiia,* no. 1–2 (1922), pp. 136–44.

"Pis'ma k triudiashcheisia molodezhi. Pis'mo vtoroe: Moral', kak orudie klassovogo gospodstva i klassovoi bor'by." *Molodaia gvardiia,* no. 6–7 (1922), pp. 128–36.

Polozhenie zhenshchiny v sviazi s evoliutsii khoziaistva. Moscow: Gosizdat, 1922, 1923. *Trud zhenshchiny v evoliutsii khoziaistva.* Moscow and Leningrad: Gosizdat, 1923; 2d ed., 1926. *Kvinnans ställning in den ekonomiska samhällsutvecklingen.* Stockholm: Frams förlag, 1926. Excerpted in *Marxisme et révolution sexuelle,* pp. 214–46. Excerpted in Schlesinger, Adolph, *Changing Attitudes in Soviet Russia; the Family in the USSR,* pp. 45–71. London: Routledge and Kegan Paul, 1949.

†"Prazdnik vesny rabochei revoliutsii." *Izvestiia* (Odessa), 19 June 1922.

Skoro (cherez 48 let). Omsk, 1922. "Inom kort." *Författarförlagets Tidskrift,* Ann-Marie Axner, trans., no. 2 (1972), pp. 18–20.

"Tvorcheskoe v rabote K. N. Samoilovoi." *Kommunistka,* no. 3–5 (May 1922), pp. 8–11. *Revoliutsionnaia deiatel'nost Konkordii Nikolaevny Samoilovoi.* Moscow, 1922.

1 9 2 3

"Dorogu krylatomu Erosu!" *Molodaia gvardiia,* no. 3 (May 1923), pp. 111–24.

Voprosy zhizni i bor'by, edited by Emelian Iaroslavskii, pp. 170–82. Moscow: Molodaia gvardiia, 1924. *La juventud comunista y la moral sexual.* Madrid: Editorial estudios sociales, 1933. "L'idéologie prolétarienne et l'amour." *Marxisme et révolution sexuelle,* pp. 183–205.

"Kak my sozvali pervyi vserossiiskii s"ezd rabotnits i krest'ianok." *Kommunistka,* no. 11 (November 1923), pp. 3–8. *Rabotnitsa,* no. 42 (1928), pp. 6–7. *Sovetskaia zhenshchina,* no. 6 (1948), pp. 9–10.

Liubov' pchel trudovikh. Petrograd: Gosizdat, 1923. Moscow and Petrograd: Gosizdat, 1924. Riga: Knigoizd. O. D. Strok, 1925 (contains only "Liubov' pchel trudovikh"). *Arbetsbiens kärlek.* Stockholm: Frams förlag, 1925. 2 ed., 1931. *Wege der Liebe.* Berlin: Malik verlag, 1925. *Abejas proletarias.* Buenos Aires, 1926. *Red Love.* New York: Seven Arts, 1927. Japanese edition, 1927. *La Bolchevique enamorada.* Madrid, 1928. *Vasilisa Malygina.* Moscow-Leningrad: Gosizdat, 1927. *De maan kameraad.* Utrecht: Door de Ploeg, 1928. *Vejen till kjaerlighet.* Oslo, 1928. *Vasia.* A play in three acts by N. A. Kresheninnikova. Moscow: Teakinopechat', 1930.

"Ne 'printsip,' a 'metod.' " *Pravda,* 20 March 1923, p. 4.

*"Norvegiia i nash torgovlyi balans." *Izvestiia,* 16 November 1923.

"Pis'ma k triudiashcheisia molodezhi; Pis'mo tretee: O 'drakone' i 'beloi ptitse.' " *Molodaia gvardiia,* no. 2 (February–March 1923), pp. 162–74.

"Anna Akhmatova: chantre de la femme nouvelle," In *Marxisme et révolution sexuelle,* pp. 135–52.

"Sestry." *Kommunistka,* no. 3–4 (March–April 1923), pp. 23–26. In *Liubov' pchel trudovikh. Sestry.* Moscow: Gosizdat, 1927.

Zhenshchina na perelome. Moscow and Petrograd: Gosizdat, 1923. *Bol'shaia liubov'.* Moscow and Leningrad: Gosizdat, 1927. *A Great Love.* Lily Lore, trans. New York: Vanguard, 1929. *Den stora kjarlighet.* Oslo: Arbeiter mag., 1930. *A Great Love.* Freeport, N.Y.: Books for Libraries, 1971.

1924

†*Otryvki iz dnevnika 1914 g.* Leningrad: Gosizdvo, 1924. In *Zvezda*, no. 4 (1924). *Ocherki o Germanii v pervye mesiatsy pervoi imperialisticheskoi voiny.* Leningrad: Gosizdat, 1925.

1925

"Kollontai, Aleksandra Mikhailovna." *Deiateli SSSR i Oktiabr'skoi Revoliutsii: Entsiklopedicheskii slovar'.* 3 parts. Moscow and Leningrad: Granat, 1925–28. Part 1, pp. 194–201. In Haupt, Georges, and Marie, Jean-Jacques, trans. *Les Bolcheviks par eux-mêmes.* Paris: Maspero, 1969. In *Makers of the Russian Revolution,* trans. C. I. P. Ferdinand and D. M. Bellos, pp. 353–60. Ithaca, N.Y.: Cornell University Press, 1974.

1926

"Brak i byt." *Rabochii sud'*, no. 5 (1926), pp. 363–78.
"Brak, zhenshchina i alimenty." *Ekran*, no. 5 (1926).
"Obshchii kotel ili individual'nye alimenty." *Brak i semia.* Moscow: Molodaia gvardiia, 1926.

1927

**"Chto dal Oktiabr' zhenshchine zapada?" *Ogonek*, no. 41 (9 October 1927).
†"Dekret na stene." *Krasnaia panorama*, no. 45 (4 November 1927), pp. 14–15. In *Nemerknushchie gody: Ocherki i vospominaniia o Krasnom Petrograde.* Leningrad, 1957.
†"Mandat v Sovet o derevoobdelochnikov." *Krasnyi derevoobdelochnik*, no. 3 (1927).
"Meksika, strana problema." *Leningradskaia pravda*, 21 October 1927.
*"Oppozitsiia i partiinaia massa." *Pravda*, 30 October 1927, p. 3.
†"Pervoe posobie iz Sosbeza." *Krasnaia niva*, no. 45 (1927), p. 39. In *Smena*, no. 2 (1927), p. 6. In *Krasnoarmeets*, 1946. In *Moskva*, no. 9 (1957), pp. 156–58. In *Vospominaniia ob Il'iche.* Moscow: Politizdat, 1959. In *Vospominaniia o Vladimire Il'iche Lenine.* Moscow: Politizdat, 1960. Reprinted as "Pervye dni Narkomsobesa," in *Izvestiia*, 6–7 November 1927. In *Nemerknushchie gody*, pp. 267–72. Reprinted as "Pervye shagi." *Sotsial'noe obespechenie*, no. 11 (1957), pp. 23–25. In *Sovetskaia zhenshchina*, no. 7 (1957), pp. 11–13.
†"Po 'bozheskim' delam u monakhov." *Smena*, no. 2 (1927), p. 39. Reprinted as "Po sotsial'nym delam u monakhov," *Don*, no. 4 (1966).
"Revoliutsionnaia Meksika." *Vecherniaia Moskva*, 22 September 1927.
†"Ruka istorii: Vospominaniia A. Kollontai." *Krasnoarmeets*, no. 10–15 (November 1927), pp. 68–71. Reprinted as "V.V.", in *Izvestiia*, 24 October 1937. In *Ob Il'iche: Vospominaniia pitertsev*, pp. 351–54. Leningrad: Lenizdat, 1970.
†"V tiur'me Kerenskogo." *Katorga i ssylka*, no. 36 (1927), pp. 25–53. Moscow: Izd. obshchestva politkatorzhan i ss.-poselentsev, 1928.
*"Veliki stroitel'." *Za kul'turnuiu revoliutsiiu* (November 1927).

"Zavetnyi porog." *Krasnoarmeets*, no. 10–15 (1927).
*"Zhenshchiny-bortsy v dni Velikogo Oktiabria." *Zhenskii zhurnal*, no. 11 (November 1927), pp. 2–3.
"Ziel und Wert meines Lebens." *Führende Frauen Europas*. Elga Kern, ed., 1st series, pp. 258–86. Munich: E. Reinhardt, 1927. *Autobiographie einer sexuell emanzipierten Kommunistin*. Iring Fetscher, ed. Munich: Rogner and Bernhard, 1970. *The Autobiography of a Sexually Emancipated Communist Woman*. Edited with an Afterword by Iring Fetscher. Salvator Attanasio, trans. New York: Herder and Herder, 1971.

1931
"Molodezh' zvala ee Solntsem." *Sbornik pamiati V. F. Komissarzhevskoi*. Moscow: Gosizdat, Khudozhestvennoi lit., 1931.

1934
"Eine stossbrigadlerin der Proletarischen Revolution." *Clara Zetkin: Ein sammelband zum gedächtnis der grossen kämpferin*, pp. 59–61. Moscow and Leningrad: 1934.

1936
"Men med hensyn till fri kjaerlighet?" *Veien frem*, 12 February 1936.

1937
†"Zhenshchiny v 1917 godu." *Rabotnitsa*, no. 31 (November 1937), pp. 12–13.

1945
†*Den första etappen*. Stockholm: Bonniers, 1945. *Förste etappe*. Oslo, 1946. *Madame Kollontayn Muistelmat*. Helsinki, 1946.
†"Iz vospominanii." *Oktiabr'*, no. 9 (1945), pp. 59–89.

1946
"Dom na Moike." *Krasnoarmeets*, 1946.
†*"Lenin dumal o bol'shom i ne zabyval o malom." *Rabotnitsa* 23 (January 1946):6. In *Vospominaniia ob Il'iche*. Moscow: Politizdat, 1959. In *Vospominaniia o V. I. Lenine*. 3 vols. (Moscow: Politizdat, 1964), v. 3, pp. 139–41.
"Molodomu pokoleniiu." *Rabotnitsa* 23 (April–May 1946):16–18.
*"Sovetskaia zhenshchina—polnopravnaia grazhdanka svoi strany." *Sovetskaia zhenshchina*, no. 5 (September–October 1946), pp. 3–4.

1947
"Lenin i rabotnitsy v 1917 godu." *Rabotnitsa* 24 (January 1947):5–6. In *Vsegda s vami*. Moscow: Pravda, 1964.
†*"Lenin v Smol'nom." *Krasnoarmeets*, no. 2 (1947). In *Utro novogo mira: Sbornik vospominanii i dokumentov o II Vserossiiskom s"ezde sovetov*. Moscow: Gosizdat, 1962. In *O Vladimire Il'iche Lenine: Vospominaniia 1900–*

1922, pp. 218–20. Moscow: Politizdat, 1963. In *Vospominaniia o V. I. Lenine.* v 2. Moscow: Politizdat, 1969.

1949
*"Pamiati Nadezhdy Konstantinovny Krupskoi." *Izbrannye stat'i,* pp. 391–94.

1957
Nezabyvaemye gody, 1917–1920. Rostov: Kniznoe izd., 1957.

1959
Vospominaniia ob Il'iche. Moscow: Gosizdat, 1959.

1962
†"Amerikanskie dnevniki A. M. Kollontai, 1915–1916." *Istoricheskii arkhiv* 1 (January 1962):128–59.
"Zvezdy." *Smena,* no. 8 (1962), p. 11. In *Vospominaniia o V. I. Lenine,* vol. 3, pp. 186–87. Moscow: Politizdat, 1969.

1963
†"Golos Lenina." *Oktiabr'* 40, no. 1 (1963):5–6.
†"Raskryvalsia novyi put'." *Pravda,* 8 April 1963, p. 3. Reprinted as "Priezd Lenina v Petrograd," in *O Vladimire Il'iche Lenine: Vospominaniia 1900–1922.* Moscow: Politizdat, 1963. In *Ob Il'iche: Vospominaniia pitertsev.* Leningrad: Lenizdat, 1970.
†"V. I. Lenin i pervyi s"ezd rabotnits." In *O Vladimire Il'iche Lenine: Vospominaniia pitertsev.* Leningrad: Lenizdat, 1970.

1964
†"Vypolniaia porucheniia Lenina." *Nedelia,* 4 July 1964.

1967
†"Skoree v Rossiiu!" *Sovetskie arkhivy,* no. 2 (1967), pp. 23–33.

1970
"Iz arkhiva A. M. Kollontai." *Inostrannaia literatura,* no. 1 (1970), pp. 226–36; no. 2 (1970), pp. 226–45.
"Leninskie tezisy." *Ob Il'iche: Vospominaniia pitertsev,* pp. 275–76. Leningrad: Lenizdat, 1970.
"Statuia svobody." *Inostrannaia literatura,* no. 2 (1970), pp. 244–45.

1972
Izbrannye stat'i i rechi. Moscow: Politizdat, 1972. Articles reprinted in this volume are marked above with an asterisk(*).

1973
Marxisme et révolution sexuelle. Judith Stora-Sandor, ed. Paris: Maspero, 1973.

1974

Iz moei zhizni i raboty. I. M. Dazhina, ed. Moscow: Sovetskaia Rossiia, 1974. Articles excerpted in this volume are marked above with a dagger (†).

BOOKS AND ARTICLES

Abrahamsen, Samuel. *Sweden's Foreign Policy*. Washington: Public Affairs Press, 1957.

Akademiia nauk SSSR. Institut istorii. *Istoriia Vtorogo Internatsionala*. 2 v. Moscow: Nauka, 1965–66.

———. *Khronika sobytii* in *Velikaia oktiabr'skaia sotsialisticheskaia revoliutsiia*. 5 vols. Moscow: Izd. Akademii nauk, 1957.

———. *Petrogradskii Voenno-Revoliutsionnyi Komitet; Dokumenty i materialy*. 3 vols. Moscow: Nauka, 1966.

———. *Revoliutsionnoe dvizhenie v Rossii v sentiabre 1917 g*. Moscow: Izd. akademii nauk, 1961.

———. *Sovety v pervyi god proletarskoi diktatury oktiabr' 1917–noiabr' 1918 g*. Moscow: Izd. akademii nauk.

———. *Triumfal'noe shestvie sovetskoi vlasti*. 4 vols. Moscow: Akademii nauk, 1963.

Aksel'rod, Pavel Borisovich. *Pis'ma P. B. Aksel'roda i Iu. O. Martova*. Russian Reprint Series, Alexandre V. Soloviev and Alan Kimball, eds. The Hague: Mouton, 1967.

Andreev, A. A. *Professional'nye soiuzy v Rossii v 1921–1922 godu*. Petrograd: Izd. Redaktsionno-izdat. otdela VTsSPS, 1922.

Anikeev, V. V. *Deiatel'nost TsK RSDRP(b) v 1917 godu (Khronika sobytii)*. Moscow: Mysl, 1969.

Anskii, A. *Professional'noe dvizhenie v Petrograde v 1917 g*. Leningrad: Leningrad. oblastnoi sovet profsoiuzov, 1928.

Anthony, Katharine. "Alexandra Kollontay." *The North American Review* 230 (September 1930):277–82.

Apter, David E., ed. *Ideology and Discontent*. New York: The Free Press, 1964.

Armand, Inessa [Elena Blonina]. *Ocherednye zadachi po rabote sredi zhenshchin (Doklad na Vserossiiskom soveshchanii organizatorov otdelov po rabote sredi zhenshchin 28 marta 1920 g. v Moskve)*. Moscow, 1920.

———. *Rabotnitsy v Internatsionale*. Moscow: Gosizdat, 1920.

———. "Vseros. soveshchanie organizatorov otdelov po rabote sredi zhenshchin." *Pravda*, 24 October 1919, p. 4.

Arvatov, B. "Grazhdanka Akhmatova i tov. Kollontai." *Molodaia gvardiia*, no. 4–5 (1923), pp. 147–51.

Assarsson, Vilhelm. *I Skuggan av Stalin*. [Stockholm]: Bonniers, 1963.

Avrich, Paul H. "Russian Factory Committees in 1917." *Jahrbücher für Geschichte Osteuropas* 11 (1963):161–82.

Baevskii, D. "Bol'sheviki v Tsimmerval'de." *Proletarskaia revoliutsiia*, no. 5 (1935), pp. 27–48.

Bailes, Kendall E. "Alexandra Kollontai et la nouvelle morale." *Cahiers du monde russe et soviétique* 6 (October–December 1965):471–96.

Balabanoff, Angelica. *Impressions of Lenin.* Isotta Casari, trans. Ann Arbor: University of Michigan Press, [1964].

———. *My Life as a Rebel.* New York: Harper and Bros., [1938]. Reprint. Bloomington: Indiana University Press, 1973.

———. *Die Zimmerwalder Bewegung.* Frankfurt: Verlag Neue Kritik, 1969.

Barmine, Alexander. *One Who Survived.* New York: Putnam's Sons, 1945.

Baron, Samuel H. *Plekhanov, the Father of Russian Marxism.* Stanford: Stanford University Press, 1963.

Beatty, Bessie. *The Red Heart of Russia.* New York: The Century Co., 1918.

Bebel, August. *Woman Under Socialism.* Trans. from the 33rd edition by Daniel de Leon. New York: New York Labor News Company, 1904.

Berkman, Alexander. *The Bolshevik Myth (Diary 1920–1922).* London: Hutchinson, [c. 1925].

Bez nikh my ne pobedili by: Vospominaniia zhenshchin-uchastnits Oktiabr'skoi revoliutsii, grazhdanskoi voiny i sotsialisticheskogo stroitel'stva. Moscow: Politizdat, 1975.

Bobroff, Anne. "The Bolsheviks and Working Women 1905–20." *Soviet Studies* 26 (October 1974):540–67.

Bochkareva, E. I., and Liubimova, S. *Svetlyi put'.* Moscow: Politizdat, 1967.

Body, Marcel. "Alexandra Kollontai." *Preuves*, no. 14 (April 1952), pp. 12–24.

Boheman, Erik. *På vakt: Kabinettssekretarare under Andra Världskriget.* Stockholm: Norstedt, 1964.

Bol'shaia sovetskaia entsiklopediia, 1st edition, s.v. "VKP(b)," by A. Bubnov.

Bol'sheviki v period podgotovki i provedeniia velikoi oktiabr'skoi sotsialisticheskoi revoliutsii. Leningrad: Politizdat, 1947.

Bonch-Bruevich, Vladimir Dmitrievich. *Izbrannye sochineniia.* 3 vols. Moscow: Akademiia nauk, 1959–61.

Brak i byt; Sbornik statei i materialov. Moscow: Molodaia gvardiia, 1926.

Branting, Hjalmar. "Alexandra Kollontay utvisad!" *Socialdemokraten*, 21 November 1914, p. 3.

Bronin, Ia. "K kharakteristike platformy rabochei oppozitsii." *Proletarskaia revoliutsiia*, no. 11/94 (November 1929), pp. 3–25.

Browder, Robert Paul, and Kerensky, Alexander F., eds. *The Russian Provisional Government 1917.* 3 vols. Stanford: Stanford University Press, 1961.

Bryant, Louise. *Mirrors of Moscow.* New York: Thomas Seltzer, 1923.

———. *Six Red Months in Russia.* New York: Doran, [1918].

Bukharin, N. I. *Rabotnitsa, k tebe nashe slovo!* Moscow: Gosizdat, 1919.

Bunyan, James, and Fisher, H. H., eds. *The Bolshevik Revolution, 1917–1918.* Stanford: Stanford University Press, 1934.

Chamberlin, William Henry. *The Russian Revolution 1917–1921*. 2 vols. New York: Macmillan, 1960.

Cohen, Stephen F. *Bukharin and the Bolshevik Revolution*. New York: Alfred A. Knopf, 1973.

Communist International. 1st Congress, Moscow, 1919. *Pervyi kongress Kominterna, mart 1919 g.* Moscow: Partizdat, 1933.

———. 2d Congress, Moscow, 1920. *Vtoroi kongress Kominterna, iiul'–avgust 1920 g.* Moscow: Partizdat, 1934.

———. 3d Congress, Moscow, 1921. *Tretii vsemirnyi kongress Kommunisticheskogo Internatsionala; Stenograficheskii otchet.* Petrograd: Gosizdat, 1922.

———. Executive Committee, 1st plenum, 1922. *Compte rendu de la conférence de l'exécutif élargi de l'Internationale Communiste.* Paris: "L'Humanité," 1922.

Communist Party of Great Britain. *Work Among Women*. London: Communist Party of Great Britain, 1923.

Conquest, Robert. *The Great Terror*. New York: Macmillan, 1968.

Curtiss, John Shelton. *The Russian Church and the Soviet State, 1917–1950.* Boston: Little, Brown, 1953.

Dangulov, Savva. *Dvenadtsat' dorog na Egl.* Moscow: Sovetskaia Rossiia, 1970.

Daniels, Robert V. *The Conscience of the Revolution*. Cambridge: Harvard University Press, 1960.

———. *Red October*. New York: Scribners, 1967.

Debo, Richard Kent. "Litvinov and Kamenev—Ambassadors Extraordinary: The Problem of Soviet Representation Abroad." *Slavic Review* 34 (September 1975):463–82.

Deutscher, Isaac. *The Prophet Armed: Trotsky, 1879–1921.* New York: Vintage, 1954.

———. *The Prophet Unarmed: Trotsky, 1921–1929.* New York: Vintage, 1959.

———. *Soviet Trade Unions*. London: Royal Institute of International Affairs, 1956.

Dmitrenko, S. L. "X s"ezd RKP(b) o edinstve partii." *Vestnik Moskovskogo universiteta, Istoriia*, no. 3 (1971), pp. 27–44.

Documents on German Foreign Policy. Series D (1937–45). 13 vols. Washington: Government Printing Office, 1956.

Dokumenty vneshnei politiki SSSR. 19 vols. Moscow: Politizdat, 1960–74.

Draper, Theodore. *The Roots of American Communism*. New York: Viking, 1957.

Duranty, Walter. *I Write as I Please*. New York: Simon and Schuster, 1935.

Dybenko, Pavel Efimovich. "Dybenko, Pavel Efimovich." *Deiateli SSSR i Oktiabr'skoi Revoliutsii; Entsiklopedicheskii slovar'*. 3 parts. Moscow and Leningrad: Granat, 1925–28. Part 1, pp. 128–33.

Edmondson, Linda. "Russian Feminists and the First All-Russian Congress of Women." *Russian History*, 3, part 2 (1976):123–49.

Eichenbaum, Vsevolod Mikhailovich. *Nineteen-Seventeen, the Russian Revolution Betrayed*. Holley Cantine, trans. New York: Libertarian Book Club, 1954.

Elgström, Anna Lenah. "Alexandra Kollontay, Sovjets ambassadör." *Tidens kvinnor*, pp. 11–20. Stockholm: Steinvicks bokförlag, 1944.

Engel, Barbara Alpern, and Rosenthal, Clifford N., eds. and trans. *Five Sisters: Women Against the Tsar*. New York: Alfred A. Knopf, 1975.

Engels, Friedrich. *The Origin of the Family, Private Property, and the State*. New York: International Publishers, 1940.

Ermanskii, A. "Vserossiiskii zhenskii s"ezd." *Sovremennyi mir*, no. 1–2 (January 1909), pp. 108–12.

Evans, Richard J. *The Feminists: Women's Emancipation Movements in Europe, America, and Australasia 1840–1920*. New York: Barnes & Noble, 1977.

Fainsod, Merle. *International Socialism and the World War*. New York: Octagon Books, 1973.

Farnsworth, Beatrice. "Bolshevik Alternatives and the Soviet Family: The 1926 Marriage Law Debate." In *Women in Russia*, edited by Dorothy Atkinson, Alexander Dallin, and Gail Warshofsky Lapidus. Stanford: Stanford University Press, 1977.

———. "Bolshevism, the Woman Question, and Aleksandra Kollontai." *American Historical Review* 81, no. 2 (1976):292–316.

Ferro, Marc. *The Russian Revolution of February 1917*. J. L. Richards, trans. Englewood Cliffs: Prentice-Hall, 1972.

Fischer, Louis. "Love and Work." *The Nation*, 22 June 1927, p. 700.

Fischer, Ruth. *Stalin and German Communism*. Cambridge: Harvard University Press, 1948.

Fortunato, E. "Nash drug Aleksandra Kollontai." *Neva*, no. 3 (1959), pp. 182–87.

Fréville, Jean. *Une Grande Figure de la Révolution Russe: Inessa Armand*. Paris: Éditions sociales, 1957.

"Kollontai i Finland, på stormigt Ålands hav i fängelse och sjuglasvagn." *Folket i Bild*, no. 51–52 (1944), pp. 10–11, 80–81.

Futrell, Michael. *Northern Underground*. New York: Praeger, 1963.

Gaisinskii, M. G. *Bor'ba s uklonami ot general'noi linii partii: Istoricheskii ocherk vnutripartiinoi bor'by posleoktiabr'skogo perioda*. 2d ed. Moscow and Leningrad: Gosizdat, 1931.

Gay, Peter. *The Dilemma of Democratic Socialism: Eduard Bernstein's Challenge to Marx*. New York: Collier, 1962.

Geiger, H. Kent. *The Family in Soviet Russia*. Cambridge: Harvard University Press, 1968.

Gerhard, Karl. *Om jag inte minns fel*. Stockholm: Bonniers, 1952.

Glickman, Rose. "The Russian Factory Woman, 1880–1914." In *Women in Russia,* edited by Dorothy Atkinson, Alexander Dallin, and Gail Warshofsky Lapidus. Stanford: Stanford University Press, 1977.

Goldman, Emma. *Living My Life*. 2 vols. New York: Alfred A. Knopf, 1941.

———. *My Further Disillusionment in Russia*. New York: Doubleday, Page, 1924.

Gripenberg, G. A. *En beskickningschefs minnen*. 2 vols. Stockholm: Natur och kultur, 1960.

Hagglof, Gunnar. *Diplomat*. London: Bodley Head, 1971.

Halvorsen, Carsten. *See* Johansson, Gustav.

Hannah, Gayle Durham. "Political Equality for Russian Women: An Unfulfilled Promise of the Revolution." Paper presented at the Midwest Slavic Conference, Cleveland, Ohio, May 1975.

Harrison, Margaret Elton. *Marooned in Moscow*. New York: Doran, 1921.

Hauge, Kaare. "Alexandra Mikhailovna Kollontai: The Scandinavian Period, 1922–1945." Ph.D. dissertation, University of Minnesota, 1971.

Haupt, Georges, and Marie, Jean-Jacques. *Makers of the Russian Revolution*. C.I.P. Ferdinand and D. M. Bellos, trans. Ithaca: Cornell University Press, 1974.

Hayden, Carol Eubank. "The *Zhenotdel* and the Bolshevik Party." *Russian History* 3, part 2 (1976):150–73.

Höglund, Zeth. "Den lyckliga trons lotusblomma." *Morgon-Tidningen*, 18 April 1954, n.p.

———. *Minnen i fackelsken*. 3 vols. Stockholm: Tiden, 1951–60.

———. "Den skamliga utvisningen." *Stormklockan*, 28 November 1914, p. 1.

Honeycutt, Karen. "Clara Zetkin: A Socialist Attempt to Combat Woman's Oppression." Paper presented at the Second Berkshire Conference on the History of Women, Cambridge, Mass., October 1974.

Iakushina, A. P. "Iz istorii antivoennoi deiatel'nosti bol'shevikov pod rukovodstvom V. I. Lenina." *Voprosy istorii KPSS*, no. 2 (1962), pp. 155–62.

Iaroslavskii, Emelian. "Moral' i byt proletariata v perekhodnyi period." *Molodaia gvardiia*, no. 3 (May 1926), pp. 138–53.

———. *Protiv oppozitsii*. Moscow: Gosizdat, 1928.

Igumnova, Z. P. *Zhenshchiny Moskvy v gody grazhdanskoi voiny*. Moscow: Moskovskii rabochii, 1958.

International Conference of Women Communists, 1st Congress, Moscow, 1920. *Otchet o pervoi mezhdunarodnoi konferentsii kommunistok*. Moscow: Gosizdat, 1921.

International Socialist Congress. 7th Congress, Stuttgart, 1907. *Compte rendu analytique publié par le secrétariat du Bureau socialiste international*. Brussels: D. Brismee, 1908.

———. 8th Congress, Copenhagen, 1910. *Compte rendu analytique . . . .* N.d.: "Volksdrukkerij," 1911.

Itkina, A. M. *Revoliutsioner, Tribun, Diplomat: Stranitsi zhizni Aleksandry Mikhailovny Kollontai*. 2d ed., enlarged. Moscow: Politizdat, 1970.

"Itogi vserossiiskogo Soveshchaniia zagubzhenotdelami." *Kommunistka*, no. 1 (January 1922), pp. 2–3.

Izmailov, N. F., and Pukhov, A. G. *Tsentrobalt*. Moscow: Politizdat, 1963.

Jados, Stanley S., ed. *Documents on Russian-American Relations*. Washington: The Catholic University of America Press, 1965.

Jakobson, Max. *The Diplomacy of the Winter War*. Cambridge: Harvard University Press, 1961.

Johansson, Gustav [Carsten Halvorsen]. *Revolutionens ambassadör: Alexandra Kollontays liv och gärning, åren 1872–1917*. Stockholm: Arbetarkultursförlag, 1945.

Kalmanson, S. M., ed. *Polovoi vopros*. Moscow: Molodaia gvardiia, 1924.

Kan, A. S. *Vneshniaia politika skandinavskikh stran v gody vtoroi mirovoi voiny*. Moscow: Nauka, 1967.

Kanev, S. N. "Bor'ba V. I. Lenina protiv anarkho-sindikalistskogo uklona v RKP(b)." *Voprosy istorii KPSS*, no. 3 (1971), pp. 93–102.

Kaplun, S. I. *Sovremennye problemy zhenskogo truda i byta*. Moscow: Voprosy truda, 1924.

Karpetskaia, N. D. "Vovlechenie trudiashchikhsia zhenshchin Petrograda v revoliutsionnoe dvizhenie (mart–iiul' 1917 g.)." *Vestnik Leningradskogo universiteta* 21, no. 8 (1966):45–53.

Keep, John L. H. *The Rise of Social Democracy in Russia*. Oxford: Clarendon Press, 1963.

Kommunisticheskaia partiia Sovetskogo Soiuza. *Kommunisticheskaia partiia i organizatsiia rabotnits*. Moscow and Petrograd: Kommunist, 1919.

―――. *Kommunisticheskaia partiia Sovetskogo Soiuza v rezoliutsiiakh i resheniiakh s"ezdov, konferentsii i plenumov TsK* 8th ed., v. 2, 1917–1924. Moscow: Politizdat, 1970.

―――. *Vos'maia konferentsiia: Protokoly*. Moscow: Gosizdat, 1961.

―――. *Deviataia konferentsiia RKP(b): Protokoly*. Moscow: Politizdat, 1972.

―――. *Materialy po voprosu o gruppe Rabochei oppozitsii na XI s"ezde RKP: Otchet komissii i rezoliutsiia XI s"ezda RKP o nekotorykh chlenakh "Rabochei oppozitsii."* Moscow: Izd-vo. TsK RKP(b), 1922.

―――. *Sed'moi ekstrennyi s"ezd RKP(b): Stenograficheskii otchet*. Moscow: Politizdat, 1962.

―――. *Vos'moi s"ezd RKP(b): Protokoly*. Moscow: Politizdat, 1959.

―――. *Desiatyi s"ezd RKP(b): Stenograficheskii otchet*. Moscow: Politizdat, 1963.

―――. *Odinnadtsatyi s"ezd RKP(b): Stenograficheskii otchet*. Moscow: Politizdat, 1961.

―――. *Tri goda diktatury proletariata (Itogi raboty sredi zhenshchin Moskovskoi Org. RKP)*. Moscow: Izd-vo. Moskovskogo komiteta RKP, [1921].

―――. Tsentral'nyi komitet. Otdel po rabote sredi zhenshchin. *Sbornik instruktsii Otdela Ts.K. RKP po rabote sredi zhenshchin*. Moscow: Gosizdat, 1920.

―――. *Otchet otdela Ts.K. RKP po rabote sredi zhenshchin za god raboty*. Moscow: Gosizdat, 1921.

Korolev, N. E. *Lenin i mezhdunarodnoe rabochee dvizhenie, 1914–1918*. Moscow: Politizdat, 1968.

Krasnikova, A. V. *Na zare sovetskoi vlasti*. Leningrad: Lenizdat, 1963.

Krupskaia, N. K. "Inessa Armand." *Kommunistka*, no. 5 (October 1920), pp. 17–20.

―――. "Krupskaia, Nadezhda Konstantinovna." *Deiateli SSSR i Oktiabr'skoi Revoliutsii: Entsiklopedicheskii slovar'*. 3 parts. Moscow and Leningrad: Granat, 1925–28. Part 2, pp. 236–37.

―――. *O rabote sredi zhenshchin*. Moscow, 1926.

―――. *Pamiati Inessy Armand*. Moscow: Gosizdat, 1926.

―――. *Sobranie sochinenii*. Moscow and Leningrad: Politizdat, n.d.

Kuzin, V. V. *Bor'ba kommunisticheskoi partii s anarkho-sindikalisticheskim uklonom v 1920–1922 gg.* Moscow: Znanie, 1958.

Lademacher, Horst, ed. *Die Zimmerwalder Bewegung*. 2 vols. The Hague: Mouton, 1967.

Landfield, Jerome. "Kollontai and the New Morality." *The Weekly Review*, 28 July 1920, pp. 85–86.

Lavrov, E. "Polovoi vopros i molodezh'." *Molodaia gvardiia*, no. 2 (March 1926), pp. 136–48.

League of Nations. *Official Journal*. Special Supplement #139. Records of the 16th Ordinary Session of the Assembly. Meetings of the Committees. Geneva: League of Nations, 1935.

―――. *Official Journal*. Special Supplement #157. Records of the 17th Ordinary Session of the Assembly. Meetings of the Committees. Geneva: League of Nations, 1936.

―――. *Official Journal*. Special Supplement #170. Records of the 18th Ordinary Session of the Assembly. Meetings of Committees. Geneva: League of Nations, 1937.

―――. *Official Journal*. Special Supplement #174. Records of the 18th Ordinary Session of the Assembly. Meetings of the 5th Committee. Geneva: League of Nations, 1937.

Lemons, J. Stanley. *The Woman Citizen: Social Feminism in the 1920's*. Urbana: University of Illinois Press, 1973.

Lenczyc, Henryk. "Alexandra Kollontai." *Cahiers du monde russe et soviétique* 14 (1973):205–41.

Lenin, Vladimir Il'ich. *The Emancipation of Women*. New York: International Publishers, 1966.

―――. *Polnoe sobranie sochinenii*. 5th ed. in 56 vols. Moscow: Politizdat, 1958–66.

Leninskii sbornik. 3d ed. 35 vols. Moscow and Leningrad: Gosizdat, 1925.

Leonhard, Susanne. "Alexandra Kollontaj." *Aktion*, no. 15 (May 1952), pp. 44–48.

Lerner, Warren. *Karl Radek, the Last Internationalist*. Stanford: Stanford University Press, 1970.

Lichtheim, George. *Marxism: An Historical and Critical Study*. 2d ed. New York: Praeger, 1965.

Lindhagen, Carl. *I revolutions land*. Stockholm: Åhlen and Åkerlund, 1918.

"The Case for Madame Kollontay." *The Literary Digest*, 20 November 1926, p. 15.

Lore, Ludwig. "Leon Trotsky." In *One Year of Revolution*, pp. 7–10. Brooklyn: Socialist Publication Society, 1918.

Lorenson, E. G. "A. M. Kollontai v Shvetsii." *Novaia i noveishaia istoriia*, no. 1 (1966), pp. 105–11.

Lundin, C. Leonard. *Finland in the Second World War*. Bloomington: Indiana University Press, 1957.

Luxemburg, Rosa. *Rosa Luxemburg Speaks.* Ed. with an Introduction by Mary-Alice Waters. New York: Pathfinder Press, 1970.

McNeal, Robert. *Bride of the Revolution: Krupskaya and Lenin.* Ann Arbor: University of Michigan Press, 1972.

———. "Women in the Russian Radical Movement." *Journal of Social History* (Winter 1971–72), pp. 143–63.

Maiskii, Ivan. "A. M. Kollontai." *Oktiabr'*, no. 7 (1962), pp. 107–12.

Malia, Martin. "The Russian Intelligentsia." In *The Russian Intelligentsia*, edited by Richard Pipes, pp. 1–18. New York: Columbia University Press, 1961.

Massell, Gregory. *The Surrogate Proletariat.* Princeton: Princeton University Press, 1974.

Meyer, Alfred G. "Marxism and the Women's Movement." In *Women in Russia*, edited by Dorothy Atkinson, Alexander Dallin, and Gail Warshofsky Lapidus. Stanford: Stanford University Press, 1977.

Michelsen, Ellen. *Sju kvinnor ur den ryska revolutionens historia.* Stockholm: Axel Holmströms förlag, 1932.

Mikoian, Anastas I. *Mysli i vospominania o Lenine.* Moscow: Politizdat, 1970.

Mindlin, Emelian. *Ne dom, no mir.* Moscow: Politizdat, 1967.

Mints, I. I., ed. *Dokumenty velikoi proletarskoi revoliutsii.* Moscow: Ogiz, 1938.

Moscow. Institut istorii partii. *V edinom stroiu.* Moscow: Moskovskii rabochii, 1960.

Moscow. Institut Marksizma-Leninizma. *Istoriia kommunisticheskoi partii Sovetskogo Soiuza*, vol. 4: *Kommunisticheskaia partiia v bor'be za postroenie sotsializma v SSSR, 1921–1937 gg.* Moscow: Politizdat, 1970.

Nelaev, V. A. *Pavel Dybenko.* Moscow: Politizdat, 1965.

Nerman, Ture. *I vilda östern.* Stockholm: Ljungbergs förlag, 1930.

———. "Lika vacker som klok." *Röster i radio*, no. 20 (1967), pp. 14–15.

Nevolina, V. S., and Orlova, N. V., eds. "O mezhdunarodnoi zhenskoi sotsialisticheskoi konferentsii v 1915 g." *Istoricheskii arkhiv*, no. 3 (1960), pp. 106–25.

Niessel, Henri A. *Le triomphe des bolchéviks et la paix de Brest-Litovsk: Souvenirs 1917–1918.* Paris: Pron, 1940.

Nilsson, Ada. "Det stora uppdraget." *Vi*, no. 35 (1961), pp. 9–11, 38; no. 36, pp. 16–18, 37; no. 37, pp. 18–19, 40; no. 38, p. 16.

O'Connor, Richard, and Walker, Dale L. *The Lost Revolutionary: A Biography of John Reed.* New York: Harcourt, Brace and World, 1967.

Oswald, J. Gregory. "An Introduction to Soviet Diplomatic Relations with Mexico, Uruguay, and Cuba." In *The Communist Tide in Latin America*, edited by Donald L. Herman, pp. 75–115. Austin: The University of Texas Press, 1973.

Paasikivi, J. K. *President J. K. Paasikivis minnen.* 2 vols. Stockholm: Bonner, 1958.

Palencia, Isabel de. *Alexandra Kollontai: Ambassadress from Russia.* New York: Longmans Green, 1947.

Pares, Bernard. *My Russian Memoirs*. London: Jonathan Cape, 1931.

Perepiska sekretariata Ts.K. RKP(b) s mestnymi partiinymi organizatsiiami (avgust–oktiabr' 1918 g.). 6 vols. Moscow: Politizdat, 1969.

Pertzoff, Margaret. "Lady in Red: A Study of the Early Career of Alexandra Mikhailovna Kollontai." Ph.D. dissertation, University of Virginia, 1968.

Pervyi vserossiiskii s"ezd rabotnits 16–21 noiabria 1918 g. i ego rezoliutsii. Kharkov: Vseukrainskoe izd., 1920.

Pestkovskii, Stanislav. "Ob oktiabr'skikh dniakh v Pitere." *Ob Oktiabr'skoi revoliutsii: Vospominaniia zarubezhnikh uchastnikov i ochevidtsev.* Moscow: Politizdat, 1967.

Petrov, G. D. "Aleksandra Kollontai nakanune i v gody pervoi mirovoi voiny." *Novaia i noveishaia istoriia*, no. 1 (1969), pp. 67–81.

———. "A. M. Kollontai v gody pervoi mirovoi voiny." *Istoriia SSSR*, no. 3 (1968), pp. 83–97.

———. "Aleksandra Kollontai v SShA." *Novaia i noveishaia istoriia*, no. 3 (1972), pp. 128–42.

———. "Meridiany druzhby." *Moskva*, no. 1 (1967), pp. 162–69.

———. "O broshiure A. M. Kollontai 'Komu nuzhna voina.'" *Sovetskie arkhivy*, no. 5 (1968), pp. 109–11.

Petrov, Vladimir M., and Petrov, Evdokia. *Empire of Fear.* New York: Praeger, 1956.

Petrova, L. I. *Sovetskie profsoiuzy v vosstanovitel'nyi period 1921–1925 gg.* Moscow: Profizdat, 1962.

Pipes, Richard, ed. *Revolutionary Russia*. Cambridge: Harvard University Press, 1968.

Popov, N. N. *Ocherk istorii RKP(b).* 2 vols. Petrograd: Gosizdat, 1934.

Price, Morgan Philips. *My Reminiscences of the Russian Revolution*. London: Allen and Unwin, 1921.

Profsoiuzy v bor'be za pobedu Oktiabr'skoi sotsialisticheskoi revoliutsii. [Moscow]: Profizdat, 1957.

Rabinowitch, Alexander. *Prelude to Revolution: The Petrograd Bolsheviks and the July 1917 Uprising*. Bloomington: Indiana University Press, 1968.

Ransome, Arthur. *Russia in 1919*. New York: Huebsch, 1919.

Reed, John. *Ten Days That Shook the World*. New York: Vintage, 1960.

Reichenbach, Bernhard. "Moscow, 1921." *Survey* (October 1964), pp. 16–22.

Riabinskii, K. *Revoliutsiia 1917 goda*. 6 vols. in 4. Moscow: Gosizdat, 1926.

Riadom s Leninym: Vospominaniia o N. K. Krupskoi. Moscow: Politizdat, 1969.

Rigby, T. H. *Communist Party Membership in the U.S.S.R., 1917–1967*. Princeton: Princeton University Press, 1968.

Riksdagens protokoll vid lagtima riksmötet år 1915—Andra kammaren. Stockholm: Norstedt, 1915.

Rosenberg, William G. *Liberals in the Russian Revolution*. Princeton: Princeton University Press, 1974.

Rosmer, Alfred. *Lenin's Moscow*. Ian H. Birchall, trans. London: Pluto Press, 1971.

Ross, Edward A. *The Russian Bolshevik Revolution*. New York: Century, 1921.
Rossiiskaia sotsial-demokraticheskaia rabochaia partiia. Seventh Conference,
   Leningrad, 1917. *Petrogradskaia obshchegorodskaia i vserossiiskaia konferen-
   tsiia RSDRP(bol.) v aprele 1917 g.: Protokol'nye zapiski zasedanii TsK ot
   10, 16, i 24 oktiabria 1917 g.* Moscow: Gosizdat, 1925.
————. *Shestoi s"ezd RSDRP(bol'shevikov): Protokoly.* Moscow: Politizdat,
   1958.
RSFSR. S"ezd sovetov, 1st, Leningrad, 1917. *Pervyi vserossiiskii s"ezd sovetov
   R. i S. D.: Stenograficheskii otchet.* Moscow: Gos. sotsialno-ekonomicheskoe
   izdatel'stvo, 1931.
————. *Vserossiiskii s"ezd sovetov, 3–7, 8–14, 16: Stenograficheskii otchet.*
   Moscow, 1918–35.
Sadoul, Jacques. *Notes sur la révolution bolchévique.* Paris: Éditions de la
   Sirène, 1920.
Salomaa, Erkki. "Pervoe nauchnoe issledovanie o zhizni finskikh rabochikh."
   Skandinavskii sbornik 7 (1963):299–306.
Samoilova, Konkordiia N. "K mezhdunarodnomu dniu zhenshchin-rabotnits."
   Put' pravdy, 29 January 1914, p. 2.
————. "Konferentsiia rabotnits i organizatsionnaia rabota." *Pravda*, 9 Decem-
   ber 1917, p. 3.
————. *Organizatsionnye zadachi otdelov rabotnits.* Moscow: Gosizdat, 1920.
————. *V ob"edinenii-zalog pobedu (k mezh. sotsialis. dniu rabotnits 8 marta
   1921).* Moscow: Gosizdat, 1921.
"Samoilova, Konkordiia Nikolaevna." *Deiateli SSSR i Oktiabr'skoi Revoliutsii:
   Entsiklopedicheskii slovar'.* 3 parts. Moscow and Leningrad: Granat, 1925–
   28. Part 3, pp. 1–3.
Schapiro, Leonard. *The Origin of the Communist Autocracy: Political Opposi-
   tion in the Soviet State. First Phase, 1917–1922.* London: The London School
   of Economics and Political Science, 1955.
Schirmacher, Käthe. *The Modern Woman's Rights Movement.* Trans. from
   the 2d ed. by Carl Conrad Eckhardt. New York: Macmillan, 1912.
Schmitt, Karl M. *Communism in Mexico: A Study in Political Frustration.*
   Austin: University of Texas Press, 1965.
Selivanova, Nina Nikolaevna. *Russia's Women.* New York: Dutton, 1923.
Serditova, S. N. *Bol'sheviki v bor'be za zhenskie proletarskie massy.* Moscow:
   Politizdat, 1959.
Serge, Victor, and Trotsky, Natalia Sedova. *The Life and Death of Leon
   Trotsky.* Arnold J. Pomerans, trans. New York: Basic Books, 1975.
Serge, Victor. *Memoirs of a Revolutionary, 1901–1941.* Peter Sedgwick, trans.
   and ed. London: Oxford University Press, 1963.
Shelavin, K. *Rabochaia oppozitsiia.* Moscow: Molodaia gvardiia, 1930.
Shelly, Carol. "The Bolshevik Party and Work Among Women, 1917–1925."
   Paper presented at Stanford Conference on Women in Russia, June 1975.
Shklovskii, G. "Vladimir Il'ich nakanune Bernskoi konferentsii." *Proletarskaia
   revoliutsiia*, no. 5 (40) (May 1925), pp. 134–49.

Shliapnikov, Aleksandr Gavrilovich. "Fevral'skaia revoliutsiia i evropeiskie sotsialisty." *Krasnyi arkhiv*, no. 2 (15) (1926), pp. 25–43.

————. "K oktiabriu." *Proletarskaia revoliutsiia*, no. 10 (1922), pp. 3–42.

————. *Nakanune 1917 goda*. 2 vols. Moscow: Gosizdat, 1920.

————. *Semnadtsatyi god*. 3 vols. Moscow: Gosizdat, 1923–27.

————. "Shliapnikov, Aleksandr Gavrilovich." *Deiateli SSSR i Oktiabr'skoi Revoliutsii: Entsiklopedicheskii slovar'*. 3 parts. Moscow and Leningrad: Granat, 1925–28. Part 3, pp. 244–51.

Sizonenko, A. I. "Polgoda v Meksike." *V strane atstekskogo orla*, pp. 35–54. Moscow: Mezhdunarodnoe otnosheniia, 1969.

Smirnova, V. N. "Iz istorii bor'by za razoblachenie burzhuaznogo feminizma v Rossii." *Voprosy istorii, filologii, i pedagogiki*, pp. 32–49. Kazan: Izd. Kazanskogo universiteta, 1967.

Smith, Jessica. *Women in Soviet Russia*. New York: Vanguard, 1928.

Sorokin, Pitirim A. *Leaves from a Russian Diary*. Boston: Beacon Press, 1950.

Sosnovskii, L. S. *Bol'nye voprosy (zhenshchina, sem'ia i deti)*. Leningrad: Priboi, 1926.

Sovet rabochikh i krasno-armeiskikh deputatov. *Protokoly zasedanii*. Moscow: Gosizdat, 1925.

Spiridovich, A. I. *Istoriia bol'shevizma v Rossii ot vozniknoveniia do zakhvata vlasti 1883–1903–1917*. Paris: Société anonyme de presse, 1922.

Stal', Liudmilla. "Rabotnitsa v Okt'iabre." *Proletarskaia revoliutsiia*, no. 10 (1922), pp. 229–301.

Stanton, Theodore, ed. *The Woman Question in Europe*. Unabridged republication of the 1884 edition. New York: Source Book Press, 1970.

Stasova, E. D. *Vospominaniia*. Moscow: Mysl, 1969.

Stavrakis, Bette D. "Women and the Communist Party in the Soviet Union, 1918–1935." Ph.D. dissertation, Western Reserve University, 1961.

Stites, Richard. "M. L. Mikhailov and the Emergence of the Woman Question in Russia." *Canadian Slavic Studies* 3 (Summer 1969):178–99.

————. *The Women's Liberation Movement in Russia: Feminism, Nihilism, and Bolshevism, 1860–1930*. Princeton: Princeton University Press, 1977.

————. "Women's Liberation Movements in Russia, 1900–1930." *Canadian-American Slavic Studies* 7, no. 4 (Winter 1973):460–74.

————. "*Zhenotdel*: Bolshevism and Russian Women." *Russian History* 3, part 2 (1976): 174–93.

Strong, Anna Louise. *I Change Worlds*. New York: Henry Holt, 1935.

Sukhanov, N. N. *The Russian Revolution 1917*. Ed., abridged, and trans. by Joel Carmichael. London: Oxford University Press, 1955.

————. *Zapiski o revoliutsii*. 7 vols. Berlin: Izd. Z. I. Grzhebin, 1922.

Svartz, Nanna. *Steg för steg*. Stockholm: Bonniers, 1968.

Tanner, Väinö. *The Winter War*. Stanford: Stanford University Press, 1957.

————. *Vägen till fred 1943–1944*. Stockholm: Holger Schildt, 1952.

Taracena, Alfonso. *La verdadera revolución mexicana*. Mexico City: Editorial jus, 1963.

Temkin, Ia. G. *Lenin i mezhdunarodnaia sotsial-demokratiia 1914–1917*. Moscow: Nauka, 1968.

Thönnessen, Werner. *The Emancipation of Women: The Rise and Decline of the Women's Movement in German Social Democracy, 1863–1933*. Joris de Bres, trans. London: Pluto Press, 1973.

Trotsky, Leon. *The History of the Russian Revolution*. Max Eastman, trans. 3 vols. New York: Simon and Schuster, 1932.

———. *The Revolution Betrayed*. Max Eastman, trans. Garden City, N.J.: Doubleday, Doran, 1937.

———. *Sochineniia*. Moscow: Gosizdat, 1927.

———. *Stalin: An Appraisal of the Man and His Influence*. Charles Malamuth, ed. and trans. New York: Harper and Bros., 1941.

Tsereteli, I. G. *Vospominaniia o fevral'skoi revoliutsii*. 2 vols. Paris: Mouton, 1963.

Tyrkova-Williams, Ariadne. *From Liberty to Brest-Litovsk*. London: Macmillan, 1919.

———. *Na putiakh k svobodu*. New York: Chekhova, 1952.

Ulam, Adam. *The Bolsheviks*. New York: Collier, 1965.

———. *Expansion and Coexistence: The History of Soviet Foreign Policy 1917–1967*. New York: Praeger, 1968.

United States Department of State. *Papers Relating to the Foreign Relations of the United States, 1927*. 3 vols. Washington: Government Printing Office, 1942.

Utechin, S. V. "Philosophy and Science: Alexander Bogdanov." In *Revisionism, Essays on the History of Marxist Ideas*, pp. 117–25. New York: Praeger, 1962.

Vasser, M. M. "Razgrom anarcho-sindikalistskogo uklonom v partii." *Voprosy istorii KPSS*, no. 3 (1962), pp. 62–78.

Vinogradskaia, Polina. *Pamiatnye vstrechi*. 2d ed. Moscow: Sovetskaia Rossiia, 1972.

———. "Voprosy byta." *Pravda*, 26 July 1923, pp. 4–5.

———. "Voprosy morali, pola, byta, i tovarishch' Kollontai." *Krasnaia nov'*, no. 6 (16) (November 1923), pp. 179–214.

Vladimirova, Vera. *Revoliutsiia 1917 goda*. 4 vols. Leningrad: Gosizdat, 1924.

Voennaia entsiklopediia, 1912 ed., s.v. "Domontovich, Mikhail Alekseevich."

Voskresenskaia, E. "Sovetskii polpred." *Ogonek*, no. 15 (April 1962), pp. 5–6.

Vsegda s vami: Sbornik posviashchennyi 50-letiiu "Rabotnitsa." Moscow: Rabotnitsa, 1964.

Vserossiiskaia konferentsiia professional'nykh soiuzov. 3d conference, Leningrad, 1917. *Tretiaia vserossiiskaia konferentsiia professional'nykh soiuzov: Rezoliutsii, priniatye na zasedaniiakh konferentsii, 20–28 iiul', 1917 g.* Petrograd, 1917.

Vserossiiskii tsentral'nyi sovet professional'nykh soiuzov. *O roli professional'nykh soiuzov v proizvodstve*. Moscow: Pervaia obraztsovaia tip. MSNKh, 1921.

————. Komissia po izucheniiu istorii professional'nogo dvizheniia v SSSR. *Materialy po istoriiu professional'nogo dvizheniia v Rossii.* Moscow: VTsSPS, n.d.

W. "Zhenskii s"ezd i rabochaia gruppa (Pis'mo iz Peterburga)." *Golos sotsial'-demokrata* 2 (March 1909):7–8.

Wagner, Bertil. "Alexandra Kollontay—världens första kvinnliga ambassadör." *Arbetartidning*, 13 March 1962, p. 9.

Wahlbäck, Krister. *Finlandsfrägan i svensk politik 1937–1940.* Stockholm: Stockholm universitet, 1964.

Williams, Albert Rhys. *Journey Into Revolution, Petrograd 1917–1918.* Lucita Williams, ed. Chicago: Quadrangle Books, 1969.

————. *Lenin, the Man and His Work.* New York: Scott and Seltzer, 1919.

————. *Through the Russian Revolution.* New York: Boni and Liveright, 1921.

Wolfe, Bertram. "Lenin and Inessa Armand." *Slavic Review* 22 (March 1963): 96–114.

Wuorinen, John H., ed. *Finland and World War II, 1939–1944.* New York: Ronald Press, 1948.

Zetkin, Clara. *Lenin on the Woman Question.* New York: International Publishers, 1934.

Zhenshchiny russkoi revoliutsii. Moscow: Politizdat, 1968.

Zhenshchiny v russkoi revoliutsii. Moscow: Politizdat, 1959.

Zinov'ev, Grigorii. *God revoliutsii.* Leningrad, 1925.

————. *Partiia i soiuzy.* Petrograd: Gosizdat, 1921.

————. *Rabotnitsa, krest'ianka i Sovetskaia vlast'.* Petrograd: Petrogradskii sovet rabochikh i krasnoarmeiskikh deputatov, 1919.

Zorkii, Mark S. *Rabochaia oppozitsiia.* Moscow: Gosizdat, 1926.

NEWSPAPERS

Afton-Tidningen, Stockholm.
Arbetaren, Stockholm.
Arbetet, Stockholm.
Die Gleichheit, Berlin.
Golos, Paris.
Iskra.
Izvestiia.
Izvestiia TsK RKP(b), Moscow.
Kommunar, Moscow.
Kommunist, Geneva.
Kommunist, Moscow.
Morgon-Tidningen, Stockholm.
Nashe slovo, Paris.
Die Neue Zeit, Berlin.

New York Times.
Pravda.
Petrogradskaia pravda, Petrograd.
Socialdemokraten, Stockholm.
Stockholms-Tidningen, Stockholm.
Stormklockan, Stockholm.
The Times, London.
Vorwärts, Berlin.

ARCHIVAL MATERIALS

Dossier of press clippings, Bibliothèque Marguerite Durand, Paris.
Paris Okhrana Files, Hoover Institution on War, Revolution and Peace, Stanford, California.
Boris Nicolaevsky Archive, Hoover Institution on War, Revolution and Peace.

INTERVIEWS

Bertram Wolfe, Hoover Institution, July 1973.
Erik Boheman, Margit Palmaer-Waldén, Alva Myrdal, Nanna Svartz, Eva Palmaer, and Agneta Pleijel, by Sonya Baevsky and Britta Stövling, Stockholm, February and March 1976, made available to the author by Sonya Baevsky.

Index